Fine
WoodWorking
TECHNIQUES 8

Fine WoodWorking
TECHNIQUES 8

Selected by the Editors of *Fine Woodworking* magazine

The Taunton Press

Photo, p. 67, by Nikolay Zurek ©1982
Photo, p. 121, by Richard Raffan
Photo, p. 161, by Erik Borg
Photo, p. 183, by Brunner Studio
Photo, back cover, by Robert Aude

Typeface: Garamond and Univers
Paper: Warrenflo, 70 lb., Neutral pH

The Taunton Press, Inc.
63 South Main Street
Box 355
Newtown, Connecticut 06470

A FINE WOODWORKING Book

FINE WOODWORKING® is a trademark of
The Taunton Press, Inc., registered in the
U.S. Patent and Trademark Office.

International Standard Book Number 0-918804-49-3
Library of Congress Catalog Card Number 78-58221
Printed in the United States of America

CONTENTS

INTRODUCTION

Of all the techniques to be learned by the woodworker, those involving hand tools are among the most useful. To be sure, machines do the big chores like ripping and thickness-planing. But for fitting a joint just so or for shaping a delicate chamfer, mastery of hand tools—particularly planes and chisels—is an undeniable asset. In this volume, the eighth in our series of *Fine Woodworking Techniques* books, you'll learn about both the basics and the finer points of hand-tool use. You'll also find a generous selection of articles about machines, joinery, turning, finishing and things to build.

This volume is based upon articles first published in *Fine Woodworking* magazine during 1984, issues #44 through #49, plus a brief excursion into issues #50 and #51 to include our series on hand tools in its entirety. Sources of supply and price information given were current as of 1984.

HAND TOOLS

Starting Out
I. Edge-joining for the beginner

by Roger Holmes

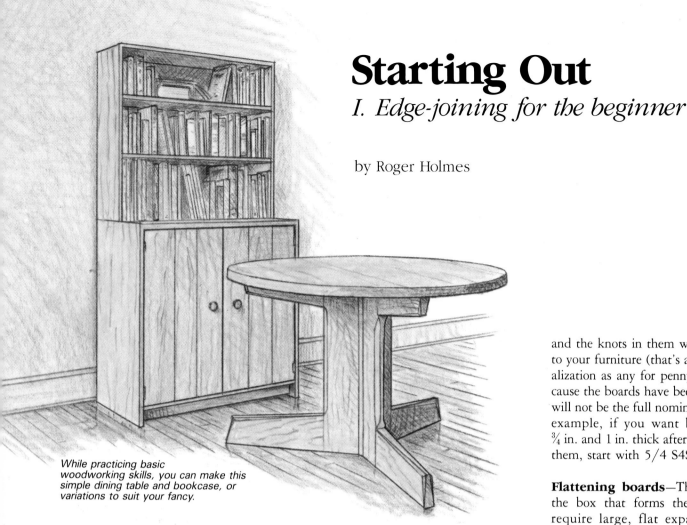

While practicing basic woodworking skills, you can make this simple dining table and bookcase, or variations to suit your fancy.

A friend of mine took a beginners' woodworking course not too long ago. She was surprised, and a little disappointed, to discover that the first two sessions were devoted not to the construction of a coffee table or a dovetailed box but to the making of a simple, ordinary board—two flat, parallel faces, and square to them, two straight edges.

Board-making is not exactly the stuff of woodworking romance. But without boards it's tough to make tables and cabinets. In this article I'll tackle board-making; in the next three articles that follow, I'll cover other basics of joinery and furnituremaking. My methods aren't definitive, but I hope they'll get you going.

Making sample joints isn't much fun, so if you don't have your own projects to practice on, you can cobble up the table and bookcase shown above as you go along. (Make the 48-in. dia. tabletop now, the table base with the next article, the bookcase with the third and fourth.) I built these pieces after my wife and I moved our meager possessions into a seven-room apartment and needed to fill up the empty spaces. The results are hardly masterpieces of design or construction, but you can generate a lot of simple furniture from them. Chests of drawers, after all, are just little boxes housed in a big box; tables, merely slabs of wood perched at various heights above the floor.

Wood—I decided to build the table and bookcase of solid wood, even though using plywood would have eliminated gluing up wide boards. I enjoy working solid wood. Curling a long shaving out of my plane gives me a great deal of satisfaction—planing plywood produces grit and dust.

There is solid wood and solid wood, however. Some woods, such as rosewood and walnut, seem to demand elegant designs. But what I wanted was utility, economy, and something easy and pleasing to work. Pine filled the bill on all counts, and I discovered a small lumberyard up the road selling it for $.30 to $1.00 a board foot.

I strongly recommend that beginners work with pine or a similarly soft, evenly grained wood such as basswood or certain varieties of fir. Mistakes are inevitable and instructive, so you might as well make them cheaply. In lumberman's lingo, you'll need 4/4 (1-in.) boards for the boxes and 8/4 (2-in.) boards for the table.

If you can, buy roughsawn (unplaned) boards. If not, buy the planed, or surfaced, boards sold at most lumberyards. The most common variety of surfaced board is designated S4S, which stands for "surfaced four sides," meaning that the boards have been surfaced on both faces and both edges. No. 2 Common pine boards are fine. They're relatively cheap,

and the knots in them will add character to your furniture (that's as good a rationalization as any for penny-pinching.) Because the boards have been surfaced, they will not be the full nominal thickness. For example, if you want boards between ¾ in. and 1 in. thick after you've flattened them, start with 5/4 S4S stock.

Flattening boards—The tabletop and the box that forms the bookcase base require large, flat expanses of wood. Roughsawn boards from the sawmill or surfaced boards from the lumberyard are seldom flat enough or wide enough. Their faces usually will be cupped across the grain, bowed, or twisted diagonally along the grain, or a combination of all these. Making wide boards by edge-joining requires flat boards, so your first task is to make them that way.

Cabinetmaking, like mathematics, proceeds logically from start to finish. Each step builds on the last, and if you miss something at the beginning, you'll likely suffer for it at the end—or sooner. If the first face isn't reasonably flat, everything that follows will be affected. The sequence is simple: After flattening one face, flatten the other while removing enough wood to bring the board to the right thickness. Then plane the edges square to the faces, and you're ready to glue up.

I think that the hand plane is the most effective tool for flattening. Its mechanical cousin, the jointer, is quicker, but the width of the jointer bed limits the width of board that can be flattened. A thickness planer can make a board uniformly thick, but it can flatten only the thickest boards. Whenever possible, I use a combination of hand and machine techniques. But even if you're blessed with a wide jointer and a planer, it helps to know how to flatten, thickness and joint the edges of boards by hand. In the process, you'll also

For a close shave

Planing with a dull tool is a thankless task. I spent much of my first woodworking year struggling with a dull plane blade, and when I finally managed a keen edge, it was a revelation. It's inevitable that, for a while, you'll be keener than your tools.

In sharpening, the end totally justifies the means, and there are dozens of equally effective routes to a sharp edge. The cutting edge of a plane blade is at the intersection of the bevel and the back of the blade. The ideal edge, like the ideal line in geometry, would have length but no thickness. All sharpening methods try to refine the bevel/back intersection to the ideal by removing steel with finer and finer abrasives.

My sharpening tools are simple: a bench grinder with a medium-grit, 6-in. carborundum wheel; an 8-in. long combination India benchstone, one side coarse, one side fine; a 6-in. long soft Arkansas benchstone; and a leather strop, a piece of belt leather impregnated with a fine abrasive such as rottenstone. (The leather alone, or even the palm of your hand, will do for a strop).

The bevel of a new plane iron is ground to about 25° and I maintain this angle, trying not to facet the bevel when grinding. Most grinders have tool rests that can be fixed, or adapted, to support the blade at the bevel angle. You can grind the cutting edge slightly convex in its length or dub off the corners to prevent making ridges in the wood when you're rough-planing. I use one plane for everything, so I grind straight across, and plane the ridges out with a few strokes of a sharp, finely set blade.

After grinding, rub a little light machine oil on the fine face of the India stone and rest the bevel on it. I hold the blade with one hand, tilt it slightly forward (about 5°) and draw it toward me. The motion can be slow or fast, but hold the blade steady—don't rock it from front to back or side to side. Tilting the blade forms a second bevel, which makes the cutting edge a little more durable.

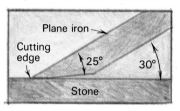

Take six to eight strokes, then feel for a burr of steel rolling over the back of the cutting edge. When the burr appears, move to the soft Arkansas stone and make about as many strokes at the same angle. Then turn the blade over, lay it *flat* on the stone, and rub it back and forth to turn the burr. Alternate on the Arkansas between the bevel and the back until the burr disappears. Then stroke the bevel and back on the leather strop, just as on the stones.

At the end of this little ritual, try to shave the hair off the back of your hand—a clean shave equals a sharp edge. If you tire of being asked about your bald hand, rest the flat side of the blade on your thumbnail, raise it slightly and push the cutting edge toward the cuticle. The lower the angle at which the edge catches on the nail, the sharper it is. If the edge isn't sharp enough, strop again; if that doesn't work, go back to the stones.

That's how I do it. Others hold the blade with both hands, move it in a circle or a figure eight on the stone, strop the edge on their pant leg, and so on. No matter how long it takes, don't get discouraged. Once you get used to it, you can sharpen a plane iron in less time than takes to read about how to do it. —R.H.

Sharpening on stone

Sharpening involves a series of simple operations, but success requires patience and persistence. Grind a 25° bevel on the blade (below), then refine the edge with increasingly fine benchstones and a leather strop. Try not to rock the blade as you push or pull it across the stones (above). When you move to the soft Arkansas stone, alternate between stroking the bevel and laying the blade *flat* on the stone to turn the burr.

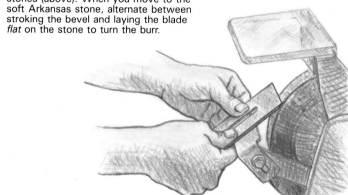

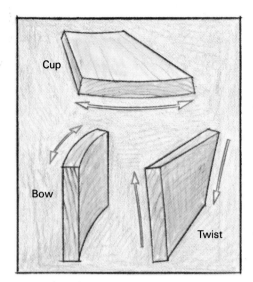

Cup

Bow

Twist

Most boards are afflicted with at least one of the problems shown at left, but can be cured with a hand plane. Hold the plane comfortably; make your whole body work for you. Extend your right index finger along the edge of the blade for added control. Begin with pressure on the plane's toe, and end with pressure on the heel.

acquire dexterity with the plane, which is handy for all sorts of work.

Selecting a plane—Locked up in a London warehouse is my collection of bench planes—eight or nine different sizes, all in working order. When I acquired them, I was teaching myself to woodwork from books and it didn't seem possible to get by with fewer than a half-dozen bench planes. I did my best with them, but the results were mixed. When I went to England to work with master craftsman Alan Peters, I packed them all, eagerly expecting Alan to reveal their secrets. The secret, he told me, was to leave them in the box and use a jointer plane.

I use a 22-in. long, 7½-lb. Stanley-Bailey #07 jointer for everything, from flattening rough lumber to slicing a few thousandths of an inch off the end grain of a 2-in. wide drawer side. The plane is at least 30 years old and cost me $35 used.

I like the jointer's size, weight and balance. Its length and width make it ideal for flattening boards and jointing long edges. It rides over low spots while slicing

Using winding sticks

You can check for twist by sighting across two identical pieces of wood called winding sticks. Get the edges at one end of each stick in your line of sight, then move your eye down the length of the edges. If the edges at the other ends don't line up, the board is twisted. Mark the high corner and the corner diagonal to it; these will have to be planed down.

off the high until everything is flat. And it's heavy enough to maintain solid contact with the wood so most of the pushing can be in the direction of the stroke.

Most important for me is the jointer's balance. Held only by its handle, a jointer remains nearly horizontal—there's about as much weight behind the handle as in front. Balance makes the plane easier to control and less tiring to use.

Every woodworker has a favorite plane. The right bench plane for a job is the one you're most comfortable with—don't be afraid to go against the book and try a plane outside its prescribed territory.

Planing—First determine where the board isn't flat. This can be done by eye, alone or aided by a straightedge, or by feel on a large, flat surface, such as a benchtop, the top of a tablesaw, or the kitchen floor (unless your kitchen floor is like mine and requires sea legs to navigate). Sight across the width of the board to check for cupping and along its length to check for bowing. If you've got a flat surface, check for twist by placing the face of the board on it, then tap each corner in turn. A twisted board will rock, supported on diagonal corners. If you haven't got a flat surface, you can use winding sticks to determine twist, as shown on the facing page.

When you've found and marked the high spots, plane them off. The first problem here is holding the board while you plane. A bench with a tail vise and benchdogs is ideal: pinched between the vise and a stop, most if not all of the board is supported by the benchtop. Lacking a built-in, wooden tail vise, you can mount a regular bench vise on the end of a bench, and bore holes in the benchtop for homemade wooden dogs—¾-in. dia. dowels with scrapwood heads work fine. An easier solution is to drive three or four nails into the benchtop in an L-shaped configuration and shove the board against them. As long as you plane toward the nails, the board won't move.

I set the plane blade to remove as much wood as possible, while still allowing for a comfortable stroke. Position the chip breaker about ¹⁄₁₆ in. back from the cutting edge and make sure that the edge is parallel to the sole of the plane. (Keep the sole and cutting edge parallel for all planing.) I lower the cutting edge as I make the first few strokes. The amount varies with the character of the board, how keen the cutting edge is, and how keen I am to shove away. If you're a hearty soul and the wood is cooperative, you can peel off a goodly shaving (maybe ¹⁄₃₂ in. thick) with each pass. Less blade, less brawn and more strokes will get the job done just as well. If you keep lowering the blade and still slice off only a wisp of wood, or none at all, chances are the blade is dull—take the time to sharpen it.

I hold and push the plane as shown on the facing page. Planing is repetitive work and is most accurately and efficiently done rhythmically, each stroke the same, or nearly the same, as the last. I like to power the stroke with my back and shoulders as well as my arms, shifting weight from front to rear

foot as the stroke progresses. Using your whole body allows you to control the plane with your hands and wrists.

I plane the concave side of a cupped or bowed board first. The plane can too easily follow the contour of the convex side, and you'd just keep planing the same curve rather than flattening it. Regardless of whether the board is cupped, bowed or twisted, it's best to plane diagonally across the board's width, because the plane is less likely to follow and maintain the contour of a long curve or to tear the grain severely. Concentrate on removing the high spots. Check your progress every now and then with a straightedge, flat surface or winding sticks. If the plane is long enough, you can use it as a straightedge, as shown above. A torn and rough surface indicates that you're planing against the grain—try planing the other way. After the face is planed, draw an arrow on it to mark the best direction for planing—the arrow will help you lay out the boards when you're ready to joint the edges.

If the planed board is wide enough to use without gluing up (a bookcase side, for example), smooth any torn grain with

Scribing the thickness

After flattening one face, scribe a line indicating the board's thickness around the edges and ends with a marking gauge. Push the gauge's fence flush to the flat face and its scribe point into the wood. Push or pull the gauge, whichever suits you.

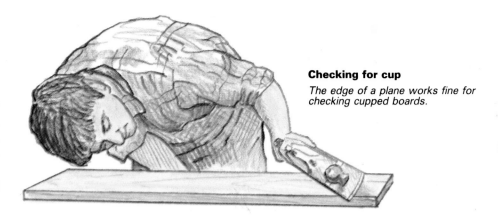

Checking for cup

The edge of a plane works fine for checking cupped boards.

a sharp plane, stroking parallel to the grain direction. Often I make these last strokes after assembling the piece. I don't sand the surfaces, because I like the look and feel of a planed surface—and sanding is no fun at all.

Flattening boards is a good way to get a feel for planing. In the old days, apprentices spent months at it, paying their dues, building up their skill and their biceps. You make lots of strokes, but there isn't a lot of risk involved. About the worst you can do is end up with thinner boards than you wanted. And if you really screw one up, try another—after all, it's just pine.

Thicknessing—When you're satisfied with the first face, you can gauge from it to flatten the second face and thickness the board. Set a marking gauge to the thickness you want (or the thickness you can get—the thinnest spot on the edges or ends), then run it around the edges and ends of the board. Now plane down to the scribe, just as for flattening.

If you don't want to thickness boards by hand, a local millwork shop might do it for you by machine. If you haven't flattened one side, make sure they do, otherwise you'll just end up with uniformly thick boards that are still cupped, bowed or twisted. Also let them know beforehand if the boards are pine—some shops won't machine resinous woods.

Edge-jointing—When you've got a stack of flat boards, a pile of fragrant shavings and a pair of sore arms, you're ready to plane the edges for gluing up. This is less strenuous than flattening or thicknessing, but more exacting. I've come to appreciate bookcases that can be made without edge-joined boards. Tabletops and deeper boxes, unfortunately, can seldom be made without gluing up boards. Once I'm resigned to necessity, I usually enjoy the technical challenge of making good edge joints.

The ideal edge joint consists of two edges, planed straight, flat and square to their adjacent faces, cemented together with a microscopic layer of glue. In practice, the edges needn't be square or flat as

5

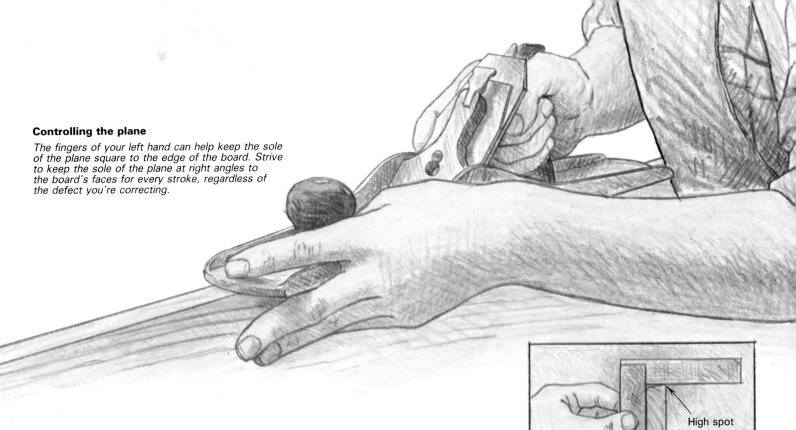

Controlling the plane

The fingers of your left hand can help keep the sole of the plane square to the edge of the board. Strive to keep the sole of the plane at right angles to the board's faces for every stroke, regardless of the defect you're correcting.

High spot

Checking the edges

Check the squareness of an edge with a try square. Sight into a light source as you slide the square along the edge. Light between the edge and the blade indicates a high spot. If high spots at each end are on diagonally opposed corners, the edge is twisted. Check mating edges with a straightedge, as shown below. If the surface isn't fairly flat, adjust the angle of one or both edges to the faces.

long as they are complementary, and if the edges are slightly concave in their length, the joints will be less prone to open at the ends. That said, I still *try* to plane edges flat and square.

Lay out the boards for the tabletop or box side on a flat surface. Arrange them so the grain pattern and colors please you. If you have a slightly bowed board, place it between straight ones—it can be pulled into alignment when you clamp up. Run all the grain-direction arrows you made earlier in the same direction, so you'll be less likely to tear the surface when planing it flat after glue-up. Finally, mark the relative positions of the boards by drawing a

large V across their faces—reconstituting the V will restore the order.

Sharpen the plane blade before edge-jointing, and set the chip breaker within $\frac{1}{32}$ in. or less of the cutting edge. Make sure the cutting edge is parallel to the sole, then adjust the iron during the first few strokes to take a heavy shaving for roughing out the edge, or a fine one for finishing.

Put the first board edge-up in a bench vise. (Long boards narrower than 2 in. to 3 in. should be planed edge-up on the benchtop between dogs or against a nail, so they won't bend under the pressure of planing.) Sight down the length of the edge to determine if it's convex or con-

Edge-planing

Edge-planing strokes should be slower and more controlled, but no less rhythmic, than flattening strokes. Power the plane with your body; orient it with your hands. Put pressure on the toe at the start, and on the heel at the finish of a stroke.

cave. Check the edge for squareness to the faces with a try square. You can sight down the edge as you slide the square along it, marking high spots as you go.

The secret to edge-planing is to always hold the plane with its sole perpendicular to the faces of the board. I extend three fingers of my left hand over the edge of the plane, where they rub against the wood, forming a fence and giving a surprisingly accurate sense of the angle of plane to face. Use your whole body to power the plane; control it with your hands. Get the edge roughly in shape with rapid strokes, but finish evenly and deliberately. (When there's a machine jointer handy, I rough out the edges on it and finish them with the hand plane to remove the tiny ridges created by the machine.)

Because planing edges is so exacting, its success depends upon all sorts of factors—chiefly, practice. So don't fuss too much with the first edge; when you feel it's straight, flat and square to the faces, plane the mating edge on the next board. Then, while the second board is still in the vise, place the first edge on the second to check the fit. The top board should rest steadily on the bottom one. If it rocks, one or both of the edges is convex and/or twisted.

A concave or convex edge is easy to see; a twisted edge is not so easy. Press down on one end of the top board and look closely at the joint at the other end. If an edge is twisted, the surfaces will touch only at one corner; if they don't touch at all, the edge is convex. (Edges may, of course, be convex and twisted at the same time—I try to correct the convexity first.) You can also check for twist with a try square. If there are diagonally opposed high spots at the ends, the edge is twisted.

It doesn't hurt if the edges are slightly concave—but not more than $\frac{1}{32}$ in. over 3 ft. To fix an excessively concave edge, take a few strokes off each end and one the full length, then recheck. To flatten a convex edge, work out from the center, taking three or four progressively longer strokes, finishing with a full-length stroke.

A twisted edge requires a more delicate fix. As when flattening a twisted face, you want to plane from corner to corner to remove the diagonally opposed high spots. If the sole of the plane is perpendicular to the board's faces, you should be able to take a shaving from just the high spot at the near end, reach a full-width shaving in the center of the edge, and nip off the other high spot at the opposite end. When you think the twist is gone, take a full-width shaving from end to end, and

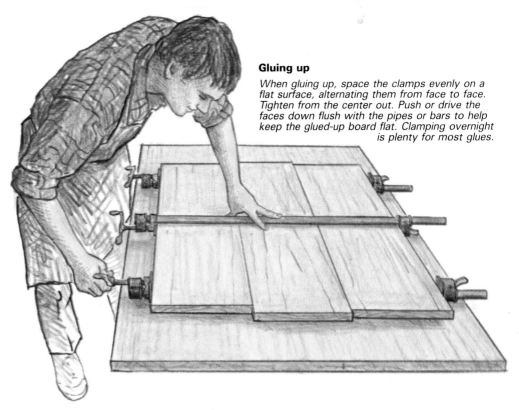

Gluing up

When gluing up, space the clamps evenly on a flat surface, alternating them from face to face. Tighten from the center out. Push or drive the faces down flush with the pipes or bars to help keep the glued-up board flat. Clamping overnight is plenty for most glues.

check against the mating edge. If the boards still rock, the mating edge may need work. This can go on for some time. Don't lose heart—think of all the skill you're accumulating.

Twisted edges need to be fixed, but it doesn't matter if mating edges are at slightly other than right angles to their adjacent faces—as long as the angles are complementary, the boards will form a flat surface. To check the surface, stack the boards edge-to-edge and place a straightedge against their faces. If the surface isn't flat, adjust the angle of one edge to its face and check them again. After edge-planing all the boards to be glued together, stack them up and make a final check for flatness.

Hand-planing mating edges is a difficult skill to master. Over and over again you'll introduce one fault while trying to correct another. When the edges are close to mating perfectly, force yourself to try one more time to correct that last niggling fault. If it still isn't right, then say the hell with it, and move on to the next pair. Among the virtues of modern glues is their ability to join edges that are far from perfectly matched. There may be gaps, the joined boards may not be perfectly flat, but they will stick together. The simple table and bookcase are nice projects because you get a lot of practice while making something useful. It's up to you how much practice you can stand before you need to see the completed piece before you.

Gluing up—When all the pairs of mating edges have been planed, I glue up with $\frac{3}{4}$-in. pipe clamps and Elmer's Glue-All (a white glue), first making a dry run to de-

termine the position and number of clamps. Place clamps 12 in. to 15 in. apart, starting and ending about 3 in. from the ends of the boards. Alternate the clamps top and bottom to equalize their pull and avoid cupping the glued-up boards.

Lay the bottom clamps on a flat surface and spread glue on all the edges to be joined. Better too much glue than too little—the excess will get squeezed out of a tight joint anyway. Place the boards on the clamps and rub the mating edges together until glue squeezes out. Draw the joints together with the center clamp, then work out toward each end. I align the faces of the boards with a 16-oz. hammer and a hardwood block, driving them down on the clamps, which helps keep the boards from cupping or twisting as a unit.

It's important that the surface of the glued-up boards lie in a single plane while the glue cures. Whether the boards lie flat or lean against a wall, you can sight over the clamps just like over winding sticks, and shim up low corners to align them.

The glued-up boards can be treated like a single board now, and cleaned off with a sharp plane. Chances are the surface will be slightly cupped, but I don't worry too much about that. The understructure of a table or the corner joints of a box can pull it fairly flat. At this point, the whole question of flatness boils down to what irritates you more: a gently rolling tabletop with wobbling plates and teacups, or seemingly endless tabletop planing.   □

Roger Holmes is an associate editor at Fine Woodworking.

Starting Out

II. Cutting a bridle joint

by Roger Holmes

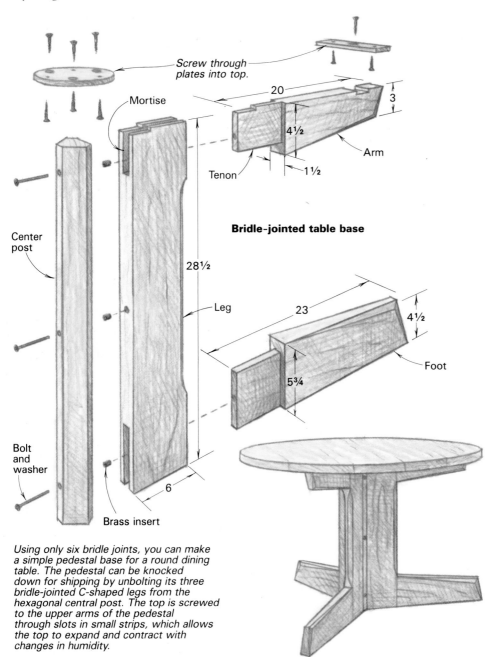

Bridle-jointed table base

Screw through plates into top.

Mortise

Center post

Tenon

Arm

20

3

4½

1½

28½

Leg

23

4½

5¾

Foot

Bolt and washer

6

Brass insert

Using only six bridle joints, you can make a simple pedestal base for a round dining table. The pedestal can be knocked down for shipping by unbolting its three bridle-jointed C-shaped legs from the hexagonal central post. The top is screwed to the upper arms of the pedestal through slots in small strips, which allows the top to expand and contract with changes in humidity.

The mortise-and-tenon is one of the most basic and versatile woodworking joints. It can be as plain as the rung-to-leg joints in any stick chair, or as complicated as some of the three-dimensional, jigsaw-puzzle joints used in Japanese house carpentry. A mortise-and-tenon can be used almost any time you need to join the end of one piece to the edge of another. They're such effective joints that it's hard to find a piece of furniture without at least one, even if only a dowel in a hole.

The bridle joint (shown above) is one of the simplest garden-variety mortise-and-tenons. Its open-ended mortise doesn't have the mechanical (unglued) strength of an enclosed mortise, but modern glues and the joint's ample gluing surface make up the difference. And a bridle joint can be made more quickly and easily. Both tenon and mortise can be cut almost entirely with a saw, eliminating the excavation that would be required to clear out an enclosed mortise (see p. 13).

When I was figuring out the base for the round pine dining table shown here, bridle joints seemed ideal. A pedestal eliminates obstruction under the table, and the C-shaped, bridle-jointed frames are sturdy enough to support the tabletop, Thanksgiving turkey and a dozen or so elbows. And the six bridle joints are all the joinery needed for the entire base. (See the first part of this series on pp. 2-7 for how to join boards for a top.)

I cut the bridle joints with a bandsaw and backsaw, then used a chisel and shoulder plane to clean up and fit them together. If you don't have a bandsaw, you can do all the sawing with a backsaw and a bowsaw or handsaw (see p. 10). A shoulder plane is a handy tool, but if you're reluctant to dish out $40 or so for one, you can trim the shoulders with a chisel.

When I knew roughly what sort of table I wanted, I designed it on the workshop floor with a piece of chalk. I drew an elevation (side view) of half the top and one frame full-scale, then fiddled with the proportions until they looked good. If you start with the drawing shown here, sketching a full-scale elevation will help fix the project in your mind. You can change the dimensions and shapes, but I think you'll find the table too shaky if you make the arms, legs or feet much less than 4 in. wide or 1¼ in. thick. The feet will get in the way if they extend beyond the top's circumference. I made the top 4 ft. in diameter, but I think the table would look better with a 5-ft. top.

When your plans are chalked out, cut three sets of arms, legs and feet for the C-shaped frames. Cut all the parts to width and length, but don't shape them yet—it's a lot easier to cut joints in rectangular stock. Next plane the parts flat and to thickness—mine were 1½ in. thick. Try to make them all the same thickness, but don't get bogged down if there's ¹⁄₁₆ in. or so variance—the parts can be planed flush after the frames are glued up. Mark the flattest face of each piece, plane the edges straight and square to it, then mark the most accurate edge (I use a little squiggle on the good face, joined to a V on the good edge). The tolerances needn't be up to edge-joining standards, but the closer the better. Don't worry about making the ends exactly square; a good sawcut is fine.

Laying out—Like any mortise-and-tenon, bridle joints require accurate, organized marking out. To avoid errors, mark all the joints at once, before cutting. You'll

Marking the shoulders

Knife the tenon shoulder lines around each arm and foot. Hold the square's stock against only the good edge or face as you go.

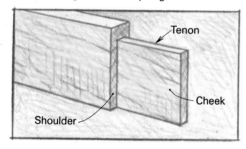

Tenon

Cheek

Shoulder

need to mark wherever a sawcut must be made. As the drawings above and below show, I marked the shoulders with a square and knife, and the cheeks with a mortise gauge, which is just a marking gauge with two pins that scribe both cheeks at once. When laying out each joint, always reference the square and marking gauge from *only* the marked good face and good edge of each part.

For the pedestal, I arranged the parts for each frame on the bench: good-face marks up, good-edge marks to the top of the arm, the bottom of the foot and the inside of the leg. Mark one end of each leg for reference, then identify both parts of each joint with the same number or letter.

Lay out the tenons first. To reduce er-

ror, I avoid measuring wherever possible by scribing dimensions directly from the parts being joined. Here, all the tenons are as long as the legs are wide, so I laid one foot across its leg in the position it would be joined, and marked the shoulder position on the edge with a pencil. Using this foot as a guide, I marked the shoulders on the remaining feet and arms. (If the tenons are $\frac{1}{32}$ in. or so shorter than the leg width, clamping will be easier and the surfaces can be planed flush after assembly.)

When you've marked all the tenon lengths, scribe the shoulder lines using a try square and a sharp pocket knife or utility knife. I've devised a little ritual to ensure that I'm scribing only from the good face and edge: First I scribe across the good face, holding the stock of the square against the good edge. Then I scribe across each edge, holding the stock against the good face. Finally I scribe across the second face, holding the stock against the good edge. The lines should connect around the piece. If they don't, the good face is probably twisted. If they come close, don't worry about it—you can take care of the discrepancy when you fit the joint. If they're way off, I'd re-plane the face, or pick another board and start over.

Lay out the ends of the mortises next. I made the tenons about 1 in. narrower than the full width of the arm and foot—the length of the mortise equals the width of the tenon, so there's less mortise to saw out. Pencil the mortise length on the good faces of the legs, then extend the line across the edges with a try square and knife.

The cheeks of the tenons and the mortises can be scribed with a marking gauge or a mortise gauge. When the mortised and the tenoned pieces are the same thickness, I make tenons about three-fifths that thickness. If the tenon is much thicker, the width of the mortise will make its walls too thin and liable to break. Cutting and cleaning up the mortises will be easier if you make the tenon thickness match a standard auger-bit and chisel size—I made the tenons for the C-shaped frames $\frac{5}{8}$ in. thick.

Set the mortise gauge and

scribe around the edges and ends of the pieces, from shoulder line to shoulder line. When setting up a mortise gauge, I set the distance between the pins, then adjust the fence so that the mortise will be centered on the edge. An easy way to set the fence is to gauge from both faces of the piece, tapping the fence until pin marks made from each face coincide. Scribe all the tenons and mortises with this gauge setting. (At the same time, scribe several offcuts from the frame pieces to use when setting up the bandsaw for cutting the joints.) Make sure you run the fence against the good faces so the

Cutting the cheeks

Bandsaw the tenon cheeks against a straight, squared-up fence. Make sure the sawkerf is in the waste, and try to saw right to the scribe, leaving half of it on the tenon. (After boring the mortises, saw them the same way.)

Saw-blade

Scribe

Waste

Marking the cheeks

Scribe the cheeks of the tenons and mortises with a mortise gauge—the setting is the same for both. Always run the gauge fence against the good face.

pieces will be aligned even if their thicknesses vary slightly. If you scribe with a one-pin marking gauge, set up once for each cheek and gauge only from the good faces. Gauging from both faces will produce mortises and tenons of varying thicknesses—a big headache.

Cutting the cheeks—Bandsawing the cheeks of the mortises and the tenons is easy, safe, and, if you set up and saw carefully, accurate. Pieces this large are best cut with a ½-in. or ¾-in. wide blade, though a ¼-in. will do if you feed slowly. Whichever blade you use, make sure it's sharp; there's no joy in burning your way through six inches of pine. My saw

Cutting the shoulders

Saw right to the knifed shoulder line with a backsaw. Holding the piece against a bench hook, angle the saw at the start and drop it slowly as the cut proceeds.

Boring the mortises

Bore a hole at the end of each mortise so that the waste will come free after you make the cheek cuts.

doesn't have a rip fence, so I attach a 2-ft. long, straight piece of pine, about 1½ in. by 3 in., to the table with two clamps.

Set up for the tenons first, starting with the cheeks farthest from the fence. Mount the fence parallel to the blade and position it so that the sawkerf falls in the waste and the cut leaves half the scribe line on the tenon, as shown in the drawing on p. 9. (Remember to place the good face against the fence when setting up and cutting). Use the scribed scrap pieces to check the setup, then saw away on the real thing. Set up and make the second-cheek cuts in the same way. Remember, the closer you are to splitting the gauge lines, the less

work you'll have fitting the joints later.

The cheek cuts for the mortises are set up and bandsawn the same way. Before cutting the cheeks, I bore a hole through the piece at the end of the mortise so the waste will come away cleanly at the completion of the second-cheek cut. I use a brace and ½-in. auger bit to bore about halfway through from each edge. A drill press will work, too, but doesn't deliver the same cheap thrill I get when the holes meet in the center.

If the cheek cuts leave half the scribe line around the mortise and the tenon, the joint should slip together snugly without much fitting. The bandsaw isn't a preci-

Handsawn cheeks

You can cut the bridle-joint cheeks with a bowsaw (shown at right) or a crosscut handsaw. A handsawn cheek requires three cuts: two diagonal and one parallel to the shoulder line, guided by the first two kerfs. It's faster to make the cuts in pairs, working both cheeks simultaneously. For the angled cuts, tilt the workpiece so you can see the scribe marks on the edge and end at the same time. Saw right to the marks, leaving half the scribe outlining the mortise or the tenon. Use your thumb as a fence to start the cut, then lengthen the stroke. With practice, slight adjustments to keep the saw on the marks will become second nature.

Handsaw each tenon or mortise cheek in three cuts. The first two kerfs will guide the third. Try to cut right to the scribed lines.

sion tool, however, so I usually adjust the second-cheek cut according to how the scrap tenon fits the scrap mortise. Better too tight than too loose; it's easier to shave the tenon down than to build it up.

When all the mortises have been sawn, square up the bored-out ends with a ½-in. or ⅝-in. chisel. Chop straight down or undercut slightly. There usually isn't much wood to remove, so I push the chisel rather than bashing it with a mallet. Holding the chisel as shown in the box on p. 13 affords good control from the bottom hand and plenty of power from the top.

What can be done by bandsaw can also be done by hand—not as quickly, maybe, but just as well. The cheeks of mortises and tenons on most furniture are small enough to be cut with a backsaw, but for the pedestal frames, you need a bowsaw or hand-

saw that can cut to a depth of 6 in. in the ends of the parts. I think that a bowsaw with a 1-in. wide blade gives more control than a handsaw, but I knew a joiner who cut perfectly good tenons—cheeks and shoulders—with a handsaw. Suit yourself; either saw takes practice. The box on the facing page outlines the basics.

Shoulders—I cut the tenon shoulders with a backsaw. It's possible to set up a tablesaw or radial-arm saw to make these cuts, but if there aren't many to do, it's just as fast to cut them by hand.

Accurate work like this demands a sharp saw. You'll also need a bench hook for holding the arms and legs while cutting the shoulders. It's easy enough to make a hook: just nail a 1x2 on each end of opposite faces of a piece of plywood or

solid wood. As shown in the drawing at the top of the facing page, the bottom strip catches the edge of the bench and your own weight keeps the workpiece in place against the top strip.

Starting the shoulder cut accurately is important. The points of the sawteeth should be flush to the knife line. I use my thumb as a fence to position the blade. Start the cut at the far edge, at an angle to the face. As the cut deepens, lower the saw gradually until the stroke extends the full width of the piece and parallel to its face. The knife line is very fine, so you can't split it like a scribe line. The wood fibers, however, will break off cleanly at the line as the cut progresses, and a close look will tell if you're veering away from the line. The cut is also self-jigging: the kerf you've already cut will help guide the saw along the uncut line. Don't hurry; make the strokes regular and smooth. With practice, you'll be able to tell by feel if the saw is perpendicular to the face or not. At first, though, you'll just have to bend down and check the angle by eye. Save the waste from the cheeks to use for clamping pads when you glue up.

After cutting the shoulders, rip the tenons to width by hand or on the bandsaw (remember, tenon width equals mortise length). I mark the width with a pencil, holding it so I can run my fingers like a fence along the tenon's edge, ensuring that the line will be parallel to the edge.

Fitting the joints—If every cut has been right on the money, the tenons should slide snuggly into the mortises, the shoulders fit without gaps. My joints, however, always need some trimming to fit right. A shoulder plane comes in very handy for this work. The rectangular steel body of the plane, usually ¾ in. or 1 in. thick, fits comfortably in one hand. The edges of the blade are flush with the sides of the body, which is ideal for planing right up to the cheek or shoulder of a tenon.

It's easier to fit the tenon to the mortise than vice versa. If the tenon is too thick, pare off the excess with a shoulder plane and a bench plane. With the shoulder plane, I take a few shavings off one cheek, hard against the shoulder, then plane the rest of the cheek down to that level with a jointer plane. Try inserting the tenon again and take more off the other cheek if necessary. Be careful to remove an even layer of wood from each cheek so they will remain parallel and make full contact with the mortise cheeks.

A loose tenon is more of a nuisance. It's

Fitting the shoulders

Clean up and adjust the shoulders with a finely set shoulder plane. To avoid chipping the far edge, reverse the plane and pull it toward you.

possible to glue on a piece of veneer to fill out the tenon's thickness, or you can clamp the slightly flexible walls of the mortise down on the tenon. If the tenon is rattling around in the mortise, cut another one. The extra practice won't do any harm, and if you're using pine, it's cheap enough that you shouldn't flinch as the mistake hits the firewood pile.

Even if the tenon shoulders have been perfectly cut, a pass with a finely set shoulder plane will smooth whatever roughness is left by the saw. Often more doctoring is required to make both shoulders tight to the mortised piece. If the knifed shoulder line is visible, plane down to it, then work by trial and error, assembling the joint and marking the high spots with pencil for removal. To avoid chipping the edge of the piece at the end of the cut, turn the plane around and pull it toward you to complete the cut. I don't usually check the shoulders for squareness as I go along, but when the shoulders are tight, I check the assembled pieces with a framing square. If they don't form a right angle, a couple of shavings off one end of the shoulders usually will fix things.

It doesn't matter how much you plane off the shoulders when making these C-shaped frames; no one will notice if one leg or arm is shorter than another. But if you're making a four-sided frame, such as for a door, you must make the shoulder-to-shoulder lengths of the rails equal, otherwise the frame won't be square.

Finishing up—Before gluing up, I tapered the arms and feet and cut the chamfers. The shape of the frame can be altered as you wish. I played around with various curves for the inside edges before deciding on the simple solution shown in the drawing on p. 8. Layout goes faster if you make cardboard templates, particu-

larly if anything is curved. I traced around tapered templates for the arm and foot, bandsawed the waste and planed off the sawmarks. Leave the ends square for clamping, then trim and chamfer them after gluing up.

The first time I made one of these frames, I cut the arm and foot chamfers with a hand plane and the leg chamfers with a spokeshave. The job got done, but it took a long time. Prodded by a friend, I later tried a drawknife. Much to my surprise, it was not the crude implement I had expected, but a tool as capable of taking thin, controlled shavings as of lopping off great chunks of wood. The next set of chamfers took a third as long.

If you drawknife the chamfers, spend some time practicing on scrapwood before slicing into the real thing.

You'll get used to the tool and discover pleasing proportions for your chamfers. The main prerequisite for successful drawknifing is a sharp blade. I sharpen mine like a carving tool: a large bevel on one side and a small bevel on the other. The small bevel helps you control the tool, which is important because a drawknife has no sole to govern its depth of cut. (I hold the blade still and move the stones over it; you may prefer the reverse. See p. 3 of this book for more sharpening tips.) A slicing cut increases control and produces the cleanest surfaces. You can

Chamfering

A sharp drawknife makes fast, accurate work of chamfering. Work to pencil lines or by eye. Sharpening the blade with two bevels (long on the top, short on the bottom) increases control for fine cuts.

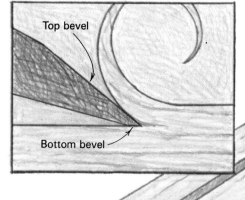

Top bevel

Bottom bevel

chamfer freehand or to penciled guide-lines. If you're after precision, finish with a plane and a spokeshave.

Gluing up the frames is a snap. Squirt glue on the tenon and mortise cheeks and spread it around with a long, thin stick. The glue film needn't be thick; just make sure that all surfaces of the cheeks are covered to ensure a good bond. (If you aren't too quick with the stick or you're gluing up in hot weather, use a white glue, like Elmer's Glue-All, instead of a quick-setting yellow glue, like Titebond.)

Slide the tenons into the mortises, pushing the tenon hard up against the end of the mortise. I pull the shoulders tight with pipe clamps, which doesn't require much pressure, then take these off and clamp across the cheeks with quick-action clamps or C-clamps, using the offcuts from the cheeks for clamping pads. Thicker pads will distribute the pressure better and produce a thinner glueline. A thick glueline might be unsightly on a door, where the edges show, but it doesn't really matter here.

When the glue has cured, plane the faces of the frames flush with a jointer plane—there can be quite a bit to plane off a misaligned joint, but no one will notice if one frame is a little thinner than another. Next trim and chamfer the ends of the arms and feet. The three frames

Gluing up

Cover the mortise and tenon cheeks with glue, then pull the joints together with pipe clamps (that's why you left the ends square). When the shoulders are tight, clamp across the cheeks, using wooden pads to distribute the pressure and protect the surfaces.

should all be the same size, with the outside edges of the arms and feet square to the outside edge of the leg. Stack the frames face to face to find the shortest one, then plane it square if necessary, checking with a framing square. Plane the other two to match, checking each against the first rather than checking with a tape measure and square. It's surprising how discrepancies that can hardly be seen can readily be detected with the fingertips.

I attached each of the frames to a central hexagonal post with three bolts. If

you'll never need to disassemble the pedestal, you could glue the frames to the post. I cut the post on the tablesaw, setting the blade at 30° to rip the corners off a 2¾-in. square. The post takes some fussing to fit. I planed three faces 1⅝ in. wide; the others finished narrower.

Bore the bolt holes in the post, offsetting the three holes at each location. Clamp the post to each leg in turn, marking through the holes onto the leg's edge, then bore pilot holes. You could lag-bolt the legs to the post, but the bolts will strip out after too many disassemblies. I used ⁵⁄₁₆-in. dia. machine bolts and brass inserts, which have wood threads on the outside and machine threads on the inside. You can buy the inserts from Woodcraft Supply. (See *FWW* #47, p. 8, for an easy way to insert these.)

I bandsawed the top round, spokeshaved the edge smooth (a rasp or file would do, too) and chamfered the arrises with a drawknife. The base is screwed to the top through small wooden strips and a wooden center plate let into the arms. Single screw holes are fine in the center plate, but slotting the holes in the strips will help allow the top to move with changes in humidity.

I don't like the look of varnished pine, so I just paste-waxed the table. This doesn't provide a great deal of protection, so we scrub it down regularly with a potato brush and hot, soapy water. I wouldn't say the table has patina, but it wears its scars well and I don't worry when a guest spills wine or the baby bashes it with his spoon. □

Roger Holmes is an associate editor at FWW. *This is the second in a series of articles for beginning woodworkers.*

Enclosed mortises

Many mortise-and-tenon joints require an enclosed mortise, rather than the open mortise of the bridle joint. Lay out the mortise using the same marking-gauge setting as for the tenon. I clear the bulk of the waste by boring a series of adjoining holes with a bit the same width as or slightly smaller than the mortise width. Bore about ¹⁄₁₆ in. deeper than the tenon length. Then slice down the cheeks with a wide, sharp chisel, splitting the gauge line. The only tricky part is keeping the chisel straight. Clean up the mortise bottom with a narrow chisel, so the tenon doesn't bottom out.

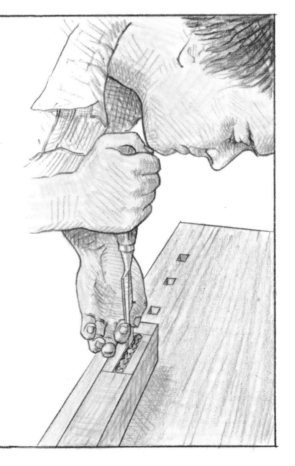

Starting Out
III. Simple bookcase joints

by Roger Holmes

I can't remember the last time I rented a house with bookshelves (or enough closets for that matter, but I own a lot more books than shirts). So for years I've lived with makeshift shelves—planks on bricks and brackets, planks wedged into alcoves. Confronted with another shelfless house recently, I finally decided to make some permanent shelves that could move with me from house to house. The result, a stack of two simple boxes, one shallow, one deep, is shown in the drawing at right.

Boxes—called carcases in traditional parlance—are the cabinetmaker's basic building blocks. Stripped down to essentials, most casework isn't much more than a box-like container, usually filled with boxy drawers. In fact, most of the furniture in my house is made of simple rectangular boxes. For example, scale down the shallow box shown on top in the drawing for a spice rack or knickknack shelves; add a mirrored door and you've got a medicine cabinet. Slide a stack of smaller boxes into the deep bottom box and you've got a chest of drawers (I'll show how to do this on pp. 20-24).

I made my boxes of pine, tailoring the depth of the upper box to the width of the boards I had on hand. I started with 10-in. wide boards for that box, but tapered the sides to add a little stability and to break the monotony of all those rectangles. The wider sides, top and bottom of the lower box had to be edge-joined and glued up.

Box joinery can be as simple or as complex as your skill and patience permit. Anybody can nail a butt joint together, and for some things that's joint enough. Secret mitered dovetails are at the other end of the scale, and I don't know many people who use them regularly. For my bookshelves, I wanted more strength than

a simple nailed butt joint would give, but I didn't want to spend a lot of time getting it. The upper box, therefore, was put together entirely with dadoes—strong, easily cut joints in which the full thickness of each shelf end is housed in a groove in the side. (If you want adjustable shelves, just dado the top and bottom shelves and support the others on dowels as shown for the adjustable shelf in the lower box.)

Because the lower box had to have a

flush, flat top, the top couldn't be dadoed into the sides. You could nail the ends of the top in rabbets in the sides, but the tongue-and-groove shown in the drawing locks together, which makes the joint stronger and much easier to assemble. The carcase bottom dadoes into the sides. Eighth-inch tempered Masonite backs strengthen both boxes, an important factor if you want adjustable shelves in the upper box. Whether you nail the back

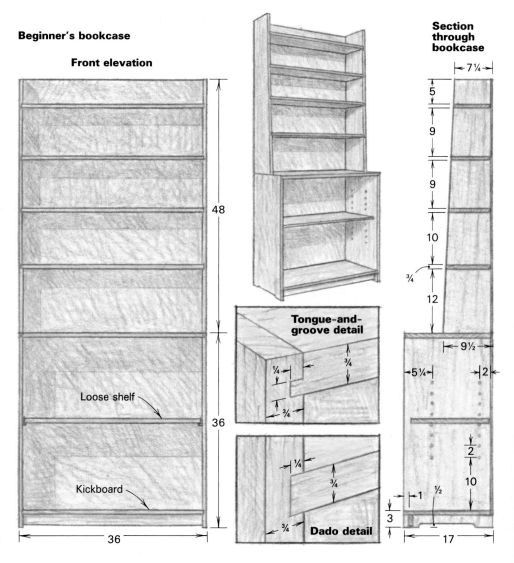

Beginner's bookcase

Front elevation

Loose shelf

Kickboard

48

36

36

Section through bookcase

7¼

5

9

9

10

¾

12

Tongue-and-groove detail

¼

¾

¾

¼

¾

¾

Dado detail

9½

5¼

2

2

10

1

½

3

17

over the back edges or into a rabbet affects only the looks, not the strength. I reinforced all the joints with finishing nails; screws would add even more strength. If the joints fit snugly and the boxes have backs, simply gluing them will be enough.

The carcase joints I've described can be cut by hand or machine. I'll explain the hand methods here, and the router and tablesaw alternatives on p. 18.

First prepare the parts. Flatten, thickness and glue up the boards, either by hand as described in the first article of this series (see pp. 2-7) or with a jointer and thickness planer. Try to make all the parts at least ¾ in. thick. The exact thickness of the shelves of the upper box and the bottom of the lower box depends on the width of the dadoes. I cut a test dado in scrapwood and thicknessed the boards to fit it snugly. Tight joints present a dilemma: The tighter the joints, the stronger the box, but the harder it will be to glue up. You should have to apply some pressure to assemble a joint dry, but you shouldn't have to hammer it home. If anything, make the shelves too thick for now—it's easier to make a board thinner than to shim a loose joint.

Next rip the boards to width and crosscut them to length. (Since the back is let into a rabbet in both boxes, the shelves have to be narrower than the sides, so that their back edge will be flush with the bottom of the rabbet.) Mark the good face and good edge. From now until you cut the joints, the top and bottom of the lower box are worked in the same way as the shelves of the upper box, so I'll just lump them all together and call them shelves.

The ends of all the shelves should be square to their edges, and the shelves should all be the same length. Your tablesaw or radial-arm saw may be very accurate, but mine leave the pieces slightly off, so I finish the job with a jointer plane. Stack the shelves so you can pick out the shortest one to square up first.

Planing end grain isn't particularly difficult, and the techniques are similar to those used for planing edges (again, see pp. 2-7). Check the end against the good edge with a framing square or a try square, and mark the high corner. Put the board end-up in the face vise. If the board is short enough, position the end only a couple of inches above the bench to cut down on chatter. Adjust the plane to take a thin shaving, then plane in from the high corner—to avoid splintering the edge, don't run the plane off the far corner. Un-

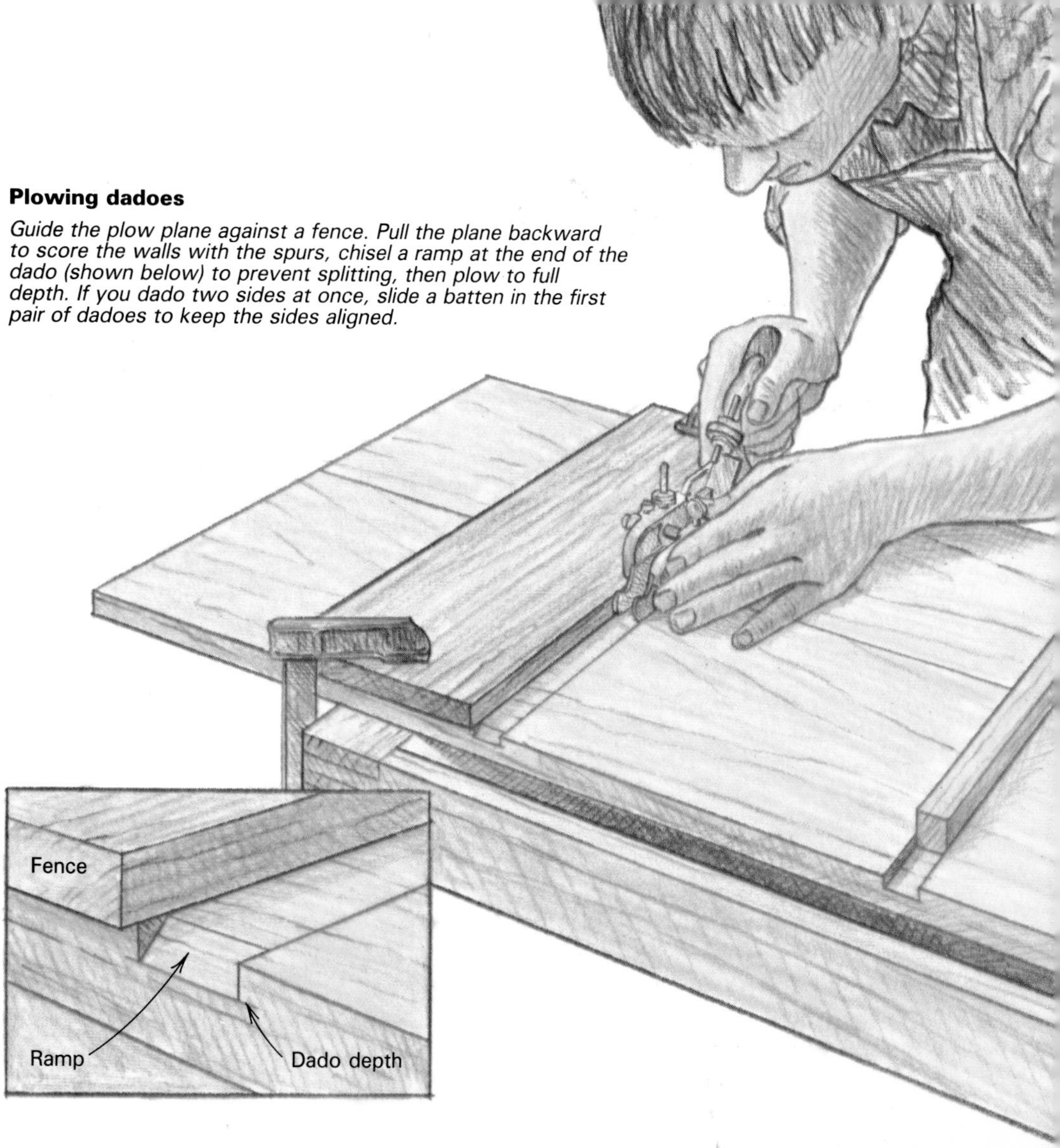

Plowing dadoes

Guide the plow plane against a fence. Pull the plane backward to score the walls with the spurs, chisel a ramp at the end of the dado (shown below) to prevent splitting, then plow to full depth. If you dado two sides at once, slide a batten in the first pair of dadoes to keep the sides aligned.

Fence

Ramp

Dado depth

less your saw is way out of whack, a couple of shavings should square the end to the good edge. The end needn't be dead square to the face, but if it's too far off, the joint won't be as strong. With the shortest shelf square, use it as a template for the rest, stacking it and the next shelf, then feeling with your fingertips for discrepancies in the ends. Square the box sides the same way.

Before I cut any of the dadoes, I pencil in their positions on the sides. Place the good edges of the paired sides together, ends flush, and simultaneously mark the locations of both walls of each dado on the two inside faces to ensure that the shelf spacing is exactly the same on both. Extend these marks across each inside face with a framing square, holding the square against the good edge. Also clearly mark the bottom of the inside face of each side. The spacing shown in the drawing on the facing page accommodates most of my books, but alter it to suit yours.

The depth of the dado isn't critical, but it shouldn't be more than half the side's thickness. A deeper dado would be stronger, but too hard to assemble. One-quarter to one-third the thickness of the side is plenty. Scribe the dado depths on the edges with a marking gauge.

Dadoing by hand is satisfying work if you're not in a hurry. You'll need a plow plane—a straightforward tool that requires a little practice. A simple metal plow plane consists of a handle attached to one of two fairly thin runners that form the body. The handled runner holds the blade and is fitted with two bars on which the other runner slides. The outer faces of the runners are set flush with the edges of the cutter, which can be one of a variety of widths. A fence, which also fits on the bars, can guide the plane along the edge or end of the work. I've had good luck plowing easy-to-work woods like pine or mahogany; harder woods are tough going. Most mail-order tool companies carry simple plow planes or slightly more complicated, and more expensive, combination planes. Prices vary—from $60 to well over $100—so shop around. The plane shown above is a Stanley #45, a more complicated molding plane that can also be used as a plow plane. I got lucky and picked it up at a garage sale for $25.

To set up the plane, make sure that the blade is razor-sharp and that the outside faces of the runners are flush with the edges of the blade. When plowing across grain, use the small spurs housed ahead of the cutter in each of the runner faces. They score the wood, which keeps the fibers from splintering on either side of the dado. The spurs should be knife-sharp and long enough to score the wood cleanly, but not so long that they tear it.

Narrow box sides are easily dadoed in pairs. Place a pair on the benchtop, inside faces up, bottom ends aligned, good edges butted together. Then clamp a wooden straightedge across them, flush with the mark for the first dado wall. Set the plane on the far edge, tight to the fence, and draw it carefully back toward you to scribe the walls with the spurs without engaging the cutter. Then chisel a ramp in the waste at the end of the dado to prevent splintering. The first few strokes establish the dado, so make them carefully—set a shallow depth of cut and keep the plane tight against the fence and perpendicular to the board's face. After two or three strokes the plane will follow its own path, so you can remove the straightedge. Most plow planes have depth stops, but I use mine only for a rough gauge; when I get down to the scribe marks on the edges, I check the depth of the groove with a steel ruler. Slide a piece of scrap into both dadoes to keep the sides aligned, and reset the fence for the next cut.

Plow-planing takes practice, so dado a few pieces of scrap before tackling the real thing. The fussiest adjustment is aligning the edges of the cutter, the faces of the runners and the spurs to cut the dado walls cleanly. As you become familiar with the tool, you'll develop little dodges to make the job more accurate and efficient.

Tongue-and-groove corner joints are not much more difficult to cut than dadoes, just a little more time-consuming. I make the tongue about one-quarter to one-third as thick as the board, whichever matches the plow-plane cutter, router bit or dado head to be used for cutting the groove. The top and bottom of the lower box are the same length as the upper-box shelves, so the length of the tongue (the groove depth) is the same as the depth of the dadoes.

Make the groove first—it's easier to plane the tongue to fit it than vice versa. Since the tongue has a shoulder, you can make the groove just slightly deeper than the tongue length to avoid having the tongue bottom out at assembly. I plow the groove by running the plane's fence attachment against the end of the side. You could also run the plane against a clamped-on fence as you did for the dadoes. Make sure that there are no high spots on the

bottom of the groove that would keep the joint from going together completely.

The tongues, created by rabbeting the ends of the top, should fit snugly in their grooves. I cut them with a rabbet plane, a narrow plane with a blade that extends completely across the sole and with faces perpendicular to the sole. One face has a spur like that on the plow plane. (You can also rabbet with a plow plane or a shoulder plane.)

First gauge the shoulder line and tongue thickness on the ends. Use a cutting gauge (a marking gauge with a small knife instead of a pin) if you've got one, because it makes a cleaner line across grain. Position the top on the bench and clamp a wooden straightedge fence on the shoulder line to guide the plane. Alternatively, set the plane's adjustable fence to run against the end of the board. Make sure that the blade and spur are sharp, and that the blade is flush with the spur face—if it's shy of the face, the rabbet will be stepped; if it's proud of the face, the shoulder will be ragged. Draw the plane backward as before to scribe the shoulder with the spur, make a ramp at the far end of the rabbet to prevent tearout, then plane away. When I'm close to the gauge lines, I try the tongue in the groove and

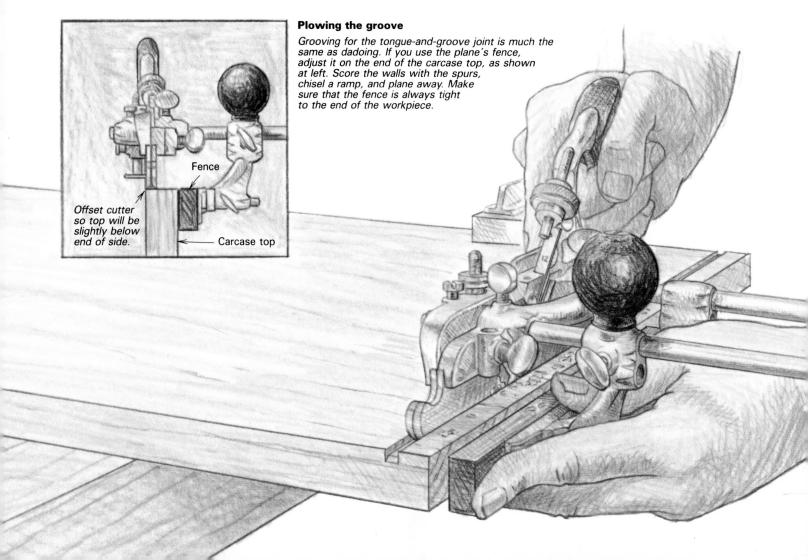

Plowing the groove

Grooving for the tongue-and-groove joint is much the same as dadoing. If you use the plane's fence, adjust it on the end of the carcase top, as shown at left. Score the walls with the spurs, chisel a ramp, and plane away. Make sure that the fence is always tight to the end of the workpiece.

Fence

Offset cutter so top will be slightly below end of side.

Carcase top

Rabbeting the tongue

As when dadoing, score the rabbet with the spur and chisel a ramp in the waste before planing. Keep the fence tight to the end, and the plane's machined spur face perpendicular to the work.

take the final cuts to fit the joint with a sharp, finely set shoulder plane.

Cutting the rabbets for the backs is the final bit of joinery required. I cut them just slightly deeper than the 1/8-in. back and about three-quarters the thickness of the sides. I rabbeted only the sides of the boxes, and butted all the horizontal pieces against the back. Rabbet the top of the lower box if you want to hide the top edge of the back. Because the rabbet runs parallel to the grain, you needn't knife the shoulder line or use the spur cutter. If you're tapering the bookcase sides, do it now.

To make sure everything fits, put the boxes together dry before gluing up. If the shelves are all the same thickness, dry assembly should go quickly. If they're not, now is the time to fit them individually to the dadoes. I thin the ends with a sharp, finely set jointer plane, planing

with or across the grain. Be careful not to take too much off—if you're not confident with the plane, it might be better to sand off tiny amounts. You should be able to assemble the joints by hand, though it may take some wiggling to get the ends to seat all along the length of the dado. If you're fitting the joints individually, mark the end/dado pairs clearly.

When you're sure the boxes will go together, clear a space in the shop and organize the things you'll need for gluing up. You should have at least two pipe clamps and a pair of stout cauls for each box—scrap hardwood at least 1 in. by 3 in. and just a bit longer than the width of the sides will do. Plane a slight crown in the cauls for the wide sides; pressure on the ends will produce pressure in the middle. I use a white glue like Elmer's Glue-All because it sets up more slowly than yellow glue.

I lay the parts on the bench to spread

the glue, then build up from a side on the floor. Protect the surface by laying the side on a clean piece of plywood or particleboard. Spread glue in all the dadoes (and grooves) in one side with a stick or a flux brush (available at most hardware stores), making sure that the dado walls are covered. Then stick the shelves in place. Align the back edges and the rabbet before you push the ends home—it's impossible to slide an end sideways in a tight joint. Work quickly, seating each end as best you can, but don't worry if they don't go down completely; you'll pull the joint tight with clamps in a minute.

When the shelves are housed in the first side, glue the second and push it down on the shelf ends, aligning the back edges and the rabbets before driving the joints home. The second side is harder to wiggle into place—a shelf or two always wants to pop out. So I get them started, then drive them down with a hammer padded by a thick hardwood block. As you've already made sure all the joints fit, you shouldn't have any nasty surprises.

Now draw the joints tight with clamps. Getting two clamps and two cauls in place on a shelf all by yourself is exasperating—enlist a friend if you can. If you can't, figure it out dry beforehand. The top of the lower box is easier to pull tight because you can rest the clamps on it. Tight joints usually will stay in place after you've

Gluing up

Getting the shelves started in the second-side dadoes can be trying. When you've succeeded, drive them home with a hammer and wooden block.

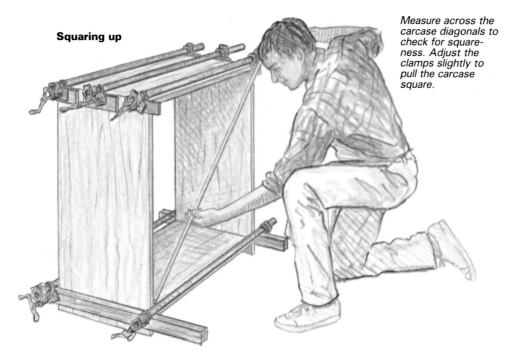

Squaring up

Measure across the carcase diagonals to check for squareness. Adjust the clamps slightly to pull the carcase square.

pulled them home; if they don't, just leave the clamps on while the glue dries.

Check the squareness of the box by measuring diagonally from corner to corner. If the diagonals aren't equal, you can adjust by pulling across the longer diagonal by hand or with a clamp (on wide boxes, clamp front and back to keep the box from twisting). Sometimes just perching the box on the floor on one corner and leaning into the diagonal corner will correct the problem—don't lean too hard, though.

When all the joints are pulled tight, carefully set the box on its side on the floor for nailing. Nails help keep the joints tight while the glue sets, and they add a certain amount of strength, particularly if the joints are at all loose. (If the joints are less than a friction fit, I'd reinforce them with screws.) Check for squareness, then drive in some finishing nails at a slight angle. Flip the box over and nail the other side.

If you're adding a back, do it now before the glue sets. A square, well-fitted back will help square up most boxes. Flush any uneven joints between shelf edges and rabbets with a chisel or plane. I painted the inside face of the back before assembly. To assemble, run a bead of glue down the rabbets and across the edges of the shelves—not too much or it will squeeze out—and nail the back in place. If the box is out of square, nail along one side first, then force the other side square as you nail it down. For extra strength, I nailed a 1-in. by 2½-in. kickboard to the sides and bottom as shown on p. 14.

Let any squeezed-out glue set to a rubbery consistency, then pare it off with a

sharp chisel. If you don't want to hang around waiting, swab off squeeze-out with a damp rag, but remember that finish won't take on those areas without thorough sanding. When the glue is dry, flush off the joints with a sharp plane. I chamfered the edges and corners of the boxes with a piloted chamfer bit and router; files and a block plane will do the job as well, if more slowly. The floors in our house are like roller coasters, so I routed out a segment of the bottom ends of the lower-box sides to make four small feet. A coping saw and spokeshave would work, too.

Adjustable shelves perch quite adequately on ¼-in. dowel shelf pegs. I made a Masonite template for the holes in the lower box; resting it on the bottom and flush with the back ensured that the holes would be in the same locations on each side. A piece of tape wrapped around the twist drill or auger bit serves as a dandy depth gauge to keep you from inadvertently drilling through the sides. I chamfered the holes with a countersink bit because I think it looks nice and it makes inserting the dowels easier.

Like all simple, quick projects, this one took me about twice as long as I had expected, so I was in no mood to apply a complicated finish. Which was just as well, because I think film finishes (varnishes and lacquers) generally make pine look terrible. A couple of coats of Johnson's Paste Wax seem to protect the surfaces well enough, and I could enlist the whole family's help in putting it on. □

Roger Holmes is an associate editor at Fine Woodworking.

Machines do it, too

Dadoes: To dado the sides on a tablesaw, set up the dado head to match the thickness of the shelves (or you can thickness the shelves to match the dado). Dado a piece of scrap and try the shelves. I fine-tune the dado width by adding donut-shaped paper shims of various thicknesses between the cutters. Set the depth for about one-third the thickness of the side.

I run the ends of the sides against the rip fence to cut the dadoes—one setting cuts the two dadoes for each shelf. I find this a faster method than using a miter gauge, and it ensures that the shelves are square to the ends. Use a miter gauge for dadoing boards less than 6 in. wide, and for dadoes in the middle of sides too long to be passed against the fence.

With the dado head set up and the fence positioned for the bottom shelf, dado both carcase sides. Most saw guards have to be removed for dadoing, so work carefully, keeping your hands well clear of the blade. Narrow boards can be tricky because there isn't much surface bearing against the fence. I find that placing my right hand near the fence as shown in the drawing below helps overcome any tendency of the board to pivot during the cut. If you're at all uneasy with this procedure, use a miter gauge to steady the board. Push the board's inside face down

Tablesawn dadoes

One fence setting cuts matching dadoes in a pair of identical, squared-up sides.

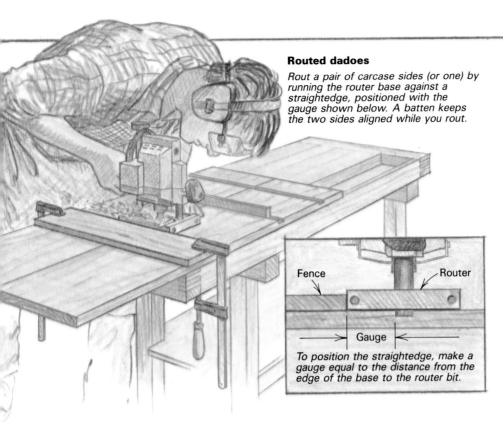

Routed dadoes

Rout a pair of carcase sides (or one) by running the router base against a straightedge, positioned with the gauge shown below. A batten keeps the two sides aligned while you rout.

Fence — Router

Gauge

To position the straightedge, make a gauge equal to the distance from the edge of the base to the router bit.

on the table so the dadoes will be uniformly deep. (Waxing the table and fence also helps.) After cutting the first pair of dadoes, reset the fence and cut the next pair and so on. (If you're making adjustable shelves, dado for the top shelf now and you're done.)

I work off one end to about the middle, then work from the other end. If the sides are square, this shouldn't cause any problems. Most tablesaws can clear up to 24 in. between the blade and fence, so this procedure will work for bookshelves up to 4 ft. tall.

Dadoes can be routed by guiding the router base against a straightedge. First make a gauge for positioning the fence, as shown in the drawing above. Narrow sides can be routed in pairs. Lay them inside-faces-up on a flat surface, aligned and tight together. Clamp the straightedge below and parallel to the first dado, positioning it with your scrapwood gauge. Rout the first dado, slide a scrapwood batten into the grooves to keep the sides aligned, and repeat the procedure for the next dado. If your router base is round, always run the same spot against the fence unless you're sure the base is concentric with the bit.

With a little thought, you can figure out various easily made jigs to speed up the process. Without them, however, I think the tablesaw is faster—it's a ready-made jig for positioning the cuts.

Grooves: On the tablesaw, set up the dado head to the right thickness and height, and run the end of the side against the fence as for dadoing. Position the groove slightly farther from

the end than the thickness of the top so you have only to plane off a little end grain to clean up the joint after assembly. If you rout the groove, guide the router base against a clamped-on fence as for dadoing, or use the adjustable fence that comes as an accessory on most routers.

Tablesawn tongues

Lay the workpiece flat on the table for the first cut. Run it end-up against the fence as shown here for the second.

Fence — Workpiece

Feather board

Blade

First cut

Tongues: You can rout the rabbet that creates the tongue by running the router base against a straightedge as for routing a dado. Rabbet a piece of scrap exactly the same thickness as the top to check bit depth. The tongue should be a snug fit in the groove, as for dadoes.

The drawback of this method is that if the top isn't uniformly thick, the tongue won't be either. The tablesaw method shown below overcomes this problem. Set up the saw with a single sharp crosscut or combination blade. Cut the shoulder first, running the end against the fence, the outside face down on the table. Make the same cut in several pieces of scrap to use for setting up the second cut.

For this second setup, the distance between the fence and the blade should equal the tongue's thickness, which eliminates the need for uniform thickness. Adding a tall wooden fence to the rip fence will help you keep the top perpendicular to the table. Few boards are dead flat, so I clamp a wide feather board to the saw table, positioned so the pressure it exerts will push the top flush to the fence for several inches on both sides of the blade. Test the setup on the scrap, then cut the real thing. (Stand to one side as you complete the cuts, in case the saw kicks the waste back.) —*R.H.*

Starting Out
IV. Build and fit a basic drawer

by Roger Holmes

I have always been fond of cabinets filled with row upon row of little drawers, each cleanly dovetailed and snugly fitted in its opening. Drawers seem full of promise and mystery. When they're closed, that is; an open drawer usually reveals much more junk than treasure. But there is pleasure in sliding open a well-made and well-fitted drawer, even if it's filled with shoelaces and paper clips.

Making drawers can be fun, too, if you don't let your ambition outstrip your ability. I'll never forget the sight of my first attempt, a little drawer barely three inches deep, buried beneath a network of pipe clamps attached in a vain attempt to pull its ill-fitting dovetails tight and its corners square. The drawer joinery shown here is more modest, but perfectly adequate. Using it will allow you to get the hang of making a drawer square and fitting it to a cabinet before you stir dovetails into the mix. And if you need lots of drawers, these are quick to make. Drawers are also well suited for mass production—if you're making more than one, do the same operation on all the pieces at the same time.

The fit of a drawer in a cabinet can be as important as the construction of the drawer itself. I always make the carcase first and then the drawers to fit it. The ideal is a snug fit, with drawer sides and carcase sides sliding against each other like the walls of a piston and its cylinder (well, as much like a piston and cylinder as your patience and the material allow). But the drawer will work even if it is looser, so fitting a drawer really well is a challenge more than a necessity—a distinction worth remembering after you've fiddled around for an unsuccessful hour trying to do it. I use the method described below when I'm trying for that ideal fit; for a less refined and much quicker method, see the box on p. 24.

The drawer joinery—locking tongue-and-groove at the front corners, dadoes for the back and sides—is a variation on the carcase joinery described in the previous "Starting Out" article (see pp. 14-19). I've hung the drawer on runners housed in its sides, which is less traditional than resting the drawer on a frame (a rail under the drawer front and runners under the

sides). Frames can stiffen a carcase, and I use at least one or two in tall stacks of wide drawers. Side-hanging the drawers saves time (no frames to make) as well as the space taken up by the frames, which can be as much as 3 in. on a four-drawer cabinet. The method below, however, can be used to fit either type of drawer.

I made the drawers of pine, but it's not the best-wearing wood for drawer sides—a hard wood would be better. Boards with growth rings more or less parallel to the edges when viewed on the end grain (called quartersawn or riftsawn) are least likely to cup and shrink, and are worth culling out of your lumber pile for use as drawer sides.

Accurate stock preparation is the key to successful drawermaking. If the parts aren't square, the drawer won't be either. Cut all the fronts, backs and sides roughly to size: front and back about 1/32 in. longer than the distance between the carcase sides; drawer sides about 1 in. less than the width of the carcase sides. I make the fronts 3/4 in. thick; the backs and sides

A side-hung drawer

This drawer is easy to make and hang in a new or existing carcase. It's fitted so its sides slide smoothly against the carcase sides.

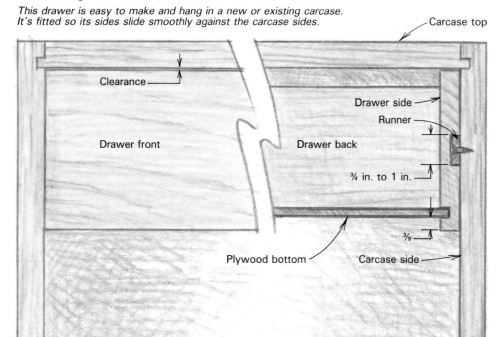

Clearance

Carcase top

Drawer side

Runner

Drawer front

Drawer back

3/4 in. to 1 in.

3/8

Plywood bottom

Carcase side

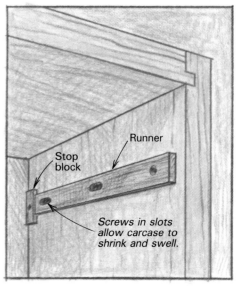

Runner

Stop block

Screws in slots allow carcase to shrink and swell.

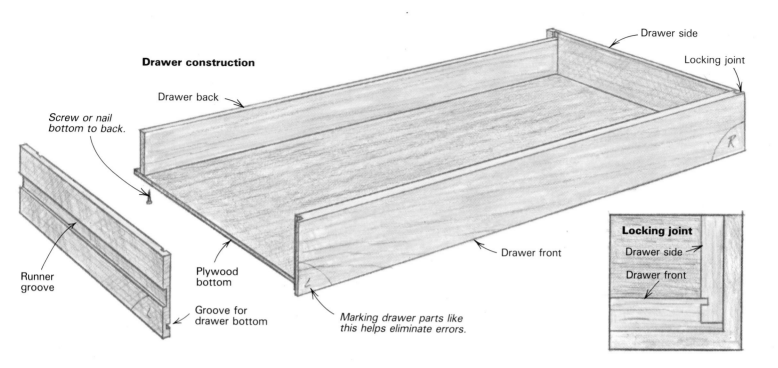

Drawer construction

Drawer side

Locking joint

Drawer back

Screw or nail
bottom to back.

Runner
groove

Plywood
bottom

Groove for
drawer bottom

Drawer front

*Marking drawer parts like
this helps eliminate errors.*

Locking joint

Drawer side

Drawer front

about ½ in. thick. Take care when flattening the pieces—twisted parts make twisted drawers. The back is dadoed to the sides, so match its thickness to a standard plow-plane blade or router bit.

Mark the good faces, then plane and mark the good edges on all the boards, checking them with a straightedge. I put the good edges on the bottom of the drawer. (A simple way to keep the pieces straight is shown above.) The ends of the pieces *must* be square to the good edges. If they're not, the drawer will certainly be twisted, and probably not be square. I usually do this planing freehand, holding the piece end-up in the vise and checking square-ness with a try square or a framing square.

A shooting board, shown in the drawing at right, is a good jig for doing the same thing, particularly if you're making lots of drawers. There's not much to a shooting board, but it must be made accurately; obviously the stop must be dead square to the guiding edge, and the sole of your plane perpendicular to the plane's sides. Use whatever plane is most comfortable for you. I use my jointer plane because of its weight and long bearing surface. (No, you won't plane the guiding edge as well as the workpiece.) Fool around squaring up scrapwood until you get the hang of the shooting board.

Square the ends of the drawer front first, planing enough off so that the front will just about, but not quite, fit between the carcase sides. Only the front end of each drawer side need be square for this construction; if you're corner-jointing the back to the sides as well, square up both ends. Unless you're sure of the dado

depths now, plane the back to exact length after you dado the sides.

Next groove the inside faces of the sides and front for the drawer bottom (it passes under the back). You can plow the grooves with a plow plane, rout them, or cut them on the tablesaw with a dado head. They shouldn't be deeper than half the thickness of the pieces. I locate them ⅜ in. above the

bottom edges, which leaves enough wood for strength without stealing too much depth from the drawer. Remember to run the bottom, good edge against the fence of whatever tool you use for grooving.

The locking joints at the front corners are a little more complicated than those for the carcase. (If you used the simple car-

Shooting board
You can square an end to an edge quickly and accurately with a shooting board, one of the simplest of jigs.

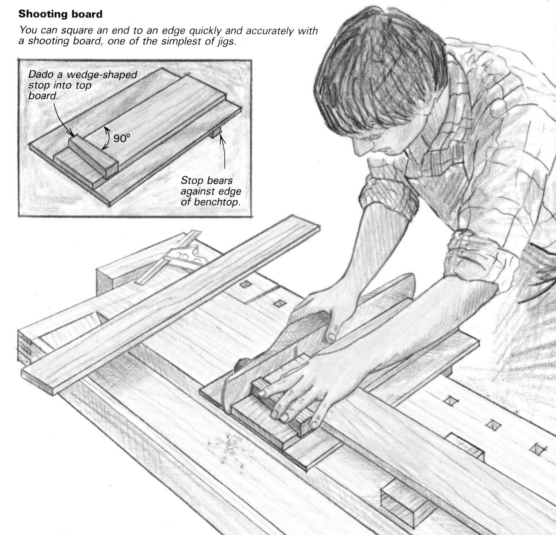

Dado a wedge-shaped
stop into top
board.

90°

Stop bears
against edge
of benchtop.

case joint shown on p. 20 for the drawers, either the end grain of the sides would show, or the tongue would have to be on the sides, running in the direction of most stress—the front would easily pull away from the sides.) This joint is fairly easy to cut on the tablesaw or with a plow plane, but I think it's too much trouble to rout. Regardless of how you cut the joint, do it accurately, because its strength depends on a close mating of the parts.

The drawings at right show proportions and the sequence of cuts on the tablesaw. I use a single blade that cuts a kerf about ⁵⁄₃₂ in. wide, which is sufficient width for the groove. Make the groove depth (cut **1**) about one-third the thickness of the side. Make cut **2** using the same fence setting as for cut **1** to ensure that the end of the drawer side will fit tight against the drawer-front rabbet. Cut the front and several pieces of scrap the same thickness as the front, then use the scrap to reset the fence for cut **3** to make a snug-fitting tongue. I make the final cut just shy of the groove bottom, so the tongue won't bottom out and hold the joint apart.

Though this is essentially a machine joint, it can be cut by hand with a plow plane as shown. I use a ¼-in. cutter to groove the side (**B**) and a ⁵⁄₁₆-in. cutter for the end of the front (**A**). Plow the groove in the side first, setting the fence using the wider cutter as a gauge. Plug the drawer-bottom groove with a tight-fitting scrap to prevent breaking it out, and remember to chisel ramps at the ends of the cuts to prevent tearout. To make the tongue, set the plow-plane fence using the groove cutter as a gauge. Plowing in end grain, at least in soft woods, isn't much more difficult than plowing with the grain, but practice on some scrap first.

Dado the sides for the drawer back with tablesaw and dado head, router, or plow plane. I place the dado about ½ in. to 1 in. from the end of the side, so there's plenty of wood on both sides of the dado for strength. One-third the thickness of the side is sufficient depth.

Next groove the outside faces of the drawer sides for the runners. The width of the runners isn't critical; I find that ¾-in. to 1-in. wide runners are easier to work with than narrower runners, and probably stiffer. I make the runner grooves ³⁄₁₆ in. to ¼ in. deep, and plow them from end to end—the drawer front will cover the groove at the front end. For drawers up to 6 in. deep, center the grooves; for deeper drawers, locate them nearer the top edge.

I think that solid-wood bottoms give a

Tablesawn locking joint

The locking joint can be cut quickly and accurately by following this sequence of cuts.

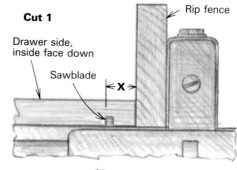

Cut 1

Drawer side, inside face down

Sawblade

Rip fence

←X→

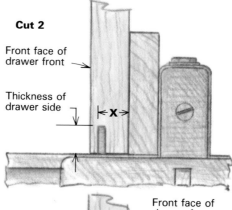

Cut 2

Front face of drawer front

Thickness of drawer side

←X→

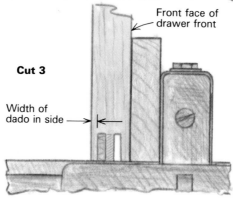

Cut 3

Front face of drawer front

Width of dado in side →|←

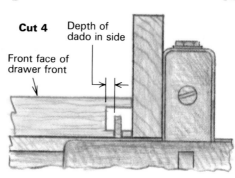

Cut 4

Depth of dado in side

Front face of drawer front

Lay out a tablesawn joint according to the sawblade thickness, as shown at left below. Lay out a plow-plane joint to match standard cutters (**A** and **B**).

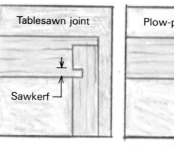

Tablesawn joint

Sawkerf

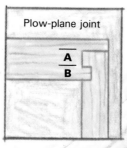

Plow-plane joint

A / B

drawer a nice heft, and raise it a notch or two in quality, but they're sure a lot more work than plywood bottoms. When I make solid bottoms, I plane them about ⁵⁄₁₆ in. or ⅜ in. thick, then thin them at the edges with a bevel or a rabbet to fit the grooves. Whether the bottom is solid wood or plywood, trim it square and fit it snugly from side to side, and so it runs beneath the drawer back. The grain of a solid-wood bottom should parallel the drawer front so it won't shrink out of the side grooves, or push the sides apart when it expands. Grain direction doesn't matter for plywood bottoms, but I run it parallel to the front anyway.

All the parts should be ready for assembly now, but first I clean up the inside faces of everything and wax them, taking care not to get wax on a surface to be glued. It's a lot easier to do this now than later. If you want more protection than wax but not a full-blown finish, brush on a coat of sanding sealer, rub it down with steel wool, then wax it.

Assembly is straightforward, but it's not a bad idea to make a dry run just to see that everything fits, and that you've got all the clamps and paraphernalia you'll need. Then spread glue in the groove and dado of one side, and insert the front and back, aligning the grooves for the bottom. Slide in the bottom and add the second side. (You can glue plywood in place, but a

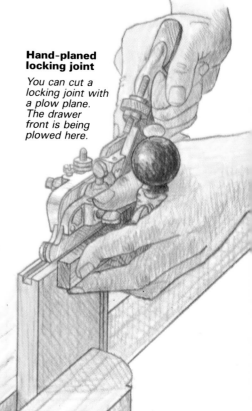

Hand-planed locking joint

You can cut a locking joint with a plow plane. The drawer front is being plowed here.

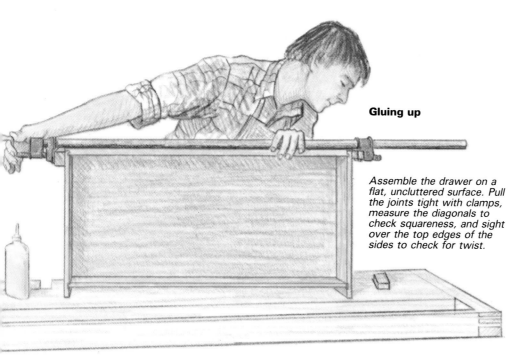

Gluing up

Assemble the drawer on a flat, uncluttered surface. Pull the joints tight with clamps, measure the diagonals to check squareness, and sight over the top edges of the sides to check for twist.

solid bottom should just be nailed or screwed to the back.) Assembling with the drawer bottom in place helps keep the drawer square. Pull the joints tight with pipe clamps, placing hardwood blocks between the jaws and the sides to protect the surfaces and distribute the clamping pressure. You can leave the clamps on while the glue sets, or drive a couple of nails in each joint and take them off.

Measure the diagonals to check for squareness. Sight over the edges of the sides or try to rock the drawer on the benchtop to see if it is twisted. If it is, you can weight the high corners; too much counter-twisting can break the joints. If the twist isn't too bad, you can plane it out when fitting the drawer to the carcase. If you find yourself planing off most of the drawer side, make another drawer. Leave the drawer on a flat surface while the glue dries.

The runners for the drawers are best made of a hard wood such as maple, cherry or oak. The easiest way to make them is to thickness a wide board to a sliding fit in the runner grooves and rip the runners off the edge. Plane the edge of the wide board after each cut so each runner will have one smooth face. I make the runners just slightly thinner than the depth of the runner grooves and about ¾ in. shorter than the drawer sides.

The runners are slot-screwed to the carcase sides to allow the sides to shrink and expand with changes in humidity. In better-quality work, the runners are housed in dadoes in the carcase sides, then screwed down. I think three #6 screws are sufficient to fasten a 15-in. runner. The screw

near the front end is fixed through a single hole so it won't move in relation to the front edge of the carcase. I make each slot by boring two holes ½ in. apart and chiseling out the waste in between. (Save a little time by boring the holes in the edge of the wide board before ripping off the individual runners.) Countersink the holes and slots so the screwheads will be beneath the runner's surface.

To install the runners, make a gauge block equal in width to the distance from the top of the runner groove to the top edge of the drawer side, as shown in the drawing below. This distance should be the same for each pair of sides on a draw-

Attaching the runners

Make a runner gauge as shown below, then butt the gauge against the carcase top to position the runner while you screw it in place.

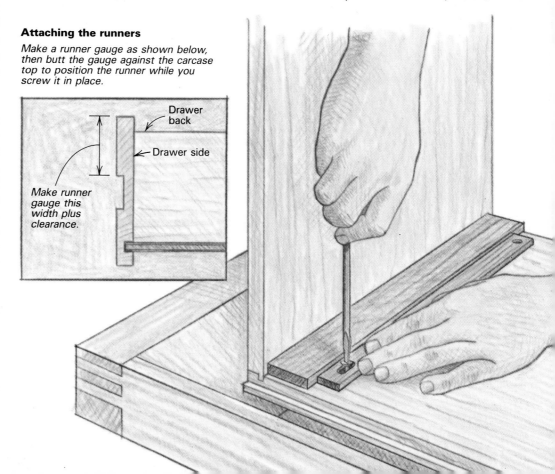

Drawer back

Drawer side

Make runner gauge this width plus clearance.

er. The block should be about as long as the carcase is deep. Lay the carcase on its side, butt the gauge into the upper corner, position the runner against the gauge about ½ in. back from the carcase's front edge, and screw the runner in place. (You'll need to bore pilot holes for the screws in hardwood carcase sides.)

The drawer sides and front will expand and contract across their width with changes in humidity. You can allow for this in the gauge, or by adding a spacer between the gauge and the carcase top, or by planing the sides down when fitting. The size of the gap will vary according to the wood used and the conditions where you live. In England, we used to fit drawers in fine work very closely because the humidity was fairly constant year round. On my first job after returning to Nebraska, I fitted the drawers tightly, only to have to plane the height of the sides later to accommodate the extreme variation in humidity from summer to winter—4-in. deep riftsawn oak sides moved more than ⅛ in. across their width. Play it safe on your first drawers.

Now you're ready to fit the drawer to the carcase. With luck, this will require only a couple of fine shavings off each drawer side and just a touch from a sanding block on the bottom edge of the runners. An assembled drawer is difficult to hold in a vise, so I clamp a piece of ¾-in. plywood to the benchtop to support the drawer for planing. The width of the ply should fit easily inside the drawer, and the

A simple slider

If you're not too bothered by how a drawer looks, or not quite so compulsive about how it fits, try this method. The sides, front and back are joined exactly the same as for the drawer on p. 20, but you don't need to groove for the bottom and the runners. Make the drawer bottom of ¼-in. or ⅜-in. plywood—Baltic birch if you can afford it, or an interior grade that permits few voids if you can't; ¼-in. tempered Masonite will work, too. The width of the drawer isn't terribly important. I leave a ¼-in. gap between the carcase sides and the drawer sides. (A large gap like this, uniform on both sides, announces itself as deliberate, and shouldn't raise any eyebrows.) I assemble the sides, back and front, then glue and nail the bottom in place after making sure it slides easily in the carcase dadoes.

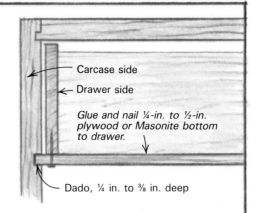

Carcase side

Drawer side

Glue and nail ¼-in. to ½-in. plywood or Masonite bottom to drawer.

Dado, ¼ in. to ⅜ in. deep

You can dado the carcase sides to accept the drawer bottom before assembling the carcase or after. If you do it after, dado before attaching the back. Either way, you'll need to fix a fence to the carcase side to guide the router or plow plane. A good trick is to make the top drawer as deep as the distance from the edge of the router base to the bit—just run the base against the carcase top to cut the dadoes. —*R.H.*

Planing the sides

Clamp a piece of plywood to the bench so it overhangs the edge enough to support the drawer for planing. Plane and sand down the sides carefully, from back to front, until the drawer slips easily but snugly into the carcase.

piece should overhang the edge of the bench by about the drawer's depth.

The initial goal when fitting is to get the drawer to slide completely into the carcase, as tight to the sides as possible. Using a sharp plane, first take a thin shaving off the back half of both drawer sides, then try the drawer in the opening. If it fits halfway, plane farther forward until it fits all the way; if it doesn't fit halfway, take more off the back. If the drawer gets hung up, remember to check the runners, too. More than once, I've planed too much off a drawer side before discovering a sticky spot on a runner. You can trim the runners with a sharp, finely set shoulder plane, or with sandpaper wrapped tightly around a square-edged block of hardwood.

When the drawer slides completely into the carcase, work the sides and runners with planes or sandpaper until it slides sweetly. Colored chalk rubbed on the carcase sides will show up high spots on the drawer sides. Finally, paste-wax all the mating surfaces. You should be able to open and shut a well-fitted drawer with only your little finger, and when the drawer is halfway out, there should be very little movement either up and down or side to side.

When the drawer fits, screw stop blocks at the back of the carcase to fix its position when closed. If the drawer front is allowed to strike the end of the runners to stop the drawer, the front will soon be popped off. (The runners are acceptable drawer stops if you stop the runner grooves about 1 in. short of the drawer front.) I like the drawer front to sit about ⅛ in. back from the edge of the carcase. To add another drawer, or a stack of drawers, just repeat the process, gauging from the drawer above to place the runners.

This all sounds like a lot of trouble, you might say, for a simple pine drawer. True, there's no need to fit this drawer with anything like the precision I've described. For that matter, there's no need to fit any drawer like this. I have drawers in my house that you can practically throw into their openings from across the room, and they still do a fine job of corralling my socks and shirts. But if your dream is to someday build one of those exquisite cabinets with lots of piston-fit little drawers, then the more practice you have, even with humble pine drawers, the more likely you are to succeed when it really matters to you. □

Roger Holmes is an associate editor at Fine Woodworking.

Pipe Clamps
Six versatile tips

Between glue-ups, the humble pipe clamp just gathers dust and gets underfoot. Here's how six readers coax double-duty out of these tools. So he always has one handy, Scott LeCocq of Arvada, Colo., uses a pipe clamp for his toolbox handle. Robert Harrigan of Cincinnati, Ohio, extended the grip of his vise with a clamp gizmo, while Philip Hahn of Blacksburg, Va., made a simple bench hold-down. Lyon McCandless of Bainbridge Island, Wash., Bernd Schroder of Half Moon Bay, Calif., and Maurice Harrington of Chicago devised pipe-clamp vises. Thom Lipiczky of West Stockbridge, Mass., suggested adding bench dogs for larger work. ☐

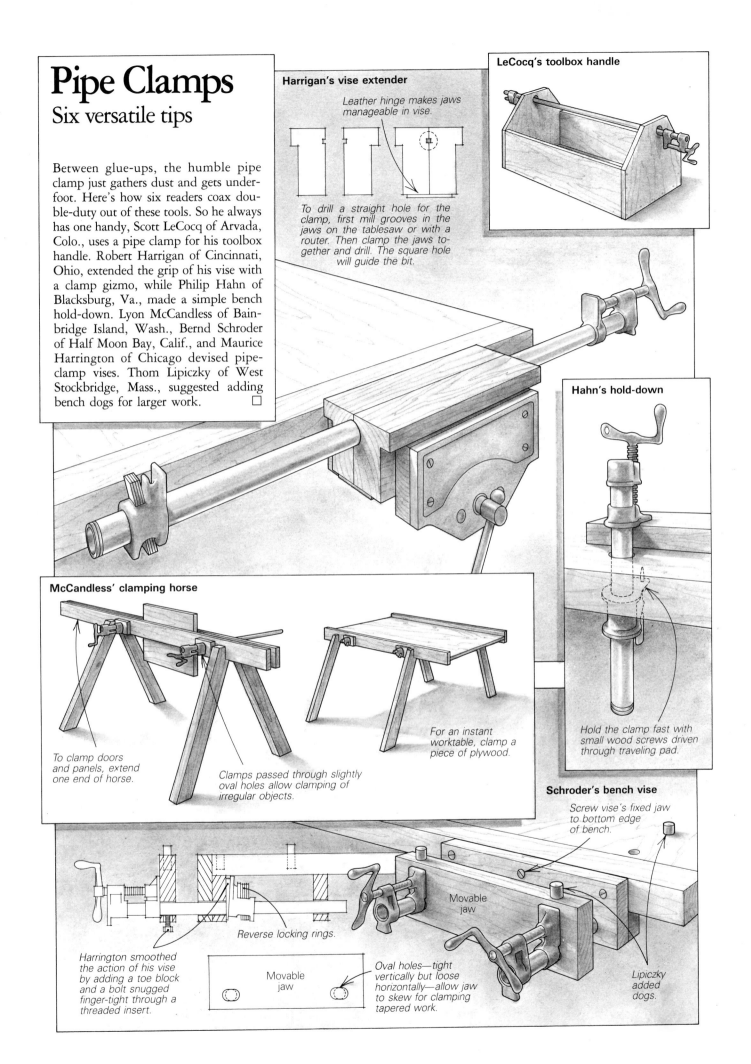

Harrigan's vise extender

Leather hinge makes jaws manageable in vise.

To drill a straight hole for the clamp, first mill grooves in the jaws on the tablesaw or with a router. Then clamp the jaws together and drill. The square hole will guide the bit.

LeCocq's toolbox handle

Hahn's hold-down

Hold the clamp fast with small wood screws driven through traveling pad.

McCandless' clamping horse

To clamp doors and panels, extend one end of horse.

Clamps passed through slightly oval holes allow clamping of irregular objects.

For an instant worktable, clamp a piece of plywood.

Harrington smoothed the action of his vise by adding a toe block and a bolt snugged finger-tight through a threaded insert.

Reverse locking rings.

Movable jaw

Oval holes—tight vertically but loose horizontally—allow jaw to skew for clamping tapered work.

Schroder's bench vise

Screw vise's fixed jaw to bottom edge of bench.

Movable jaw

Lipiczky added dogs.

Drawing: David Dann

Doweling Jigs
Putting nine to the test

by David Sloan

When you're starting out in woodworking, the dowel seems like the perfect answer to every joinery problem. Drill a couple of holes, dribble in some glue and bang in those little wooden nails. If the dowels and holes don't quite line up, a little muscular persuasion will put things right. And if the surfaces aren't exactly in the same plane, the belt-sander offers a quick remedy.

Before long, however, the aspiring woodworker will learn that dowels won't do everything. They are mostly worthless where there is much cross-grain wood movement, or any amount of racking stress, as in chairs. Sure, dowels work well when glued into end grain, because the dowel's fibers line up, and move, right along with those of the main board. Dowels are also great for aligning edge-glued joints where long grain is being mated to long grain, and they keep things from sliding around while you're clamping. They're good for quick frame joints or for lightly stressed rail-to-leg joints, and they work fine in stable, man-made boards. But in most applications, to get the best results with dowels, you need some kind of jig to get the holes lined up and square.

The various doweling jigs on the market are designed to do just that: guide a drill to make accurate, perpendicular holes in the edge, end or face of a board. Most also provide a way to drill mating holes in two boards. A few jigs can make only one type of joint, others can make several, and some are extremely versatile. Deciding which one to buy can be tough.

I tested all the commercially made doweling jigs I could find, nine of them, by making as many different joints as I could with each. I used ⅞-in. thick, 3-in. by 12-in. poplar boards, factory-made birch dowels (both fluted and spiral—I found no obvious advantage to either type), brad-point bits and yellow glue. I evaluated each jig for accuracy, versatility, ease of operation and quality of construction.

In addition to the jigs, I tested a dowel-former—a ¼-in. thick, hardened steel plate that produces a crude, but functional, dowel when you bang an oversize piece of wood through the appropriate hole (¼-in., ⁵⁄₁₆-in., ⅜-in. or ½-in.). This $15 tool could be handy if you run out of dowels in the middle of a job, or want dowels made of your primary wood. I also tried dowel-centers—metal plugs with a point on one end. These are great for curved work that doweling jigs can't handle, and they also work well on flat stock. You drill a hole, insert the right-size plug and press the piece you want to join against the point, which leaves a nice clear center mark for the other hole. You may seldom need a dowel-center, but they're cheap enough ($4.50) to keep on hand.

• • •

After finishing my tests, I had several favorites. The Dowl-it #1000 was hard to beat for speed and convenience on edge or end joints, and the Dowel-Master and Dowel Magic were really fast on corner joints. These jigs center automatically—I like that. Most times I want a dowel on center, and for the few times I don't, I can use a shim to nudge the Dowl-it off-center. With the Dowl-it and either of these other two, there aren't many jobs I couldn't tackle. But if I could have only one jig, I'd buy the Record. It takes a long time to set up, and its loose bushings are easy to lose, but no other jig can make as many different joints.

David Sloan is an associate editor at Fine Woodworking. *For more information about dowel joints, see* FWW #7, *pp. 46-49, and* #21, *pp. 68-72.*

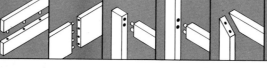

Each jig will make the joints shown in white.

Dowl-it #1000	Sugg. price $27.95	Dowel sizes ¼, ⁵⁄₁₆, ⅜, ⁷⁄₁₆, ½

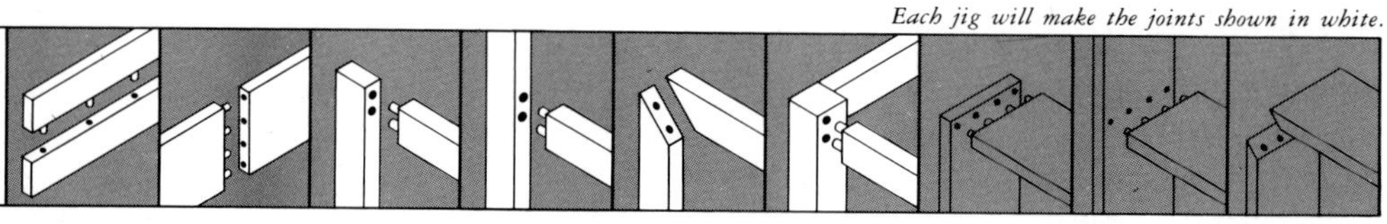

Dowl-it Model #1000—The Dowl-it jig I got didn't look like the one pictured in the mail-order catalog—the gizmo I remembered from junior high school shop. The manufacturer says it's "improved." I'm usually skeptical of "improvements" (translation: cut manufacturing costs and, most of the time, quality), but this time I was pleasantly surprised. The American-made Dowl-it is a durable tool of nicely machined steel and extruded aluminum. The hardened-steel drill guide has five holes (¼-in. to ½-in.), with sizes clearly stamped into the metal. There are no loose parts to lose and no extra clamps required. A large T-handled center screw clamps the extrusions around boards up to 2⁷⁄₁₆ in. thick, and centers the drill guide automatically and accurately. You can drill holes off-center by putting a spacer on one side of the wood.

To use the #1000, you first mark the board where you want dowels, then line up the jig's index marks with your pencil lines. You have to read these marks through a slot, which is difficult with overhead light, but this was the only design flaw I found.

Of the nine jigs tested, the Dowl-it #1000 was the handiest and most accurate for edge- or end-doweling, and it's the only one that can be conveniently used on round or odd-shaped stock.

I didn't test the Dowl-it #2000, which is basically the same as the #1000 except for six screw-in bushings that allow you to drill two identical holes parallel to each other, without moving the jig. It's easy enough to do this by moving the #1000, and besides, who needs those loose bushings?

Dowl-it #4000	Sugg. price $72.95	Dowel sizes ¼, 5/16, 3/8, ½, 5/8, ¾, 1	

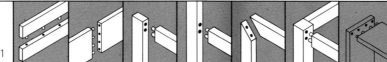

Dowl-it #4000—Weighing just under 4 lb., this behemoth was, at $72.95, the most expensive jig tested. Like the #1000, its quality is high. Two clamping heads and a steel drilling guide slide on two rods. A T-handled screw then tightens the heads. There are seven drill sizes (¼-in. to 1-in.), the three smallest in the form of pairs of threaded bushings that enable you to drill two identical holes without moving the jig. The four larger drill sizes are permanent holes.

Unless you improvise with spacer blocks, the #4000 will drill holes only in the face of a board, or in the edge or end of boards thicker than 1½ in. It can drill anywhere on the face of a board as wide as 12 in., and wider if you add longer rods. It was the only jig tested that could accommodate ¾-in. and 1-in. dia. drills.

Alignment marks incised on the jig are easy to read on wide stock, but on narrow stock, parts get in the way. No instructions came with my jig, and it doesn't center automatically, but the thing I like least about this one is that you need an Allen wrench (not supplied) to make all the adjustments. Knurled screws, which could be finger-turned, would be a great improvement.

This jig is hard to beat for drilling holes on the face of a board or a beam, but for most cabinet-scale work, it's just too massive. If you work with large, thick stock, this may be the jig for you.

Disston Dowel Magic	Sugg. price $11.40 (¼-in.)	Dowel sizes ¼, 5/16, 3/8	

Wolfcraft Dowel-Master	Sugg. price $19.95	Dowel sizes ¼, 5/16, 3/8	

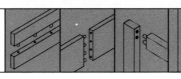
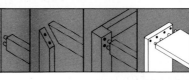

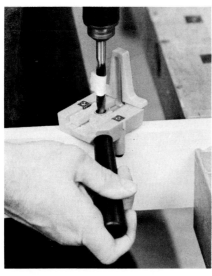

Disston Dowel Magic—This plastic contraption, imported from West Germany, drills only one size hole. You must buy a separate jig to change dowel sizes. At $11.40 for the ¼-in. model, it was the least expensive jig tested. The same jig is sold under the Coastal label.

Two plastic posts protrude from the square face of the jig, flanking a steel drill-guide bushing. A pair of machine screws with nuts clamp a sliding plastic fence to the base.

The Dowel Magic makes only 90° edge-to-face corner or "T" joints, a job it does quickly and well. It can handle stock of unlimited width, up to 1¼ in. thick. You place the jig posts astride the board's edge, which automatically centers the hole, and drill. The indexing marks don't work for edge-drilling, so you have to eyeball the location, which I found fairly easy to do. Then you slide the jig along the edge to drill more holes. Next you put dowels in the holes and clamp the mating board flat on top of the first. When you invert the jig, its slotted fence fits over those dowels to locate the holes on the face of the second board.

I tried both the ¼-in. Disston and the 3/8-in. Coastal. Base sections that were solid plastic on the Coastal were ribbed or hollow on the Disston, but this was the only difference I found, and it didn't seem to affect performance.

I wasn't thrilled about the plastic construction, but it keeps the cost down, and I don't think metal would work any better. The drill was a sloppy fit in the guide bushing. The square nuts that held the fence fell off and got lost.

Wolfcraft Dowel-Master—Similar to the Dowel Magic in design and operation, this German-made jig is very well built. Unlike the Dowel Magic, one size jig can drill all three hole sizes (¼-in., 5/16-in. and 3/8-in.). It's also more durable—aluminum extrusions, with steel drill guides. It uses dowels in the edge of one board to locate holes in the face of the second board, and it's limited to corner joints or "T" joints.

My only complaint: When I flipped the jig to drill the second board, I had to reset the depth gauge on my drill. Other than that, the jig performed well and was convenient to use.

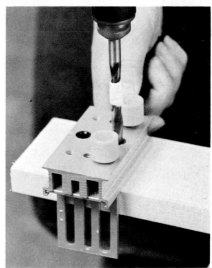

(continued on next page)

Disston Doweling Jig Clamps	Sugg. price $27.30	Dowel sizes 1/4, 5/16, 3/8						

Disston Doweling Jig Clamps—This

German-made, die-cast aluminum jig consists of two clamps: one with steel drill guides (1/4-in., 5/16-in. and 3/8-in.), and one without. The clamps are used to hold one board flat on the benchtop and the other board on edge at 90°. This jig can make only a 90° corner joint, in stock up to 15/16 in. thick.

To use the jig, you set up the boards with one clamp at each end, drill a hole in each board, loosen the clamp with the drill guides, move it, retighten it and drill two more holes, and repeat for each pair of holes. When you get to the board's other end, you have to switch the clamps to drill the last set of holes.

I liked not having to set up extra

clamps, but the jig clamps' 2¾-in. throat capacity couldn't grab my 4-in. thick benchtop. It was easy to line up the jig's indexing marks with my pencil lines on the face and edge of the boards, so I got the holes exactly where I wanted. The clamps held the boards firmly for drilling, but the drill was sloppy in the guide bushing. I also found it tedious to unclamp, move and reclamp.

When I drilled the 1/4-in. holes, I discovered that they were way off-center: 1/8 in. from one edge and 1/2 in. from the other edge of my 7/8-in. thick board. There is no way to remedy this. The 5/16-in. and 3/8-in. holes were slightly better—3/16 in. from one edge. This doesn't affect the alignment, but the dowels are too close to the outside corner.

Disston's jig (also sold under the Coastal brand for $19.95) comes in a box marked "best," while their Dowel Magic is marked "better," but I found the latter more useful and a better buy. Although the Doweling Jig Clamps made a joint with good alignment, they were inconvenient to use and will probably end up gathering dust in my shop.

HIT Products Precision Doweling Jig	Sugg. price $25.95	Dowel sizes 3/16, 1/4, 5/16, 3/8						

HIT Products Precision Doweling

Jig—This aluminum and steel jig is radically different from any other jig on the market. The two boards to be doweled are clamped edge-up, one on each side of the ½-in. thick aluminum vane on

the bottom of the jig. An aluminum arm, which holds a steel drill-guide bushing (3/16-in., 1/4-in., 5/16-in. and 3/8-in. bushings are supplied), swings from side to side over the edges. You adjust a bolt on each side of the jig to stop the arm

where you want the hole. Once the arm is set, you lock it with a wing nut, drill one hole, loosen the wing nut, swing the arm over the other board, and repeat the procedure. All the holes are the same distance from the edge of the board, though not necessarily on-center. The jig reaches to the center of a 1½-in. thick board; thicker stock can be doweled, but with holes off-center.

It took a long time to set up this jig, and using it wasn't easy. I needed a vise, a clamp, a wooden "T" spacer block (supplied with the jig), a 7/16-in. wrench to change bushings, scrap pieces, and four hands—the "T" block kept falling out whenever I tried to clamp the two boards in the vise. I finally got all my holes drilled, but despite careful rechecking, the alignment was off by 1/16 in. I blame the wing nut, which is supposed to lock the arm tight. It doesn't, so the arm wobbles around when you're drilling. I was intrigued by this jig's design, and impressed by the quality of construction, but in use it was a big disappointment.

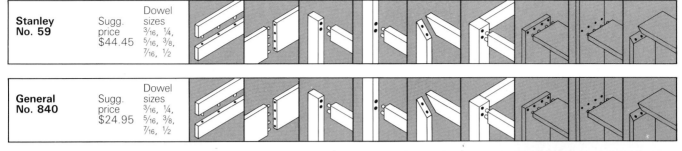
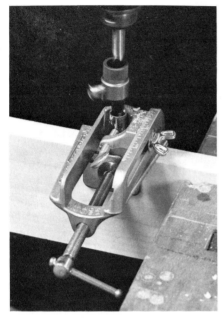

gauge is a piece of tape wrapped around the drill bit). This jig doesn't center automatically. To center a hole, you line up a mark for your bushing size on the graduated scale (which is accurate), then lock it with a thumbscrew.

The American-made No. 59 was easy to set up and performed well—one of the better ones. I liked it best for drilling a series of holes for a mortise. But the loose bushings and lack of a self-centering feature dampened my enthusiasm.

General No. 840—Also sold by Sears under the Craftsman brand ($21.49), this die-cast aluminum jig seems to be an attempt to improve upon the Stanley No. 59. It has a revolving turret with six drill-guide holes ($\frac{3}{16}$-in. to $\frac{1}{2}$-in.), instead of Stanley's loose bushings. The turret clicks in place to index the desired hole. Like the Stanley, this jig fastens on the edge or end of a board with an integral clamp. The carriage slides on two steel rods to locate holes on- or off-center. You can drill the edge, end or face of stock up to $4\frac{3}{8}$ in. thick.

The General is not self-centering. A measurement scale on one of the steel rods lets you locate the center of the hole once you've measured the board thick-

Stanley No. 59—This well-made, die-cast metal jig has a built-in screw that clamps on stock up to $2\frac{7}{8}$ in., and a sliding guide-bushing holder that can be set anywhere on the board. The jig comes with six loose guide bushings ($\frac{3}{16}$-in. to $\frac{1}{2}$-in.), which fit one at a time in the holder, and a useless, one-size-fits-all depth gauge (my favorite depth

ness. The scale is accurate, and I had no trouble using it.

This jig was easy to work with. No extra clamps are needed to set up, and there are no loose drill guides to lose. It's well made, but the turret has about $\frac{1}{32}$ in. of play. Surprisingly, this didn't seem to cause any major alignment problems. The depth gauge that comes with the jig is worthless—it's clumsy and it doesn't fit small drills properly.

 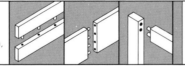

Record No. 148—This British-made jig is a complicated-looking device: Two 6-in. polished steel rods hold a stationary reference head at one end and a sliding head at the other. Between the heads, two drill-guide bushing carriers slide back and forth. You clamp a board between the heads and move the carriers to locate the holes. Five bushing sizes are supplied: $\frac{1}{4}$-in., $\frac{5}{16}$-in. (6mm), $\frac{3}{8}$-in., 8mm and 10mm. The basic jig will dowel boards up to $6\frac{3}{8}$ in. wide, but optional rods are available, in two lengths, that will extend the capacity to $12\frac{1}{4}$ in. and $18\frac{1}{4}$ in., respectively.

There are lots of adjustments, but knurled screws, some of which are slotted, so you can tighten them with your fingers or with a coin or a screwdriver,

make it easy. Except for the steel rods and screws, the jig is made of painted, die-cast metal.

The illustrated manual has good, clear instructions, in four languages. I had no trouble using the jig, but I found set-up to be time-consuming, and there were loose bushings—my only complaints.

Equipped with the 18-in. rods, the Record is the most versatile of the jigs tested, but it can't handle round stock. It performed well, though it could stand some improvement. The play in the bushing-carrier assemblies, for example, could be eliminated if these were machined instead of cast and painted.

Some of the other jigs are faster and easier to use, but if you want one that does it all, this is the one to buy. □

A Patternmaker's Carving Tips

And a portable carving kit for whittling wherever you are

by Wallace C. Auger

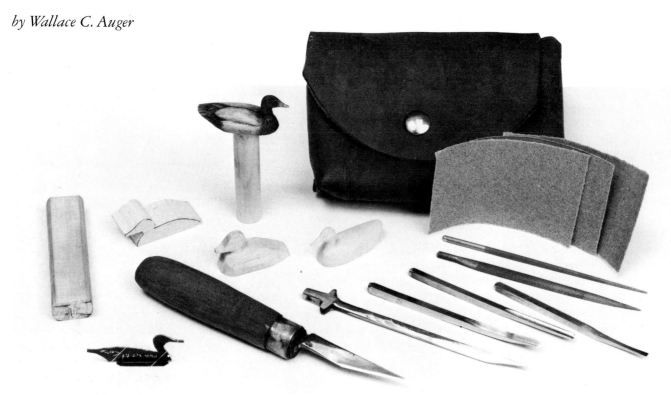

The author enjoys carving miniature decoys, but doesn't like to be tied to his bench, so he devised a carving kit that fits in a belt pouch. In the process, he discovered that small tools don't need bulky handles. The template shown was cut from a soft-drink can.

When I was an apprentice patternmaker thirty years ago, the old guys in the shop weren't eager to share what they knew. If an old-timer thought you were watching, he'd turn a little, so that his shoulder blocked the view, or he'd switch to some other work until you went away. So mostly I learned from workers my own age, but I picked up a lot just from the way the older guys moved their elbows. I'd catch a glimpse of what they were doing and try it myself. It didn't take long to learn that the main trick was to choose the right tool and cut in the right direction.

Any carving has problem areas, places where the wood won't cut cleanly in the direction you're working. Experience and practice will show you ways around the problems, but without a teacher, experience can take a long time. A miniature duck decoy is as good a practice field as any. You'll find the same problems there as in larger carvings or in more purposeful things such as cabinet and drawer handles. Whatever you want to make, here are some general carving hints that will smooth your path.

Few tools are needed to start. Because I like to get outdoors, I assembled a small kit that lets me carve miniature decoys anywhere (photo, above). I could probably get by with the knife alone, but the other tools make some jobs easier, as you will see.

First of all, you can't carve something until you know what it looks like, and general knowledge isn't enough. Anybody would recognize a pine cone, for instance, but how many of us have ever really looked at one? Is it egg-shaped or conical? How does each scale taper into the main form? Do the scales

run straight up and down, or do they spiral? You won't know unless you look. A carver must anticipate these questions— and a lot more—before starting to cut.

Ducks are symmetrical, which makes it fairly easy to make templates. For a miniature, carved from a single block, you need only a side-profile template (figure 2). But the outline will only start you off; you will have to thoroughly understand the three-dimensional shape you're aiming for. I'll give you tips about duck anatomy as we go along. For any other carving project, the same kind of knowledge and understanding is necessary—there is nothing more frustrating than to carve a block of wood to the point where it *almost* looks right, and not know where to go from there.

In any carving, get close to the final shape in the easiest way—use a saw. For a miniature decoy, I cut the blank profile with a jigsaw. For a larger blank, I bandsaw, cutting not only the side view but the top as well. On a larger bird, quarter-size and up, the head is usually carved separately, then glued on. This saves wood, and also allows you to bandsaw both profiles of the head, as is done with the body. Making the head separately allows you to shift the head template on the carving block so that the long grain of the wood goes in the same direction as the bill. If you tried to cut the whole bird from one block, and wanted a lifelike pose with the bill pointing slightly down, chances are you'd end up with short grain in the bill, which would be liable to break. For the same reason—grain direction—wings and wing tips that stand away from the bird are carved separately, even on miniatures.

Pick a wood that works well. Jelutong is my favorite, but

basswood or any other soft, even-textured wood works well, too. White pine is good for larger birds, but it's a little too weak for miniatures. Some people use sugar pine for full-scale decoys, but I avoid it for miniatures because its large sap pockets can bleed through the final finish, even after you think you have sealed them.

Let's say you have your block sawn out. The first problem is how to hold it while you work. On a little carving, one hand is enough to power the tool, but your other hand will tire quickly if you try to grip the bare blank. On a larger carving, you'll want both hands free to manipulate your tools, so attach a handle to the blank. For miniatures, just screw the blank onto a wood screw epoxied into the end of a dowel. For larger carvings, you can hold the handle in a vise, or you could make the bench I use, shown on p. 32. It securely holds a blank at virtually any position.

The prime tool in my kit is a patternmakers' knife I made from a file many years ago. Actually, these days I prefer a laminated-blade Swedish carving knife, such as those sold by places like Woodcraft. Wille Sundqvist carved spoons with one of these knives in *FWW* #38, pp. 84-88, and demonstrated a lot of carvers' grips and knife strokes.

A laminated blade sharpens faster than a solid-steel blade. Don't just unwrap the knife and start carving, however. It comes from the factory as a general-purpose knife, and it should be modified for the job at hand, as shown in figure 1. First, grind away most of the blade. It is false economy to have more steel in the blade than you need—the point will be too far from your hand to control. Then taper the blade so that it ends in a point, and sharpen as in the drawing, with a crowned bevel.

Many people will tell you that this is wrong, that the bevel has to be flat. Well, it depends on the job you want to do. A flat bevel will give a knife good control for long, straight cuts. But woodcarvers make a lot of scoop cuts as well as straight cuts and cuts across the grain. The most difficult cut is a tight scoop. A straight bevel tends to dig in and scrape at the bottom of a scoop (a hollow grind is even worse), but a crowned bevel helps guide and support the cutting edge. Think of a knife blade as if it were a bandsaw blade. If you try to make a tight curve with a wide blade, the blade binds. When a knife blade binds, its leverage splits off a chunk of your carving. So the tighter the curve, the narrower the blade should be. But, just as for a bandsaw, the narrower the blade, the harder it is to keep a constant curve. That's why a patternmakers' knife is shaped the way it is. It promotes a slicing cut, and, in addition, somewhere along the length of the blade there's the right width and the right crown for the scoop cut you want to make.

Begin to rough out a miniature decoy blank with the knife by cutting away the waste at both sides of the head to center the neck on the body. First, slice a line along the shoulder, aiming at the base of the neck, a little more than 1/16 in. deep. This is a stop cut, and it has to be as deep as or deeper than the shaving you plan to take from the side of the neck, because its purpose is to prevent the second cut from splitting ahead of the blade through the block. Be sure to slice when you use a knife, especially when making the stop cut. If you wedge the blade through instead of slicing, you won't have any control—chances are you'll cut the head right off, and maybe your finger, too. Make a series of stop cuts, taking shavings off the sides of the head to meet them, until the

Fig. 1: Shaping the blade

Grind away surplus metal to make the knife blade easier to control. The rounded bevel makes tight scoop cuts without digging in.

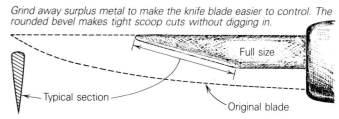

Fig. 2: A miniature mallard, one-twelfth scale

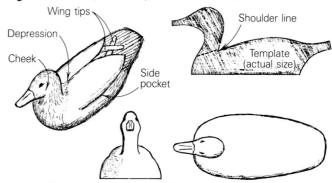

Templates and sizes vary slightly according to species.

head and neck are squared off to the right width.

When slicing a stop cut, begin at the tip of the blade and end with the thicker part. You have more control with the thicker part of the blade because it's closer to your hand, and its shape will also help prevent the blade from going too deep. To control a cut, you must steadily decrease pressure during the slice. This lets you ease the cut to a halt. If you are right-handed, use your left thumb to help power the cut. Stop cuts, in general, are necessary anytime you don't want a cut to go too far. In scoop cuts, as you cut down from each side to the center, every cut can be thought of as a stop cut—each one prevents the wood from splitting out ahead of the blade on the next cut. When slicing a scoop cut, however, slice from the thicker part of the blade toward the tip. It takes less force to move the thinner part of the blade around the curve, and you'll be better able to maintain control as you ease through.

Next, round the body. On larger carvings, I'd recommend a wide, shallow gouge for this job, but the knife works fine on miniatures. When roughing out, you can take wood away quickly. Work from the high point on the body toward the ends—it's best not to cut uphill into the wood grain; cut down from each side. Use lighter cuts as you get closer to the line of dimension.

When making cuts, you'll find it best to work both hands together. By rocking your hands—something like a scissors action—you will maintain control throughout the cut, instead of having the blade run away from you. You will take a lot of wood off at the front and rear of the body, but aim for a wide curve, like a raindrop, that blends into the curve of the breast below the neck. When cutting from the center of the body back toward the tail, I'd recommend that a beginner make a template of the side of the bird. The template should fit the curve when the bird is finished. It also will show you where you must remove a lot of wood, and it will save you from "finishing" a bird before it has the right overall shape. For instance, don't waste time making a smooth curve along the corners of the block until you have roughed out the top-view profile. When roughing out, you don't have to be too fussy—there's still plenty of wood if you make a mistake.

Perhaps the best carving tip I can give you is to pay attention to every cut. This is second nature to me after so many years of carving, but beginners often let their attention wander, and lose the chance to learn how the wood, the tool and the hands work together. If the wood tends to split or tear, you should figure out how to deal with the problem while you still have enough wood left to experiment. With the knife, simply changing the slicing angle can make a big difference. Change cutting actions and directions until you find what works. Remember which cut worked best for each trouble spot—it will also work well as a finishing cut. Slice rather than wedge whenever possible, regardless of what tool you are using. With the wide, shallow gouge I mentioned earlier, for instance, I make my share of straight-ahead cuts, but I use it more like a knife wherever I can, holding it slightly askew and slicing with it. Even when making a straight-ahead, cross-grain cut, you can get a gouge to slice if you rotate it a little as you go.

Keep the edges of your tools sharp, of course. When I'm carving larger work in my shop, the minute I feel an edge beginning to drag through the wood, I touch it up on a buffing wheel charged with gray compound. The setup doesn't have to be elaborate—I chuck a 3-in. dia. felt wheel in my drill press, right next to my bench. When I take my kit outdoors, with such small pieces of soft wood, I don't bother to bring sharpening gear along. The edges last long enough.

Ducks fold their wings beneath the feathers along the sides of their bodies. The wing fits into an area called a side pocket, and it pushes the side feathers out, away from the body. I use a V-parting tool to define the top of the side pocket. I could outline the side pocket with the knife, but the parting tool does the job in one stroke, whereas the knife would take two. The parting tool is easier and safer for the job, and its shape helps ensure that both grooves are the same size. Because the V-parting tool has such a small job, I removed its handle. The modified tool worked so well that I removed the handles on my gouge and straight chisel, too, grinding away any sharp edges on their tangs. The V-parting tool and the gouge originally came from a small Marples tool set, but I made the chisel from an old file.

The gouge also has a limited job: it hollows out the areas beneath the tail and the depression on the back behind the neck. The straight chisel makes the low spot between the wings and the tail, outlining the wing tips at the same time: I first make a stop cut by pressing the edge straight down into the wood for the required depth, then I use the same tool to clear the waste—something like chip-carving.

You should be able to detail most of the top of the bill with the point of the knife. For the tight curves around the neck, I use a round file. On the head, a couple of strokes with the round file make the groove above the duck's cheeks. I use a half-round to smooth broader curves, such as around the bill and along the sides of the head. To smooth the sides of the head above the cheek line, lay the edge of the half-round file on the cheek line, then gradually slide the file away from it during the stroke. If you try to file parallel to the line, the file may too easily wander, cutting into and lowering the cheek. When rounding the cheek below the line, begin at the line and roll the file away from it during the stroke.

A duck has a slight depression on its back, which channels water from the high point of the body forward, so that it can roll off at both sides of the neck. This is one of the small things most people don't notice, but if you omit it, the carving will look chunky and lifeless. Make the channel with the gouge and smooth it with the half-round file, being careful not to make the base of the neck too narrow—the neck should be about as wide there as it is just below the head, with the thinnest part about halfway up. This is the time to lower the surface of the wing tips slightly, so they look as if they are emerging from the feathers that cover them.

After sanding a little, you're ready for detailing. For this part of the job, it's best to have the carving on a handle, but the handle can be smaller than the one used for carving. I burn-in feather texture with a fine-point woodburner controlled by a rheostat, adjusting the heat according to how fast I want to work. I recommend sealing any wood before painting it. Shellac or lacquer works well. After sealing, I paint the bird with artists' acrylic colors.

A nicely painted miniature decoy sells for about $20. They are $\frac{1}{12}$-scale, an inch to the foot, the same scale as most miniature furniture, so they fit right into a scale-cabinetmaker's room displays. I've sold my share, but now I carve mostly for myself. I don't like to think of my carving as a business, because that would take a lot of the fun out of it. I'd like to make a set of all the American waterfowl, more than fifty species if you count the geese and swans, and I find that one of the nicest parts of decoy carving is researching the birds. I've learned much from bird books and magazines, but they often disagree, particularly about colors of bills and iridescent feathers. So once in a while I go to the park or to the zoo and look at the real thing. I'm retired now—I can go look at ducks whenever I want. □

Wallace Auger carves in Fairfield, Conn. Duck carvers will enjoy the book Decoys, The Art of the Wooden Bird *by Richard LeMaster (Contemporary Books, 1982).*

Bench for larger carvings

The carving blank is screwed to a round anvil that fits into pivot blocks. The round post swivels, too, allowing the work to be turned and locked in any position. —*W.C.A.*

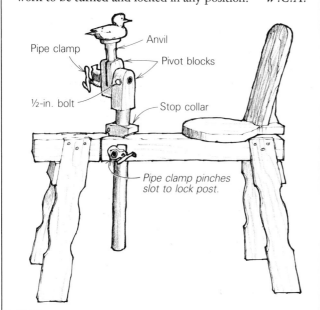

Pipe clamp

Anvil

Pivot blocks

½-in. bolt

Stop collar

Pipe clamp pinches slot to lock post.

Drawing: Jim Richey

Sharpening Screwdrivers

by Michael Podmaniczky

In 1964 I was blessed with a Latin teacher who was as happy to avoid the drudgery of classical studies as his charges were. His nonacademic interests were wide and varied, and he was easily sidetracked by his resourceful students. On one such rambling day, while discoursing on the development of the internal combustion engine by BMW, he observed that in order to make some vital adjustment, a properly sharpened screwdriver was necessary. This brought a back-row dozer to sudden, albeit sleepy, attention:

"Sharpen a screwdriver, sir?"

"Indeed, scholar Westcott . . . sharpen a screwdriver."

I don't remember just what tangent we managed to steer the screwdriver tale toward, but the vignette came back to me the other day when I was asked about the same thing.

The first requirement for a screwdriver is that its blade positively engage the slot of a (wood) screw well enough to remain in place while you turn and tighten the fastener. The second is that this must be accomplished without mangling the surrounding wood, or, if the screw is to be countersunk and plugged (as is usually the case in boatbuilding), without deforming the bung hole. Screwdrivers straight from the hardware store don't perform either task very well, but with a little "sharpening" they will.

Since the screw manufacturer kindly provides a slot across the whole width of the screw head, you might as well take

Grind away.

advantage of it. You therefore want a screwdriver tip that's exactly as wide as the screw head and that fits tightly in the slot, so as to bear along its entire width. Thus you really need a *set* of drivers, individually matched to each and every screw size you use.

A screwdriver tip that's too wide will overhang the ends of the slot. When driving a countersunk screw, it will ream out the bung hole, resulting in a poorly fitting and unsightly bung. If you're trying to tighten down a screw flush with the surface, that last turn will score the wood around the head, or raise nasty burrs on brass hardware and fittings.

Most manufacturers make screwdrivers with spade-shaped tips, which means that the blade will make the hole even bigger as it goes deeper into the wood. You can prevent this by grinding the tip to a constant width.

A screwdriver tip that's too thin will bear only at its corners, defacing the screw slot and increasing the likelihood that the tip will jump out of the channel and gouge the woodwork. This problem, bad enough with flat-head screws, is even worse with round-heads because the slot is so shallow at the extremes. Ask yourself why you push so hard when tightening a fastening with a stock tool. The answer is that you're trying to keep the tip from parting company with the slot.

Because the threads of a screw do all the work, pulling it

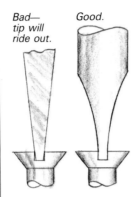

Bad—tip will ride out.   *Good.*

tightly into the wood, you should have only to apply torque; forward pressure should be unnecessary. But the faces of a stock screwdriver taper slightly, preventing the blade from squarely contacting the slot's sides, and the tip therefore tends to ride up and out when torque is applied. The harder you twist, the greater the tendency of the tip to pop out, and the greater the force required to keep it jammed in place. If the tip does jump out, all the force you're exerting will be directed at the surrounding wood—too bad! Yankee-style screwdrivers can apply only as much "push" as the spring is strong, and they invariably pop out if not dressed properly. The result is a less-than-decorative "Yankee doodle" across your pride and joy.

The solution is to dress the tip of the screwdriver so that its faces are parallel to the sides of the slot. Bits designed to be power-driven with an electric drill are invariably ground this way by the manufacturer—they would be lethal otherwise. You can grind a screwdriver to the correct shape as easily as you would hollow-grind the bevel on a chisel. The tip will wear in use, and now and then you'll have to go to the grinder to square up rounded edges. Such touch-ups will gradually shorten the blade, but you should be able to drive a few thousand screws before you have to hollow-grind the blade again.

For major-league screw installation, such as in boat planking, maximum torque is supplied by a brace and screwdriver bit. Once in a great while, this may even break a screw, but a properly sharpened screwdriver bit will engage the slot so well that even a screw that's been broken above the threads can be coaxed out of the bung hole by turning it counterclockwise with the brace and gently pulling it. Try that with a stock bit.

The ultimate touch, the *pièce de résistance* of the craftsman's ego, is to ever so slightly grind away the corners of the sharpened tool to make the tip conform perfectly to the beveled edges of the screw slot.

There you have it. The screwdriver with the right stuff is actually one of a set, each driver ground to match a particular screw size. You can take virtually any old screwdriver and true it up to do its job, but I prefer to begin with what are variably called "cabinet" or "cabinetmakers' deluxe" screwdrivers. These have a constant-dimension round shank for literally generations of sharpening. With one of these, you're half-way to having a well-dressed screwdriver already. □

Trim corners.

Michael Podmaniczky is a boatbuilder and Windsor chair maker. He lives in Thomaston, Maine.

Japanese Measuring and Marking Tools

More than simple utility

by Toshio Odate

墨付道具

While I was returning home from a seminar in Atlanta recently, the word *shokunin* came to mind. This Japanese word is defined by both Japanese and Japanese-English dictionaries as "craftsman" or "artisan," but such a literal description does not fully express the deeper meaning. The Japanese apprentice is taught that *shokunin* not only means having technical skill, but also implies an attitude and social consciousness. These qualities are encompassed in the word *shokunin,* but they are seldom written down.

The relationship of a *shokunin* to his tools is very close, for it is through the tools that the work of the *shokunin* is created. When I was being trained as a *tategu-shi* (sliding-door maker), we celebrated the tools every New Year's Day. We cleaned them and our toolboxes and put them in the *tokonoma* (a special, decorated corner of the house or sometimes the shop). We put a small piece of rice paper on each box, and on top of that two rice cakes and a tangerine. This simple gesture is the traditional way of thanking the tools for their hard work and for the crucial part they play in the *shokunin*'s life.

In the past ten years, some of these tools have enjoyed popularity among Western woodworkers, but problems exist in knowing how to get the best performance from them. Though Japanese tools often look simple when compared to Western tools, they are really very complicated to use, performing best through the *shokunin*'s preparation, ability and experience. Though the knowledge is usually acquired through long apprenticeship in Japan, in America, especially, knowledge of new things is often gained through experimentation. In some countries, this freedom to experiment is unknown, but, in America, I realize that it is a natural outgrowth of interest in and respect for personal opinion, not recklessness or carelessness.

In my book *Japanese Woodworking Tools: Their Tradition, Spirit and Use,* from which this article is adapted, I had the opportunity to write about the *shokunin*'s tools. Here I will talk about some of the marking tools used by both the *tategu-shi* and the carpenter as well as other woodworkers. I will be very happy if you understand not only the tools, but a little bit about the spiritual relationship a *shokunin* has with them.

Sumitsubo—The carpenter usually begins his work by outlining on the ground with string the shape of the house to be built. Then he chooses the wooden columns and beams from the timber on the site and marks directly on them with the *sumitsubo* (ink pot) and *sashigane* (square). The same tools are used by *tategu-shi* to mark out the rails and stiles of sliding doors. The line made with the *sumitsubo* is similar to that made with a Western chalk line (a chalk-covered string unwound from a reel, stretched between two points and snapped to mark a straight line). But instead of coarse string and chalk, the *sumitsubo* uses fine silk line and ink, which comes in both liquid form and as small solid chips.

The *sumitsubo* is an important tool, symbolic of the carpenter's spirit. When I was an apprentice, it was customary for the master carpenter to come to the site at the beginning of construction and, with the *sumitsubo,* to snap one line on a major timber. After this, his work for the day was considered done, and he was paid for the full day. An ancient custom at the end of construction of a shrine or a temple was to leave the *sumitsubo, sashigane* and *chona* (adze) in the building as treasures.

Because the *sumitsubo* is such an important spiritual symbol, it has maintained its ornate, formal style even though other woodworking tools have been simplified. Today you can buy *sumitsubo* in every Japanese tool store. They are available in three sizes: large, about 30 cm (11⅝ in.) long; medium, about 24 cm (9⅜ in.) long; and small, about 18 cm (7⅛ in.) long. The medium-size *sumitsubo* is the most commonly used.

The *sumitsubo* is used with a piece of bamboo called a *sumisashi.* One end functions as a pen for fine work such as marking joints, and the other end as a brush for writing characters, numbers and signs, as shown in figure 1. The carpenter presses the *sumisashi* across ink-soaked cotton in the well of the *sumitsubo* as the ink line is being drawn out. To make a *sumisashi,* cut the shape with a chisel or knife; use a razor blade to split the pen end into approximately 40 pieces about 1¼ in. to 1½ in. deep to separate the fibers so that they will hold ink. Then relieve the sharp corner. This relief is called the *kaeshi,* which means "return." The *sumisashi* is used by pulling it toward you. When you are making a long line and the last part of the line is getting lighter because the brush is running out of ink, you can reverse the *sumisashi* to use the ink stored on the *kaeshi,* then go back over the line.

To prepare the *sumitsubo* for use, soak the cotton in water, then wring it out and pull it evenly into a shape about twice the size of the ink pot. Place half the cotton in the pot, letting the other half hang over the side. Next, pull the end of the line through the mouth of the *sumitsubo* from the outside, and pass it over the cotton and then through the hole between the pot and the wheel. Tie the line to the groove in the wheel the way you would tie a fishing line to a reel, then insert the wheel. Thread the handle into the wheel and start reeling in the line. Stop reeling about 2 ft. from the end of the line. Tie the free end of the line to the *karuko,* a small piece of wood with which

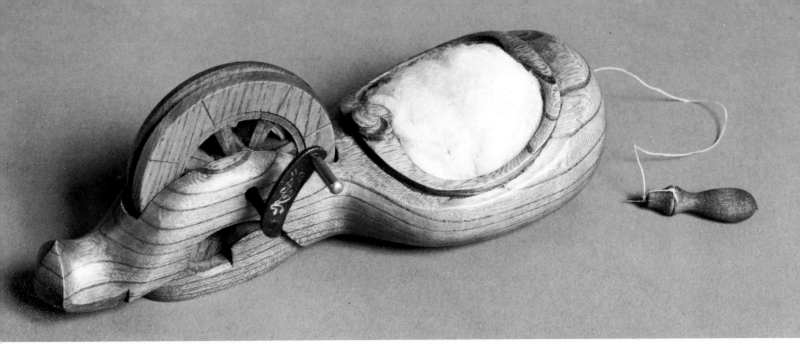

The sumitsubo, or ink pot, is symbolic of the Japanese carpenter's spirit. Used like the Western chalk line, you snap a mark by plucking the silk line straight up, then releasing.

Fig. 1: Sumisashi (bamboo pen)

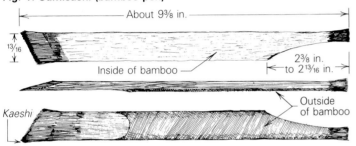

About 9⅜ in.

13/16

Inside of bamboo

2⅜ in.
to 2¹³/₁₆ in.

Kaeshi

Outside
of bamboo

to pull out the line, shaped so that it can be easily grasped. The *karuko* (which means "porter") has a steel pin at one end with which to hook the line after it is tied.

Put enough liquid ink into the pot to soak the half of the cotton pad that is there. Spread chips of ink evenly on the cotton in the pot and fold over the other half of the cotton so that the line is in the middle. Now pour just enough ink onto the cotton to soak the top layer. The chips will slowly dissolve into the cotton. The next time you wish to use the *sumitsubo* and the cotton is dry, you do not have to add ink—plain water will do. Now, to ink the line, anchor the *karuko* in a piece of wood and pull the line out about 10 ft. to 15 ft. While walking back, press the cotton with the *sumisashi* so that the line will be well saturated with ink. Then reel in the line. Do this two or three times and the *sumitsubo* will be ready for use.

Snapping the line—A *sumitsubo* has many advantages. Not only can it make a long, straight line in very little time on flat surfaces, it can also mark straight lines on curved or twisted surfaces such as logs. Skilled carpenters also use it to make beautiful, light, curved lines, such as for marking out the boards at the gable ends of Japanese roofs. They do this by snapping the line at an angle to the wood instead of straight up and down.

To snap a straight line, plant the *karuko* on the wood you wish to mark. Walk the *sumitsubo* back while pressing on the cotton with the *sumisashi*. When enough line is out, put your left thumb between the pot and the wheel to stop the wheel from turning. Using your left index or middle finger to tighten the line, press down the line where you want it. Now stretch your arm as far out as possible and, with your right fingers, lift up the line and snap it. (If you pick up the line close to its end, you won't have the necessary spring in the line.)

Sashigane—The word *kane* (or *gane*) means "steel," but in woodworking it means "square." So the woodworker saying "see the *kane*" means "check the square." A *sashigane* is used very much like a Western carpenter's framing square, but the markings, material, shape and size are quite different. The *sashigane* has a long history. I have read in *Daiku Dogu No Rekishi*, by Teijiro Muramatsu, that its predecessors came from China, where a square is known to have existed in the second century. In Japan, *shokunin* may have been using squares as early as the eighth century, but these had no measurements on them.

Today there are two types of *sashigane* used. Traditional *sashigane* use the traditional Japanese measurement system, and have different markings on the front and back. This is the square I used when I was a *shokunin*, and the one I still prefer. Modern *sashigane* have the same metric gradations front and back. Figure 2 on p. 36 shows the markings on my traditional *sashigane*. In the Japanese measurement system, there are *mo*, *rin* (10 *mo*), *bu* (10 *rin*), *sun* (10 *bu*), *shaku* (10 *sun*), *ken* (6 *shaku*), and *jo* (10 *shaku*). The unit *ken* (about 6 ft.) is an essential measure. The Japanese *tatami* (grass mat) measures 6 *shaku* (1 *ken*) by 3 *shaku* (½ *ken*). Japanese rooms are often proportioned according to the number of *tatami* that will be used to cover the floor.

The front face of the *sashigane* is calibrated in *sun*. The markings on both the tongue (short arm) and the body start at the outside corner of the square. These markings are only on the outside edge. On the back face, the outside edge of the body, which is based on *sun* multiplied by the square root of 2 (*sun* x 1.4142), is called *ura-me*. The uses of the *ura-me* are far-ranging. Carpenters use this edge to determine the maximum-size square timber that can be cut from a log by laying the *sashigane* across the smallest diameter of the log. This works

Photos: Brian Gulick

Fig. 2: *Sashigane* (square)

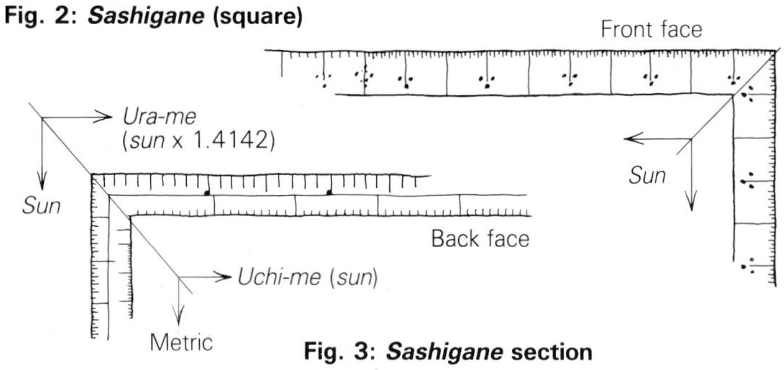

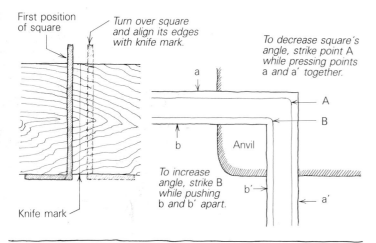

Front face

Ura-me
(sun x 1.4142)

Sun

Uchi-me (sun)

Sun

Back face

Metric

Fig. 3: *Sashigane* section

Sumisashi

Space prevents
ink from smudging
when sashigane
is moved.

Press edge to wood to
measure accurately.

Fig. 4: Judging the squareness of a *sashigane*

*Square is true if, when in second
position, it's parallel to knife mark.*

First position
of square

Turn over square
and align its edges
with knife mark.

To decrease square's
angle, strike point A
while pressing points
a and a' together.

a

A

B

b

Anvil

To increase
angle, strike B
while pushing
b and b' apart.

b'

a'

Knife mark

Fig. 5: Types of marking gauges

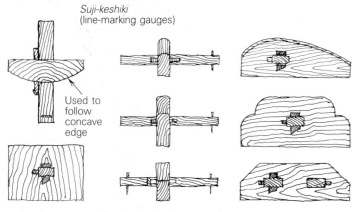

Suji-keshiki
(line-marking gauges)

Used to
follow
concave
edge

Fig. 6: Marking-gauge blades

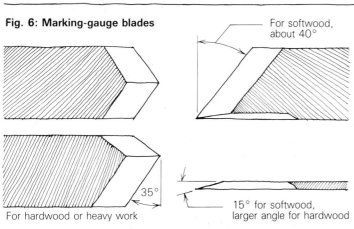

For softwood,
about 40°

35°

For hardwood or heavy work

15° for softwood,
larger angle for hardwood

---

mathematically because each side of a square inscribed in a circle is equal to the diameter of the circle divided by the square root of 2.

Until about 55 years ago, *sashigane,* like other tools, were forged by blacksmiths from iron. Today, I do not know of any blacksmiths making *sashigane* by the old method. Instead, *sashigane* are made from copper, brass, German silver (an alloy of copper, zinc and nickel), steel or stainless steel. Steel *sashigane* rust easily, and it is difficult to see the lines, so many *shokunin* do not like them, even though they are stronger than the others. At the time of my youth, many *shokunin* did not like stainless-steel *sashigane* because the color was too bright and its shine was cold and harsh. My master said, "It never gives me calmness." Stainless steel does not have this effect on me, and this is the type of *sashigane* I use today.

Shape and squareness—The *sashigane* is much smaller and narrower than the Western framing square, and also much more flexible. It is sensitively designed—for example, the blade is contoured so that when used with the *sumisashi,* as shown in figure 3, the space between the edge of the square and the surface to be marked allows the square to be moved without smudging the ink. Yet by holding the edge of the square flat against the surface, very accurate measurements can be taken.

The *sashigane* is the basis for all marking. If it is not square, then the entire building will not be true, so you must check that the angle is correct from time to time. I will explain how to check for squareness, as shown in figure 4.

Begin by preparing a board about 1 in. thick by 12 in. wide by 30 in. to 36 in. long. Dress its face as flat as possible and plane one edge straight and square to the face. Then put the square on the board and draw a line with a marking knife along the square's edge. Reverse the square and hold its edge to the knife mark. If the edge is parallel to the mark, that is good, and the *sashigane* is square. But if they are not parallel, follow these steps. If the angle is too large, strike point A gently with a hammer while pressing the tongue and body together on an anvil, either alone or with the help of an assistant. Don't strike too hard, as you might stretch the steel badly. If the angle is too small, strike point B while pushing apart at the points indicated. Continue this procedure and test again until the square is true.

Keshiki—Marking gauges, or *keshiki,* are used mainly by *tategu-shi* and other woodworkers who use small materials. Many *shokunin* make their own, but *keshiki* are also available in tool shops that carry Japanese tools. There are different sizes, shapes and types for different work (figure 5). I will talk here about the most common, the *suji-keshiki,* or line-marking gauge. This tool is used to scribe a single line parallel to the edge of the piece of wood. Most *suji-keshiki* have a simple flat fence and a single beam to hold the blade. The fence, which must be square to the beam, is usually held in place with a wedge, but sometimes with a nut and bolt. The blade, either made from an old bandsaw blade or purchased, is a forced fit in the beam.

In general, Japanese marking gauges are similar to their Western counterparts. With the exception of the mortise gauge, however, all Japanese gauges use blades instead of pins, for marking both across the grain and along it. A blade, which cuts, leaves a finer mark than a pin, which scratches. Like other Japanese tools, marking gauges are used on the pull stroke. Most are adjusted in the same manner by tapping the beam with a hammer, as shown in the photos on the facing page.

Suji-keshiki are traditionally made of white or red oak, which has the hardness and tenacity the tool needs. Today, however, *suji-keshiki* are also made from rosewood and ebony. Rosewood and ebony *keshiki* should be used with a wedge of a softer, more resilient wood, such as oak or maple. Wedges made of these woods will compress when tapped to allow fine adjustment and will hold the fence tightly in position. Here are some points to consider if you are making your own *suji-keshiki*. Fences may be made in a variety of shapes and sizes. Common beam lengths are 3½ in. to 7 in. and common thicknesses are ⅜ in. to ⅝ in., but size the beam to fit your hand and work. The width of the beam may vary, and depends on the size of the blade; naturally, a wide blade in a too-narrow beam could split the beam.

The beam should slide easily in the fence, but not be loose. The wedge hole in the fence should be tapered, with the larger opening on the outside of the fence. The angle of the wedge and wedge slot have to match perfectly, otherwise the wedge may press on just one point of the beam, which could change the angle of the beam to the fence. In addition, a wedge that does not fit correctly will not hold the beam tight.

The blade of the *suji-keshiki* is beveled on one side to form the cutting edge, and that side usually faces the fence; as the blade cuts, the bevel keeps pulling the fence into the edge of the wood. Blades can be made in a number of different shapes, as shown in figure 6. I make my blades from a piece of broken bandsaw blade or any other hardened steel, but they can also be purchased. To set the blade in the beam, first insert the beam into the fence and tighten it. Then draw a line on the beam showing the location of the knife, usually about ½ in. to 1 in. from the end. This line should be exactly parallel to the fence. Now draw another line starting at the same position at the front, but skew it out one pencil-mark width at the back. (Skewed away from the fence, the blade will push away from the fence slightly in use, helping to pull the fence into the wood and allowing greater accuracy.)

Start the slot for the blade by making a small hole on the end of the line at the front of the gauge. I usually use a spade-tipped gimlet for this, or a drill. Saw down the skewed line with a coping-saw blade. If necessary, widen the top of the slot with a chisel. The thickness, but not the width, of the blade must be tight, otherwise the beam might split. (In case the blade is loose in the slot, you can add a wedge to tighten it.)

Suji-keshiki can also be made with two beams on one fence, so that you can mark two lines, as for mortising. For this, the bevels on the blades should be opposite each other, facing toward the inside of the mortise. This will leave a clear guide for the mortise chisel. *Suji-keshiki* can be adapted to do many different jobs. For example, if you have a gauge with one beam and you need to make many sets of parallel lines a certain distance apart, as when marking mortises, cut a piece of wood the width of that distance for a spacer and notch it to take the beam. Mark once with the piece in place against the fence and once without the piece. □

Toshio Odate's book, Japanese Woodworking Tools: Their Tradition, Spirit and Use, *is available for $24.00 from The Taunton Press. In addition to the chapter on marking tools, the 192-page volume covers saws, chisels, planes, sharpening stones and some specialized tools with no Western counterparts. Odate, who lives in Woodbury, Conn., conducts frequent workshops on Japanese tools and teaches sculpture at New York's Pratt Institute. Drawings by the author.*

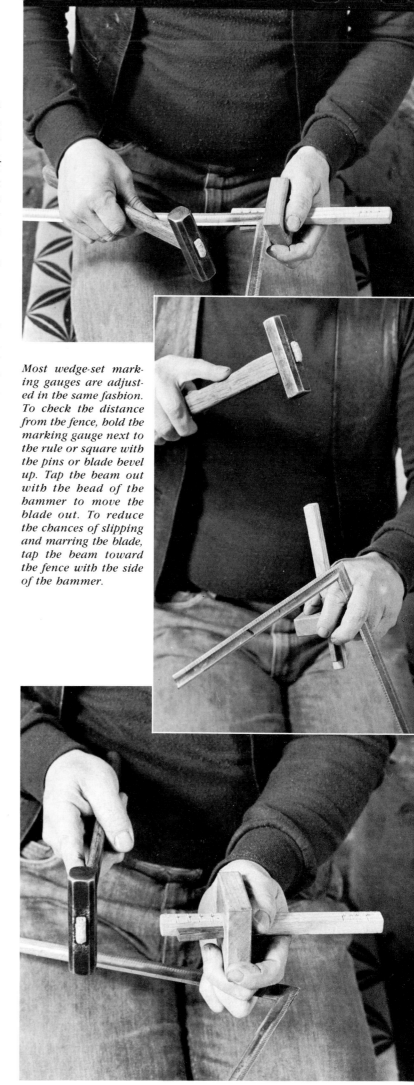

Most wedge-set marking gauges are adjusted in the same fashion. To check the distance from the fence, hold the marking gauge next to the rule or square with the pins or blade bevel up. Tap the beam out with the head of the hammer to move the blade out. To reduce the chances of slipping and marring the blade, tap the beam toward the fence with the side of the hammer.

Files in the Woodshop

They're often a good alternative to abrasives

by Henry T. Kramer

Point

Length

Face

Heel   Edge

Tang

Fig. 1: Parts of a file

Files seem to be poor country cousins in a typical woodworker's shop, often neglected by even skilled craftsmen. But it's wrong to ignore a tool that can be so useful and that frequently is the best tool for shaping, smoothing or sharpening.

Files can true up all kinds of tools, especially new planes and spokeshaves. They sharpen saws, scrapers, cold chisels, axes and screwdrivers. Files can also smooth knicks and dents in everything from drill bits to drive shafts. They're efficient and economical alternatives to abrasives for shaping both wood and metal—they last a long time, and there's a size, shape and cutting grade for almost any carving or smoothing job you might encounter.

You may not consider a file a precision tool, but I've brought the badly hogged sole of a 22-in. jointer plane to within ±0.00125 in. of dead flat with only three files. And it doesn't take as much time or experience as you might think. As in any woodworking or metalworking, the slogan is "Measure twice, cut once." Stress the word "cut": you'll never learn how to use a file properly until you realize it's a cutting tool, not one that abrades the work.

More than 650 types of files are available today, but I'll discuss only 10 groups of "American Pattern" files that include about 170 files useful to woodworkers. The American Pattern designation is a traditional one stemming from post-Civil War days when Americans first began manufacturing files on a large scale, instead of importing them from Europe. These American Pattern files usually are coarser than their European or "Swiss Pattern" counterparts. I won't consider Swiss Patterns here, since they are finishing tools used by jewelers and modelmakers and too fine for most woodshop jobs, or circular-tooth files designed for soft, ductile metals such as copper, brass and aluminum.

The terms commonly used to describe files are fairly self-explanatory and probably already part of your vocabulary (figure 1). Most files have cutting teeth on both faces and both edges, but some have one or two smooth or "safe" edges so that they can be used in tight corners without accidentally damaging adjacent areas.

The "cut" of a file describes how its teeth are arranged. Single-cut files have one set of continuous, parallel teeth running in one direction. These files are designed primarily for sharpening or finishing metals. Double-cut files have intersecting sets of teeth forming sharp, diamond-shaped points designed to remove material faster. They'll cut wood quickly, though not as fast as a rasp, which has freestanding, clog-resistant teeth. Rasps and rifflers (small shaped rasps) are made primarily for woodworkers, carvers and farriers. Rasps come in several combinations of length and tooth grade, but all you really have to know is that in similar lengths and grades, the wood rasp is the coarsest, the cabinet rasp is a little finer, and the patternmakers' cabinet rasp is the finest. These cut wood rapidly, but leave a rough surface which can be smoothed with a wood file. In addition to regular rasps, there is also a tool called a shoe rasp, or four-in-hand, which is a combination of rasps and files that looks a lot more useful than it really is—its toothed surfaces are too short for an effective cutting stroke.

Any file can be used on wood, but you may find that the majority are too fine and clog up too quickly to be of much use. The coarseness of a file is controlled by two factors: the grade or size of tooth used, and the file's length. Today it's hard to find more than three grades of teeth: bastard, second-cut and smooth. Years ago, rough, coarse, dead-smooth and dead-dead-smooth grades were also available. The grade usually is stamped on the heel of the file, but this doesn't give you an exact gauge of the tooth size unless you also consider the length of the file. Within any one grade, a longer file has larger, coarser teeth than a shorter file, and fewer teeth per inch. There appears to be no industry-wide standard, but generally a file that's one grade finer and 2 in. longer has the same size teeth as its coarser, shorter counterpart. Thus, an 8-in. second-cut or a 10-in. smooth has the same size teeth as a 6-in. bastard. If you find a number on the heel of the file, it's a Swiss Pattern type; 00 is the coarsest and 6 the finest.

The two files designed for wood are the wood file (essentially a 10-in. coarse half-round) and the cabinet file, which has somewhat finer teeth than the wood file. Any double-cut bastard file, 10 in. or longer, can be effective, however, as long as you keep the teeth clean. Regardless of the type, a file's teeth face forward and won't cut anything when going backward—they'll just get dull. Don't move your file back and forth like a saw. Pick it up on the return stroke.

A file's name is based on several things: the shape of its cross section, such as flat, square, round or half-round; its use, such as for sharpening an auger bit or a chainsaw; or from traditions that no longer clearly speak for themselves—a mill file, for instance, is a single-cut flat file originally used for sharpening mill saws. The way in which files are identified in a catalog or a store may seem mysterious, but it's simply a

Single-cut

Double-cut

Rasp

combination of the file's length, name and tooth grade. For example, you'd ask for a 16-in. flat bastard when you really want to rip off material and have a lot of working room, or a 4-in. mill smooth when you want the smoothest surface an American Pattern file can produce.

Taper files, for sharpening handsaws, are a special case. Tapers are made with only one grade of tooth, but the size of the tooth increases according to the degree of slimness and the length of the file. The four sizes are regular, slim, extra slim, and double extra or extra extra slim. To sharpen a saw without damaging the teeth, you must use the correct size file. For a 5- to 5½-pt. ripsaw, I recommend using a 7-in. regular. For an 8-pt. crosscut saw, use a 6-in. slim, 7-in. extra slim or 8-in. double extra slim. For a 10-pt., a 5-in. or 6-in. extra slim does the job best. For an 11-pt., use a 5-in. extra slim or a 6-in. double extra slim. A 12-pt. calls for a 5-in. extra slim; a 12½- to 16-pt., a 5-in. double extra slim. The number of points on a saw equals the number of teeth per inch, plus one.

A table describing files of probable interest to woodworkers is shown at right. The metalworking files that a woodworker would likely find most useful are the 4-in., 6-in., 12-in. and 14-in. mill smooth; the 4-in. mill bastard; the 12-in. hand second-cut; the 12-in. hand bastard; the 14-in. flat second-cut; the 4-in. flat smooth; a 5-in. extra slim taper; and a 5-in. double extra slim taper.

I'm not suggesting that you immediately buy all these files, but as you learn how useful they can be, you'll probably want to, if you can find them. It's a vicious circle: merchants cannot be expected to stock files if there is no demand, and woodworkers can't be expected to demand tools they don't know about. If you do buy files, I recommend that you avoid foreign-made American Pattern files, which don't seem to amount to much. I've also found that files packed in plastic bubbles don't seem to be of the same quality as those sold in machinists' supply houses.

• • •

One of the first things you should do with a new file is put a handle on it. An uncovered tang is dangerous: you can drive it through your palm. If you want a removable handle, buy one with a threaded ferrule or built-in clamp. It's cheaper to make your own hardwood handles with ferrules of thin copper, brass or steel pipe. Once you've fitted a ferrule onto your handle blank, use a bit the size of the tang end to drill a hole slightly deeper than the tang's length. Then open the top half of the hole with a drill the size of the middle of the tang. Insert the tang in the hole, hold the file, and bang the end of the handle with a mallet or on a bench or other hard surface, driving the handle onto the tang. Another way to enlarge the hole is to take a worn-out file with the same size tang, heat the old tang to a red glow, and shove it down the hole. Keep a bucket of water nearby in case the handle catches fire.

You should use different files for wood, soft metal and steel. A file that has been used on a hard material will not cut as well on a softer one. So if you want to use a file on wood, don't use it on anything else. Except for small sharpening files, new files that will be used on steel should be broken in first, to eliminate any irregularities that might cause teeth to break off or dull. To do this, file for a total of about an hour on a soft metal such as brass or aluminum. Properly broken in, a file will last a long time, cutting about the same throughout its life. When it does go, this will happen quickly and you'll

FILES FOR WOODWORKERS		
Name and cross section	Cut*	Description
Mill	S	For sharpening sawblades and scrapers, shaping and smoothing wood and metal, drawfiling, fitting, and truing. These files are tapered in width and thickness. Every woodworker should have a selection of these.
Flat	D	The standard machinists' file for shaping and quick removal of material. Tapers in width and thickness. Used for forming grooves, squaring holes and filing in sharp corners. Good for starting jobs that the mill file will finish.
Hand	D	Same as the flat file, but tapers only in thickness. Has one safe edge, making it useful for filing in corners where one surface should not be filed. Good for rough, heavy work.
Warding	D	Tapers to a fine point. Useful for getting into tight spots, such as when you are fitting plane irons and frogs.
Pillar	D	Narrower than a flat or hand file. Has two safe edges and no taper. Useful for filing slots.
Half-round	D	The flat side is useful for filing on flat and convex surfaces; the rounded back is good for filing on concave surfaces. You don't need a half-round often, but when you do, nothing else will do. The rounded backs of finer, shorter half-rounds have single-cut teeth.
Wood	D	Essentially a coarse half-round. Specifically designed to resist clogging when used on wood. Available in 10-in. length only.
Cabinet	D	Another file designed for wood. Thinner and with a shallower back and finer teeth than the wood file. Available in 8-in. and 10-in. lengths.
Taper	S	For sharpening 60° teeth on handsaws.
Three-square	D	A general-purpose file for working in angular corners of more than 60°.
Square	D	A flat file with a square cross section.
Round (Rat-tail)	S&D	A tapered file used for dressing the insides of holes and small-radius curves. Round files longer than 10 in., except the 12-in. smooth, have double-cut teeth. Others have single-cut.
Chainsaw	S&D	Has special teeth designed for sharpening chainsaws. This file is not tapered.
Auger-bit	S	A double-ended file with each end tapering to a point. Has safe edges on one end, safe faces on the other end. Very handy for sharpening the cutting edge and spurs of auger bits.

* S is single-cut; D is double-cut.

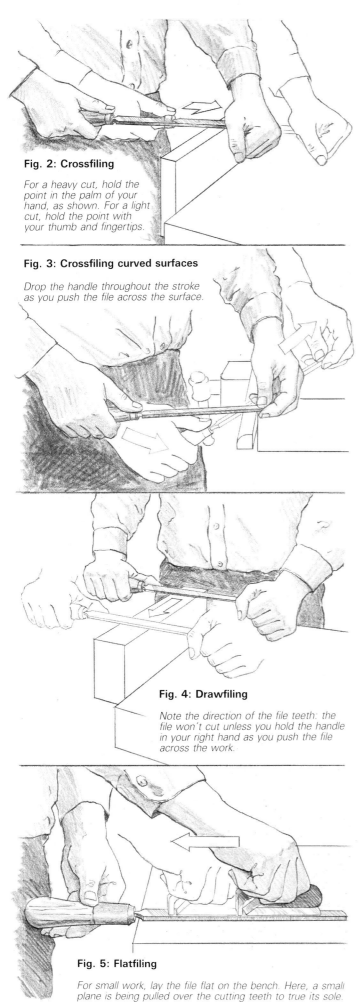

Fig. 2: Crossfiling

For a heavy cut, hold the point in the palm of your hand, as shown. For a light cut, hold the point with your thumb and fingertips.

Fig. 3: Crossfiling curved surfaces

Drop the handle throughout the stroke as you push the file across the surface.

Fig. 4: Drawfiling

Note the direction of the file teeth: the file won't cut unless you hold the handle in your right hand as you push the file across the work.

Fig. 5: Flatfiling

For small work, lay the file flat on the bench. Here, a small plane is being pulled over the cutting teeth to true its sole.

know it. Files can be resharpened, but it's impractical and dangerous in the small shop. It's best to buy a new file.

There are three common ways of filing: crossfiling, drawfiling and flatfiling. In crossfiling, which most people consider the only filing method, you usually push the file across the work, but it is sometimes done with the file held so that its long axis and the long axis of the work coincide (avoid this variation on narrow edges, or you're liable to round them). Clamp the work firmly at elbow height. Put one foot in front of the other, and stand up straight. Don't hunch over your work. For heavy filing, hold the handle of the file with your thumb on top and the point in the palm of your other hand (figure 2). To make a lighter cut, hold the handle the same way, but place the thumb of your other hand on the point and curl your fingers around the file. Think of your arms and shoulders as a parallel-motion machine swinging from the shoulders, and push the file across the work, maintaining a constant angle to the work. When filing a flat surface, first catch the vertical angle by rocking the file on the surface until it's flat. Do this each time you've stopped. On very thin material, hold the file at an angle to make a shearing cut, so the file teeth don't catch. From time to time, change the lateral angle of filing—errors in maintaining the vertical angle and any high spots will stand out clearly after only a stroke or two. If a wavy surface appears, try clamping the piece more securely, using less pressure on the file, or try a finer file.

Crossfiling with a taper file is a useful technique for notching a bar or other surface, say, to start a hacksaw cut. Notch an edge and file at a slight angle. You can crossfile a rounded or cylindrical surface if you drop the handle end of the file throughout the stroke (figure 3).

Drawfiling (figure 4), which usually is done with a single-cut mill file, is very useful to woodworkers. It's slower than crossfiling, but you'll find it easy to control the cut and produce a smooth surface. It also has the advantage of letting you file the entire surface in one continuous stroke. Drawfiling is a sharpening or finishing stroke, so don't use any more pressure than needed to feel the file cut.

Position the work so that its long axis runs away from your body, not from side-to-side. Hand position is important to ensure that the teeth are in a cutting position. If you're holding the file wrong, it won't cut—it'll just get dull. Grip the handle in your right hand, lay the file across the work at the desired angle, and grasp the point in your left. The file should be held at a right angle to the direction of the stroke. Now push. If you bear down too hard, the teeth will dig grooves and the file will walk to one side. If you are left-handed and feel uneasy with the handle in your right hand, or if the shape of the work requires it, you can hold the file handle in your left hand, but then you must use a pulling stroke. The rule is: Push stroke, handle in right hand; pull stroke, handle in left. To distribute wear evenly on the file, most workers move it slightly to the left or right between strokes.

If you want an even finer finish, wrap emery paper around the file and polish with the same drawfiling stroke. You may want to begin with 320-grit and work down to 400, then 600. Use a little light oil on the paper when sanding metal.

A good drawfiling exercise is squaring up a cabinet scraper with a 6-in. mill bastard and a 4-in. mill smooth (if you can't find the latter, use a 6-in. mill smooth or a 4-in. mill bastard, but go easy). First, use a straightedge to check that the scraper's long edge is flat or slightly convex, depending on your

Treatise on files and rasps

by Dick Burrows

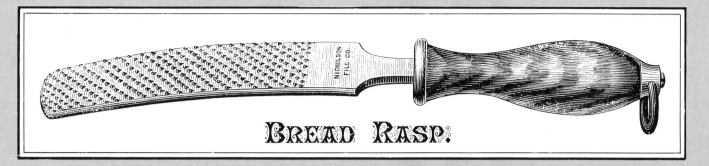

BREAD RASP.

Ever try to use a rasp on bread? The practice was quite fashionable among "many of the better class of English and French people" in the late 19th century when the Nicholson File Company published *A Treatise on Files and Rasps.*

High-class bakers of the day felt that bread baked quickly and hard was sweeter and tastier than bread prepared in the conventional way, once you got past the thick, singed crust. So they ordered a curved, nickel-plated rasp (above) with an enameled handle—just the thing to get rid of the crust and create lots of bread crumbs.

The bread rasp is just one of the unusual items described in the Nicholson treatise, a catalog and description of files and rasps developed to meet the needs of every specialized trade and industry. The Early American Industries Association, which recently reprinted the book, calls the slim, 80-page volumn a classic of hand-tool literature, and the engravings reproduced from the original volumn add to the nostalgia. The work is a delight to those who favor hand tools and relish the history of tools.

Many of the files available when the book was published are no longer manufactured, but the information on using and caring for files is still pertinent. And the historical glimpses are especially informative in light of Nicholson's role as a pioneer manufacturer of machine-cut files.

The text is concise, crisp and easy to follow. The files, rasps and scrapers are well illustrated, and their uses are clearly described. There are enough details—such as discussions of the lengths of file teeth needed for penetration in various types of metals, and the relationship between tooth angle and tool control—to satisfy most students. □

A Treatise on Files and Rasps may be ordered from the EAIA, PO Box 2128, Empire State Plaza Sta., Albany, N.Y. 12220 ($7.95 to EAIA members; $13.50 to non-members). Engraving reprinted courtesy of the EAIA.

preference. Use the 6-in. mill to straighten the edge if needed. Then, holding the same file at a slight angle to the direction of the stroke and with the file's face flat on the side of the scraper, take off any hook left from the previous sharpening. Now drawfile the whole edge until it's square to the scraper sides. Start with the 6-in. tool and finish up with the 4-in. Crossfile lightly along the sides to remove any lip left by drawfiling, then burnish.

Flatfiling can be a useful technique for small work—work that generally is less than 3 in. long and no more than 1¼ in. wide, really too small to be handled easily with other hand-filing methods. Start by laying the file flat on a table or a bench. If the file is handled, let the handle hang over the edge, or put the file in a fairly large machinists' vise. Now draw the article to be filed over the cutting edges of the teeth. This is a handy way to flatten the sole of an ordinary thumb plane, and most rabbet planes are narrow enough to be flat-filed (figure 5). Most rectangular-section files have slightly convex faces, and some people may think that this would work against a flat surface. Actually, this convexity is intended to help achieve flatness when crossfiling, and it seems to have the same effect when flatfiling, especially if the work is reversed every four or five strokes.

Files look rugged, but like any other cutting tool, they need care. Keep them separated in racks, not thrown loose in a drawer or stuck in an old can. Given a chance, two files try to cut each other, with bad results for both.

Keep your files clean. A file card with a brush on its back is useful here. The card's stiff, short teeth work well on large-toothed files, and the short-bristle brush does the job on all files, if used frequently enough. Generally, it's best to use the brush more frequently than you think necessary. Files clog or "pill or pin up" once in a while, and this condition can both mark the work and stop the cutting. To clean a file, try a medium-grade power-driven wire wheel, holding the file so that the wires run down the gullets of the teeth. Alternatively, you can make a pinning tool from ⅛-in. brass or hard copper rod. Hammer the end of the rod to the rough shape of a double-bevel chisel and file to a smooth, slightly round edge with sharp corners. The edge should be thin enough to touch the bottom of the gullets between the rows of teeth. Put on your magnifying glasses, take a deep breath and get comfortable, and pick each "pin" out, one by one.

In addition to cleaning the files, you should also clean the metal surfaces that you file. Filing can leave metal fragments in the pores of iron, which, as in the case of a plane sole, can be transferred to the wood. Don't trust your eye: the surface may look clean, but it's not. Clean it with an oiled rag. Besides, any newly filed metal surface needs a coating of light oil right away, unless you live in Death Valley. The best lubricants and rust preventives are things people like to argue about, but anything is better than nothing. I don't think that the files themselves should be oiled, because oil can make them slip and more prone to clogging. Files will rust, however, and when they do so badly, that's it. So keep them dry. At the first hint of rust, use the wire-brush wheel. □

Henry T. Kramer, a retired reinsurance specialist, is an amateur woodworker and metalworker living in Sommerville, N.J.

Auger Bits

How to tune these deceptively simple tools

by Richard Starr

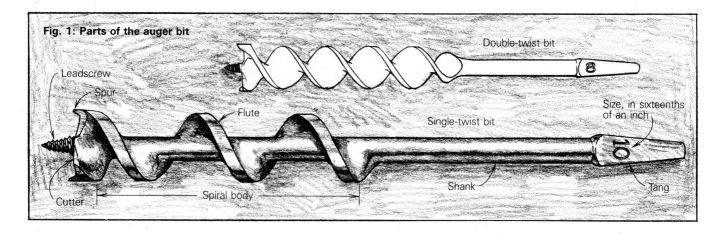

Fig. 1: Parts of the auger bit

Double-twist bit

Leadscrew
Spur
Flute
Single-twist bit
Size, in sixteenths of an inch
Shank
Tang
Cutter
Spiral body

I once knew an auto mechanic who didn't believe in gremlins. He felt that it was natural for a car to run well—if it didn't, there was a good reason. Like a car, an auger bit should work well. If you have a bit that has lost its bite and requires hard pushing to get it to drill, you needn't put up with its misbehavior. There's nothing mysterious going on; something specific is amiss, and it usually can be fixed. Even new bits can be tuned to cut more smoothly and easily.

The auger bit has probably the most complex shape of any piece of steel in the shop, with several parts that must work in concert. First into the wood goes the leadscrew, which pulls the bit forward with enough force so that once it gets a bite, no further pressure is required on the head of the brace. Next, the spurs score a circle in the wood, severing fibers across the grain so that the cutters, which follow the spurs, can lift a shaving without tearing the walls of the hole. The spiral flutes lift the shavings away from the cutters, while bearing against the walls of the hole to keep the bit running straight and true. To allow the bit to turn freely, the spiral body of an auger must be slightly smaller than the hole diameter. The diameter of the hole is determined by the distance between the tips of the spurs, so the manufacturer makes clearance for the flutes by flaring the spurs outward slightly.

There are many variations on this basic design. Some are intended for rough construction work and for power drive. The two varieties suitable for use in a hand brace are the solid-center single-twist bit and the double-twist Jennings type (figure 1). The double-twist is reputed to do a better job of lifting shavings from a hole, and it has more flute surface bearing on the walls of the hole to keep it boring true. On the other hand, the single-twist bit is less likely to bend, because of its sturdy core, and is cheaper to manufacture. In practice, the differences are insignificant.

While many rough-construction bits have a single cutter and one spur, workbench bits have two of each. Each of the paired parts does only half the work that a single cutter or spur would have to do. Because wood is removed more gently

this way, less effort is required and a smoother hole results. A well-tuned bit is balanced: the spurs do equal work and the cutters take shavings of equal thickness.

The pitch of the leadscrew determines how fast the bit will cut. Bits available at hardware stores are usually single-twist types with coarse-pitch or fast screws, while most of the double-twist bits have fine-pitch leadscrews. The slow-lead bits take thinner shavings and leave a smoother surface. Fast bits are harder to turn because they take a bigger bite, and in harder woods the effort required may be excessive. By using a brace with a wider sweep (twice the radius of the crank), you can reduce the amount of force required to turn any bit. Most braces today have a 12-in. sweep, but I prefer a 14-in. sweep for bits larger than ¾ in. in diameter. These braces are no longer made, though they can be found at flea markets.

Auger bits sold in the United States are made in ¹⁄₁₆-in. increments, from ½ in. to about 1½ in. in diameter. The bit diameter is usually stamped on the tang with a number that represents sixteenths of an inch: a number 14, for example, is a ⅞-in. bit. Most auger bits are made to cut ¹⁄₆₄ in. oversize, unless they are designated as doweling bits (made by The Irwin Co., PO Box 829, Wilmington, Ohio 45177), which are sized right-on. Doweling bits are shorter than regular auger bits, being about 4 in. to 5 in. long, with flutes about 2½ in. long.

If an auger bit doesn't drill well, any of the three cutting parts—leadscrew, spurs or cutters—may be the culprit. First, check the screw. It should have a sharp point and clean, undamaged threads along its full length, or it will load with ground-up fibers, preventing it from biting. Bent threads can sometimes be straightened with the point of a knife. If this fails, true them with a small jewelers' file. Remove as little metal as possible but as much as necessary—a low section of thread will cause less resistance than a pinched section. Even broken points can sometimes be filed to shape.

Spurs are often too long and thick, even on new bits. A long spur, by scoring the wood much deeper than the thick-

The single-twist auger on the left is new, while the bit on the right is a well-cared-for veteran with modified spurs. Starr drilled sample holes in cherry with these bits, then cut the wood in half (below). You can see the difference in scoring depth—the new bit scored too deeply. The thinner, shorter spurs of the modified bit made the smoother surface at right.

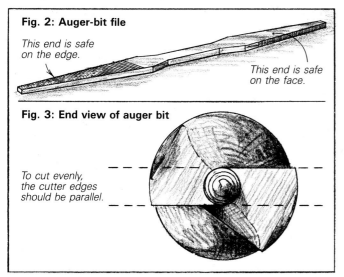

Fig. 2: Auger-bit file

This end is safe on the edge.

This end is safe on the face.

Fig. 3: End view of auger bit

To cut evenly, the cutter edges should be parallel.

When sharpening a cutter with an auger file, it's easy to file accurately if you support the bit against a piece of scrap wood.

ness of the cutter's shaving, wastes effort. A thick spur wedges its way through the wood rather than cutting cleanly. On the other hand, if the spurs are too short, the cutter will reach the surface of the wood first and tear out unsevered fibers, leaving rough walls. A spur that's too thin will dull quickly and may bend. Since the spurs are flared to provide clearance for the flutes, shortening them reduces the hole diameter slightly, but since most auger bits are designed to cut $\frac{1}{64}$ in. oversize, this may not be a problem.

Use an auger-bit file (available from mail-order tool suppliers and hardware stores) to sharpen or modify the spurs. Its tapered ends let you work on wide or narrow surfaces. One end has no teeth on the face, while the other end is safe on the edge, as shown in figure 2. This allows you to file without damaging adjacent surfaces. You can finish up with an auger-bit stone, but I'm satisfied with the edge I get from the file.

To file spurs, I secure the shank end in a vise and support the upper end of the bit with my left hand. Since the spur is thicker at its base than at its tip, you should file the entire inside surface to avoid thickening the spur's profile as the spur gets shorter. If you wish to thin down the entire spur, file the base thinner first, then work all of the inside surface. Though only the tip actually cuts wood, any nicks along its leading edge will scrape the walls of the hole, so these should be filed out. Never file the outside edge of the spur, except to gently brush away burrs. To check that the spurs are of equal length, drill into a board with the bit square to the surface, watching to see if one spur touches the wood first. If it does, shorten that spur slightly and try again.

Dull cutters make a bit difficult to turn, and may even cause the leadscrew to slip and load up. Even new cutters may need a touch-up, but be sure to file on the flute or bevel side, not on the leadscrew side. Most problems with cutters come from filing the wrong side. To file, I hold the bit in my left hand, and press its business end firmly against a piece of scrap wood for support. A 30° bevel angle is about right. A damaged cutter may be filed back quite a bit, but be sure you file both cutters to maintain balance. You can judge this by looking at the end of the bit—the cutter edges should appear parallel, as shown in figure 3. To fine-tune, drill a hole, compare the shavings made by each cutter, and file a little more off the cutter that makes the thicker shaving. If the cutters are filed back a lot, check the spurs for depth of cut; they may need to be shortened.

Have you ever noticed how difficult it is to drill into end grain with a regular auger bit? The spurs are the problem. They have no function in end grain, and just get in the way. You can recycle a damaged auger bit for use in end grain by grinding off the spurs. The leadscrew does tend to follow the grain, so for really accurate deep holes in end grain, grind the leadscrew off too. Then use a file to angle the cutters toward the center where the leadscrew was, so that the end of the bit resembles the point of a machine drill. You'll have to start the hole with another bit that still has its lead.

It takes experience to get the hang of filing auger bits. Practice on some worn or damaged ones. If the back of your tool cabinet doesn't contain the usual pile of ineffective bits, you can probably pick some up cheap at a flea market. You'll be surprised how easy it is to resurrect them. □

Richard Starr is a teacher and the author of Woodworking with Kids *(The Taunton Press). Photos by the author.*

Make a Hook Scraper

by Tom Vaughn

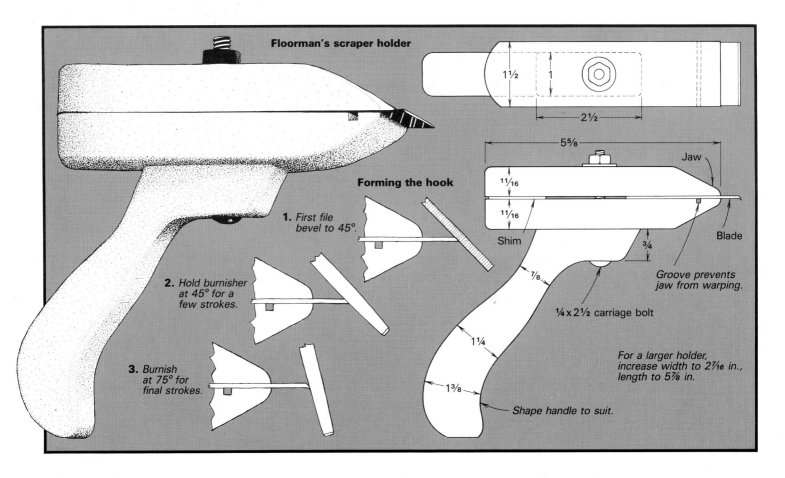

Floorman's scraper holder

1½   1   2½

5⅝

Forming the hook

1. First file bevel to 45°.

2. Hold burnisher at 45° for a few strokes.

3. Burnish at 75° for final strokes.

11/16

11/16

Shim

Jaw

Blade

¾

⅞

Groove prevents jaw from warping.

¼ x 2½ carriage bolt

1¼

1⅜

For a larger holder, increase width to 2⅟₁₆ in., length to 5⅞ in.

Shape handle to suit.

The phrase "laid, scraped and finished" was still part of the tradesman's lingo in 1948 when I started installing parquet flooring. Needing an efficient tool to smooth large surfaces, as well as the tight corners formed by baseboards and stairs, workmen made special hook scrapers, like the one shown here. In principle, this hook scraper works the same as a regular cabinet scraper, but its pronounced hook works better than a cabinetmakers' small burr for scraping big areas, and the wooden holder makes it less tiresome to use. A thin shim at the back of the jaws directs the pressure to hold the blade at the very tip.

You can make the holder out of any hardwood, though maple is my favorite. The drawing shows a small holder, but you could make the jaws up to 2⅟₁₆ in. wide and ¹³⁄₁₆ in. thick. Shape the handle any way you wish and glue it to the bottom jaw. Blades can be made by cutting up a regular scraper blade or an old backsaw. A trick for cutting the hard steel used in these tools is to score a line on opposite sides of the blade with a carbide-tipped machinists' scriber, then clamp the steel in a vise and smack off the waste with a hammer. It should break cleanly. You can also cut steel with a tungsten-carbide blade in a hacksaw.

To form the hook, mount the blade in the holder so it protrudes about ½ in. With the holder on its side and braced by your knee atop a toolbox or an 18-in. high bench, file a 45° bevel on the top face. Work it until you have a sharp edge and

can feel a wire burr on the back side. Remove the weak part of the burr by passing it over a board or the edge of your toolbox.

Now you're ready to burnish the hook. I burnish with a tapered-triangle steel (like a butchers' steel and available at many woodworking supply stores), but any smooth, rounded, hardened steel object like a screwdriver shank will work. With the holder still on its side, start with the burnisher at the far end of the blade and draw it up toward you. Hold the burnisher at 45° to the blade for three or four hard pulls, then progress to 75° for a few more passes. You should have a nice hook now.

To use the scraper, grasp it as you would a handsaw, hold it at about 30° to the surface and draw it briskly toward you. It should pull a small shaving, not crumbs. Light scraping—the inside corner of a carcase, for example—can be done one-handed, but for heavier work, press downward with your other hand against the back of the jaws. Continual burnishing will bend the hook over so much that it won't cut well. You can file a new hook, or renew the old one for a while by inserting the point of a small oval burnisher (sold by jewelers' and gunsmiths' supply houses) under the hook and restraightening it. □

Thomas Vaughn is a commercial cabinetmaker in Phoenix, Ariz. He has worked at Colonial Williamsburg and at the National Park Service in Yorktown, Va.

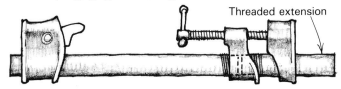

Reversing pipe clamps

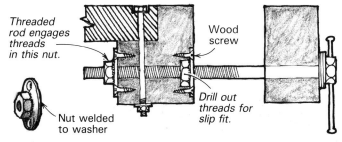

Threaded extension

It's handy to be able to reverse a pipe clamp so it can be used to push something apart. In fact, special clamp heads are sold for this purpose. As a thrifty alternative, if you add a short section of pipe to the head as shown, you'll be able to reverse any standard pipe clamp at will.

Screw the head on backwards and stop about halfway. Now screw the short 6-in. piece into the clamp head in the normal fashion. Reverse the shoe, and you have an efficient spreading clamp. —*T.D. Culver, Cleveland Heights, Ohio*

Extending pipe clamps

This simple method gives you a clamp of almost unlimited length. Just slot the ends of two short sections of pipe and install a heavy chain with bolts, as shown in the sketch. By removing one of the bolts and pinning a new chain link, you can extend the chain to 30 ft. if needed. Unlike pipe clamps, which must be flat to work, the chain will bridge minor obstacles without loss of pull. An added bonus is that the chain requires little storage space. —*Harold R. Olsen, Fox Island, Wash.*

Outdoor workbench

I made a version of the outdoor workbench shown in *FWW #33*, p. 18, by substituting a sliding-head pipe clamp for the bench hold-down, and it works like a charm. Instead of tying up a whole clamp, I took just the sliding head from the standard clamp (which has a fixed foot at the other end, fits ¾-in. pipe, and is available from Constantine, 2065 Eastchester Rd., Bronx, N.Y. 10461) and attached a different piece of pipe to the log with metal straps at the side and over a standard pipe elbow at the bottom, which grips the log for purchase. This way, I can take the head indoors with me at the end of the day to avoid rusting, and I can slide it back onto its regular pipe for other projects, too. As a bonus, I find that the pipe sticking up makes it easy to shift the block around. —*Don Anderson, Sequim, Wash.*

Quick tip: When turning, you can scribe critical lengths with a simple gauge. In scrapwood, drive screws the correct distance apart so that their points protrude, then press this against the roughed-out cylinder. —*Jim Ryerson, Guelph, Ont.*

Bench vise improved

Joe Laverti's homemade bench vise (*FWW #37*, p. 24) is a fine idea. But because the heavy steel screws project from the bench, the vise is a potential leg-bruiser. From my school days, I remember a shop teacher hurrying down the aisle between the benches and smacking his leg into an open vise. He was badly injured and the memory has never left me. With a couple

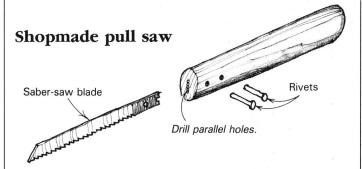

Threaded rod engages threads in this nut.

Wood screw

Drill out threads for slip fit.

Nut welded to washer

of modifications, as shown in the sketch, Laverti's vise can close up like a regular vise and thus be safer.

My vise uses two threaded rods. At the front end of these, I welded a nut and drilled through it to install peened-over bars for handles. —*Al Glantz, Winthrop, Wash.*

Quick tip: My dust-removal system is an ordinary vacuum with a strong magnet clamped to its nozzle. The magnet holds the nozzle just where I need it. —*G. Kramer, Ashland, Ore.*

Shopmade pull saw

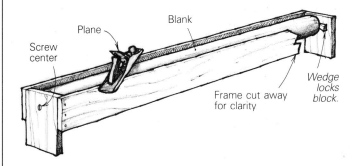

Saber-saw blade

Rivets

Drill parallel holes.

I don't own a saber saw, but I do buy the blades—they make the handiest small saws in my shop.

First, choose a drill bit the same thickness as the sawblade and drill four or five holes side-by-side in the end of the handle blank. Using the blade as a template, mark the location of the rivet holes on the side of the blank. Now clamp the blade upright in a vise and tap the handle over it. Drill holes where marked, rivet the blade securely in place, and shape the handle to suit. *Stefan During, Texel, Holland*

Turning without a lathe

Screw center

Plane

Blank

Frame cut away for clarity

Wedge locks block.

If you've got a 4-ft. post to turn and only a 3-ft. bed on your lathe, the drawing shows a way out of the dilemma. Bandsaw or tablesaw the blank octagonal, mount it in a scrapwood cradle and plane it round. Position the wood-screw mounting centers the desired radius beneath the parallel sides of the cradle. The final strokes of the plane will rest on the sides of the cradle to ensure a uniform and accurate circumference. —*Blaine Foule, Lincoln, Neb.*

MACHINES

A Swing-Away Drill-Press Table

Versatile accessories help sand and rout

by R.J. DeCristoforo

The drill press is one of the most versatile tools in any woodworking shop, but you need special accessories to get the most from it. Many times these accessories aren't available commercially and you must make them. Here's an auxiliary swing-away table with custom-made inserts that will help you use your drill press for drum-sanding inside or outside curves, pattern-sanding and pin-routing. When the jig isn't needed, it swings out of the way, and can be used as a platform for other tools.

To construct the jig, cut two 1½-in. thick pieces of maple, birch or other hardwood, 5¼ in. wide by 19½ in. long. Clamp the pieces edge-to-edge and use a hole saw or a fly-cutter to make a hole the same size as your drill-press column. Locate the hole so that its rim is 2 in. from the end of the jig and its center is directly on the joint line.

Unclamp, and draw the outside profile on one of the pieces, as shown in figure 1. After sawing and sanding it, use it as a pattern to mark the mating piece. If you have a bandsaw, you can speed up the process by taping the pieces together and cutting both at the same time. Locate and drill the hole for the ⅜-in. carriage bolt that tightens the jig on the drill-press column.

Mark the centerline for the strap hinge on one half of the jig. Before cutting along this line, mark the location of the hinge screws, or, better yet, install the hinge and then remove it. Replace the hinge after making the cut and rounding the corner of the cut-off

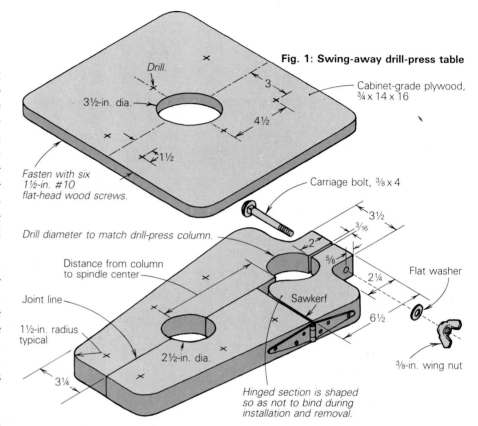

Fig. 1: Swing-away drill-press table

Drill.

3½-in. dia.

3

4½

1½

Cabinet-grade plywood, ¾ x 14 x 16

Fasten with six 1½-in. #10 flat-head wood screws.

Carriage bolt, ⅜ x 4

Drill diameter to match drill-press column.

Distance from column to spindle center

Joint line

1½-in. radius typical

3¼

2½-in. dia.

3½

3/16

2

5/8

2¼

6½

Flat washer

Sawkerf

⅜-in. wing nut

Hinged section is shaped so as not to bind during installation and removal.

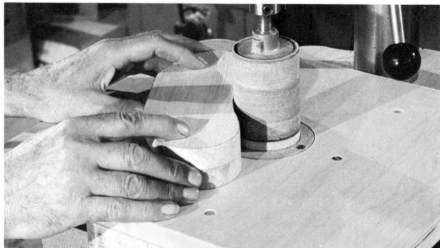

Sanding pattern tacked to underside of workpiece rides against guide disc.

Fig. 1A: Inserts

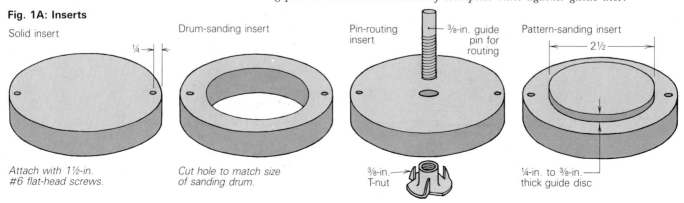

Solid insert

Drum-sanding insert

Pin-routing insert

⅜-in. guide pin for routing

Pattern-sanding insert

2½

¼

Attach with 1½-in. #6 flat-head screws.

Cut hole to match size of sanding drum.

⅜-in. T-nut

¼-in. to ⅜-in. thick guide disc

piece. Remove just enough material from the corner to allow the hinged section to swing around the drill-press column. Glue the two table pieces together.

Make the top piece now, but don't cut any of the holes yet. Center the top on the base and attach it with six 1½-in. #10 flat-head wood screws. The front edge of the top should be flush with the front of the base piece. Now center the assembly on the drill-press table, secure it with the carriage bolt, and, with the drill press, drill a small pilot hole through both top and base. Take the two pieces apart, and cut the 3½-in. hole through the top and the 2½-in. hole through the base. Sand all parts carefully and then screw the top to the base. Finish with lacquer or shellac, followed by paste wax.

Now use your bandsaw, fly-cutter or hole saw to make the inserts shown in figure 1A. All the inserts are 3½ in. in diameter, to fit snugly into the jig. The solid insert provides a good surface for normal drilling and helps prevent tearout. The drum insert, designed for a 2½-in. drum, supports the workpiece so that its edges can be sanded square to surfaces. To sand inside areas, put the workpiece in place before you lower the drum.

To make the insert for pin-routing, drill the hole for the pin and T-nut while the insert is locked in the table. This ensures that the router bit and the pin, which is made from a cut-off ⅜-in. bolt, will be perfectly aligned. Alignment is crucial since a pattern, exactly the size and shape of the part you need, is tack-nailed to the bottom of a rough-cut piece. Moving the pattern along the pin enables the router bit to transfer the shape of the pattern to the rough-cut piece. Use a similar alignment procedure in making the pattern-sanding insert, which serves as a guide disc when pieces are being drum-sanded to size. Have the insert in place and mark the location of the guide disc while your sanding drum is mounted in the chuck. The sander and the guide disc must be perfectly concentric. The pattern rides the disc, so the work is sanded to match. Remember that this is a sanding operation—workpieces should be sawn as close to the line as possible. □

R.J. DeCristoforo, of Los Altos Hills, Calif., is a woodworker and author of numerous articles and books on woodworking. Photo by the author.

An Oscillating Spindle Sander
Taiwanese drill press spins and bobs

by Wesley P. Glewwe

An oscillating vertical spindle sander, whose drum moves up and down as it spins, doesn't leave the scratches that a conventional drum sander does. With a few inexpensive parts, you can turn a cheap Taiwan-made benchtop drill press into a durable, efficient oscillating sander, for a fraction of the cost of a manufactured unit, and you won't need to do any welding or machine work.

Not all Taiwanese drill presses are suitable for conversion. The one I used is about 23 in. high, weighs just under 50 lb., and costs less than $100. Made of cast iron, it has a ½-in. chuck, a ⅓-HP single-phase motor, and stepped pulleys for variable speeds. These machines are sold under many different names (American, Duracraft, Chicago, Intergram, Sterling, Central, Guardian, etc.), but all brands are about the same. Larger, more expensive Taiwanese drill presses, about 30 in. to 38 in. tall, cost more and can't be modified because of the way the head casting is attached.

The drill-press motor will rotate the sanding drum, but you'll need to buy a reduction motor to move the spindle up and down about ¾ in. to ⅞ in. There are two types of reduction motors: one with

Photos: Blumenfeld Photography

With a few extra parts, Glewwe converted a Taiwanese drill press into this oscillating spindle sander. The sanding drum moves up and down as it rotates, eliminating scratches. The particleboard cabinet has a plastic-laminate top with different size inserts, shown hanging on the cabinet, that lift out for drum-changing.

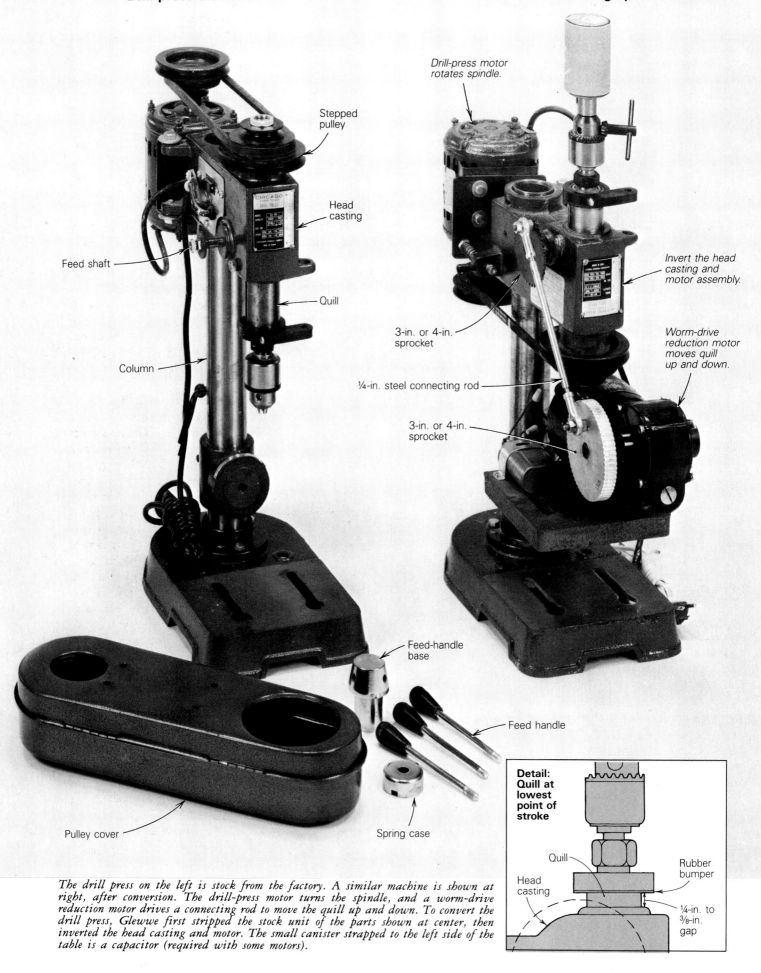

Drill press dismantled . . .

. . . becomes oscillating spindle sander

Stepped pulley

Head casting

Feed shaft

Quill

Column

Drill-press motor rotates spindle.

Invert the head casting and motor assembly.

Worm-drive reduction motor moves quill up and down.

3-in. or 4-in. sprocket

¼-in. steel connecting rod

3-in. or 4-in. sprocket

Feed-handle base

Feed handle

Pulley cover

Spring case

Detail: Quill at lowest point of stroke

Quill

Head casting

Rubber bumper

¼-in. to ⅜-in. gap

The drill press on the left is stock from the factory. A similar machine is shown at right, after conversion. The drill-press motor turns the spindle, and a worm-drive reduction motor drives a connecting rod to move the quill up and down. To convert the drill press, Glewwe first stripped the stock unit of the parts shown at center, then inverted the head casting and motor. The small canister strapped to the left side of the table is a capacitor (required with some motors).

50

a sun-gear mechanism, and one with a worm-gear assembly. Either type will do, but the worm-gear motor is easier to mount because the shaft is perpendicular to the axis of the motor. Buy a motor with at least $\frac{1}{20}$ HP, rated continuous-duty with an output speed between 25 RPM and 60 RPM. My motor is a 115-volt AC, $\frac{1}{15}$-HP worm-gear type with a 60:1 ratio and an output speed of 28 RPM. It was made by Bodine Electric Co. (2500 West Bradley Pl., Chicago, Ill. 60618), but I bought it at a surplus house (Surplus Center, 1000-1015 West "O" St., PO Box 82209, Lincoln, Neb. 68501) for about $30.

Two 3-in. or 4-in. sprockets form the crankshafts that oscillate the spindle. One fits on the reduction-motor arbor, the other on the drill-press feed shaft. Each sprocket must have a setscrew or some other means of locking it on the arbor. You can substitute gears or pulleys for the sprockets, or you can make the crankshafts from flat bar stock—they don't need to be round.

The connecting rod between the sprockets is made from an 8-in. length of $\frac{1}{4}$-in. steel rod, capped by two rod ends with $\frac{1}{4}$-in. bearing inserts (available from Alinabal, Division of MPD Corp., 28 Woodmont Rd., Milford, Conn. 06460). Buy the kind with female threads where the rod attaches.

Begin the conversion of your machine by removing the stepped pulley on the quill shaft. This is a press-fit and may be tough to get off. To loosen it, give the shaft end a few sharp taps while a helper tugs on the pulley. Be careful not to break the flanges. After you get the pulley off, remove the sheet-metal pulley cover, then replace the pulley on the quill shaft. If you can't get the pulley off, just cut the cover off with a hacksaw.

Next, remove the quill-return spring, which is in a case on the left side of the head casting, and slide out the feed shaft and handle assembly. Remove the three feed handles, and with a pin punch, drive out the pin that secures the feed-handle base to its shaft. Remove the base, which is also a press-fit.

The small end of the feed shaft is slotted for the spring (which you've removed). Epoxy a metal shim in this slot to prevent the shaft from crushing when you tighten the sprocket on the shaft. Slide the feed shaft back through the head casting, and slip a few washers on the end of the shaft to take up the space originally occupied by the spring.

Now lift off the entire head assembly and invert it on the column. There are three cast-iron ribs on the inside of the head assembly. If the inverted head assembly won't slip over the column, file off the burr on the center rib.

One crankshaft sprocket goes on the feed shaft, but first drill a $\frac{1}{4}$-in. hole $1\frac{1}{8}$ in. from the center of the arbor hole for the connecting-rod end. Mount the sprocket on the shaft. Drill a $\frac{1}{4}$-in. hole through the other sprocket, 1 in. from the center of the arbor hole, and mount this sprocket on the gear-reduction motor arbor. Making sure the table isn't tilted, position the reduction motor on the worktable. Line up the upper and lower sprockets with a straightedge, and bolt down the motor.

Rotate the upper sprocket so that the rod-end hole is at four o'clock. At this position, the low point in the quill-shaft stroke, there should be a $\frac{1}{4}$-in. to $\frac{3}{8}$-in. gap between the head casting and the rubber bumper on the quill shaft. If there isn't, remove the sprocket, slide out the feed shaft, rotate it slightly, and replace it. Put a scrap piece of wood in the gap temporarily to prevent the quill from dropping while you're measuring. Now rotate the lower sprocket, by running the reduction motor, so that the rod-end hole is at six o'clock. At these positions, the quill will be at the bottom of its stroke. Now you're ready to measure for the connecting rod.

With the sprockets in the right posi-

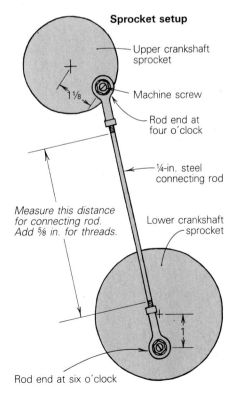

Sprocket setup

— Upper crankshaft sprocket

$1\frac{1}{8}$

— Machine screw

— Rod end at four o'clock

— $\frac{1}{4}$-in. steel connecting rod

Measure this distance for connecting rod. Add $\frac{5}{8}$ in. for threads.

Lower crankshaft sprocket

1

Rod end at six o'clock

tion, measure the distance between the rod-end threads and add $\frac{5}{8}$ in. to allow for threads. Cut the $\frac{1}{4}$-in. rod to this length and thread the ends with a die that matches the rod-end threads. Just start the rod into the rod ends—you'll need to make adjustments later. Mount the rod assembly on the sprockets with machine screws, and add lock washers and nuts, finger-tightened.

Test the action by quickly switching the reduction motor on and off. Don't plug in the drill-press motor yet. The upper sprocket should make less than half a revolution, then reverse direction. You'll probably have to adjust the length of the connecting rod to get a smooth up-and-down motion. The easiest way to make this adjustment is to turn the connecting rod farther in or out of the rod ends, but you can also raise or lower the worktable or the head casting. Don't allow the reduction motor to run continuously until you get a smooth stroke of about $\frac{3}{4}$ in. to $\frac{7}{8}$ in. with no "thumps" at the top or bottom of the quill's stroke.

You can mount the sander underneath an existing workbench in your shop, but I built a particleboard cabinet to house mine. Plastic laminate makes a good work surface for the top. The spindle protrudes through a hole in a removable insert in the worktable that lifts out when you want to change drums.

I usually plug both motors into an outlet box controlled by a single switch. Sometimes you may want only the spindle to rotate, and with this setup, all you have to do is unplug the reduction motor.

In my machine, I use 3-in. long sanding drums with $\frac{1}{2}$-in. dia. shanks (available from Singley Specialty Co., Inc., Box 5087, Greensboro, N.C. 27403). I like the kind with a clamping mechanism to hold regular sheets of abrasive paper, so I don't have to buy abrasive sleeves. These drums come in diameters from $\frac{3}{4}$ in. to 3 in. Use the larger ones for long, sweeping curves, and the smaller ones for short arcs and scrollwork.

For best results, feed the work against the rotation of the drum, and keep it moving to avoid burn marks. You also risk burns if the drum turns too fast, so adjust the rotation speed by moving the V-belt on the pulleys. □

Wesley Glewwe is a retired FBI special agent. He lives in West St. Paul, Minn., and makes wooden-gear clocks as a hobby.

Machining Backwards

Power-fed climb-cutting reduces tearout

by Lew Palmer

Several years ago some friends decided to expand their repertoire of woodworking machinery, so that they could better fill their rapidly increasing orders for oak accessories. On their list of must-haves was a nifty SCM R-9 overarm router, a power-fed affair which they ordered tricked out with all the options. But when they started running their new line of oval mirror frames on it, alas, they suffered a staggering number of ruined pieces, which threatened their anticipated profits.

An anguished call to their machinery supplier brought forth a knowledgeable rep. He took a quick look at their procedures and promptly prescribed the cure: use the power feed to climb-cut, and thereby eliminate almost all machining rejects.

He was right. And the solution to their router problem also worked on their shaper and their more sophisticated machinery to come—and for me. I've found climb-cutting to be one of the most important machining techniques for any profit-minded (thus waste-conscious) woodworker.

Climb-cutting is nothing more than power-feeding (*never* hand-feeding, for that would be terribly dangerous) in the same direction that the knives of your shaper (or whatever) are rotating. This forces each knife to remove only a tiny slice of wood with each cut, which largely eliminates blowouts. The method contrasts with the traditional way cabinetmakers machine wood: feeding against cutter rotation, a technique probably necessitated by hand-feeding, but one that can cause the wood to lift and tear unpredictably.

Climb-cutting, and therefore power-feeding, are indispensable in my shop, where I often have to machine stock to precise dimensions and profiles—stock that's too expensive to replace. I do it on a rather hefty (1500-lb., 1½-in. dia. spindle) SCM TC-120 shaper, equipped with an 8-speed, 3-roller Univer power feed. This attachment offers a relatively slow 2.7-meter-per-minute (about 9-FPM) feed rate which I prefer when shaping unusually deep raised panels. I regard the power feed as essential, even on those rare occasions when I do not

climb-cut. Only a power feed can safely feed material at an optimum, consistent rate, hold it flat and indexed against the table and fence, and shield the operator from blown material.

To me, the only acceptable power feeds are the industrial models you can securely bolt to your shaper table. They weigh in at 150 lb. or so, one reason to operate a more massive shaper. These power feeds consist of a multi-speed 3- or 4-wheel drive unit, a base, and a post-and-arm assembly that allows you to position the feed variously. They retail from industrial woodworking ma-

Normal cutting vs. climb-cutting

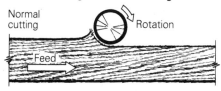
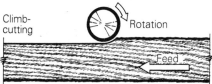

Feeding against cutter rotation allows feeding by hand, but the cutter tends to lift and tear out the wood. Climb-cutting virtually eliminates tearout, but necessitates using a power feed, or else the cutter will grab the stock.

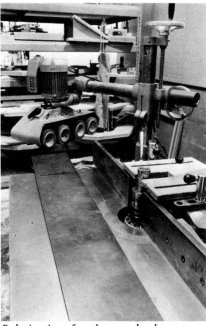

Substituting for the standard two-part shaper fence, Palmer's one-piece fence, used in conjunction with the Univer power feed, makes for safe, precise shaping.

chinery suppliers for $1100 to $1500, with the more expensive ones offering more speeds and feed wheels. For maximum versatility, instead of hard-wiring the feed to a box, you can attach a plug to one end of the cord and plug it into a receptacle on the side of the shaper. Then you can easily transfer it to another machine, such as a tablesaw.

These feeds, for the most part, are limited to working linear stock. One technique I've found advantageous for jointing, profiling and dimensioning a large amount of stock is to feed material against a one-piece auxiliary fence, instead of or in addition to the standard two-part shaper fence (photo, below left). A piece of straight phenolic plastic, steel, or even Baltic birch plywood will suffice. My fence, for example, is ½-in. thick steel plate, 6 in. by 84 in., slotted to allow for bolting to the shaper table on the operator's side of the spindle. I position the feed so that the first and second infeed wheels straddle the spindle, and I tilt the feed toward the auxiliary fence, so that the stock is held tight.

The auxiliary fence has two shortcomings. When you need to profile extremely narrow or thin stock, the feed wheels can't grab it properly. In such situations, I use a thinner fence (¼ in. or so), or I rabbet the side of a Baltic birch fence, which creates a flat running surface and raises the stock above the face of the fence. For wide stock that won't fit between the auxiliary fence and the spindle, a dimension dictated by the size of the shaper table, I revert to the regular shaper fence, which straddles the spindle.

While climb-cutting linear stock has eliminated up to 20% of the waste and machining hassles I once suffered, the technique's real advantage is with curved stock, where some part of the material must necessarily be machined against the grain, as with my neighbors' oval picture frames. Power-feeding curved stock requires more sophisticated equipment than I have, such as the R-9 overarm router, but for those shops moving into such production, cutting backwards may be a big step forward. □

Lew Palmer has a cabinet shop in Carmichael, Calif. Photo by the author.

Vintage Machines
Searching for the cast-iron classics

by Tom Howell

Inspecting a roomful of vintage, cast-iron woodworking machines gives a fascinating glimpse into American industrial history. Engraved with colorful phrases like "hand-built on the banks of the Wabash," these behemoths exhibit the proud, hands-on craftsmanship and attention to detail rarely found today. To me, the finest general-purpose woodworking machines ever made were those produced between 1930 and 1960.

I have equipped my factory, where we build woodworkers' benches, with more than 40 of these machines. Most people who see them in operation—from hobbyists to full-time professionals—seem overwhelmed by their size and power, and by nostalgia for a bygone era when me-ticulous labor, cheap materials and over-engineering were the rule. Romanticism aside, cost is what matters most: my vintage machines deliver about 95% of the performance of new industrial tools at about 20% of the cost. For example, one new industrial-quality tablesaw model sells for $8,000 to $9,000. I bought an equivalent, used, cast-iron model for $1,000, spent about $500 restoring it, and ended up with a high-quality saw for about the cost of a trade-tool-quality saw. And my saw won't wear out every couple of years, or depreciate in value. While such bargains can be hard to find, similar comparisons can be made for other tools most needed by woodworkers, especially jointers, bandsaws and planers. If you want something special, like a 30-in. planer, but don't have bundles of cash, old machines are the only way to go.

The cast-iron classics aren't for everyone, of course. Economically, they make the most sense for professionals who continually do the kind of heavy sawing, planing and shaping for which these machines were designed. For the commercial shop just starting out, buying used industrial machines is an economical road to top-notch equipment. I wouldn't rule these beauties out for the hobbyist, though. If you find decent old equipment at a

Large cast-iron woodworking machines like this 1930s planer may be obsolete by today's industrial standards, but they can give a small shop top-notch performance at scrap-iron prices.

fair price and have room for it, there's no reason why it can't be used for lighter work. Just restoring a machine can be rewarding, particularly for the tinkerer who has the same affection for old tools that some people have for vintage cars. But if you're not mechanically inclined, you'd be better off sticking to consumer- or trade-quality tools, which also represent some excellent used bargains. The Sears tablesaws of the '40s and '50s are, in my opinion, among the best light-duty machines ever made.

Thousands of vintage machines are lying dormant in factories, warehouses, salvage yards and other crannies of industrial America, especially near wood-manufacturing centers. Tracking them down may take a little time, though. For a start, find out which school systems, utilities, prisons, government installations or construction companies in your area regularly hold sales. Of late, electric utilities have become an excellent source—some are unloading tons of woodworking equipment bought to make concrete forms for nuclear plant projects since canceled. Many good bargains come through large, poorly advertised government disposal sales. The best way to get on the mailing list for these sales is to buy something, even something small, at an auction or sale—you'll soon be on everyone's list. A trip to the junkyard may turn up serviceable old machines bought as scrap from people unwilling or unable to repair them. Also check publications. The *Classified Exchange,* a monthly national newsletter (available for $20/yr. from Box 34908, Memphis, Tenn. 38184), lists hundreds of older machines. Visit nearby woodworking shops and plants for equipment that has been taken out of service. Auctions are great fun, but set limits on what you will bid, or else you might suffer bidding fever.

Finally, if you prefer a dependable sellers' warranty, search out a reputable dealer in used production-woodworking machines. Most have on-site restoration facilities and will give a one-year warranty or a one-year buy-back or trade-in, although the best bargains are machines that are not in peak condition.

If you go shopping for old machinery, you should allow enough time to check each machine carefully, and be willing to spend a little money to get the quality, production capacity and investment value offered by good vintage equipment. Throughout this evaluation, your primary concern should be how much time and money it will take to get the machine into your shop in accurate, running condition. Try to anticipate all costs—everything from paint and transportation (which usually is at least 2% to 5% of the machine's price) to new blades and cutterheads. Even if you enjoy fiddling with machinery, you should realize that restoration work will cut down on your woodworking time. You probably won't be able to find parts either, and will have to pay a machine shop to make them. You may have to replace motors, rewire your shop, install three-phase power or upgrade your dust-collection system. And remember that some of these tools may be too big for your shop (I have one tablesaw with a table as big as a queen-size bed).

Before doing a detailed evaluation, make a quick survey of the machine's general condition to see if it is even worth serious study. Be critical. For every ten machines you look at, figure on rejecting nine, due to price, condition or other factors.

One quick way to sort prospects is to consider weight—buy machinery the way you buy potatoes, by the pound. These machines are about 95% cast iron, and that's what you're buying. The remaining 5% includes bearings, shafts and motors, which have to be periodically replaced anyway. In general, don't pay more than $.30 per pound for defunct machine frames requiring a great deal of restoration, or more than $1 per pound for a completely rebuilt machine with a sellers' warranty. New machines usually are more than $3 per pound. If you can't get the old machine for less than half the cost of a new one, forget it.

If the machine looks promising, make a detailed analysis of its condition. First of all, the machine body should be 100% cast iron, not steel or sheet metal. Cast iron is very heavy (a woodworking machine can't be too heavy) and will absorb vibration, thereby increasing safety and accuracy. It does have one fault, however: it cracks easily, and such cracks are difficult to repair. I'd reject any machine with a crack that goes through the metal or that is wide enough to stick a piece of paper in. A crack that's at least an inch long and wider at one end than at the other is liable to grow if the machine is subjected to much vibration. Rust less than $\frac{1}{16}$ in. deep usually isn't a problem.

Identifying specific brands is easy. The makers cast their name, the city of manufacture and the serial number into the base of each unit—an iron-clad guarantee of a machine's authenticity. The first two digits of the serial number usually indicate year of manufacture; for example, "49-103" would indicate the hundred and third machine built in 1949. If the manufacturer is still in business (many of them aren't anymore), the serial number may help you obtain blueprints and other information, such as the name of the original owner. You're likely to find about 50 brands in your search for vintage machines (see box, below left, for several). The one I've encountered the most is one of the best, Yates-American. Still operating in Beloit, Wis., today the company manufactures only custom molders and surfacers averaging about $80,000 apiece, but it does have some parts for its old bandsaws, lathes, tablesaws and planers.

Once you're satisfied that the cast-iron base is in good shape, check the electrical system, which may include one or more motors, a starter, wiring and controls. Each motor should have a nameplate, stating its type, RPM and voltage. A majority of industrial machines are three-phase, 440-volt, though some may be 220-volt. Most homes are wired for single-phase, 110-volt current. Converting equipment from three-phase to single-phase is expensive and in many cases it may not be worth it. Besides, three-phase motors are much more efficient, so you're better off installing three-phase power in your shop, if possible. If you can't get three-phase or can't afford the conversion, consider buying a phase converter, which turns ordinary single-phase current into three-phase. (For more on three-phase current, see *FWW* #24, pp. 57-58, and #26, pp. 10-16.)

Next check the starter. If your shop is large enough to be regulated by the federal Occupational Safety and Health Administration (OSHA), you must replace any manual starters with more expensive magnetic starters—not a bad idea even in a small shop. In the event of a power failure, a tool with a magnetic starter won't restart until it's reset; with a manual starter, a stalled machine will restart as soon as power is restored, and could send pieces of wood flying all over the shop. Make sure that the controls work. Also figure out how much wire you'll need to install the machine. With some big machines, you may have to add a larger electrical service and more breakers and panels. Brace yourself for higher electric bills—big machines built in the days of cheap energy really consume the kilowatts.

After checking the electrical components, give the machine a good old-fashioned going-over. Think about where the stress points on a machine are—shafts, gears, fences and adjusting devices—and inspect these areas for warp, wear and cracks. Use your hands as well as your eyes; often you can feel play and wear in something like a shaft better than you can see it. If you can fit the edge of a business card between gear teeth or if teeth are missing, it's a sure bet the machine has been used heavily and will need work. Have a straightedge handy to check all tables and beds for flatness; grinding a table down can be expensive. If you find a machine that runs, insist on operating it yourself. Bring wide, warped boards to test planers, or tough hardwoods to test saws. Run the machine for as long as the owner will let

Vintage makes

Some of the makers of large cast-iron woodworking machinery are still in business, though their product line may have changed over the years. Here's a rundown on twelve such companies and the type of tools they made.

Yates-American, 2280-T Kennedy Dr., Beloit, Wis. 53511; all stationary tools.
Diehl Machines, 981 S. Wabash St., Wasbash, Ind. 46992; saws.
Delta (Rockwell), 400 N. Lexington Ave., Pittsburgh, Pa. 15208; all stationary tools.
Mattison Machine Works, 545 Blackhawk Park Ave., Rockford, Ill. 61108; all stationary tools.
Newman Machine Co., 5077 Jackson St., Greensboro, N.C. 27403; planers.
S.A. Woods (div. of Yates-American), 100 Rockton Rd.,
Roscoe, Ill. 61073; surfacers.
Porter-Burke Machinery Co., 730 Plymouth Ave. NE, Grand Rapids, Mich. 49505; all stationary tools.
Powermatic, McMinnville, Tenn. 37110; all stationary tools.
Oliver Machinery Co., 450 South St. NW, Grand Rapids, Mich. 49504; saws.
Tannewitz Inc., 3944 Clay Ave. SW, Grand Rapids, Mich. 49508; saws.
DeWalt, 715 Fountain Ave., Lancaster, Pa. 17604; saws.
Beach Mfg. Co., Post St., Montrose, Pa. 18801; sanders.

you. As you operate it, think about safety. A dangerous machine is an asset to no one. Plan on installing proper guards on every moving part, belt or chain. Also, old blades and cutters may be cracked and dangerous, so inspect them carefully or count on buying new ones.

Check the bearings, which usually will be worn and often are hard to replace. Most machines built before World War II have babbitt bearings, which is fine but lowers resale value. If the bearings are damaged or leak grease or oil, consider whether they can be repaired easily (see *FWW #38* for an article on how to repair babbitt bearings). If the machine has ball bearings, bring them up to speed to see if they chatter or get hot. Some machines have six large bearings—at $50 apiece for replacements, you're talking about a quick way to spend $300. Some bearing sizes are no longer made, so you might have to enlarge the machine fittings to accept standard-size bearings. Look at the machine's grease fittings (there could be two dozen)—if they're plugged, dry or corroded, you can bet the machine hasn't been serviced regularly.

Some dealers or manufacturers may stock parts for the machine, but don't get your hopes up. Fortunately, old machines are unabashedly low-tech and don't have all that many moving parts, so almost any custom machine shop can make the parts that you need, but you'd be wise to get at least three bids on each job.

Regardless of how good a machine looks, though, if it won't meet your specialized needs, don't buy it. If you're in business, a good used machine should be able to pay for itself in three years or less. But whether you're an amateur or a professional, I think you'll find that these machines are a joy to work with. □

Tom Howell, president of Tennessee Hardwood Company, gives tours daily at his plant, 800 W. Main St., Woodbury, Tenn. 37190. Three-phase power converters are available from Ronk Electrical Industries, 106 E. State St., Nokomis, Ill. 62075; Arco Electric Corp., PO Box 278, Shelbyville, Ind. 46176; and Cedarberg Industries, 5408 Chicago Ave. S, Minneapolis, Minn. 55413.

Used machines and abused buyers
by Chuck Seidel

As one who couldn't make a living as a woodworker, I went to work selling industrial woodworking machinery. Since I've had the benefit of being both buyer and seller, I'd like to offer a few tips for those shopping for used equipment.

First and foremost, let the buyer beware! Every day I visit furniture plants, cabinet shops and other woodworking operations, and it is astonishing how much junk is offered for sale. Less than 10% of what I see is suitable for purchase; the rest is either broken down or worn out, obsolete, or too specialized for most shops.

Although it's unreasonable to expect the average buyer to know as much about machinery as a dealer does, there are some rules of thumb that may save you grief. ***Beware of auctions.*** Auctions may seem like great places for bargains, but they often bring premium prices for equipment (why do you think sellers love to hold them?). Also, unless you can buy large quantities of equipment (without caring too much what kind it is), the time and expense involved in attending the auction—not to mention the cost of transporting the machinery back to your shop—may turn an apparent bargain into an expensive item.

Also remember that many people who attend auctions are canny and experienced buyers who will bid up to a reasonable price and then drop out, leaving novices to bid up to stratospheric levels. Unless you know what you're doing, you can get burned.
Beware of machinery over 15 years old. Though it may be romantic to think "they made 'em better in the old days" and "a good machine is a heavy machine," in reality many old machines are a

pain in the neck. The 24-in. vintage planer you "stole" for $1500, and which "needs a little work," may not be such a bargain when you discover that the company went out of business in 1920 and parts haven't been made for years. You may be even more chagrined when you get a $350 bill for transporting that 4,000 lb. of antique cast iron five blocks.

It's wrong to dismiss today's machines as inferior to products of the past. Ask any old hand to compare changing belts on his new Timesavers wide-belt sander with changing the drums on his old Solem. The former is a two-minute job; the latter can mean hours of wrestling chunks of steel and crawling around inside the machine.

By and large, today's industrial machines have superior bearings and motors, are more efficiently designed, and are quieter and safer. They may not be as heavy as their predecessors, but they're heavy enough. A lot of old machines are dinosaurs, and about as efficient.

Ask yourself whether you are in the woodworking business or the machinery-restoration business. You should also question if you can afford to spend a week of production time trying to get a machine going, keeping in mind that the time and money required increase in proportion to the age of the machine.
Know what you are buying. There are thousands of machinery manufacturers, many with product lines decades old. If you're unsure of what you're buying, get the model and serial numbers of the machine and its motor. A call to a local dealer may help you avoid an expensive pitfall.

A case in point is a buyer I heard of who was congratulating himself on finding a

wonderfully preserved, vintage 12-in. tablesaw. It looked almost new and sounded great. But when he got it home, he discovered that it had a tilting table and couldn't be adjusted to make a square cut.

Never buy a machine you can't see under power and under load. Look for signs of abuse—if a machine doesn't look good, it probably isn't. Examine the motors and wiring. Few people do this, but this precaution makes sense when you consider, for example, that a new motor for a Unisaw costs more than $600. Older machinery most likely has had its motors replaced, often with motors unsuited to the equipment. Old wiring tends to become brittle and may break or short out, leaving you with an expensive rewiring bill.

The best rule, however, is that no matter what you do, proceed carefully and with circumspection. Believe it or not, the most common machines—tablesaws, jointers and shapers—are the hardest to find, especially if economic conditions are good. When products are selling well, shops want to hang on to every bit of production capacity they have, running these useful tools until they're just about shot. I guarantee that if you walk into the largest, most mechanized furniture factory in the world, you'll find an old tablesaw or two stuck off in a corner somewhere.

If you can't afford to buy new equipment, be prepared to spend some time finding good used machinery. There are bargains out there, but if they were easy to find, they wouldn't be bargains. □

Chuck Seidel is a woodworker and sales representative for a Dallas, Tex., machinery dealer.

Patternsawing
Identical pieces without much fuss

by Jim Cummins

W hen I bought an old building and moved my shop into it, I removed hundreds of square feet of wainscoting to make room for insulation and new electrical wiring. I used the salvageable pieces in refurbishing, but when the sheetrock and pegboard went up, I was left with innumerable splintery tongue-and-groove strips, which I sawed into short lengths to fit my woodstove. The pile filled one shop corner to the ceiling.

The first winter took care of only half the pile, but spring brought me an idea that would get rid of the rest, get my new shop some publicity, and raise a little money for the local guild of craftsmen besides. How? By patternsawing birdhouses, inviting the public to an open-house assembly party, and selling the birdhouses—one free to new guild members, $4 apiece otherwise.

The drawings show a few patternsawing setups for both the tablesaw and the bandsaw. With the appropriate setup, you can cut inside curves, outside curves or in a straight line to produce exact multiples. These ideas aren't new, and most woodworkers will be familiar with at least one or two of them, but listing them together in this article may suggest even more possibilities. (For another patternsawing idea, see *FWW* #47, p. 8.)

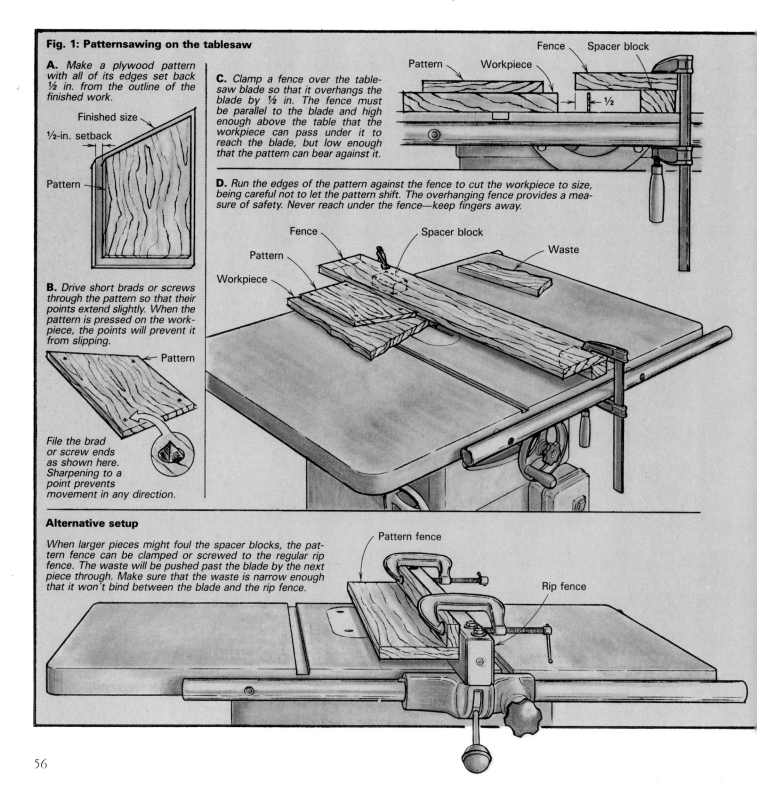

Fig. 1: Patternsawing on the tablesaw

A. Make a plywood pattern with all of its edges set back ½ in. from the outline of the finished work.

Finished size

½-in. setback

Pattern

B. Drive short brads or screws through the pattern so that their points extend slightly. When the pattern is pressed on the workpiece, the points will prevent it from slipping.

Pattern

File the brad or screw ends as shown here. Sharpening to a point prevents movement in any direction.

C. Clamp a fence over the tablesaw blade so that it overhangs the blade by ½ in. The fence must be parallel to the blade and high enough above the table that the workpiece can pass under it to reach the blade, but low enough that the pattern can bear against it.

D. Run the edges of the pattern against the fence to cut the workpiece to size, being careful not to let the pattern shift. The overhanging fence provides a measure of safety. Never reach under the fence—keep fingers away.

Fence   Spacer block
Pattern   Workpiece
½

Fence   Spacer block
Pattern   Waste
Workpiece

Alternative setup

When larger pieces might foul the spacer blocks, the pattern fence can be clamped or screwed to the regular rip fence. The waste will be pushed past the blade by the next piece through. Make sure that the waste is narrow enough that it won't bind between the blade and the rip fence.

Pattern fence

Rip fence

In each setup, the workpiece is fastened to a pattern that controls the line of the cut by bearing against a fence—you don't have to eyeball curved cuts and you don't have to change fence adjustments to make straight cuts of various widths or at various angles. The reference edges are on the pattern, which means that you can saw irregular scraps to size with the first cut, without initially having to establish clean edges to run against the fence.

The pattern and the workpiece usually are held together by something like nails, brads or sharpened screw points driven through the pattern so that their tips protrude just enough to catch the workpiece and hold it flat. With this method, there's no slow jigging and clamping from one workpiece to the next, which is an advantage over other production setups. In my case, I just lined up a couple of pieces of wainscoting side-by-side on the saw table, and pressed the tongue and groove together. Then I could slap the pattern on top, which automatically held things in place, and cut the work to size without having to do a lot of extra trimming. Instead of driving brads through the pattern to keep the work from shifting, I covered the entire bottom of the pattern with non-slip rubber tape. You could use sandpaper, too, but I wouldn't recommend either of these methods for very large pieces.

Patternsawing worked great in my shop. Over the course of about five hours, we made 54 birdhouses, recruited 22 new guild boosters, and raised about $120 in cash for the guild. As a bonus, I had beady-eyed, perky little wrens outside my bedroom window all summer long. I watched four little birds grow up and fly away, and never had to set my alarm clock once until September. □

Jim Cummins is an associate editor at FWW.

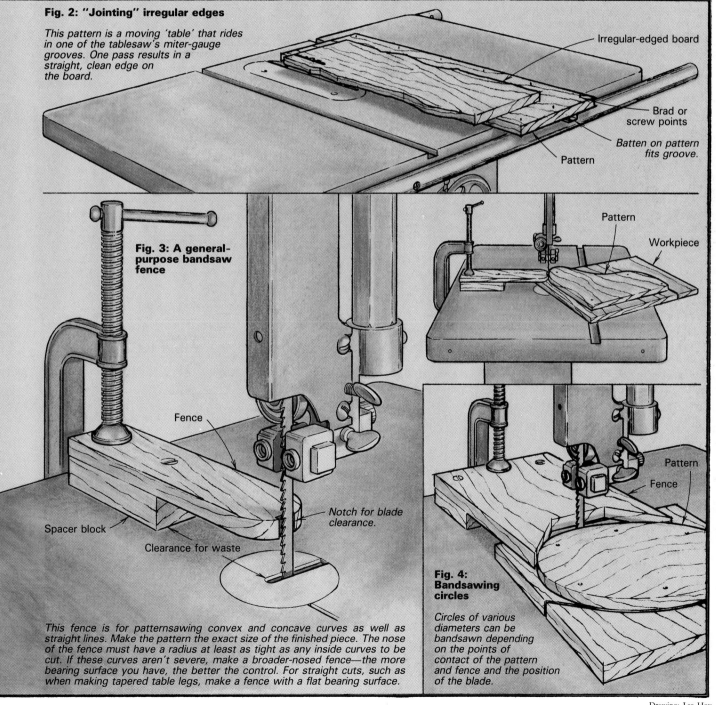

Fig. 2: "Jointing" irregular edges

This pattern is a moving 'table' that rides in one of the tablesaw's miter-gauge grooves. One pass results in a straight, clean edge on the board.

Irregular-edged board

Brad or screw points

Batten on pattern fits groove.

Pattern

Fig. 3: A general-purpose bandsaw fence

Fence

Spacer block

Clearance for waste

Notch for blade clearance.

This fence is for patternsawing convex and concave curves as well as straight lines. Make the pattern the exact size of the finished piece. The nose of the fence must have a radius at least as tight as any inside curves to be cut. If these curves aren't severe, make a broader-nosed fence—the more bearing surface you have, the better the control. For straight cuts, such as when making tapered table legs, make a fence with a flat bearing surface.

Pattern

Workpiece

Pattern

Fence

Fig. 4: Bandsawing circles

Circles of various diameters can be bandsawn depending on the points of contact of the pattern and fence and the position of the blade.

Drawing: Lee Hov

edited and drawn by Jim Richey

Tablesaw guard

Plug fits rip-fence rail.
Acrylic guard
⅝-in. steel rod

Unlike most other tablesaw-blade guards, which after the user has had a couple of frustrating experiences are left hanging on the wall, this guard is quite usable. The guard's main advantage is that it remains in place for most operations, including dado and molding cuts. If it's not needed for an operation, the guard swings out of the way in seconds, or can easily be removed completely from the saw. The inexpensive guard also acts as a hold-down—a safety bonus.

Make the guard shield from ¼-in. thick clear acrylic. The guard frame is a length of ⅝-in. cold-rolled steel bent into a U shape. Turn two metal or wooden plugs and attach them to the arms of the frame as shown in the sketch. The plugs should be sized to pivot easily in the holes in the ends of the back rip-fence rail. The frame fits on the saw by springing slightly so that the plugs snap into the holes.

—*K.L. Steuart, Ladysmith, B.C.*

Thickness-planing on the jointer

Tage Frid, in *FWW* #19, p. 94, describes how to thickness boards on the jointer. Frid's jig is a precision wooden affair that requires removing the jointer's fence to work. Here's a simpler way. From a signmaker obtain two 1-in. strips of flexible magnetic sign backing and glue each to a hardwood strip to produce two ½-in. thick sticks as long as the infeed table. Glue a hardwood block on the end of each strip to keep it from creeping into the cutterhead.

Before using the setup, first joint one face and both edges of the board to be thicknessed. Rabbet the edges, as shown on the workpiece in the sketch.

Now snap the two strips in place on the infeed table so that the rabbets ride the strips like rails. Run the workpiece down

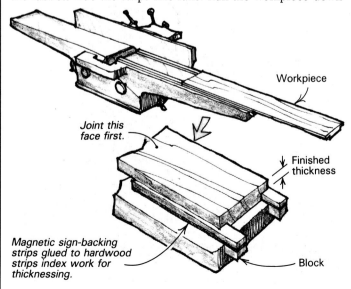

Workpiece

Joint this face first.

Finished thickness

Magnetic sign-backing strips glued to hardwood strips index work for thicknessing.

Block

the rails, across the cutterhead and onto the outfeed table. In this manner, it is the uniform rabbet that indexes the work; the irregular face doesn't touch the infeed table at all. Start with a light cut, then gradually lower the infeed table with each pass until the rabbets are only 1/16 in. deep. On the last pass, just skim off the wood down to the rabbets to produce the final thickness.

The magnetic strips can easily be adjusted to different-width boards, and there's no need to remove the jointer's fence to use them. When the job is done, it takes all of three seconds to convert your thickness planer back to a jointer.

—*Robert Edmondson, Bowmanville, Ont.*

Squaring bandsaw cuts

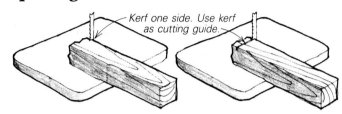

Kerf one side. Use kerf as cutting guide.

Here's a bandsaw trick that lets you true the end of a turning square without pausing to use a try-square. All you have to do is begin a crosscut on one side of the blank, then turn that side up and use the mark as your cutting line. As long as your bandsaw blade is at 90° to the table, you can't miss.

—*Jim Ryerson, Guelph, Ont.*

Raising panels with the router

I wanted to make some raised panels, but I didn't want to invest in a shaper and special cutters. My solution was to raise the panel with a ¾-in., 2-flute helical end mill in my router. All that's needed is a simple jig to tilt the router base to 15°. I fitted four lengths of 15/32-in. drill rod through the existing holes in my Makita router base and epoxied two outriggers to the ends, one on each side of the router. The low outrigger acts as a fence against the edge of the panel. In the sketch below, the tongue that will fit the frame's groove has already been milled on the tablesaw, but you could just as well do this step afterward.

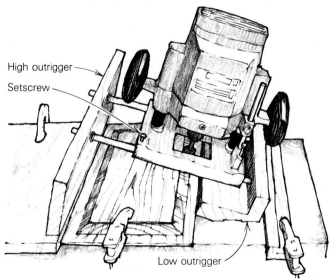

High outrigger
Setscrew
Low outrigger

The high outrigger rides atop the panel or, if the panel is narrow (as in the sketch), atop a board of the same thickness clamped to the bench. By adjusting the position of the high outrigger, you can slightly change the router's angle, if desirable. By adjusting the low outrigger, you can adjust the location of the bevel on the work.

—*Edward M. Rosenfeld, Gunley, Ala.*

Scroll Saws Compared
Precision for a price

by Silas Kopf

A scroll saw, or jigsaw as it's also called, is the right tool for cutting intricate shapes in wood and soft metal. For years, my Rockwell 24-in. scroll saw served me well, cutting veneers for the marquetry work which is my livelihood. But then I discovered some fancy, expensive scroll saws that perform so well that I bought one, and mothballed my faithful old machine.

Like the Rockwell, conventional scroll saws have a reciprocating blade, the lower end of which clamps into a chuck that's driven by the crankshaft. The upper end of the blade clamps into a chuck on a spring-loaded sleeve at the end of the rigid saw frame. The blade is pushed and pulled from the bottom end, while the spring at the top end struggles to keep tension on the blade. This tension is not constant throughout the stroke, however, and blade breakage is common.

The saws I tested for this article—the Hegner line from West Germany and the Excalibur from Canada—are designed differently from conventional scroll saws. Two arms, one above the table and one below, are connected at one end by the sawblade, and at the other by an adjustable tensioning rod. Only the lower arm is connected to the motor. Each arm pivots on a shaft, and they remain roughly parallel as they rock up and down. The blade is mounted so that it can pivot at its ends from front to back. The whole system—arms, blade and tensioning rod—maintains the shape of a parallelogram. As the blade moves downward on the cutting stroke, it moves forward slightly; on the upstroke, it moves back.

These saws produce an extremely clean cut that needs no sanding. Because tension on the blade remains constant throughout the stroke, sideways deflection is minimal, allowing the use of very fine blades. I quickly discovered that blades break much less frequently with this type of saw than with a conventional scroll saw. In fact, it isn't easy to break one. It's possible to cut a right angle by quickly turning the workpiece 90°. This small turning radius makes the most intricate shapes possible.

Unlike conventional scroll saws, the Hegner and Excalibur saws don't require any guides or support behind the blade. For cutting marquetry, I find this feature especially useful because my vision is unobstructed all around the cut. It's also

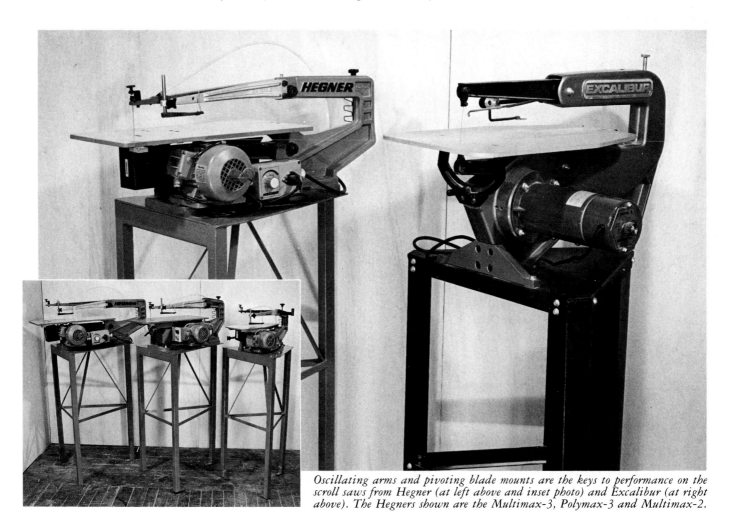

Oscillating arms and pivoting blade mounts are the keys to performance on the scroll saws from Hegner (at left above and inset photo) and Excalibur (at right above). The Hegners shown are the Multimax-3, Polymax-3 and Multimax-2.

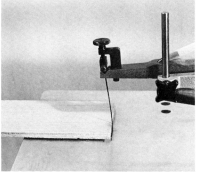
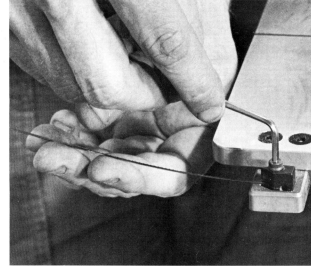

It's not easy to break a blade on these saws. Kopf pushes hard against a fine blade to prove the point. Both the Excalibur mount (above left) and the Hegner mount (above right) allow the blade to pivot from front to back. Even 8/4 maple poses no problem for these scroll saws, as shown below. They'll easily cut intricate curves in thick hardwood.

A holder on the Hegner saw (top) makes it easy to mount the blade ends in the clamps. Excalibur blades are mounted right on the saw (bottom). Inserting a steel hair pin keeps the blade mount from moving under the torque of the Allen wrench.

easy to manipulate around very tight curves since you can get your fingers on all sides of the blade.

The Hegner saw made its U.S. debut in 1978, and there are now three different models: the Multimax-2, Multimax-3 and Polymax-3. The Multimax machines are direct-drive, single-speed saws with an optional add-on variable-speed control. The Polymax-3 is a heavy-duty, belt-driven, 4-speed industrial saw. The Multimax-3 and Polymax-3 have an adjustable, 2-position stroke length. The shorter stroke offers better control on intricate curves.

The Excalibur saw came on the market in January 1983. There's only one model, and it's currently available with either a single-speed motor or a variable-speed DC motor. The variable-speed motor senses load changes and supplies the power needed to maintain the same stroke rate regardless of load. Equipped with this motor, the saw can cut as slowly as 3 CSM (cutting strokes per minute), and even in a hard material like brass, it delivers a constant stroke. You can actually lean your weight on the upper arm and feel the surge of power as the motor compensates for the load. I wasn't strong enough to stop the saw, even at very slow speeds.

One of my favorite Excalibur features is the wide table that

tilts both left and right. The narrower Hegner table tilts only to the left. Unlike the Hegner, the Excalibur's oscillating arms are supported on both sides by the saw frame, which seems sturdier. There's a power take-off on one end of the motor, so a flexible-shaft tool can be connected for drilling starter holes for internal cuts. The Excalibur brochure recommends weighting or bolting the saw to the floor, but I found that this wasn't really necessary with any of the machines.

The blade on the Hegner saw is mounted in two small pointed clamps that allow it to pivot. A holder attached to the saw table makes it easy to mount the blade in the clamps: you place a clamp in the holder, insert the end of the blade, and tighten the clamp with a hex wrench.

Although I found it easy to change blades in the holder, the clamping system proved frustrating when I was making interior cuts with fine blades (larger blades were no problem). For this type of cut, I have to slip the end of the blade through a hole in the work, and then into the clamp while the thing's mounted on the machine. Sometimes I was able to get it easily; other times I just couldn't. For piercing work with fine blades, the Hegner clamping system is a drawback.

The Excalibur has a different blade-mounting system: the

	Excalibur	Hegner Multimax-2	Hegner Multimax-3	Hegner Polymax-3
Throat	24½ in.	14¼ in.	25 in.	19½ in.
Maximum cutting depth	2¼ in.	2 in.	2⅜ in.	2 in.
Stroke length	¾ in.	¾ in.	⅜ in. or ¹¹⁄₁₆ in.	⁹⁄₁₆ in. or ¹⁵⁄₁₆ in.
Table	14 in. by 24 in.; tilts 45° left, 20° right	7¹⁄₁₆ in. by 15⅜ in.; tilts 45° left	10¼ in. by 20⁷⁄₁₆ in.; tilts 45° left	10¼ in. by 19¼ in.; tilts 45° left
Weight with stand	99 lb.	50 lb.	92 lb.	111 lb.
Cutting strokes per minute (CSM)	1650 (single-speed); 3 to 1800 with variable-speed*	1660 with standard single-speed; 150 to 1660**	1200 with standard single-speed; 150 to 1200**	700, 1100, 1270 and 1600 (4-speed belt drive only; no variable-speed option)
Blades	Standard 5-in. flat-end scroll-saw	Standard 5-in. flat-end scroll-saw	Standard 5-in. flat-end scroll-saw	Standard 5-in. flat-end scroll-saw
Warranty	2 years for home use, 180 days for commercial use	2 years (1 year on electrics)	2 years (1 year on electrics)	5 years (1 year on electrics)
Price	$1285 (variable-speed)	$859 (single-speed)	$1499 (single-speed)	$1899

* 3-speed pulley model available soon ($950 without a motor)
** with optional variable-speed regulator ($319)

blade pivots in clevis mounts. The blade clamp on each mount holds fine blades tightly, but thicker blades have a tendency to slip out of the clamps.

All the saws have an automatic air pump that directs a stream of air to blow sawdust away from the cutting line. The air pump on the Hegner saws is a plastic bellows, while the pump on the Excalibur is a piston concealed in the saw frame.

For intricate cuts in veneer, I found that a variable-speed saw is a necessity. The single-speed machines are much too fast. Without the variable-speed regulator, I couldn't control the cut with the precision needed for the double-bevel cutting method I described in *FWW* #38, pp. 61-65. The Polymax-3 set at the slowest speed (700 CSM) and the shortest stroke length (⁹⁄₁₆ in.) was also satisfactory for marquetry.

I tried cutting some ¹⁄₂₈-in. thick sheet brass with the recommended blades for metal, and all the machines performed well. Here, too, I preferred the variable-speed models.

All the saws, including the single-speed Hegners, did a fine job on ½-in. thick pine. With the heavier sawblades required for thicker stock, mounting the blade for an interior cut was quite easy on the Hegner.

My final test was to saw 8/4 walnut and maple—the maximum thickness recommended for these machines. It was remarkable how easily these saws cut stock that seems better suited to a bandsaw. The Multimax-3, with its 1200-CSM top speed, cut the maple more slowly than the others, but still performed well. On this thick stock, the Hegner left a perfectly square cut, but the Excalibur cut bowed outward slightly in the middle, enough to trap pieces on tight, intricate curves. I had to make relief cuts and remove the cut-out sections in pieces. Slowing down the rate of feed seemed to improve things, but this would slow down production.

Making a recommendation about these machines is diffi-

cult. Because of their cost, they're not for everybody. (But with a price tag of over $1300, a new Rockwell scroll saw is no bargain, either.) You'd have to get a lot of use from one of these machines to make it pay for itself.

If I were making toys, puzzles or signs, I'd choose one of the Hegner saws—if price were no object, the Polymax-3—because of the blade mounts and the nice square cut in thick stock. The Hegner saws are well engineered, and I like the fact that all the machinery is exposed. Nothing to hide. I also like the Hegner's safety feature that stops the saw immediately if a blade breaks. On the Excalibur, a broken blade can damage the work before you can stop the machine.

Because I use a scroll saw for marquetry, and rarely cut more than a few layers of veneer at a time, I bought the variable-speed Excalibur. Fine blades are easier to mount for interior cuts, and a table that tilts both ways is an important advantage for double-bevel cutting. If a blade breaks during a cut, I can restart an interior cut at the original drill hole, tilt the table to the other side, and saw in the other direction. The lower price of the Excalibur also influenced my decision.

There are at least two other companies manufacturing scroll saws with designs similar to the machines discussed here, but I wasn't able to include them in my test. An American-made line of scroll saws is available from RBIndustries, Inc., 201 First St., Pleasant Hill, Mo. 64080. Woodmaster Power Tools, 2849 Terrace, Kansas City, Mo. 64108, also sells a saw. Pedal- and motor-powered scroll-saw kits are sold by Tool Company, PO Box 629, 1306-G S. Commercial, Harrisonville, Mo. 64701. □

Silas Kopf is a professional furnituremaker in Northampton, Mass. He wrote about marquetry in FWW #38, and his work is pictured in #45, p. 69.

Souped-Up Spade Bits
Ideas for special-purpose, low-cost boring tools

by Mack Philips

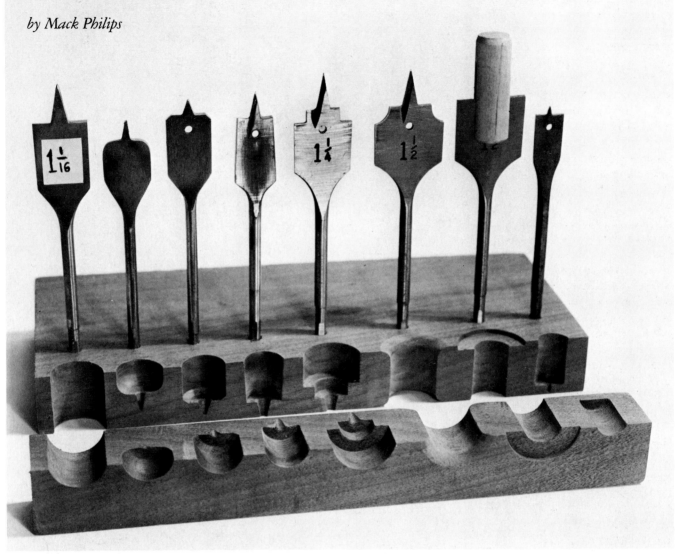

For those special wood-boring jobs, inexpensive spade bits are easy to modify to produce the holes shown here. Bit at left has been shaved ⅟₁₆ in. less than standard size; others have been reshaped with sharpening equipment, belt/disc sanders, motor tools and files.

When I need to drill an odd-size hole, or want a special contour, I usually just grab a spade bit and regrind it until it's exactly what I want. The procedure is inexpensive, quick and quite satisfactory. Some possibilities, explained later in this article, are shown in the photo above.

Besides being cheap, spade bits are made of relatively soft steel and are easy to alter. A regular bench grinder will do the job, but I've found that my Dremel belt/disc sander is even handier. Coarse belts remove metal quickly without heating up too much, and fine belts leave a good cutting edge. In addition, a motor tool such as the Foredom or the Dremel can help shape curves, using mounted stones of an appropriate diameter. Most bits are soft enough that you can even file them to shape if there's no motor tool around.

Spade bits typically have about 7° clearance on the cutting edges, about 5° on the sides. After you change the shape, restore these clearances. Tilt your grinder's tool rest or table to

grind the same angles as on the unmodified bit. If the bit won't lie flat on the rest, put a small block of wood under the bit's face so that the shank is raised out of the way.

Clearance angles don't have to be absolutely adhered to. The main idea is to relieve the edge so that it can penetrate the wood and take a shaving without the metal behind the edge getting in the way. There is a compromise here: if the edge has been relieved too much, the bit will dull quickly and begin to chew up the work or, in hardwoods, to burn it. For cutting softwoods, the edge requires a larger clearance angle than it does for cutting hardwoods. The standard spade bit is ground to work well in softwoods, but dulls faster in hardwoods than it really has to. If you're going to be drilling hardwoods, try a little less relief at first and see how the bit cuts. You can always increase clearance if needed.

Except at the very corners, the sides of a straight spade bit don't actually cut. The clearance angle at the sides is more for the sake of reducing friction than for efficiency in cutting. Keep this in mind when you're grinding contours. Visualize the action of the bit as it works into the wood and make sure that the clearance is in the right place. On curved sections, maintain the larger clearance angle through the whole extent of the curve. In a stepped bit, relieve the bottom cutting edges more than those on the sides.

Notice, too, that the manufacturer usually grinds larger spade bits so that the corners project slightly ahead of the cutting edge. With the point in the wood, the corners enter next, which aids stability during the cut.

Getting the shape symmetrical is important, but I've found that a bit does not have to be absolutely precise to do a good job of cutting. To get as close as possible, first coat the bit with machinists' layout dye and scribe the shape you want on the bit, measuring as accurately as you can on each side of a centerline. Then grind away material alternately from each side, a little at a time to avoid overheating. Quench the bit in water often. If you notice the metal beginning to change color (the first change is to yellow or bronze), you're grinding too fast and the heat has begun to affect the temper. Quench the bit immediately and slow down.

For odd-size holes, simply take the next larger bit and grind its sides a little. Lumberyard dowels, for instance, are notoriously off-size, either too loose or too tight in the hole they're supposed to fit. If you're trying to get a press-fit hole from a nominal-size bit, just kiss the sides with the grinder. It won't take much. Make trial cuts in scrapwood to avoid going undersize.

Round-bottomed and beveled-corner holes result when you grind curves or chamfers on the corners. This modified bit is good for making finger holes, or for holes where you want bottom clearance.

Tapered bits make holes for candle sockets, chair rungs and special wedge joints. A tapered bit cuts the full length of its side. If you find that a tapered bit is burning the wood, increase the side clearance angle.

For a stepped hole, grind steps on the bit. One useful purpose for this bit is to space nesting tubes in a hole. The larger diameter locates the larger tube, and the smaller bore locates the smaller tube on center.

You can easily make a neat rounding-over bit by grinding a concave radius on the corners. To use this bit, first drill a small pilot hole through the workpiece. Form the radii on both sides of the work with the rounding-over bit. Then drill the main hole through.

A spotfacer is a counterbore that relieves the surface for a bolt head or a plug. I make piloted spotfacers by epoxying an appropriately sized slotted dowel over the center of the bit. If the dowel doesn't cover the sides of the point, grind them away. Run these bits at a fairly low speed to prevent heat buildup from softening the epoxy. You can use the same trick to enlarge an existing hole on-center.

If necessary, to keep the point from coming through the work, you can shorten it to as little as ⅛ in. or so. This works best when the manufacturer hasn't sharpened the point by grinding a groove down its faces, but you can work around this, too. I've found it best to rough off most of the point with a grinder and then do the final shaping with a file. ☐

Mack Philips is a midwest-based freelance writer who specializes in woodworking. Photo by the author.

Drawing: David Dann

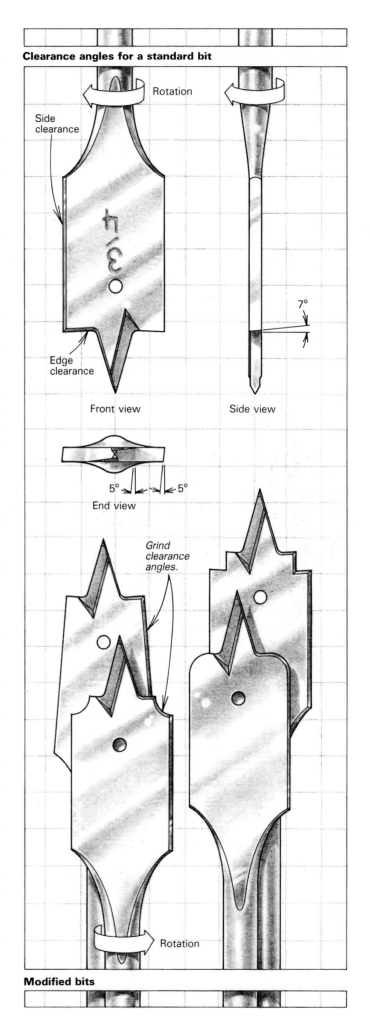

Clearance angles for a standard bit

Side clearance

Rotation

Edge clearance

7°

Front view   Side view

5°   5°

End view

Grind clearance angles.

Rotation

Modified bits

Shop-Built Sharpener
Salvaged garbage disposal grinds a keen edge

by Tom Dewey

Jeffrey C. Carts

Author photo

Salvaged parts keep the cost of this water-cooled sharpener below that of similar store-bought machines. Above, after honing the bevel on a plane blade, Dewey opens the machine's hinged port and removes the burr from the back of the blade. A steady stream of water keeps the edge from overheating. The nut in the foreground locks the tool rest at the desired angle.

Nearly everyone agrees that the best cutting edge comes from hand-sharpening on water or oil stones, but it takes time and practice to get a perfect edge. I'm not very fast at hand-sharpening, and in my production shop, where time equals food on the table, I can't justify the luxury of hand-honing. Instead, I wanted to build an inexpensive machine that would speed both jobs—something with a water-cooled horizontal wheel, a wide selection of abrasive grits, and a solid, adjustable tool rest. My first two versions had problems, but the one shown here works fine.

The grinder took me a little more than a day to build, using a salvaged garbage-disposal unit, a few parts and some scrapwood. I use a 60-grit stone and/or 7-in. abrasive discs, either store-bought or homemade, ranging from 36-grit to 600-grit. The grinder can sharpen blades as wide as 2½ in.

A garbage-disposal motor (usually ⅓ HP or ½ HP, and 1725 RPM) is ideal for a water-cooled grinder because it is designed to run in a vertical position, has a waterproof seal on the shaft to keep the motor dry and has built-in overload protection. When a disposal stops working properly, usually it's because the food choppers have worn out—often the motor is still in good shape. Few people bother to have broken disposals repaired, opting for replacement instead. Check with a local plumber and you probably won't have much trouble finding a unit with a good motor. (New disposals from Sears are as cheap as $50.) You can use almost any brand, but try to avoid models labeled "automatic self-reversing" or "auto-grind," because they'll re-

quire some rewiring. You'll have to make some mechanical modifications to any unit.

The food-grinding chamber must be cut away to expose the chopper plate on the end of the motor shaft, as shown in the drawing. If your unit has a stainless-steel liner in the grinding chamber, pry it out before cutting the case. Anything goes in this removal operation—sawing, chiseling with a cold chisel—but be careful not to crack the casting. It may take plenty of penetrating oil before you can loosen the retaining nut and unscrew the plate from the shaft. If the plate has a recessed nut, the shaft won't be long enough to mount the stone and discs. You'll have to make another plate from ¼-in. thick acrylic, a worn-out circular-saw blade with the teeth ground off, or exterior plywood.

Most of the other modifications should be clear from the drawing, and I'd suggest that you do them in this order: Plug the drain opening in the side of the disposal case with a piece of wood and file the wood flush with the outside of the housing. Epoxy the laminated-plywood ring that supports the table to the case, and drill a hole through both the ring and the wooden plug for a new copper-tubing drainpipe.

The table can be any convenient shape and size. Mine is round because I happened to have a small sink cutout handy. Glue and screw the table to the plywood ring, level with the top of the case, then cement plastic laminate on the table, overlapping the edge of the disposal unit.

Add the splash guard (mine is a section of heavy PVC plastic

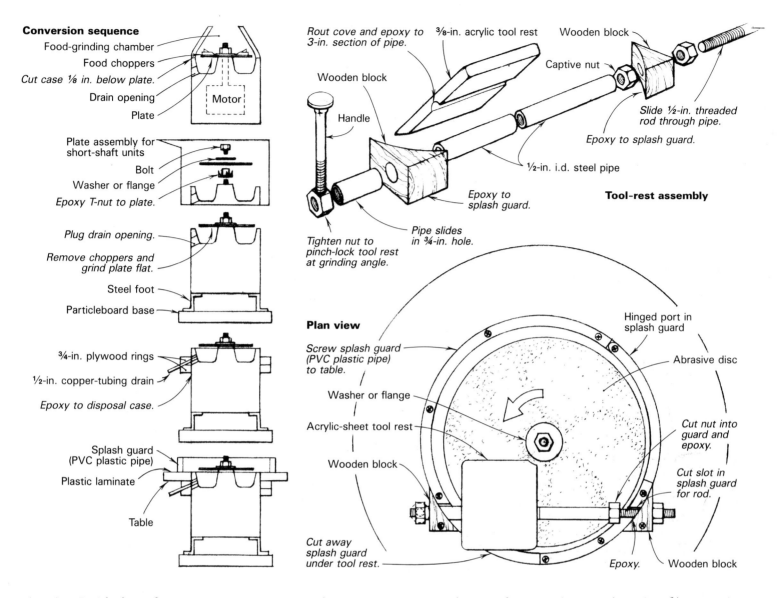

Conversion sequence

Food-grinding chamber
Food choppers
Cut case ⅛ in. below plate.
Drain opening
Plate
Motor

Plate assembly for short-shaft units
Bolt
Washer or flange
Epoxy T-nut to plate.

Plug drain opening.
Remove choppers and grind plate flat.
Steel foot
Particleboard base

¾-in. plywood rings
½-in. copper-tubing drain
Epoxy to disposal case.

Splash guard (PVC plastic pipe)
Plastic laminate
Table

Rout cove and epoxy to 3-in. section of pipe.
Wooden block
Handle
Tighten nut to pinch-lock tool rest at grinding angle.
Pipe slides in ¾-in. hole.
Epoxy to splash guard.
½-in. i.d. steel pipe
⅜-in. acrylic tool rest
Wooden block
Captive nut
Slide ½-in. threaded rod through pipe.
Epoxy to splash guard.

Tool-rest assembly

Plan view

Screw splash guard (PVC plastic pipe) to table.
Washer or flange
Acrylic-sheet tool rest
Wooden block
Cut away splash guard under tool rest.

Hinged port in splash guard
Abrasive disc
Cut nut into guard and epoxy.
Cut slot in splash guard for rod.
Epoxy.
Wooden block

pipe that I picked up from a construction site—wooden rings epoxied together would work as well). Seal the joint with silicone caulk. Note that the splash guard is positioned slightly to the left of center to make room for wide blades on the tool-rest side. For deburring the backs of plane blades, I cut a hinged port in the side of the splash guard.

Next cut two slots in the splash guard for the tool-rest pivot rod. Mark off a 25° line on the side of the guard as shown in the photo on the facing page. I cut two shallow slots, then gradually deepened them until the top of the tool rest lined up with the 25° line. When fitting this assembly, make sure that the rod is high enough off the plate for abrasive discs to slip underneath. I cut away a section of the splash guard under the rear of the tool rest so the rest can be tipped up for changing discs.

To provide a continuous flow of water to the disc, I use a plant-watering gadget called Water Whiz (available from Edmund Scientific, 101 E. Gloucester Pike, Barrington, N.J. 08007). It comes with a 50-ft. hose which attaches to a faucet and provides any flow from a spray to a stream. I heated the plastic wand of the Whiz and bent it into shape. The Whiz is fastened to the grinder with two metal broom-hanging clips from the hardware store. To get rid of waste water, run a length of garden hose from the copper drain tube to a sink or a catch bucket.

I added a light, then mounted my grinder/honer on a 30-gal. drum filled with about 100 lb. of sand for stability. Casters on the bottom allow the setup to be rolled about the shop.

The workhorse of the grinder is a 6-in. dia., ³⁄₁₆-in. thick, 60-grit resin-bond stone (available from Foley-Belsaw Co., 90472 Field Bldg., Kansas City, Mo. 64111). This stone gives a very good edge and cuts quickly. You'll need to make a plastic or aluminum bushing to reduce the center hole of the stone to fit the garbage-disposal shaft.

For occasional coarser work, I use 36- to 80-grit, cloth-backed auto-body grinding discs fastened with contact cement to ⅛-in. thick acrylic discs (Brodhead-Garrett Co., 4560 E. 71st St., Cleveland, Ohio 44105, sells ⅛-in. acrylic sheet). For honing, I cut my own discs from silicon carbide paper and cement them to acrylic discs. The finer grits—400 and 600—produce a beautiful sheen. Abrasives can be mounted on both sides of the acrylic discs—coarse on one side, fine on the other—to cut down on storage and handling. You can sharpen blades by sliding them back and forth on the tool rest, or by holding them in one place—it doesn't seem to make much difference. By rolling gouges on the rest, several different profiles are possible and the bevels will be consistent from corner to corner.

I normally grind with the stone, then hone with 180-grit or 320-grit, or both, for a really fine edge. A buffing wheel whisks off the wire edge. It's hard to resist "going all the way" with the polishing grades. It's easy to get hooked on seeing such nicely polished edges come off a shop-built machine. □

Tom Dewey is a cabinetmaker in Coudersport, Pa.

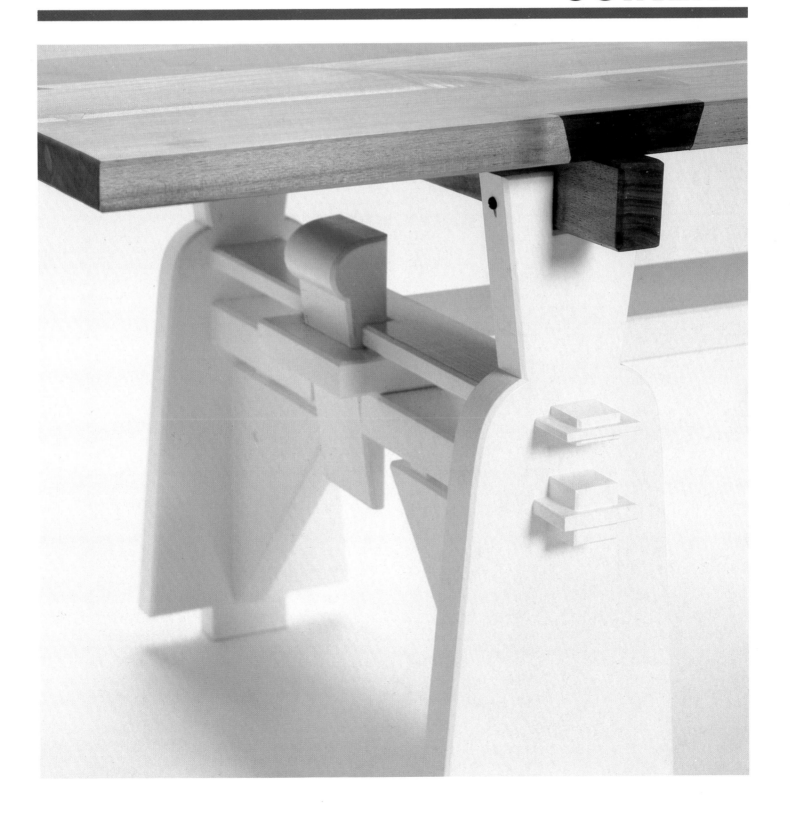

Making 50 Tables
Jigs and fixtures do the job

by Peter Pennypacker

After years of throwing countless pots, a potter friend surprised me when I asked if he was still challenged by his work. "I'm finding new enjoyment in pottery by simplifying the steps," he said, "streamlining the process, enjoying the exactness of efficiency."

Not long ago, I found out what he meant when I helped a fellow woodworker with a furnituremaking operation entirely new to me—a limited production run. Until that time, I had built only one-of-a-kind furniture, all commissioned by clients after lengthy discussions about how a certain design should look. I'd found one-off work gratifying and certainly instructive, since I often had to experiment with new tools, techniques and materials to satisfy my customers' demands.

Competence and speed came with practice, but my work still consumed enormous amounts of time, and with the time came a large price tag. I began to feel that some of my pieces assumed a more exaggerated posture than handcrafted, functional furniture ought to have. I became uneasy with the preciousness I was bestowing upon single works. I was anxious to find more efficient work patterns, and to repeat some of my favorite pieces, applying the refined technique and clarity of vision I'd learned from the first tries.

I was eager to try a production run. I had seen fine examples of production-run furniture from the more discerning manufacturers—much of it slippery-looking stuff from Italy—so I knew it could be done well. But did it take a factory? Joe Tracy provided the answer. He had just contracted to build 50 oak restaurant tables and needed help. A woodworker trained at the Rochester Institute of Technology, Tracy specializes in one-of-a-kind furniture, but he has also done a fair amount of production work. He has a natural ability for designing and engineering jigs and fixtures for the process.

Working with Tracy, I learned that in a moderate-size, well-organized shop with good though not prohibitively expensive machines, limited production is an enjoyable—and profitable—way to work. Jigs that favor choreographing repeated movements into concise, economical patterns produce a great quantity of work with minimum effort. And with just two of us working, there was always a variety of tasks to choose from, relieving tedium and making the process relaxing and rewarding. With careful planning and Tracy's simple, effective jigs, we were able to produce each table, from raw lumber to final finish, in a little less than eight hours. Henry Ford and the Puritan Ethic hummed over our shoulders.

The 50 tables were for the newly rebuilt Jordan Pond House restaurant, a historic landmark in Acadia National Park, near Tracy's home/shop on Maine's Mt. Desert Island. When the Pond House was nearing completion, Tracy had

Could you build one of these tables in eight hours for $225? Joe Tracy and Peter Pennypacker did. Using the production methods described in this article, they made 50 of them.

taken the rather bold step of designing and building an unsolicited prototype dining table that he thought would harmonize with the restaurant's contemporary decor. The Acadia Corporation overseeing the work was impressed with his initiative, but not convinced his design would hold up to commercial abuse.

Undaunted, Tracy built another prototype. Though sturdier, his second design was still a beauty—a delicate, flared leg-and-apron piece that shows the influence of James Krenov, with whom he had worked for six months in Sweden during 1972. The table's white oak top was supported by red oak aprons joined to the legs with floating tenons, a joint that's strong and readily made with Tracy's equipment.

This time the design was approved, and Tracy was asked to quote prices for four sizes of tables. Working out a time/cost sheet, he outlined each construction step on paper, drawing on his experience to calculate how long each would take and adding a 10% safety margin for potentially troublesome operations. To figure labor costs, Tracy multiplied the total number of hours by his $20 hourly shop rate, which, for this job, included our hourly wages plus shop overhead—the mortgage, power and heat bills, machine loans and maintenance, and incidentals. To this figure, he added the prices of lumber, lacquer and varnish, glue, screws, abrasives, and $150 to rent a truck to haul the finished tables to Pond House.

The price came to $225 per table, a figure within 5% of what a big Maine furniture company had quoted for a somewhat heavier-handed design. Because he was a local craftsman, the Acadia Corporation gave Tracy the job. The risk of making the prototype had paid off.

Tracy's 30-ft. by 40-ft. shop, on the ground floor of his house, seemed too small to hold the hundreds of parts we would be making. His equipment includes an old but accurate 10-in. tablesaw, a drill press, an ancient 34-in. bandsaw, a real prize of a machine called a Steton Combinata (planer, jointer, mortiser and knife grinder), a 1-in. spindle shaper, and a beast of a stroke sander that impressed us by speedily sanding the tabletops. Despite his limited floor space, Tracy's big machines are spaced well apart to allow plenty of swing plus room to dolly parts from one machine to another.

While Tracy designed and built the production jigs, I began thickness-planing and cutting to width and length 1700 bd. ft. of red and white oak. Milling the lumber was pretty tiresome—the only shortcut we could take was to rip stock to width first, bypassing the task of facing warped or twisted wide boards on the jointer. Following Tracy's detailed cutting list, I crosscut each part to rough length, then to final length, using stop blocks on the tablesaw miter gauge to ensure consistency. Cutting the longest pieces first and using the offcuts for shorter components minimized waste.

Before working with Tracy, my experience with jigs and fixtures had been limited to the occasional stop block or router template. I hadn't felt the need to construct jigs for single pieces. Tracy was soon to enlighten me on jigs and fixtures. Old woodworking texts suggest that a jig clamps the work and guides a cutting or shaping tool to produce identically shaped parts, independent of the operator's skill. A fixture, on the other hand, merely holds or positions the work, leaving the tool to be guided by other means. Tracy put it more concisely: a jig is portable, a fixture attaches firmly to the

Tracy's table design adapted readily to jig and fixture work.

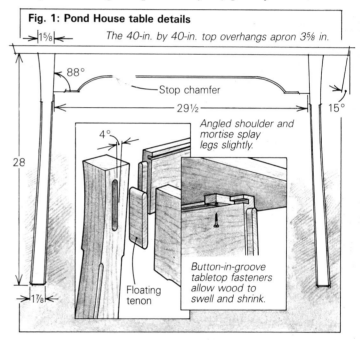

Fig. 1: Pond House table details

The 40-in. by 40-in. top overhangs apron 3⅝ in.

1⅝

88°

Stop chamfer

29½

15°

Angled shoulder and mortise splay legs slightly.

4°

28

Button-in-groove tabletop fasteners allow wood to swell and shrink.

Floating tenon

1⅞

machine or tool. Either way, the purpose is to increase the accuracy, safety and consistency of machine work.

Jigging is most useful when you must make many identical parts, as in our table job, but there are good reasons for jigs when fewer pieces are required. Safety is probably the best one, especially if you're making small, odd-shaped or hard-to-hold pieces, which are liable to be hurled or kicked back when fed past a whirring cutter. A well-designed jig will solidly grip the stock, so you can feed it with your hands well away from the danger zone. A jig also promotes an orderly work rhythm that lessens the chance of an accident. In addition, the consistency of jigged parts all but excludes the inaccuracies that would otherwise have to be corrected at assembly.

Obviously, there's a break-even point. Sometimes too few parts are needed, or they're so complicated that you'd spend more time devising the jig than you would making the pieces by hand. Yet even in this case, Tracy, like other woodworkers who derive as much satisfaction from process as from prod-

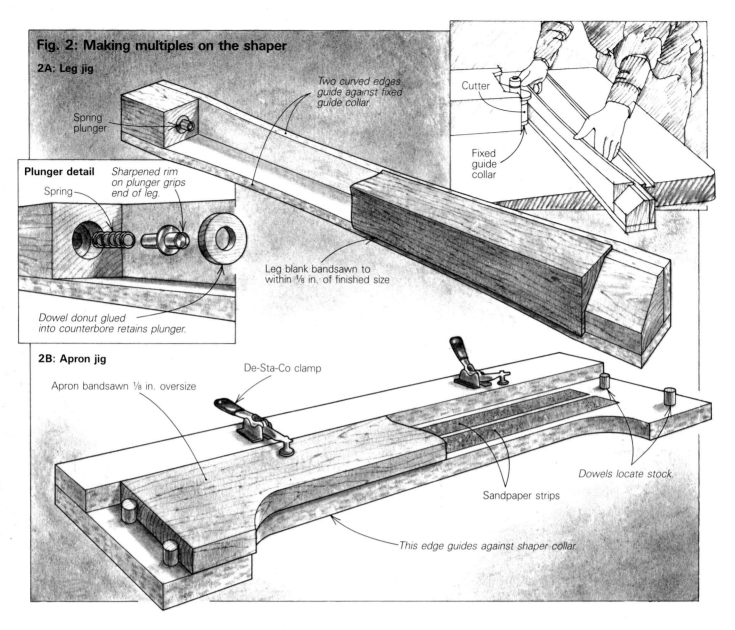

Fig. 2: Making multiples on the shaper

2A: Leg jig

Spring plunger

Two curved edges guide against fixed guide collar.

Cutter

Fixed guide collar

Plunger detail

Spring

Sharpened rim on plunger grips end of leg.

Dowel donut glued into counterbore retains plunger.

Leg blank bandsawn to within ⅛ in. of finished size

2B: Apron jig

De-Sta-Co clamp

Apron bandsawn ⅛ in. oversize

Dowels locate stock.

Sandpaper strips

This edge guides against shaper collar.

uct, will sometimes go ahead with the jig anyway. He designs much of his furniture with repeat commissions in mind, reasoning that a jig hung on the wall is a lasting resource that will save him the trouble of rethinking the problem months later when another job arrives.

Tracy's jigs for straight or angular parts are usually guided by a fence clamped or screwed to the machine table. Jigs for curved pieces are fed past a single-point guide—the fixed collar on his shaper or a router pilot bearing. Whether straight or curved, Tracy's jigs have some common features, the most important of which is a way to position and clamp the wood so that it won't slip or fly out under the stress of cutting. Blocks, fences or pins can be arranged so that blanks go into the jig only in the correct position. Quick-action toggle clamps (available from De-Sta-Co, PO Box 2800, Troy, Mich. 48007) are best for anchoring the blank, though screw hold-down clamps do a good, if slower, job. If a jig has no flat surface for mounting clamps, the blank can be held between blocks by a spring plunger, as in figure 2A. As extra insurance against slippage, Tracy glues strips of sandpaper to the jig's supporting surfaces.

Controlling a jig is vital, so Tracy puts handles on his, or makes them big enough so there's plenty of material to hold on to. Also, so it can be aligned with the machine's guiding

fence or collar before the blank engages the cutter, he extends each jig at least 3 in. beyond each end of the blank. Most of the jigs we used were made of ¾-in. medium-density fiberboard, with pine fences and stop blocks glued and screwed in place. Fiberboard, also called Baraboard, is ideal for jigs—it is dimensionally stable, can be accurately shaped, and won't wear out when repeatedly passed by fences and guide collars. Plywood also makes decent jig stock, if its interplies are free of voids. Applying lacquer or spray graphite to the edge of a jig eases its passage.

For the table job, Tracy designed the shaper jigs illustrated in figure 2. Even though his shaper has a 1-in. spindle and plenty of power, shaping the raw blank in a single pass would have provoked chattering or a dangerous kickback. To avoid this, we used the jigs as templates, marking out the curves and bandsawing off most of the waste to within ⅛ in. or so of the finished profile. The pieces could then be shaped safely and smoothly in one pass by running the jig against the fixed guide collar attached to the shaper. To make the legs, I first bandsawed the waste off all the blanks. Next, with a blank in the jig, I shaped one curved side, then flipped the jig 90° to shape the other. The aprons were similarly shaped, using a version of the jig shown in figure 2B for each of the four different length aprons (for the four different size tables).

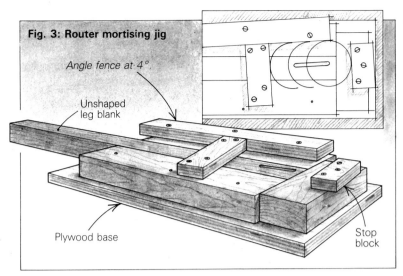

Fig. 3: Router mortising jig

Angle fence at 4°.

Unshaped leg blank

Plywood base

Stop block

To mill angled mortises in 200 legs, Tracy bolted a 4° ramp to his Steton Combinata. A mirror taped to the machine lets him view the action.

If production work is to proceed apace, like parts should be stacked together to be machined as units of work. These table aprons, which have been shaped, mortised and grooved, await assembly. The box contains the floating tenons that will join aprons to legs.

I had never used a shaper of this size before, and I was a little intimidated by its size and power. With only small amounts of wood to remove, however, the process was smooth and free of kickbacks. By the end of the job, shaper work felt safe. Shops not equipped with spindle shapers could adapt these jigs to routers, using ¼-in. tempered Masonite templates to guide a bit's pilot bearing. A 2-HP router driving industrial-quality ½-in. shank bits would do the job, but to minimize the cutting load, waste should be bandsawn to within 1/16 in. of the finished surface. These router techniques are described in *FWW* #35, pp. 46-53.

As our job progressed, I began to understand why so much factory production furniture is so lifeless. Churning out chairs or tables by the thousands, a big furniture plant would squander its profit on the extra steps and special tooling that distinctive designs require. Tracy proved to me that a resourceful small-shop craftsman needn't be similarly constrained. To accentuate the sweep of each table's flared legs, for example, Tracy splayed them slightly by cutting 88° shoulders on the ends of the aprons and milling the leg mortises at a 4° angle, as shown in the construction detail in figure 1. The operation added one jig, but without this refinement the tables would have looked just ordinary.

I cut the 88° shoulders (before shaping them) on the ta-

blesaw miter gauge fitted with a stop block. To mill the mortises in the shaped legs, we bolted a 4° ramp to the Combinata's mortising table and cut all the mortises on one side of all the legs before reversing it to mortise the other side. After milling 400 mortises on this machine, I can only sing its praises. It made what could have been a time-consuming chore a concise process that took about two minutes per leg. If you don't have a slot-mortiser—and most of us don't—you could dowel the legs, or use the router jig shown in figure 3.

As material went from rough to final size, the pieces became stacks of multiples, crisscrossed on dollies, sorted by size or function. Parts were processed as units of work, the entire pile passing through one operation before moving on to the next. This saved us hours of redundant set-up time, and is the key difference between production and one-of-a-kind work, where, at best, you're more likely to carry individual parts through a series of steps to completion or, at worst, move them around the shop in chaotic bundles.

Tracy varies the order of events according to the job. He shapes parts before cutting joints, as long as the part isn't so odd-shaped that it can't then be accurately fixed in the joint-cutting machine. Sometimes, though, a mortise or a tenon offers a handy way to hold the part in the shaping jig, so it makes more sense to cut joints first. Sanding should come

Gluing up tabletops can be a slow, frustrating job. To speed it along and minimize sanding later, Tracy aligned the surfaces of the clamped-up boards with the pressure of a hydraulic jack, above. He fabricated a Plexiglas ramp, left, to allow the curved edge of each leg to feed uniformly against the router's chamfering bit.

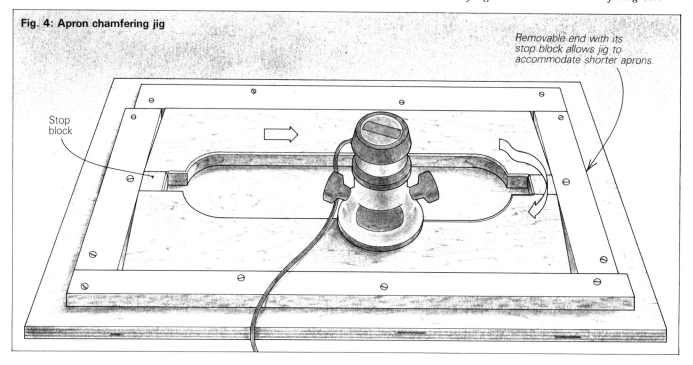

Fig. 4: Apron chamfering jig

Removable end with its stop block allows jig to accommodate shorter aprons.

Stop block

after joint-cutting. That way, you can manhandle pieces without fear of damaging them and you won't ruin the accuracy of your joinery by knocking off the crisp reference edges.

Next we began the detail work that makes the Pond House tables look more like one-of-a-kind custom work than the fruit of a production run. First, I stop-chamfered the four edges of each leg. Because two sides of each leg are curved, feeding them over a flat router base would produce an uneven, tapered chamfer. We solved this problem with a Plexiglas ramp clamped to the router base. It kept the leg edges in uniform contact with a 45° chamfer bit. The jig shown in figure 4 speeded the stop-chamfering of the aprons.

We had several hundred boards to pick from for gluing up the 50 tops. Finicky grain- and color-matching could have eaten up weeks, so Tracy set a reasonable minimum standard and sorted the boards accordingly. To eliminate the usual pounding and cursing, and to minimize having to sand boards whose surfaces were misaligned, we suspended a hydraulic pump on a long pipe anchored to a ceiling beam. We rolled our glue-up table under this setup and used the jack's pressure—distributed by a 2x4 batten—to force the boards into the same plane. Spreading the glue with a 3-in. paint

roller, we could glue up a top in three minutes.

In a crowded restaurant, the squared corner of a dining table can be a leg-jabbing, purse-snagging menace. Tracy eliminated this hazard by rounding the corners and undercutting the tabletop edges by 15°. The tops were first sized on the tablesaw, with the arbor set to cut the 15° undercut, then the corners were rounded with a saber saw set to the undercut angle. We used one of the router methods illustrated in figure 5 to clean the rounded corners. The top edges of each tabletop were eased with a roundover bit whose pilot bearing Tracy modified with a brass bushing.

By now we had 450 table parts neatly stacked around the shop. We were ready to glue up the bases, which went faster than I expected. I swabbed glue in both leg and apron mortises, inserted a floating tenon, and drew the joints up with leather-padded bar clamps. After 30 minutes in clamps, the table bases were stacked, to await touch-up sanding. Tracy, meanwhile, sanded the tops on the stroke sander. To pinpoint irregularities, he positioned a fluorescent light behind the sander, throwing oblique, shadow-making light across each top.

Finally, we were ready to spray-finish the tops and bases. While I carried out the last barrel of chips and sawdust, Tracy tacked up plastic sheeting to create a makeshift spray booth

Fig. 5: Edging the tabletops

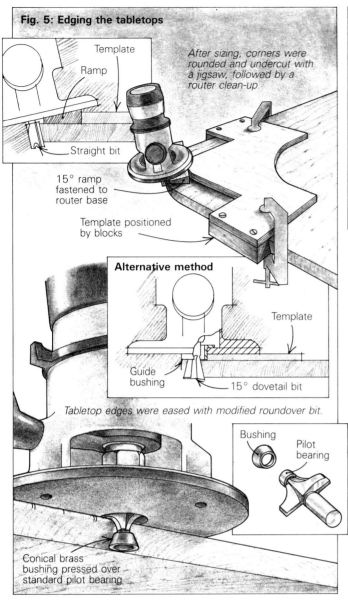

Template

Ramp

After sizing, corners were rounded and undercut with a jigsaw, followed by a router clean-up.

Straight bit

15° ramp fastened to router base

Template positioned by blocks

Alternative method

Template

Guide bushing

15° dovetail bit

Tabletop edges were eased with modified roundover bit.

Bushing

Pilot bearing

Conical brass bushing pressed over standard pilot bearing.

Fig. 6: Cutting buttons in one pass

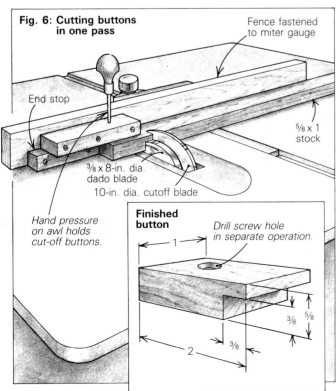

Fence fastened to miter gauge

End stop

⅝ x 1 stock

Hand pressure on awl holds cut-off buttons.

⅜ x 8-in. dia. dado blade

10-in. dia. cutoff blade

Finished button

Drill screw hole in separate operation.

1

⅜

⅝

2

⅜

Fig. 7: Carrying handle and drying rack

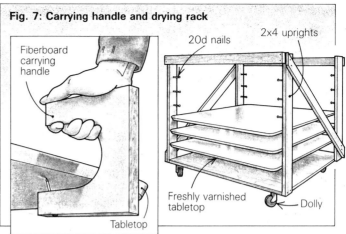

Fiberboard carrying handle

20d nails

2x4 uprights

Freshly varnished tabletop

Dolly

Tabletop

in the corner of the shop, ventilated by the exhaust fan. His spraying equipment consists of a good-quality gun with a separate pressure feed tank and 1½-HP compressor.

Since the tabletops would see heavy commercial use, they needed a tough, water- and alcohol-resistant film. Tracy chose a natural resin varnish called Rock Hard (available from H. Behlen & Bros., Rt. 30 N., Amsterdam, N.Y. 12010). The bases received a nitrocellulose lacquer, tinted to match the tops. Each top and base took three coats of finish. Since lacquer dries almost immediately, we stacked the bases as they were sprayed. Rock Hard, however, is a slow-setter. As we sprayed the tops, we grabbed them with the shopmade carrying handles shown in figure 7, and stacked them in a 2x4 rack bristling with 20d nails to allow air movement between the tops. When the last coat was dry, we buffed the tops to a flat sheen on the stroke sander, using fine Scotch-Brite pads glued to an old belt.

When we delivered the tables to Pond House, we fastened the tops to the aprons with wooden buttons let into mortises, as shown in figure 6. Tracy's final touch was to brand his logo into each table apron. I remember that the day was beautiful. Spring was in the air and the island sparkled. We had done it.

The tables have seen two seasons of hard use, and apart from a few dings and dents, they show little sign of wear. Tracy keeps extra parts on hand in case they're needed and the jigs stand ready for another run. The tables were so well-received that the Acadia Corporation ordered additional furnishings, including display cabinets for the restaurant gift shop, cash register stands, and several large *shoji*-style folding screens papered in birch bark, a material much in vogue when Pond House was first built.

This production run led me to agree with Tracy's philosophy. Mass production needn't compromise the quality of a piece of furniture. The production prototype can be as vital a design vehicle as any one-off piece. Imagination and skill must remain paramount—properly developed designs and techniques can produce high-quality multiples. Efficiency helps create comfortable and competitive work patterns. Many small shops are more than capable of completing a job like this, which will pay the bills during many lean months of custom furnituremaking. □

Peter Pennypacker lives in Sullivan, Maine. Photos by the author.

Seat-of-the-Pants Chair Design

A scrapwood mockup solves basic problems

by Jeremy Singley

For me, chair design is a choreography of happy accidents. Since I've never "thought up" a design that didn't turn out to be pretentious, I've learned to stumble onto new ideas gracefully. Thus my most trusted guide is the seat of my pants. That's how it should be. After all, my head may be the seat of my thought, but I don't sit on my head.

I usually begin with nothing particular in mind—rarely even so much as a sketch—but start right in by experimenting with scrapwood, cordwood and leftover chair parts to create various combinations of forms. I see—or, rather, feel—what works and what doesn't work. With perseverance (and a little luck), I may discover the means to bring together a tree and a human body in a way that is pleasing to both.

The best way to encourage this sort of serendipity is to build the design around a person, so I invariably start with a living, breathing body (my own or a helper's) and sit it on a crate. Then I proceed like a tailor to cut, tack together and try my scrapwood pattern against this live model. Patterns that work I earmark for subsequent reproduction in fine hardwood. Those that don't work return to the firewood pile. This way, only my posterior or my model's suffers my mistakes, and the public is spared yet another "—uh . . . very nice" chair. My firewood pile receives the majority of the shapes I try.

A wooden apple crate is my starting point. On this I might place a 20-in. by 20-in. square of plywood as a seat. I position the crate near a wall to give my model something to lean against, but for now this is all the back my chair-in-progress has. By shimming the plywood with blocks and wedges, I can create a variety of heights and cants for the seat. By moving the crate closer to the wall or farther away from it, I can adjust how far back my model leans. If I'm designing a dining or writing chair, I pull a table up to the crate to see how the two work together. This method lets me interpolate a set of comfortable and functional overall dimensions.

Once I have a seat position that seems comfortable for my first model, I retest the seat by using other models or by "altering" the one I have. To see what would happen if my model were a different height, I put blocks under the model's feet to simulate longer legs, or under the crate to raise the seat so that the model's legs seem shorter. Often I find I must adjust the dimensions to develop a compromise that will be reasonably comfortable for a wide range of people.

At this stage, I begin to play with specific contours for the seat. To determine a cross-sectional contour that will cradle my model's derrière comfortably, I experiment with bandsawn scrapwood blocks taped to the plywood's top surface, as shown in figure 1.

When I've found a shape that seems to work, I ask more

Jeremy Singley is a full-time woodworker in East Middlebury, Vt.

questions. What if my model were fatter or thinner? And—the question often overlooked by chairmakers—what if my model were the opposite sex? A healthy woman could hardly fit into some chairs I've seen. Others, where a woman apparently was the model, are so spacious that a slender man could get lost in them. Once again I collar a variety of different size models, or make the one I'm using seem thinner by spreading the bandsawn shapes apart, or fatter by pushing the blocks together (making the seat seem wider makes the model feel smaller, and vice versa). Pushing the shapes together across the width of the seat, but not in its depth, approximates how a woman's hips would fit the seat. Spreading the shapes across the seat width will make the seat fit a woman as if she were a man. Next I run through the slouch test: Can the model shift about upon the seat and still be comfortable?

I follow a similar procedure to determine the form of the chair's back. Without worrying about how the back will be attached to the chair, I hand-hold strips of bandsawn or bent scrapwood, or bent lengths of electrical cable, plastic water pipe, metal strapping, cardboard or other materials against my model's back. Since a chair back must support people in a variety of positions as they shift, lean or slouch, I avoid a literal interpretation of my model's back, looking instead for gradual, grand sweeps that support the back over broad areas.

When a likely back form has been found, I cobble it to the prototype seat firmly enough to be leaned against (sometimes I just nail it to 2x4s leaned against the wall). I then test it with models who are taller, shorter, wider, narrower, or bent more or less than the original model, or I again use shims or other tricks to simulate more sitters. In this way, I make sure that no part of the back will bother the backbone, shoulder blades or hip bones of a wide range of individuals. This test also helps me determine the tilt of the chair's back and the distance between the chair back and the seat's front edge.

Once I've evolved a set of functional seat and back forms,

Fig. 1: Seat mockup

Bandsawn blocks can be shaped and moved to fit model.

Masking tape

Bandsawn blocks

Plywood base

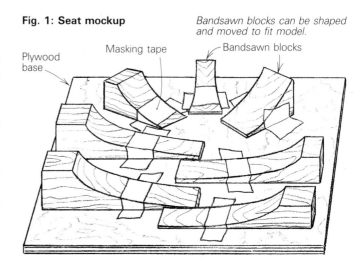

Singley's Wainscot chair began as a trial splat leaned against a wall and a seat supported on a paint can.

Simplicity is the key in this Cheshire chair—turned tenons in round holes, and a sawn rather than steamed crest.

I've reached the end of the piecemeal stage of design, when the chair has only the most nebulous structure. The next step is to choose from among my forms (some forms won't work, but these may find their way into future designs) and see if any suggest a particular mode of construction. Whether my precarious pile of scraps will end up a Windsor, a Wegner or a what's-it must now be decided.

This is the hard part for me. I can't seem to accept that the decision is not mine to make: it's up to the chair. Sometimes this isn't a problem because the parts I've tacked and leaned together make themselves into a chair before I have a chance to meddle with them. In a case like this, I haven't found the chair, the chair has found me. The Wainscot chair shown in the photo at left above, for example, is hardly more than the original scrap board that was leaned against the wall as a trial splat (drawing, right), with the seat and crest— parts from a different chair that were pirated from my inventory shelves—balanced, respectively, upon a five-gallon paint can and the top of the trial splat.

At other times I may undertake a more traditional chair type. My goal here is to make an existing chair design more attractive, or simpler, or more functional, or, if possible, all three. My version of the fan-back chair, the Cheshire chair shown in the photo at right above, is such a case.

Both the Wainscot and Cheshire chairs show my way of hooking the parts of a chair together: from functional part to functional part via the most direct route. Thus turned tenons in round holes, sawn curves rather than steamed bends, and simple, machine-cut joints predominate. Wherever a part or a process can be eliminated, I do so. I follow this standard most

rigidly for dining chairs, which must be affordable in multiples, and which tend to look cluttered around a table unless each is rather austere.

At the other end of the scale is the personal chair—such as the rocker or the executive's desk chair—where the cost of the additional comfort and visual appeal that can be attained with complex steambends and joints is justifiable. I have never found complexity a virtue in itself, however. The fact that a technique is difficult or different is no reason to include it in a design; it's usually a good reason to leave it out.

Getting from the apple crate to the finished hardwood chair is a matter of recording the relative proportions, locations and angles of the protochair's scrapwood parts so that they can be reproduced. The specific procedure for determining the chair's dimensions varies with the particular type of chair, the individual designer, and the situation. To outline them all would require a book. A look at how one chair might evolve, however, will give a general idea of this process and the thinking and experimenting that precede it.

Let's say I've decided to build a fan-back chair. This decision determines the general form of the chair: since the fan-back is a Windsor, we know we're talking about a scooped seat of solid wood, as opposed to a slatted, upholstered or webbed seat. Since in this case the seat is the part of the chair I'm most interested in improving, I begin here. After drawing a centerline on the plywood trial seat, I make tape-on contours, like those shown in figure 2 on p. 76, adjusting their shapes and their positions on the plywood seat until I've developed a seat scoop that works.

Because the chair back largely determines the seat's outline, I resist the temptation to fool with the seat any more at this stage and I go right to the back. I cut out a flat cardboard or scrapwood crest, stick dowels (to serve as spindles) onto it with glaziers' putty or tape, and lean the works against the wall behind the seat. Then I re-arrange the parts until they look right.

I use a generous number of dowels to determine the spindle layout. If a chair has too few spindles, I've found that they end up being spaced too far apart to act as a team, and will instead be felt as individual edges digging into the sitter's back. I also use an even number of dowels, since an odd number will put a center spindle where it is unlikely to get along well with the sitter's spine.

Once I've found a back that looks right, I make a firmer version that I can have models try to see if it feels right. To keep the bottoms of the dowel spindles from being forced off the seat when the model leans back, I make a shallow, oversize hole in the seat at each spindle's proposed location. Then I bandsaw a scrapwood crest, drill holes for the tops of the two outermost spindles (called post or king spindles), and cut notches for the inner (pawn) spindles. I fit the king spindles into their shallow seat holes, add the crest, and lean the whole assembly against the wall. I insert the pawn-spindle dowels, cut somewhat over-length, into their seat holes and into the crest notches. The "chair" is then sat in (figure 2A).

The advantage of this lackadaisical method of non-construction now becomes apparent. Say the curve of the crest is wrong. I can throw it away and bandsaw another. If the seat holes are wrong, I can bore new ones. If the holes start to overlap, I make the new ones deeper than the ones they intersect, to keep the dowels from wandering.

Eventually my "chair" will look like figure 2: one old crate, one chunk of used plywood with a million holes in it, a lot of odd scrapwood affixed to the plywood, a rough bandsawn crest cut from an old 2x6, perhaps ten dowels, at *least* a mile of tape, and a variety of blocks, shims, wedges and reject parts everywhere. But when I sit in it, it feels good. Voilà! Now to make it pretty (and portable).

First, I bandsaw a scrapwood crest rail with the front view of my first, flat trial crest and the top-view curve of the second, notched trial crest. I tape this new crest in front of the notched crest, so that it appears to be mounted on the spindles. The seat's plan view comes next. This is fairly easy to determine. The back edge is a curve ⅞ in. or more behind and usually (but not always) parallel to the curved centerline of the spindle holes, the width is whatever looks good with the back, and the shape will usually suggest itself from the former two dimensions and from the seat's scoop. I label the scoop blocks, trace their positions onto the plywood, and remove them. I cut out a paper pattern (figure 3) in the shape suggested by the back and scoop, with a slot or hole for each spindle, and I lay the pattern over the mockup's plywood seat. With the pattern and the back in place together, I stand back and take a look. If the pattern looks bad, I burn it. If it looks good, I laminate a trial seat blank by edge-gluing softwood scraps together.

Fig. 2: Ugly comfort

Tape, dowels, shaped blocks and scrapwood make a comfortable, but crude, chair.

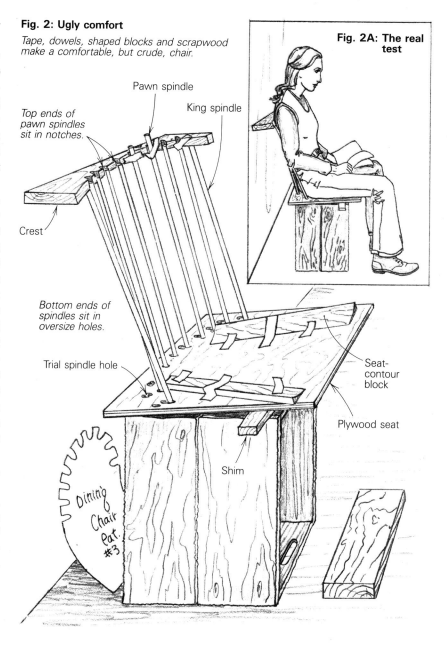

While the glue is drying on the scrapwood seat blank, I follow the procedure outlined in the box on pp. 78-79 to transfer the position and angle of the king spindles onto a duplicate paper seat pattern, but without spindle notches. Each spindle has an angle at which it tilts, and an axis along which this angle is aligned and measured.

At this time I also make a paper pattern of the crest's shape, and record on it both the spacing between the king-spindle holes and the number of pawn spindles. Then I kill time by roughing out stock for the legs and spindles, leaving the dimensions oversize, since I don't yet know exactly what size these members will be.

By now the glue on my scrapwood seat blank is dry, and the real fun begins. I trace the pattern of the proposed seat shape onto the scrapwood blank, transferring the pattern's centerline and the king-spindle locations to the wood as well. Then I bandsaw out the seat. I may later bevel the edge, but for now I cut it square.

Next I scoop the seat using an adze, an inshave and a fish-tail gouge, with the scrapwood tape-ons derived in the first step serving as guides. I place the seat on my apple-crate test stand at the altitude and cant I settled on previously, and

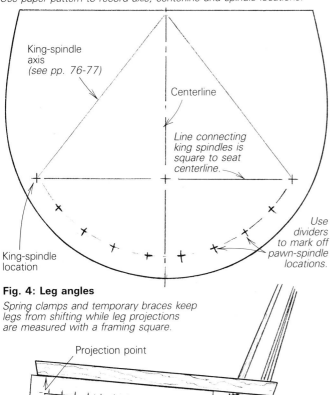

King-spindle
axis
(see pp. 76-77)

Centerline

Line connecting
king spindles is
square to seat
centerline.

King-spindle
location

Use
dividers
to mark off
pawn-spindle
locations.

Fig. 4: Leg angles
*Spring clamps and temporary braces keep
legs from shifting while leg projections
are measured with a framing square.*

Projection point

Fig. 4A: Flexible fastener

*Stapling bent wire
to chair bottom
allows legs to be
repositioned until
they look right.*

3/16-in. hole

Leg

Clamp

Framing square

Temporary
braces

shape, taper its ends, or make its top edge thinner; I turn thinner spindles; I turn fatter spindles; I throw it all in a corner and forget about it for a week.

Finally, like birthing pains, just at the point when it seems hopeless, it all comes together. I'm ready to build a real chair. Using my scrapwood parts and paper patterns as models, I laminate a hardwood seat blank and bend a hardwood crest blank (see *FWW* #8, pp. 40-45, for an article on steam-bending), or, as with the Cheshire chair, saw and smooth a hardwood crest. While the glue is drying on the seat blank—and the bent crest blank, if one is needed, is seasoning in its form—I set the softwood protochair back on its pedestal and think about legs. I cut four lengths of 1-in. dowel to approximate length, and wedge them with wads of glaziers' putty between the chair seat's bottom and the floor. This gives me something to look at that I can easily shift around.

Once I have an idea of leg positions and lengths, I turn some softwood or green-wood prototype legs to suit, shaping their contours in a way that I hope will be pleasing. These legs are hooked to the softwood chair bottom with staple-nails and bent lengths of wire coat hanger as shown in figure 4A.

Now the chair can stand on its own (but I don't dare sit in it yet!). If it looks right the first time, I can expect to wake up at any moment, because I'm dreaming. Most likely it won't seem right until I've pulled the staples and shifted the leg positions, bent the wires to change the splay of the legs, and/or turned new legs and refined their contours.

When I've arranged the legs so that they look right, I tie them together with braces and spring clamps, measure the distances between their bottom ends, and take a projection of the front legs' splay (figure 4). Then I turn the chair over. With the splay measurements just taken, I check that the legs haven't shifted, then I lay out the leg positions and axes on the bottom of the seat, using the same method I used for the king spindles. These positions and axes are recorded on the back side of the paper pattern, along with the leg angles. Now I turn a set of hardwood legs, bore tenon holes in the softwood seat bottom, and dry-assemble the complete protochair.

Even at this stage, I'm not committed. If the chair with real spindles and legs leaves me only lukewarm, I can plug the offending tenon holes with dowels, rebore at another position or angle, and try again.

Despite the lack of glue, the chair can now be sat in if blocks are nailed to the floor around the leg bottoms to keep the legs from spreading outward. Often this final test leads to some sawing-off of the ends of the front or back legs.

The rest, for the woodworking half of me, is denouement. The hardwood seat and crest are worked up, finished, bored, test-assembled and checked for accuracy. The tenons are kerfed with a veining tool to prevent air-lock as the parts are driven home, a small dab of glue is spread on the walls of each hole but not on the tenon (to eliminate the chance of excess glue bead) and the chair is glued up. That's when, for the designer half of me, the excitement becomes a fever. What began as a vague possibility waiting to be discovered in my firewood pile now exists: a chair.

Is it perfect? After all the previously described fussing and tinkering, I must confess it's not. But that doesn't dampen my enthusiasm, it only makes me itch to build another chair that's a little different, and then another. For me, chair design is not a process with an end. Good design, after all, cannot be created; it evolves.

sit in it. If it feels good, I go on to the next step. If it doesn't, I make adjustments. If it's still not right, I put it aside for future reference—somewhere within reach of the woodstove—and make another.

By now I generally have enough information to get a feel for the chair's overall proportions. Judging from the bulk of the seat and crest, I gauge the spindle diameters that should look right. If I'm not sure, I cut out a couple of trial spindles, square in cross section, on the bandsaw and see how they look when tried against the seat and crest. Then I turn a set of finished hardwood king spindles. I lay out the seat's spindle holes according to my pattern and bore the holes, using the method described in the box on pp. 78-79.

Finally, I insert the king spindles in the seat and crest, measure how long the pawn spindles need to be to span from seat to crest (allowing for tenons), and turn these spindles. I dry-assemble the chair seat and back, and try the whole thing out on the test stand.

I have never reached this stage and been happy with the result on the first try. I make adjustments: I chamfer the seat bottom to make the seat appear thinner; I cut the seat smaller, or glue on stock to make it bigger; I change the crest's

Boring angled holes

When the novice chairmaker gets out his drill bits and protractor, it usually isn't long before he's stumped. How do you get the spindle and leg holes at the correct angles? It can be puzzling, because each of these chair parts involves a compound angle—an angle at an angle—as shown in figure 5.

We could measure the two angles with a protractor, but I find that it's better to do as loggers do: consider a compound angle as one angle leaning in a particular direction. To a logger, the direction in which a tree leans is the axis along which it will fall, at least on a windless day. To determine that direction, the logger walks around the tree at some distance, sighting its trunk against an object hanging plumb from his fingertips, such as a key chain. When the tree appears to be perpendicular to the ground, he is standing on the fall line.

I apply the same trick when making a real chair from a scrapwood prototype, such as the one described on pp. 74-77. On the prototype, I sight the axis line of the spindle—its "fall line." Perpendicular to the axis, I sight the lean-angle of the spindle. Then I set a drill press to bore the lean-angle, align the spindle axis with the bit, and bore the hole. I use a radial drill press because the head, not the table, tilts, making it easier to hold and align seat blanks on the table. When you understand the principles, however, you can adapt the method to a regular drill press by making an auxiliary table that tilts the work.

To determine the spindle axis, I set up my trial plywood seat and mark on it a centerline. Then I add the trial king spindles in the position I want.

I now stand a try square on the flat plywood seat and slowly move it to the left or right until the vertical edge of the square's tongue is parallel to the king spindle's centerline. I mark the point where the tongue's edge meets the seat (figure 6). The process is repeated for the other king spindle. Then I draw the spindles' axis lines—corresponding to the direction in which each spindle leans—as shown in figure 7. The two lines should either meet at the seat's centerline, or run off the front edge of the seat at points equidistant from the centerline. If they don't, I check whether the back is on straight, measuring the crest's height from the plywood at each end and comparing the back's diagonal measurements from the top of one king spindle to the bottom of the other one. If that's not the problem, I check the

crest for twist by sighting the side view of one king spindle against the other (they should line up), and by sighting down from above to see if the crest is symmetrical to a line connecting the two king-spindle holes (line A–B in figure 7). If none of this resolves the error, I split the difference. One has only so much patience.

Now, to determine the lean-angle, I hold a protractor along a sight line perpendicular to a spindle's axis line (figure 8). The protractor's hairline should split the centerline of the spindle (I use a protractor with a clear plastic tongue). It's best to hold the protractor dead-upright and read with your eye at the same level as the protractor's base—sighting across the seat's horizon. The lean-angle shown on the protractor, which will be the same for both king spindles, is the angle at which the drill press will be set.

I use Powerbore bits for spindle holes. To set up for drilling, I transfer the centerline, the crossline A–B, the

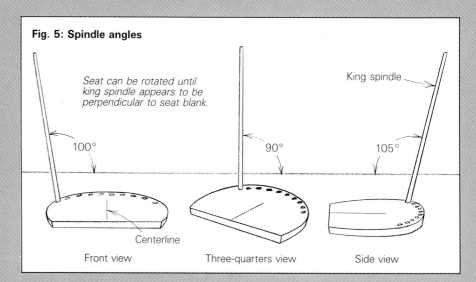

Fig. 5: Spindle angles

Seat can be rotated until king spindle appears to be perpendicular to seat blank.

King spindle

100°   90°   105°

Centerline

Front view   Three-quarters view   Side view

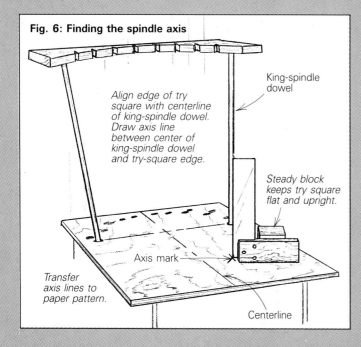

Fig. 6: Finding the spindle axis

Align edge of try square with centerline of king-spindle dowel. Draw axis line between center of king-spindle dowel and try-square edge.

King-spindle dowel

Steady block keeps try square flat and upright.

Axis mark

Transfer axis lines to paper pattern.

Centerline

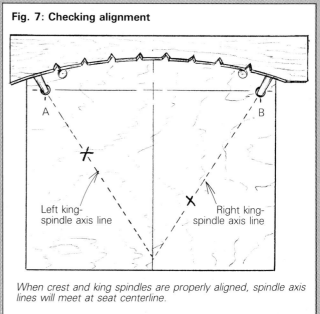

Fig. 7: Checking alignment

A   B

Left king-spindle axis line

Right king-spindle axis line

When crest and king spindles are properly aligned, spindle axis lines will meet at seat centerline.

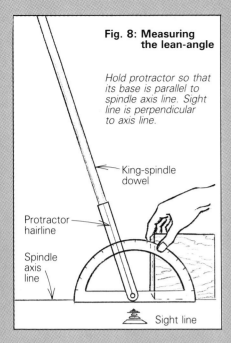

Fig. 8: Measuring the lean-angle

Hold protractor so that its base is parallel to spindle axis line. Sight line is perpendicular to axis line.

King-spindle dowel

Protractor hairline

Spindle axis line

Sight line

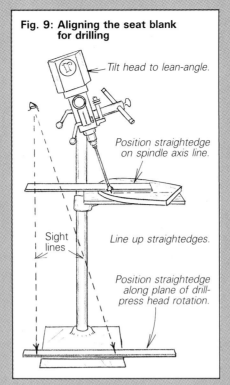

Fig. 9: Aligning the seat blank for drilling

Tilt head to lean-angle.

Position straightedge on spindle axis line.

Sight lines

Line up straightedges.

Position straightedge along plane of drill-press head rotation.

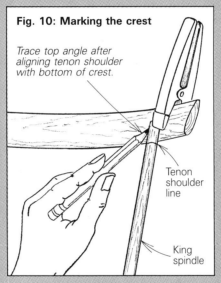

Fig. 10: Marking the crest

Trace top angle after aligning tenon shoulder with bottom of crest.

Tenon shoulder line

King spindle

hole locations and the axis lines from the prototype seat to the seat blank. One critical adjustment remains: the axis line on the seat must be set on the table in the exact plane in which the head of the drill press tilts. This plane should be parallel to the front edge of the press base, but to be sure I check by chucking an eyebolt in the press and tilting the head all the way to one side. I drop a plumb line from the eyebolt and mark the point on the floor. The process is repeated in the other direction. Connecting the points with a straightedge placed on the drill-press base shows the plane in which the head tilts, and along which the axis line must be set. If this plane doesn't correspond to the front of the press's base, I rotate the head assembly about the column until it does. Then I mark the position with matching scratch marks on the column and head. After that, I just use the scratch marks to check press alignment.

After setting the press at the spindle's lean-angle, I place the seat on the press table and align the spindle's axis with that of the press. To do this, I lay a straightedge along the spindle axis line of the seat and, with the machine turned off, I lower the quill until the tip of the bit's center brad pierces the hole location on the blank. Then I rotate the seat blank until the top straightedge is parallel to the bottom straightedge (or, on my drill press, to the front edge of the base), as in figure 9. When everything lines up, I bore the hole, then I move the seat to the other spindle location, align that axis, and bore that king-spindle hole.

At this point, I have a seat blank with two king-spindle holes. I make the king spindles, based on the trial ones from the prototype, and plug them into the seat. Now I can set up to drill the rest of the spindle holes in the seat and in the prototype crest rail. (With these parts assembled, I can refine the design, including the outline of the seat itself.) To find the angles for the spindle holes, I clamp the crest rail to the king spindles and trace off the angles of their top tenons, as shown in figure 10. Then I bore the holes as shown in figure 11. Now I can mount the crest on the king spindles and drill the pawn-spindle holes with a hand-held electric drill (figure 12), eyeballing the drill's alignment from point to point.

To drill the seat's pawn-spindle holes, I use a bit extension with the power drill. I set up the notched crest made before the model sat in the prototype, as explained on p. 76, and run the extension in the notches (figure 13). —*J.S.*

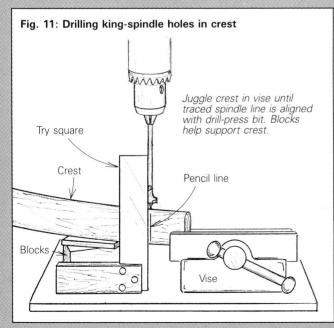

Fig. 11: Drilling king-spindle holes in crest

Try square

Crest

Juggle crest in vise until traced spindle line is aligned with drill-press bit. Blocks help support crest.

Pencil line

Blocks

Vise

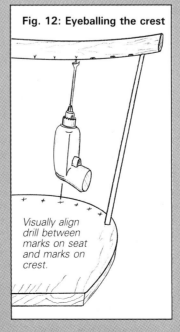

Fig. 12: Eyeballing the crest

Visually align drill between marks on seat and marks on crest.

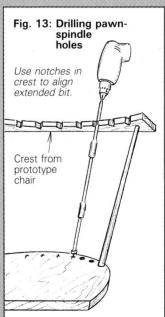

Fig. 13: Drilling pawn-spindle holes

Use notches in crest to align extended bit.

Crest from prototype chair

Making a Blind Finger Joint
Miter hides the router-cut fingers

by James A. Rome

The finger, or box, joint is one of the strongest choices for drawer, box or carcase construction. It's easy to make and easy to clamp, and there's a lot of long-grain to long-grain contact—the ideal gluing situation. In some applications, the finger joint is also quite handsome, but in others, the exposed end grain of through fingers clashes with the overall design. For that reason, I developed a method of making a joint that looks like a simple miter but retains the finger joint's strength.

Most of the steps in making my blind finger joint can be done on a router table and tablesaw, but some have to be performed by hand.

The completed joint is shown in figure 1E. The slots and fingers are cut on a router table using the jig shown in figure 2. Both halves of the joint are identical, each beginning with a finger and ending with a slot, so when one board is flipped over, the two parts mesh together.

After struggling with a small, metal router table, I built a big wooden one with a ¾-in. birch plywood top. I routed two grooves in the tabletop from front to back for the finger-joint jig to slide in. My router table has an adjustable fence which, for this job, acts as a stop behind the jig. A board clamped to the table would also work as a fence.

A note about routers: My first experiments using a Sears Craftsman 1½-HP router were unsatisfactory. No matter what I did, my slots were 0.011 in. oversize. I wrote to Sears about the problem, and received an answer from Singer, manufacturer of the router. Their specs permit runout of up to 0.007 in. at a distance of 1 in. from the collet. Since my bit was cutting farther from the collet, I got even more runout. Thus, the Sears router proved unsuitable for the job. I now use a Hitachi TR-12 plunge router, which cuts a slot accurate to within 0.001 in. With the router mounted on the table, however, it requires herculean strength to push upward against the router springs to adjust the depth of cut.

The jig must be rigid and accurately made to guarantee precision in the finished joint. I waxed the two hardwood runners on the bottom so that they would slide easily in the table grooves. Two screws countersunk into the side of one runner can be backed out to rub the side of the groove for a tight fit.

Router-bit diameter determines finger and slot width. I used a ½-in. straight-flute bit to make fingers and slots ½ in. deep, ½ in. wide and ¾ in. long, but you can change these dimensions for different size fingers. To index

Fig. 1: Steps in making the blind finger joint

Cut slots with ½-in. router bit.

A. *First pass hogs waste.*

Chisel cleans out corners.

B. *Second pass squares up slot.*

C. *Define miter with tablesaw blade set to slot depth.*

D. *Cut miter with tablesaw blade set to 45°.*

Chamfer corner.

E. *Finish miter with dovetail saw and chisel.*

45°

Fig. 2: Jig for cutting blind finger joint

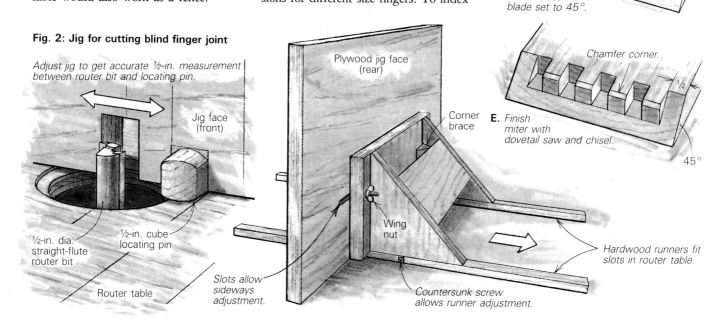

Adjust jig to get accurate ½-in. measurement between router bit and locating pin.

Plywood jig face (rear)

Jig face (front)

Corner brace

Wing nut

½-in. dia. straight-flute router bit

½-in. cube locating pin

Router table

Slots allow sideways adjustment.

Countersunk screw allows runner adjustment.

Hardwood runners fit slots in router table.

Drawing: Ken Daniel

To cut first slot, clamp board vertically against jig face (left), right-hand edge against locating pin. First slot, placed over pin, locates next cut. Pencil lines on jig and router table make it easy to square up board. Bolts in jig face allow sideways adjustment of jig. After cutting slots, Rome readjusts router bit and makes a second pass with board horizontal (right;, a light cleanup cut that flattens bottom of slots. Jig slides back until it stops against router-table fence shown at far right, behind jig.

the fingers, I installed a ½-in. cube-shaped locating pin in the front of the jig, as shown in figure 2. If you want larger or smaller fingers, make a pin with faces equal to your router-bit diameter. For ⅜-in. fingers, for example, use a ⅜-in. router bit and a ⅜-in. locating pin. Board width must be an even multiple of finger width. Finger length before mitering, as shown in figure 1A, must equal stock thickness. To make the joint shown, I used a board ¾ in. thick and 5 in. wide.

With the preliminaries out of the way, here's how to make the joint. The trick is to rout the slots between the fingers two times—once vertically, to remove the bulk of the waste, and once horizontally, to square off the round corners left after the first pass. With the jig set in the router table, adjust the router so that the bit extends ¾ in. above the table, to set the length of the fingers. Now adjust the fence behind the jig so that, pushed back against the fence, it stops when the front of the router bit extends ½ in. in front of the jig's face. Adjust the jig sideways to get exactly ½ in. between the locating pin and the router bit, as shown in figure 2. Clamp the board vertically against the face of the jig, with one edge against the locating pin as shown in the photo at left above. Use a square to ensure that the board is exactly vertical. (It's a good idea to test the setup using scrapwood before risking good stock.)

Cut one slot by pushing the jig toward the fence until it stops. Check the measurements and make any necessary

adjustment. To cut successive slots, position the slot over the locating pin and repeat the process, going from right to left. Do not cut a slot on the left edge, however. This edge must be mitered by hand later. The board at this point should look like the one in figure 1A. Cut the mating board in the same manner.

Next, lower the router bit so that it extends ½ in. above the table, and adjust the fence so that when the jig is pushed back against it, the bit extends ¾ in. in front of the jig's face. For this step, hold the board horizontal, with the slots and fingers down (photo, above right). Place the second slot from the left over the pin. Make a cut, move the board to your left one slot, and recut the remaining slots in the same way.

The first slot on the right of the board (shown at arrow in figure 1B) can't be recut with the jig. After cutting all the other slots on both halves of the joint, remove the jig from the table, put this slot over the router bit (with the router turned off), and clamp a guide board on the table against the right-hand edge of the board. Adjust the fence so that it stops the cut at the ¾-in. point and recut the last slot without the jig. After the second pass with the router, only the corners need to be cleaned up with a chisel.

On the tablesaw, adjust the rip fence so that it's ¼ in. away from the far side of the blade and adjust the blade height to ½ in. With the slots downward, and the end against the fence, cut a slot through the end of each half of the joint (figure 1C).

To recut far right-hand slot, a guide board clamped to router table substitutes for jig.

Cut the miter on the tablesaw with the blade at a 45° angle. I screw a wooden fence to the crosscut/miter gauge, make a cut through the fence, and use that kerf as a reference to see where the blade will cut. For accuracy, I clamp the board to the fence. The joint should now look like the one shown in figure 1D.

Now the outer finger and uncut slot in each board must be cut by hand to a 45° miter (figure 1E). I'm partial to a Japanese dovetail saw (*dozuki*) for this operation. Use the existing miter to guide the saw, or make a 45° guide block.

The final step is to chamfer the outer edge of each finger. When the joint is assembled, the fancy cabinetwork is invisible, but the joint is incredibly strong. □

James A. Rome is a full-time plasma physicist and part-time woodworker in Oak Ridge, Tenn. He wrote about jointer-planers in FWW #43. Photos by the author.

Knockdown Furniture
Form follows junction

by Curtis Erpelding

Although I design and make furniture for private clients, my pieces usually incorporate knockdown features. I like to devise designs suitable for mass production because I believe that functional, well-crafted furniture should be affordable. Because assembly time is eliminated, knockdown furniture is economical to produce commercially, and the pieces can be shipped disassembled, in compact packages. This economy and convenience are particularly relevant now, when people live in smaller spaces and move frequently. But the heart of my interest in knockdown design lies beyond function or practicality.

What interests me fundamentally is the concept that machined pieces of wood can lock together into a new form in ways that take into account the wood's physical properties. The basic problem becomes how to join (and later separate) two pieces of wood using gravity, friction and, occasionally, metal fasteners.

In 1980, the Design Arts Program of the National Endowment for the Arts (1100 Pennsylvania Ave. N.W., Washington, D.C. 20506) awarded me a one-year project grant to explore knockdown wooden furniture design. I had to satisfy three grant requirements: First, I was to continue my work in applying knockdown design to standard household and office furniture. Second, I was to develop three knockdown prototypes that would be suitable for mass production. And third, I was to research the possibility of having my designs commercially produced.

The three prototypes I decided on were a platform bed, a stacking chair with a circular seat, and a shelf system that leans against the wall. Each presented challenging design problems. In the beginning, I had intended to make detailed drawings and mockups to establish dimensions and proportions before building the actual prototypes. This goes against my usual practice. Normally I start with a fairly firm idea, work out the joinery details hastily on paper, cut a practice joint, and then plunge right into building the piece. When it works, this method saves a great deal of time. When it fails, the results are disastrous. Each procedure must be done correctly the first time, and design changes must be anticipated in advance, or they will interfere with the already completed part of the project. Sometimes I'm stuck with a half-completed piece of furniture and the prospect of having to start over again. For the grant project, I wanted to avoid this by doing drawings and mockups. Intentions may be noble, but bad habits die hard. As much as I tried, I kept reverting to my usual method. Somehow, for me, the design process has to involve this element of immediate risk. Either get it right the first time or blow the whole project.

Of the three projects, the platform bed, designed for a Japanese futon mattress, most closely approaches my notion of a pure knockdown design because it is built without glue or

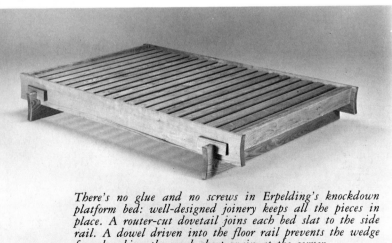

There's no glue and no screws in Erpelding's knockdown platform bed: well-designed joinery keeps all the pieces in place. A router-cut dovetail joins each bed slat to the side rail. A dowel driven into the floor rail prevents the wedge from breaking the weak short-grain at the corner.

Photos: Joseph Felzman Studio, except where noted

metal fasteners. The rail-to-rail joint locks the parts and circumvents a troublesome characteristic of traditional bridle joints: an increase in humidity causes wood to expand across the grain, locking a tight-fitting bridle joint. This is fine for conventional furniture, but I had learned in earlier experiments with bridle-joint construction that knockdown structures would freeze solid in the middle of a humid summer. To solve this problem, I modified the bridle joint by tapering it (figure 1). This joint tightens under load, yet because of its geometry, it easily loosens when force is applied in the opposite direction. Simply wiggling one of the rails, or tapping upward lightly, breaks the assembly.

The tapered bridle joint wouldn't hold the pieces together by itself, so I added a wedge that fits into an angled notch in the floor rail. This wedge, which has a compound taper, locks the joint by forcing the side rail tightly against the side of the notch in the floor rail. The bed can be lifted and carried by the side rails, and the joint won't slip.

I cut most of the modified bridle joint on the radial-arm saw. To accommodate expansion, I cut both parts of the joint slightly wider than the thickness of the rails. The tapered face in the floor-rail part was surfaced with a router on an angled jig, and I feathered all sharp edges of the joint with a chisel.

The round cap that protrudes from the top edge of the floor rails is the end of a dowel, driven 4 in. into the rail. The dowel strengthens the weak short-grain, keeping the wedge from breaking it off.

In keeping with the solid-wood construction, I opted for slats, rather than plywood, to support the mattress. The soft, cotton futon mattress is used without a box spring, and traditionally it's unrolled right on the floor. The slats had to be thick enough and spaced closely to provide a firm platform for the futon, yet not so close as to interfere with ventilation. The obvious solution was to cut individual pockets in the side rails for the ends of each slat, while leaving enough space for the slats to expand without locking. I tapered both the sides of the pockets in the rails and the dovetails on the slats 15° so that the joint can swell without locking. I cut the joint with a 1-in. dovetail bit in a router using a jig that cuts both the pockets and the dovetails (figure 2). To cut the slats, I used a router with a smaller-diameter base.

The skirts at the head and foot of the bed are installed after the bed is assembled but before the wedges are driven in. The ends of each skirt are stop-slotted and slip over splines in the side rails. The outside face of the skirts is planed concave to match the radius on the ends of the rails.

With the bed, I suppose, I drifted furthest from the grant requirement that my design prototype be manufacturable. I don't pretend for a moment that this bed could be easily manufactured—although with simpler joinery it could, conceivably, be a production prototype.

While joinery was the major design feature of the knockdown bed, this is not true of the three-legged stacking chairs. Here, most of the joinery is straightforward and expedient—socket-head cap screws.

I was aware of precedents to this design. Finnish designer Alvar Aalto made spiral-stacking, circular-seat chairs, and Rudd International manufactures a stacking chair (*FWW* #30, p. 34), but both designs have four legs and don't knock down. Hans Wegner designed a three-legged stacking chair, but it does not stack on the rotational principle. I felt that my

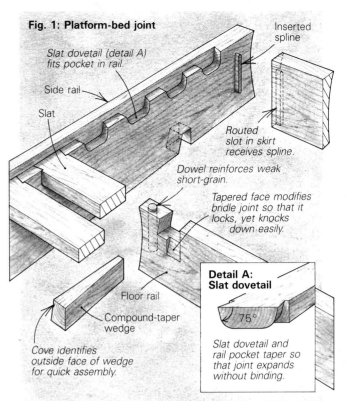

Fig. 1: Platform-bed joint

Slat dovetail (detail A) fits pocket in rail.

Side rail

Slat

Inserted spline

Routed slot in skirt receives spline.

Dowel reinforces weak short-grain.

Tapered face modifies bridle joint so that it locks, yet knocks down easily.

Floor rail

Compound-taper wedge

Cove identifies outside face of wedge for quick assembly.

Detail A: Slat dovetail

75°

Slat dovetail and rail pocket taper so that joint expands without binding.

Fig. 2: Two-way router jig for pocket dovetails

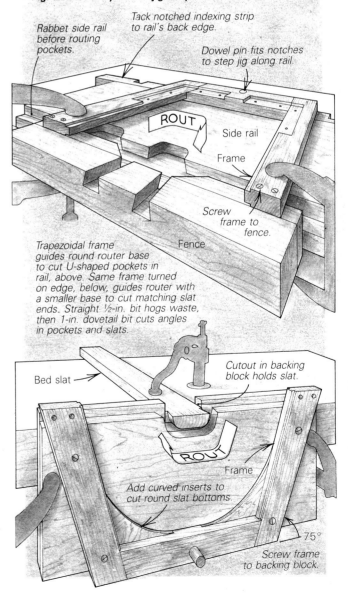

Rabbet side rail before routing pockets.

Tack notched indexing strip to rail's back edge.

Dowel pin fits notches to step jig along rail.

ROUT

Side rail

Frame

Screw frame to fence.

Trapezoidal frame guides round router base to cut U-shaped pockets in rail, above. Same frame turned on edge, below, guides router with a smaller base to cut matching slat ends. Straight ½-in. bit hogs waste, then 1-in. dovetail bit cuts angles in pockets and slats.

Fence

Bed slat

Cutout in backing block holds slat.

ROUT

Frame

Add curved inserts to cut round slat bottoms.

75°

Screw frame to backing block.

A *splined key joins the ends of Erpelding's chair-seat rim at the rear leg, above. The legs are fastened to the rim with socket-head cap screws threaded into propeller nuts mounted in a reinforcing block inside the rim. The curved clamping blocks of the chair-seat rim-bending form, below, which fit inside the laminated rim when it's being glued up, are shown resting on the metal pins that align the laminates.*

In these knockdown spiral-stacking chairs, every piece was laminated and bent, then joined together with metal fasteners.

design was different enough to justify pursuing.

The final chair design evolved after many paper incarnations. I built a few models, but the mockups only frustrated my thinking. So I put the chair project on the back burner, and returned to it nearly a year later, visualizing a circular seat rim with legs and back supports coming off at points of a circumscribed hexagon. With an idea of what dimensions the chair would need to stack, I began building the bending forms. I guessed, and hoped the calculations were correct, but I could perfect the design only by building the chair.

I bent the backrest by clamping $\frac{1}{16}$-in. ash laminates in a cone-shaped form. The curve of the backrest tapers in radius from top to bottom to follow the bend in the upright back supports. Since the human back also tapers from shoulder to waist, this makes a comfortable chair.

The outside diameter of every seat rim had to be identical, or at least within a $\frac{1}{32}$-in. tolerance, or the chairs might not stack. The rim could have been glued up around a circular form and machined true later, but my shop isn't equipped to do this easily. Instead, I built a peripheral bending form, clamping up the seat rim inside it with curved blocks on the inside surface of the rim. Metal rods projecting from the bottom position the laminates in the same plane during glue-up. To ensure color and grain continuity in the set of chairs, I cut the outside laminate of each rim from the same piece of

wood. Planing each laminate before glue-up kept sanding to a minimum. I cut the laminates to a length just shy of the outside circumference. After removing the glued-up rim from the form, I slotted the break with a slotting cutter in a router, and fitted the joint with a key where it joins at the rear leg. I glued an additional reinforcing piece across the joint inside the rim. All of the rims have exactly the same outside diameter.

I drilled the rims and installed propeller nuts (available from Selby Furniture Hardware Co., 17 E. 22nd St., New York, N.Y. 10010) from the inside. Flat-head socket cap screws fasten the legs and back supports, which are also form-bent laminations, to the rim. I put an emery-cloth spacer between the rim and the legs to prevent slippage, and to serve as a shim so that the legs clear the seat rim of the chair underneath when the chairs are stacked.

There were few aesthetic decisions in this chair's design. Having stated the problem—a three-legged, knockdown, stacking chair—the design evolved in a purely functional and geometric way. Nearly all of the design decisions—the thickness and width of the members, the radii of the bends, the choice of fasteners and seat cushion—were arrived at as the simplest solution to the stated problem.

The third prototype, a leaning shelf system, was a reworking of an earlier design inspired by Italian designer Vico Ma-

Knockdown leaning shelves are supported by both the wall and the floor. The horizontal braces under the shelves add strength and allow a longer shelf span.

A wedge joint holds the shelves together. The compound taper of the wedge in a dado forms a sliding dovetail and locks tight.

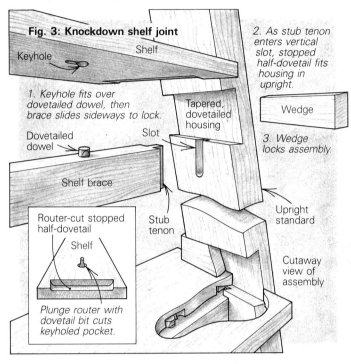

Fig. 3: Knockdown shelf joint

Keyhole

Shelf

1. Keyhole fits over dovetailed dowel, then brace slides sideways to lock.

Dovetailed dowel

Slot

Shelf brace

Tapered, dovetailed housing

2. As stub tenon enters vertical slot, stopped half-dovetail fits housing in upright.

Wedge

3. Wedge locks assembly.

Router-cut stopped half-dovetail

Shelf

Plunge router with dovetail bit cuts keyholed pocket.

Stub tenon

Upright standard

Cutaway view of assembly

gistretti. With minimal material and no bracing, the bookcase is very sturdy because weight is distributed between wall and floor. The design eliminates the need for shimming or fastening where floors slope, and the piece lends itself well to knockdown design.

I had originally intended to use metal hardware—a bolt passed through the upright standard and threaded into a nut embedded in the end of the shelf. While doodling, however, I came up with the wedge joint which, because it involves wood alone, fit my design philosophy more neatly. At first I used a wedge with a narrow tongue on the top edge which slid into a groove in the upright, but now I use a simpler joint. I've replaced the tongue and groove with a compound-taper wedge that acts like a sliding dovetail (figure 3).

To cut the edges of the dovetailed dadoes in the standards, I used a router with a 1-in. dia. dovetail bit, after wasting the material between with a ½-in. straight bit. A router-cut dovetail pocket on the underside of the shelf end fits into the dovetail-shaped bottom edge of the dado.

The horizontal braces under the shelves add strength and make a longer unsupported span possible (for ¾-in. shelving, 30 in. is about maximum before sagging occurs under load). The braces also stiffen the assembly against racking, act as a stop for books on the shelf below, and center each shelf with respect to the upright standards. The brace attaches underneath the shelf with a keyholed-pocket dovetail. Dovetailed dowels are driven into the edge of the brace, and dovetail slots are cut into the bottom of the shelf with a plunge router. The dowels enter the slot in the hole where the router bit was plunged in. The assembly locks tight when the brace is slid toward one end. A stub tenon on each end of the brace fits into a slot cut into the upright.

I am just now entering the third phase of the grant—researching the possibility of mass-producing the prototypes. Although I received only a one-year grant, I spent more than two years, on and off, working on the prototypes, and I am by no means finished with revisions.

To make an object is to arrange components into a new system. The assembly of parts can be final, the intersections fixed with glue, or it can be temporary—knockdown design. For me, the intersection of the components, the joinery, defines the form—not the other way around. Form is significant only insofar as it is incorporated into the structural integrity of the whole. The knockdown approach focuses on the relationships between the structure's components, and adds a new dimension to form—reconstructability. □

Curtis Erpelding is a professional woodworker and designer in Seattle, Wash. He wrote about making slip joints with the radial-arm saw in FWW #32.

Veneering
Preparing substrates is the first step

by Ian J. Kirby

Polished veneers: apple (top), padauk, maple burl, curly koa.

Veneering can lead to furniture designs that just aren't possible with solid wood. Lots of furniture has the shape it does because of wood's hygroscopic nature—you have to allow wood to expand and contract. Once you master veneering, however, you don't have that restriction. You can turn particleboard and fiberboard into dimensionally stable panels that are as attractive as any piece of solid wood, opening up a whole new world of design possibilities.

A veneer is simply a thin layer of wood, which can be glued on top of another material. At its best, veneering produces superb results. Done badly, it's a mess. You must plan every step before you begin. Unlike other woodworking, you don't start with a large plank and carve it down; you begin with a small piece and build it up to the size you want.

Veneering allows you to use woods that would be too expensive (rosewood or ebony) or just too unstable (burls or crotches) to be worked in solid form. Veneers have been available for centuries, of course, but what has now brought veneer into the small-shop woodworker's province is the advent of man-made substrates, the material onto which the veneer is glued. Particleboard and medium-density fiberboard have changed the whole nature of veneering.

In this article, the first in a series on veneering, I'll discuss veneers (p. 89), substrates and how to prepare them for veneering. The article beginning on p. 91 deals with the application of veneers.

•   •   •

Until the turn of this century, woodworkers had to make their own solid-wood substrates for veneering, and that was a real problem. If you veneer solid wood, laying the grain of the veneer at right angles to the grain of the solid wood, the veneer will come under tremendous stress as the substrate shrinks and expands, and can crack or delaminate. Even if you orient the grain of both materials in the same direction, you'll just have ordinary wood with a different wood glued onto it—with all of solid wood's moisture-related problems.

The traditional solution was to make large panels out of many small panels within frames, the assumption being that each little panel would shrink and expand less than one large panel would. It seems to have solved the problem in many cases, yet it shouldn't. Lots of little bits of wood will expand and contract collectively as much as one big piece of wood.

Today you can sidestep all of these problems by using particleboard or fiberboard as the substrate. These materials are so stable that seasonal movement is negligible. Probably the best substrate is medium-density fiberboard (MDF). It is made by breaking down wood into its fibrous form, then pressing the fibers back together again with an adhesive. All

MDF is basically the same: it has no grain, is square-edged and uniform throughout, and weighs about 48 lb. per cubic foot. It's a material that is very stable, but so boring that it cries out for the application of something with a little more life. Veneering both sides of a 5/8-in. thick MDF board produces a board thick enough for most furniture designs. You may have trouble finding MDF, since it is made primarily for industrial use. Some large lumber companies do carry it, although they may require a substantial minimum order. Professional woodworkers in your area may be able to recommend a local source of supply. Allied Plywood Corp. (which has seven warehouses along the East Coast) and Paxton Lumber Co. (which is headquartered in Kansas City, Mo., but has warehouses in several states) handle both MDF and furniture-quality particleboard. These materials are also available through some Georgia-Pacific Corp. service centers.

Plywood isn't a good substrate for veneering. Since it's made by gluing together layers of wood at right angles to each other, it has decent dimensional stability, but it can warp and twist. Particleboard, which is made by gluing wood particles together, is dimensionally stable, but some people get into an awful mess because they veneer onto building boards, not furniture-quality boards, which are multilayered boards with very smooth surfaces. Surface irregularities of the coarser building boards are liable to telegraph through the veneer. You can recognize furniture-quality boards (sometimes called industrial-grade) because they are oversize—a 4x8 sheet really measures 4 ft. 1 in. by 8 ft. 1 in. Building board is always 4x8, because builders commonly work to a 16-in. module.

The edges of man-made boards are just as boring as their surfaces. If the edges are going to show, you have to cover them in some way, as shown in figure 1. The usual technique is to glue a lipping of solid wood or veneer onto the edge of the substrate, clean it off, and glue veneer on both surfaces of the entire panel, including the lipping. Veneering the edges has one disadvantage: the edges will remain square after they're veneered. The only thing you can do to improve the appearance and to help prevent chipping is to soften the veneered edges with sandpaper. You could make a softer edge by applying two or three layers of veneer so that you'd have more material to radius. One of the nice things you can do with veneer lipping, however, is to accent the edge treatment. If you wanted a five-veneer lipping, you could glue on three layers of the surface veneer and two layers of a different color veneer. This colored border picks out the edge and gives the job a lot of life.

For more shape on the edges, or what in woodworking terms is called molding, use solid-wood lipping. Other edge treatments include gluing on strips of leather, Naugahyde or even metal, such as fine copper foil.

In any case, decide what the lipping's width will be before you cut your substrate to size. The procedure is to first determine the size of the finished veneered panel, including the lipping. Then determine the width of the edge treatment, and subtract twice that from the length and width of the finished panel to get the dimensions of the substrate.

I prefer to glue the solid-wood lipping around the edge of the substrate before it's veneered. This gives enough material to mold the edges, and the surface veneer blends into the lipping, making the whole piece seem more cohesive. It's common to make the lipping of the same material as the surface veneer, but don't sacrifice a rare, exotic hardwood like ebony for lippings. Use a multilayer veneer lipping instead.

Lippings can be either mitered or butt-jointed at the corners, depending on the quality of the piece and the effect you want. With thin lippings, you can just about eliminate the visual effect of the butt joint by radiusing the corner. If you wish to miter the lipping, it's best to miter the lippings for the long edges before gluing them to the panel. If you do it this way, the lipping must be glued on very accurately, with no slippage along its length. On the short edges, when you're filling in, you have to cut the miter correctly at each end, and the length must be dead-accurate. Alternatively, you can glue the lipping on first and then cut the miters, but then you've got only one shot at getting them right.

The most common fault in making lippings is to have them too wide. The lipping should be the width needed to accommodate the molding on the edge, plus a safety margin of no more than $\frac{1}{8}$ in. So, if you want a $\frac{3}{4}$-in. thick edge rounded to a semicircle, all you need for lipping is $\frac{3}{8}$ in. plus a little, since $\frac{3}{8}$ in. is the radius of a $\frac{3}{4}$-in. circle.

The main reason for keeping lippings as narrow as possible is the shrinkage differential between the stable man-made substrate and the solid-wood lipping. After a few months, a wide lipping may shrink and show through the veneer, a condition known as telegraphing. Cost is also a consideration—you'd be surprised how much material goes into the lipping.

The simplest way to apply lipping is to keep the wood for the lipping wider than necessary until after it's glued onto the substrate. It will serve as its own clamping block, so you don't need a lot of clamps and battens, as you would if you

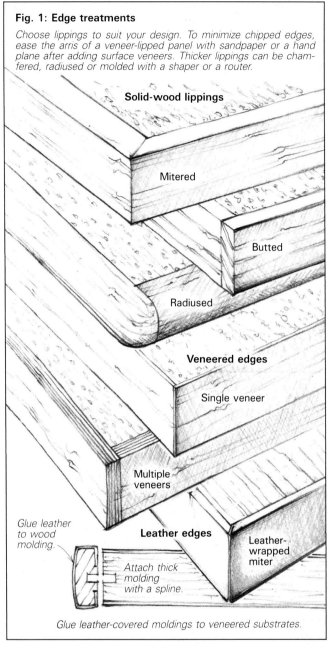

Fig. 1: Edge treatments

Choose lippings to suit your design. To minimize chipped edges, ease the arris of a veneer-lipped panel with sandpaper or a hand plane after adding surface veneers. Thicker lippings can be chamfered, radiused or molded with a shaper or a router.

Solid-wood lippings

Mitered

Butted

Radiused

Veneered edges

Single veneer

Multiple veneers

Glue leather to wood molding.

Leather edges

Leather-wrapped miter

Attach thick molding with a spline.

Glue leather-covered moldings to veneered substrates.

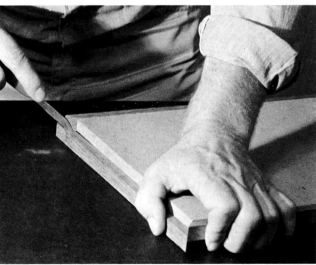

With the mitered lipping glued to the panel sides, use a marking knife to scribe the miters on the end lipping.

tried to glue on thin lipping (figure 2). After the lipping is glued onto the panel, you can quickly cut it to width. The lipping stock should be just slightly thicker than the substrate, at most $\frac{1}{16}$ in. more on each side. You could make it the same thickness as the panel if you could position it exactly when you glue it on, but this is difficult. Leave a small amount on each face and plane it flush after glue-up. The lipping need be only $\frac{1}{16}$ in. or so overlong at each end. Don't try to buy insurance by leaving excessive amounts of wood everywhere. It's tough to remove before you glue on the veneer.

The key to spreading a thin, even coat of glue on the substrate edges and the lipping is to use a narrow paint roller (the bubble pack it comes in makes a good reusable glue tray). You don't need any exotic joinery to secure the lipping: once the lipping is glued on, it's never going to come off in conventional use. In fact, I once put lipping on without glue—I just pinned it, leaving the pins proud so that I could remove them. I veneered the top and bottom, then took the pins out. Try as I might, I couldn't break the lipping off.

White PVA glue is fine for both veneer and lipping. Don't put excessive amounts of glue on either surface. Remember, you're going to have to deal with the accrued amount from both of them coming together. All you've got to do is wet the surface with glue. If the surface has dry patches, it won't adhere. If you put on too much glue, you'll get dribbles and they'll be a problem when you trim the lipping, whether with a router or a plane. All you want visible are little beads of glue. If you trim this lipping with a router trimming bit, the bit's pilot needs to travel on an absolutely clean surface, otherwise it will hit glue bumps and won't flush the lipping. If the pilot has a clear path, you can set the bit to no tolerance and clean the lipping perfectly.

The alternative is to plane off the excess lipping by hand, using a jointer plane. Clamp the panel to the bench. Put the toe of the plane on the surface and plane in a circular motion across the grain, with the substrate acting as a register for the toe. Careful, though—once the plane gets down to the substrate, stop. Don't remove lipping by planing straight along the grain. It's too easy to tip the plane and taper the lipping. Planing across, rather than with, the grain gives you a slightly less smooth surface, but that doesn't interfere with the gluing on of veneer. The thing you've got to guard against is lifting the plane's toe off the substrate, else you'll lose the absolutely flat surface. Keep a straightedge handy to check your work. Clearly, it's bad practice to glue on the lipping with $\frac{1}{4}$ in. of excess on each side, or to put it on high at one point and down at another. It's easy to get it on, but you pay the price when you have to remove the excess. Nothing other than care and accuracy will do. Cleaning up the lipping is not done rapidly. You can't do it accurately with a belt sander.

Once the lipping is absolutely level with the substrate, the panel is ready for veneering. If you're not going to veneer right away, cover the panel to keep off dust and contamination. Contrary to an old popular practice, there's no need to scuff the surface with a toothing plane; glue doesn't need a rough surface to work. The surface is now as flat as it's ever going to be—scuffing will only ruin it. □

Ian J. Kirby is an educator, designer and cabinetmaker. He recently moved his woodworking school from Vermont to Cumming, Ga. Drawings by the author. For more on particleboard and fiberboard, see FWW #29, pp. 76-81.

Fig. 2: Two ways to apply solid-wood lippings

A. *Wide lipping stock serves as its own clamping block. Rip to size after the glue has cured.*

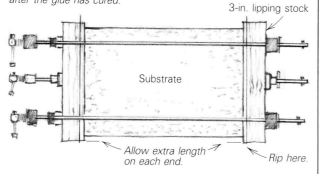

3-in. lipping stock

Substrate

Allow extra length on each end.

Rip here.

B. *Put stock wide enough to make two lippings between two panels, glue, and clamp them together. When the glue has dried, rip the stock to size the lippings, and repeat for the other edges.*

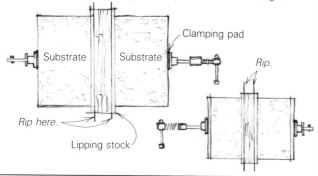

Clamping pad

Substrate Substrate

Rip.

Rip here.

Lipping stock

Spread an even coat of white glue on the substrate edge with a small paint roller before applying the lipping.

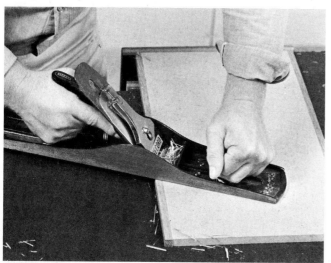

Rest the toe of the jointer plane firmly on the substrate to prevent tapering the lipping.

Getting on the good side of veneer

Veneers come in three types: sawn, sliced and rotary-cut. Sawn veneer is the oldest form, and was very common in Europe in the 1700s. It's simply a piece of wood, any thickness up to ⅛ in., sawn from a log or a board and then planed. Sawn veneer hasn't been used much in recent years, though modern band resaws offer a good chance for its revival, especially since any wood can be sawn into veneer. Modern resaws saw wood thinly and accurately, and because they make a very fine kerf, thus minimizing waste, they're economical, too.

Rotary-cut veneer, which generally is confined to the manufacture of plywood, is made by mounting a whole log on a giant lathe and peeling off veneer as if it were wallpaper. It's rarely used as a surface, show-wood veneer in furniture, although it can look nice, as in some birch plywoods used for drawer bottoms and carcase backs. Rotary-cut veneer can be very thick (⅛ in.) or very thin. Only diffuse-porous woods that grow abundantly in plywood-manufacturing areas, such as lauan in Southeast Asia and birch in Europe, are rotary-cut.

Woodworkers are most concerned with sliced veneer. Any wood can be sliced: hard, soft, ring-porous, diffuse-porous, fast-grown, slow-grown—it doesn't matter. Essentially, a guillotine-type knife is brought down through a block of wood to slice off thin pieces, usually ½2 in. to ½8 in. thick. The veneer doesn't lose any measurable thickness during drying. Veneers can be sliced thinner, but I find that ½0 in. is about the thinnest that can be handled easily in a small shop.

Sliced veneers are most commonly available in 6-ft. to 8-ft. lengths, the size of most slicing machines, but lengths of up to 16 ft. can sometimes be found. Widths of up to 30 in. are possible, but getting a wide piece of veneer doesn't have the same attraction as getting a wide piece of wood does. It's easy to cut, match and join veneers together to create the widths and grain patterns needed for any job. Wide veneers frequently are rougher and coarser in the center than on the edge, so they can be difficult to smooth and finish.

Veneer-cutting technology is complicated, and the only thing that most woodworkers need to understand is that there is considerable cracking of wood tissue during the slicing process

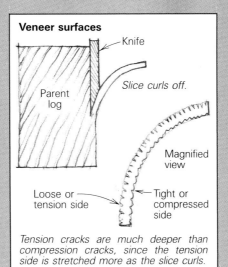

Veneer surfaces

Knife

Parent log

Slice curls off.

Magnified view

Loose or tension side

Tight or compressed side

Tension cracks are much deeper than compression cracks, since the tension side is stretched more as the slice curls.

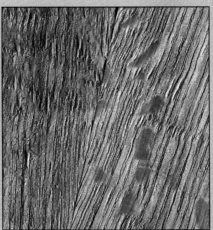

Bookmatching shows the difference between compression and tension surfaces. Compression side, right, has more sheen and is smoother than tension side.

Veneer bent along its grain with the tension side up will bend a great deal without audible cracking. With the compression side up, the radius of the curve will be greater and you'll hear cracking before the piece actually breaks.

and the two sides of each veneer piece will have very different characteristics. Two different surfaces are created as each new slice curls off the parent log, as shown in the drawing (for more about knife checks, see *FWW* #12, pp. 83-85).

This difference is important when you're deciding which side to glue to the substrate. By putting the smoother compression side up (the tight side), you'll have the more cohesive side of the veneer on the outside, with the deeper cracks of the tension (loose) side against the substrate. Smooth-side-up is best for hand-woodworking, because when you clean and sand you will go through the small compression cracks and get to the solid part of the veneer much more easily.

These two surfaces also affect bookmatching. If you have a highly figured veneer 6 in. wide and you want a 12-in. panel, you might be tempted to open two consecutive pieces like a book and put them together so that the pattern matches down the center (you can do this since veneers are stored in bundles or swatches in the order in which they were sliced). This works in solid wood, but with veneer you expose one tight side and one loose side. The visual effect when finish is applied to bookmatched veneers can be quite poor. A surface that looks fine all through the process suddenly takes on a different feel, because the tight and loose sides will absorb the finish differently and that makes the surfaces reflect light differently.

There are several ways to tell which side is which. You can rub the surfaces with your hand—the loose or tension side will be rougher. Or you can look at the stuff, and generally the side that looks smoother is the tight or compression side, and it will have more sheen than the loose side. Neither of these methods is reliable, though. The best way to differentiate between the two sides is to bend the veneer and imitate what was happening to it when it came off the machine. With the tension side up, it will bend sharply without any audible or visible cracking. If you turn it over and do the same thing on the other side, you'll feel greater resistance and hear cracking. Thus the side that is less prone to bending is the compression side; the other is the tension side. —I.J.K.

Miniature log-house joint

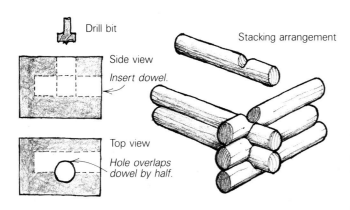

Drill bit

Stacking arrangement

Side view

Insert dowel.

Top view

Hole overlaps dowel by half.

This simple little jig makes joints on dowels or short tree branches for a miniature log house.

Choose a drill bit the same size as the dowels or sticks to be used in the house, then drill a block of wood from two sides, with the second hole overlapping half of the first. To use the jig, insert a dowel in the first hole and use the other as a guide for the drill bit. Note that the distance between the overlap and the end of the first hole will determine the overhang of the miniature logs, which assemble as shown in the sketch above. — *Gerald Robertson, Angus, Ont.*

Laminated mortise-and-tenon

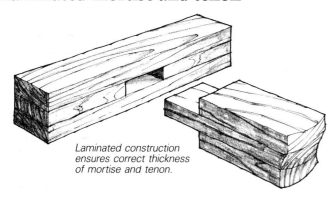

Laminated construction ensures correct thickness of mortise and tenon.

Laminating can eliminate tedious chopping and sawing when making mortise-and-tenon joints. Simply glue up the parts to be joined in three layers. Leave slots in the middle layer to form mortises and projections to form tenons.

There are several things to watch for. First, leave the tenon shoulders a little long and saw them off square after laminating—it is virtually impossible to line up the shoulders exactly when gluing. Use temporary spacer blocks to help hold the mortise dimensions during glue-up.

Because you use thinner stock, you save some wood with this method. You also get a near-guarantee of a perfect fit in the thickness, which is critical to joint strength. One additional advantage is the ease with which you can make the mortises fishtailed in shape by crosscutting the ends of the middle lamination at 5° or so. That way, the tenons can be wedged in the final assembly, yielding a strong, permanent joint.

— *Sam Bush, Portland, Ore.*

Routing spline slots in mitered frames

The simple jig shown in the sketch at right above is extremely useful for routing blind spline slots in spline-mitered frames. Nail or glue together scraps of the frame lumber into the configuration shown in the sketch. The workpiece should fit accurately into the slot, where it can be pinched in place with a clamp. A plunge router is desirable, both for ease of

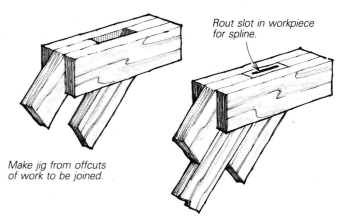

Rout slot in workpiece for spline.

Make jig from offcuts of work to be joined.

starting the cut and because it has a built-in fence for centering the slot. I imagine, however, that with a little courage a regular router would do—you could add an integral fence to the jig itself by tacking on more scraps, shimming them with cardboard where necessary. I scribed marks on the jig to show where to start and stop.

— *Jim Small, Newville, Pa.*

Cabinet latch

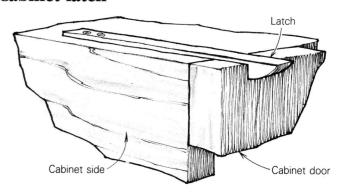

Latch

Cabinet side

Cabinet door

To make this handy latch for tool-cabinet doors, bandsaw the shape shown in the sketch from a 6-in. long, ¾-in. thick piece of springy hardwood, such as ash. Screw the latch to either the top or the side of the cabinet.

— *James F. Dupler, Jamestown, N.Y.*

Hammer-eye joint for chair spindles

The best way to join brace spindles to back bows in Windsor chairs is a hammer-eye joint, shown at right. This joint is tapered top and bottom, glued, and wedged from the top. Flare the bottom of the hole with a taper reamer and the top with a round file, taking care to enlarge the top hole only with

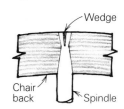

Wedge

Chair back

Spindle

the grain, so it will fit the elliptical shape of the wedge-expanded spindle. To taper the ends of the spindles, I use a "precision pencil sharpener" made from a rabbet plane

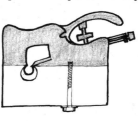

clamped or screwed to a block of wood, as shown at left. Drill a hole through the block and ream the hole at an angle, so the reamed edge is parallel to the surface of the block. Now plane down the block until about ¹⁄₁₆ in. of the hole is exposed. Screw or clamp a rabbet plane over the reamed part of the block so that the plane's blade will shave the spindles to shape. Run each spindle about ½ in. beyond the blade, so its tip will be round, ready for wedging, rather than tapered.

— *David Sawyer, E. Calais, Vt.*

Laying Veneer
Meeting the small shop's pressing needs

by Ian J. Kirby

Furnituremaking with solid wood is like whittling: you chip away at the tree until you end up with the pieces you need. Working veneer is just the reverse: you stick the bits together to build up furniture elements of the exact size and shape you want. This means you have to think about the work in a different way—you have to plan ahead instead of making dimensional decisions as you go along.

This difference in thinking is in fact the most difficult aspect of veneering. The work itself, the techniques, is well within the skills, tools and budget of the small-shop woodworker. And, you'll find that veneering has three distinct advantages for furnituremaking: you can make panels of any size; you can use woods of rare beauty; and, a design bonus unique with veneered panels based on dimensionally stable substrates, you don't have to allow for moisture-related wood movement, as you would with solid wood.

Any veneered panel is assembled from three components: a substrate or base material, some lipping or edge treatment, and the veneers themselves. Preparing the substrate is the first step, but this is relatively easy with ordinary woodworking tools and dimensionally stable medium-density fiberboard (MDF) or furniture-grade particleboard. For the photos to illustrate this article, I used a piece of ⅝-in. MDF about the size of a cabinet door or small tabletop, and glued a mitered lipping of solid wood onto its edges. This way, the edges can be radiused or shaped in some way, and the finished piece will have the look and feel of solid wood. (For an article on preparing substrates and attaching lippings, see pp. 86-89 of this volume.) Once you've glued on the lippings and planed them flush with the surfaces of the substrate, you're ready to apply the veneers.

Normally pieces of veneer are taped together to make sheets as wide as the panel. Veneers commonly are available in lengths up to 8 ft., so usually it's not difficult to find

A must-have for veneer work is a press to hold the veneers to the glued substrate while the glue cures. On Kirby's combination veneer press/woodworking bench, flat torsion boxes form the bed and top cauls; bar clamps and cambered battens apply the pressure.

pieces as long as your panel. For very long panels or for special effects, you can join several pieces to make strips as wide as the panel, then end-join the wide strips to make one long sheet. Veneers are easy to cut and join, so you have considerable design freedom here. Books on traditional veneering usually illustrate a variety of patterns, such as bookmatched mirror images or herringbone patterns, but these patterns are somewhat old hat and unnecessarily restrictive. You can match and join veneers in any way you like to create any type of pattern that appeals to you. The only rule for joining veneers is visual—what does it look like? Use your imagination. Experiment with combinations of grain directions and angles, with different species, and with bands, circles and other shaped inlays. Try aligning the grain or color of the veneer so that it accents the lines of the piece you're making.

No matter how much cutting and taping is done, the aim is to prepare a single veneer sheet that's no more than ½ in. larger all the way around than the panel to which it will be glued. A bigger overhang would just get in the way. Covering the entire panel at once enables you to make the veneer joints virtually invisible, without having to cope with glue squeeze-out between pieces, and to position the sheet accurately before placing the panel in the veneer press.

Both sides of the substrate must be veneered, usually at the same time; otherwise, the panel will be unbalanced and will invariably cup. The cupping results from a complex interaction of the glue, substrate and veneers, and from the shrinkage of

When crosscutting veneer, make two hard passes with a sharp knife, then press down on the straightedge while pulling the veneer up to break along the scoring (top photo). A veneer saw, guided against a board, is better for fragile veneers.

these components due to moisture changes. You should use a similar species and thickness of veneer on both sides of the panel to maintain a balance. Don't expect a thin, porous veneer to balance a thick, dense one.

For top-notch work, it's common to glue two layers of veneer on each side of the panel. The first veneer, the underlay, is usually an easily worked, mild species such as Honduras or African mahogany. This layer helps prevent the lippings from telegraphing through, and seems to give a richer, more solid feel to the work. Once the underlay has cured and been cleaned, it's covered with a show-wood veneer—anything from a burl or crotch to some exotic species such as ebony. Normally the top veneer is laid with its grain at right angles to that of the underlay veneer. If the top veneer and the underlay are different colors, lip the underlay with a 1-in. to 2-in. band of the top veneer, unless you want this color difference to highlight the edge.

With a fragile material such as burl or crotch veneer, it's common practice to reinforce the delicate material by gluing it onto a thick underlay veneer such as poplar. Those new to veneering should avoid very delicate materials, however, as well as old, cracked or washboard-like veneer, until they have mastered the techniques and gained more experience. There are ways to reconstitute badly buckled veneer, such as pressing it between damp layers of paper to flatten it, then slowly drying it to the proper moisture level, but these techniques can be troublesome and undependable. There are so many types of veneer readily available today, you can save yourself a lot of trouble by buying high-quality, flat veneer to begin with.

Other than conventional woodworking tools, all you'll need to begin veneering are a veneer press (see box, p. 95), a shooting board (see drawing, facing page), a glue roller and some veneer tape, which is available from most veneer suppliers. You could buy a veneer trimmer, which is a wooden knife-blade holder that looks like a handsaw handle, but a chisel and a knife work well to start with. A sharp knife (a Swiss Army knife is ideal) is good for cutting veneers, but for some hard and tough veneers, you might want a veneer saw, which has a barrel-shaped, serrated blade with no set. Oddly enough, this is also a handy tool for cutting very fragile veneer, such as burl.

Once you've assembled all your tools, you're ready to select, mark out and cut the veneers. To avoid damaging the workbench, cut on the wide surface of the shooting board. To crosscut veneer, hold the knife firmly against a metal straightedge (use the back for cutting to avoid damaging the accuracy of the chamfered edge), press hard as you cut, and chop down when you get to the second edge to prevent splintering. Make two hard passes, then break the scored veneer along the straightedge. The cut end will be slightly ragged, but that doesn't matter if it will be part of the waste overhang. If you want to join veneers end-to-end, however, knifing all the way through the veneer will produce a good joint line. It's rarely necessary to plane end grain.

When cutting along the grain, knife all the way through. Make light strokes, keeping the blade vertical and tight against the straightedge. These knifed edges are not good enough for a butt joint, so you'll have to true them with a jointer plane on the shooting board before you can tape them together.

If the veneer is mild and flat, you can plane up to a dozen

For butt joints, the sheets of veneer must be straight-edged. Hold the veneers in place on the shooting board while truing the edges with a jointer plane.

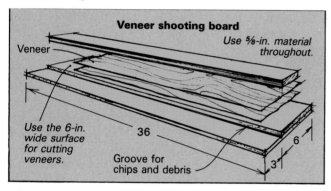

Veneer shooting board

Use ⅝-in. material throughout.

Veneer

Use the 6-in. wide surface for cutting veneers.

36

Groove for chips and debris

6

3

sheets at once; if it's anything but flat, two may be the limit. To use the shooting board, lay the plane on its side and position its sole ⅛ in. from the shoulder of the rabbet, then move the veneers to the sole. Line up a piece of wood with the rabbet shoulder and hold the veneers down by pressing hard on the top board. You'll be able to see only the top veneer, so you'll have to gauge from the shavings whether you're planing all the sheets. The amount of material removed is small, usually not enough to significantly affect bookmatching or any other pattern you're striving to achieve. When you think you've planed through all the chipouts and wavering edges, split the package apart and check the edges. If there isn't a good edge on each sheet, put the package back together and repeat the procedure.

If the edges look true, you can test the joint by putting two veneer edges together and using your fingers to press down the veneers as you check individual points along the joint. The points should come together perfectly, with no gaps. If the joint is tight at each checkpoint, it likely will be tight along its entire length. You may not be able to put the whole joint together at once, as you would with solid wood, because buckles in the veneer can distort the edges once the veneers are released from the shooting board. Pressing the edges flattens them out as they were on the shooting board.

If you're satisfied with the joint, you're ready to tape the veneers together. Veneer tape looks like brown packing tape, but it's much thinner and stronger. Don't use the thicker packing tape or masking tape, which can cause depressions in the veneer when it's pressed. Tape the top or face side only—

never put the tape between the veneer and the substrate, as the tape will show through and it may delaminate.

When taping, the joint is first pulled tight by strips of tape placed at right angles to the joint line. A single long strip placed over the joint helps hold the pieces together and prevents glue from oozing through during pressing. Tear the tape into 5-in. to 6-in. strips, which allows about 3 in. of tape on each side of the joint. Tear the tape—don't cut it—so that you have a feathered edge which is unlikely to mark the veneer. To join flat veneers, place the tape strips 9 in. apart; on buckled pieces, put them 2 in. to 3 in. apart, or as the material demands. First moisten the tape with a damp sponge—warm water on the sponge will make the glue grab a little better, which helps with oily woods such as teak. Attach one end of the tape to the first piece of veneer, pressing hard to make it stick. Then, holding the joint together with one hand, pull hard on the tape to stretch it slightly and attach it to the second veneer. After all the cross tapes are on, put a length of tape over the joint line, leaving the tape about ¼ in. to ½ in. short at each end so that you can check if the joint is tight. At this stage you could run a wooden roller over the tape strips to make sure they're secure. I've never found a

To temporarily join veneers into sheets, stretch pieces of veneer tape across the seams on the face side. The tape keeps the veneers from moving around in the press.

Finish the edges of the veneered panel with a jointer plane, after first trimming with a veneer trimmer, router or knife.

roller to be a vitally important tool, but it's something you should try for yourself.

There are two methods of applying veneer to the substrate: hammer-veneering by hand, or by using a veneer press. Hammer-veneering isn't really done with a hammer but with a squeegee-like tool that presses down the veneer onto a substrate covered with hot hide glue. The glue holds when it coalesces, and the trick is to be pressing on the veneer when the glue grabs. This isn't a skill that can be acquired on the first try, or even the second. Dealing with more than a few square feet of veneer compounds the problem—I think you will find a veneer press to be a much more efficient alternative.

If you use some form of press, any of the modern cold-curing glues work well. White PVA glue is cheaper than yellow glue, and it doesn't set up as quickly, so there is more time to prepare the panels. It will cure in the press in three to four hours, depending on temperature. Urea-formaldehyde glue (such as Weldwood Plastic Resin) can be used, although it takes at least five to six hours to cure at 65°F. Don't use contact cement—it is absolutely out of the question. Contact cement remains elastic and doesn't harden the way woodworking glues do. It is also more prone to attack by the solvents in some finishes.

With a paint roller, apply a thin, even coat of glue to the substrate only. Don't put glue on the veneer, or it will curl and be difficult to control. On a properly glued panel, only little beads of glue will be squeezed out all around the edges. If you apply too much glue, it will be pressed through the veneer's pores and the surface will be glazed. If this happens, the panel isn't ruined—the glue can be cleaned off, so it won't affect the finish—but it will take a lot of work planing, scraping and sanding to remove the glazing. Gauging the amount of glue required is a matter of experience. You'll find that different substrates will soak up different quantities of glue.

Place one sheet of veneer taped-side-down on the bench, and after covering one side of the substrate with glue, position it on the veneer. Apply glue to the second side of the substrate and place the second piece of veneer on it, taped side up.

If the joint line has to be centered, pencil a centerline on the edge of the substrate before you begin, then align your mark with the joint line. If precise alignment isn't important, position the veneer by gauging the overhang with your fingertips.

The panel must be placed in the press so that pressure first hits along the panel's centerline and then spreads out to the edges. The spreading pressure prevents glue from being trapped in the center of the panel. If excessive amounts of glue remain trapped in the center, the veneer can ripple.

When the panel is taken out of the press, the first thing to do is determine if there are any unglued areas. To check for bubbles, which are usually caused by a lack of glue, tap the panel with your fingernail—there'll be a change in tone where the veneer has lifted. To reattach the veneer, slit into the area with a thin-blade knife, ease in glue with the blade or a syringe, and clamp the section down.

The next step is to remove most of the excess veneer from the panel edges with a veneer trimmer, a trimming bit in a router, or a knife. The greater the excess overhang, the more difficult this process becomes. In any case, what you're trying to do here is to get close; the final edge is achieved by planing. If the edge is to be radiused or shaped, do it now.

At this point, the veneer tape should be removed. One way to do this is to moisten it, give the water about two to three minutes to soften the glue, and pull off the tape. Running an ordinary household iron over the moistened tape also makes it easier to remove. Be careful with water; don't use too much, and try to keep it on the tape so that it doesn't spread onto the veneer. Don't wash off the residual glue left by the tape—blot up excess water with paper towels as soon as the tape is removed and let the area dry before proceeding.

The final cleanup is done by planing, sanding or scraping, or a combination of the three. Careful use of a sharp, finely set jointer plane produces the best surface. Not all veneers will plane, however, and you can't make sweeping generalizations about which species can be planed. You'll have to experiment with each batch of veneer you use. If you sand from start to finish, start with 180-grit, followed by 220-, then

Bench-pressing veneer

A veneer press must have an extremely flat bed and some system for selectively applying pressure to a panel. The press I've designed, and for which I have applied for a patent, uses three torsion boxes: one acts as the bed of the press and the other two are movable cauls that go over the veneer assembly before it's pressed. The torsion boxes are made by gluing fiberboard skins over core strips on 7½-in. centers; the voids between the strips are filled with resin-coated-paper honeycomb. A torsion box is very flat, stable and strong. (For more on building torsion boxes, see *FWW* #32, pp. 96-102.)

Pressure is applied to the veneered panel with a series of clamps and cambered battens (detail A). The cambered side of each batten is oriented toward the panel. One batten is placed on top of the caul, another is placed under the bed, directly below the top batten, and the clamps on each end are tightened. Because the battens are cambered, they transfer the pressure from the center first to the outside edges as the clamps are tightened in unison.

Place the panels in the center of the press on a platen, a ⅛-in. thick fiberboard plate treated with wax so that residual glue can be removed. The veneer and substrate assembly must be in the middle of the platen and sandwiched between it and a second platen. Now add the top caul and battens. It's easy to assess how close to put the battens. As shown in detail B, clamping pressure is diffused in a fan of about 90° from the clamp head. Use enough clamps to ensure that the pressure fans overlap. If both top cauls are used with the bench shown here, ten battens are needed: five on the top and five on the bottom. (For more on pressure fans, see *FWW* #31, pp. 86-89.)

Once the battens are in place, tighten the clamps enough to put a little pressure on the battens. By looking at the gaps between the battens and caul on each side of the centerline, you can make sure you're applying pressure equally. Continue to tighten the clamps on each side until you see the battens flatten out over the area being pressed. You can sense the same amount of pressure coming through the clamp bars.

Don't overtighten the clamps, especially if the panel you're veneering is narrow. If overtightened, the caul will bend around the edges of the panel and leave an area of low pressure or no pressure in the panel center. The glue will migrate to the low-pressure area and the veneer will ripple as it dries. To avoid this washboard center, use a straight-edge to check the top edge of the caul to make sure it doesn't become convex as you tighten the clamps. Also, when pressing narrow panels, place dry spacers the same thickness as the veneered panel on each side of the panel to help prevent the caul from bending. —I.J.K.

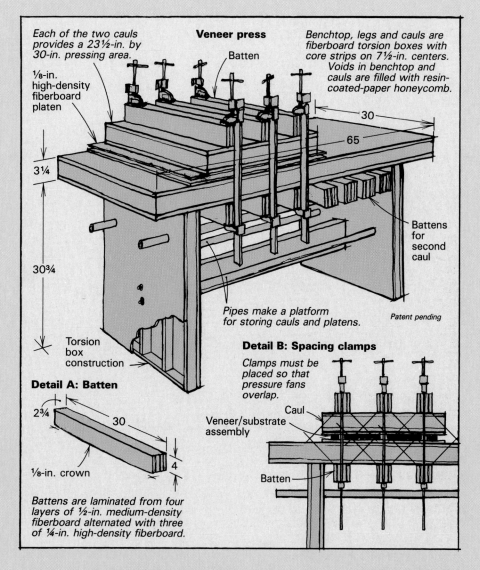

Each of the two cauls provides a 23½-in. by 30-in. pressing area.

⅛-in. high-density fiberboard platen

Veneer press

Batten

Benchtop, legs and cauls are fiberboard torsion boxes with core strips on 7½-in. centers. Voids in benchtop and cauls are filled with resin-coated-paper honeycomb.

3¼

30

65

30¾

Battens for second caul

Torsion box construction

Pipes make a platform for storing cauls and platens.

Patent pending

Detail A: Batten

2¾

30

4

⅛-in. crown

Battens are laminated from four layers of ½-in. medium-density fiberboard alternated with three of ¼-in. high-density fiberboard.

Detail B: Spacing clamps

Clamps must be placed so that pressure fans overlap.

Caul

Veneer/substrate assembly

Batten

300- or 400-grit. Avoid wet-or-dry paper—the dark abrasives can cause unsightly smudges on light woods. Be careful when sanding, especially near the edges. An awful lot of bad things happen when people let loose with a sanding block or a power sander. Check the edges frequently with a straightedge to make sure you aren't softening or rounding the area 1 in. to 2 in. from the edges. Rounding the edges with a sander is the hallmark of the careless. It shows dramatically once the work has been polished as a lack of crispness and cleanness. It's not easy to describe—it's just a sloppy look about the whole thing. The scraper, to me, is the crudest of cutters—it's difficult to scrape without marking the veneer wherever the scraper is put down or taken off the panel.

Any finish can be used on veneered panels, but the solvents used in the finish may attack the glue. The first coat of finish should be applied sparingly, especially if you're using polyurethane or another material with a great deal of solvent. Applying one or two thin coats creates a barrier against solvents. After the thin coats, proceed as you would with solid wood.   □

Ian J. Kirby is a designer, cabinetmaker and educator. He operates a woodworking school in Cumming, Ga. See pp. 86-89 for his article on preparing substrates. For more on hammer-veneering, see FWW #10, pp. 52-54.

Laying Plastic Laminates
Understanding the basics of this ubiquitous "veneer"

by Jack Gavin

Let me say, before any purists dash off angry letters to the editor, that I don't consider plastic laminates to be fine woodwork. As a custom cabinetmaker, however, I've laid miles of the stuff, and for every solid cherry secretary or walnut armoire I do, I am offered ten Formica kitchens. So knowledge of the skills has become an economic necessity. Also, a lot of furnituremakers are discovering that new laminate products and techniques add a colorful dimension to their work.

Plastic laminates had their beginning at the turn of the century when Dr. Leo Bakeland, a Belgian scientist, invented Bakelite, the first plastic. Bakeland offered his invention to the Westinghouse Company as an electrical insulator, but Westinghouse wasn't interested. A young Westinghouse chemist named Dan O'Connor, however, impregnated paper and cloth with Bakeland's resin and formed his own company in Cincinnati, Ohio. He called the new product and the company Formica: "for mica," since mica was the premium insulator of the day.

Formica was originally used for such diverse products as radio vacuum-tube bases and gears for the Model-T Ford. In the late 1930s, the idea of laminating a thin surface of this abrasion-resistant plastic to counters and tabletops was tried. After World War II, the idea caught on and grew into a multi-million dollar industry.

Plastic laminates are made of six or less layers of kraft paper (depending on the thickness) that are impregnated with phenolic resin (Bakelite), and then covered with a sheet of colored or patterned paper and sealed with a layer of melamine plastic. Although "Formica" has become the generic name for decorative plastic laminates, there are a number of other laminate manufacturers besides the Formica Corp. Nevamar, Wilsonart, Lamin-Art, and Melamite are some of the many different brands, each a quality product. I've seen 30-year-old countertops that were beginning to wear through, showing a brown tone from the kraft paper beneath, but you can expect an even longer life than that from the modern surfaces, provided that they are well cemented to the proper core material (see box, p. 98).

Laminates come imprinted with simulated wood grain, simulated stone, stripes, grids, raised designs and a seemingly infinite variety of colors. Prices range from 60¢ per sq. ft. to about $3.50 per sq. ft., depending on brand and design. Each company has color charts and makes boxes of samples of their different varieties, and a supplier will be happy to give you one of these for the brand he carries. Plastic laminates are usually stocked in widths up to 5 ft. and in lengths up to 12 ft. Instead of asking your supplier what he's got, tell him what size you need and he'll probably have something close to it, or he can order it for you. You also have a choice of two thicknesses, $\frac{1}{16}$-in. and $\frac{1}{32}$-in., called horizontal and vertical grade, respectively. Use horizontal grade whenever possible—particularly on surfaces subject to abrasion. Vertical grade is cheaper, and is good for curved surfaces, but it will show core irregularities on flat surfaces. Some laminates come with a plastic film over the surface. Leave it on until the job is done—it's there to protect the surface from your tools.

Visually check each sheet for damage. Unlike wood, scratched plastic laminate cannot be fixed. The sheets can be transported flat in a truck, or rolled and tied. If you roll a sheet, make sure you tape the inside edge to prevent the laminate from scratching itself as it is unrolled.

Seams where edges join can be filled with a product called Seamfil, available from laminate suppliers. It's a lacquer-

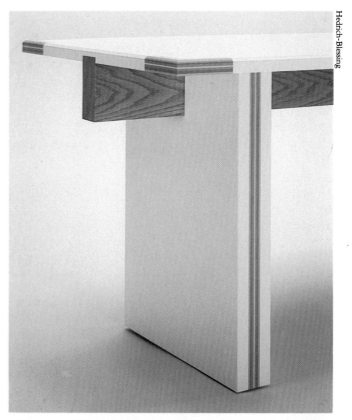

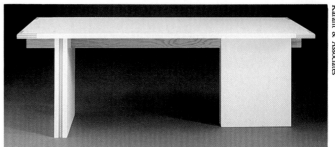

New laminates, such as Formica's ColorCore, offer decoration beyond the usual wood-surface treatments. This table, designed by Milton Glaser, is detailed with ColorCore epoxied into a multicolored sandwich and then sliced into thin ribbons.

based compound that dries very quickly. It comes with color charts that tell how to mix an exact match to whatever color plastic laminate you buy. A filled seam never looks as good as a single piece, however, and Seamfil won't fix scratches.

Cement—The standard glue for plastic laminates is contact cement, and several types are sold by stores that sell laminates. Contact cements have a bad reputation for gluing wood to wood, but when one of the materials is stable and nonporous, as plastic laminate is, contact cement forms a permanent bond. These cements are neoprene rubber dissolved in various solvents. Spread on both surfaces and allowed to dry, the rubber coatings stick to each other when the sheets are pressed together. For all-around use, I recommend the regular industrial grade.

A word of warning here. Industrial contact cement is *extremely* flammable, so much so that if the vapors are allowed to collect in a small room, something as insignificant as a cigarette or a pilot light can ignite them explosively. Work in a well-ventilated area, and even so, *always* wear an organic-vapor mask. The solvents in industrial contact cement are the same as in airplane glue, and we all know the effects of sniffing that. Some suppliers may refuse to sell industrial cements to amateurs, or may carry them only in commercial-size 5-gal. pails. If that's the case (it may even be the law in your area), then use whatever cement you can get. In any event, heed the label, both for safety warnings and for application instructions. Hardware-store cement is less explosive than industrial cement, and there's a nonflammable latex-based contact cement, too, but it takes significantly longer to dry. Otherwise, all types are worked the same way.

One type of cement is specially formulated for use in spray guns, but spraying isn't practical except for large production shops—you can spend up to $3,000 just for the gear.

Cutting laminates—I cut most of my plastic laminate on a tablesaw, using a triple-chip blade. So the material won't slip under the fence, I tape a strip of ¼-in. plywood or hardboard to the table next to the fence and run the laminate over it. The laminate sheets must be cut slightly larger than the piece they'll be laid upon, say, ⅛ in. oversize all around. They'll be trimmed flush after application.

The tablesaw gives the quickest and most precise cut, but a plastic scribe or tinsnips work, too. To cut with a scribe, mark the face side and score repeatedly, then crack with the scoreline over a table edge. The break will run diagonally through the thickness of the sheet, so leave the sheet about ⅜ in. to ½ in. oversize in all directions. Tinsnips leave small cracks perpendicular to the cut, requiring a ½-in. allowance.

Order of events—We'll go into detail as things come up, but here's the general plan for, say, a countertop. First, trim the core to its final size. Then cut a big piece of plastic laminate for the top surface and narrow strips for all the core edges you plan to laminate. Remember to cut the laminate slightly oversize. Next, apply cement to both of the core's long edges and to the laminate strips that will cover them, taking care to keep cement off adjacent surfaces and edges. Laminate the long edges and trim the surplus flush. Follow the same procedure for the short edges. Finally, cement the top piece and trim it flush. If the job calls for a splashboard, laminate it as a separate piece and attach it later. For structural pieces such as

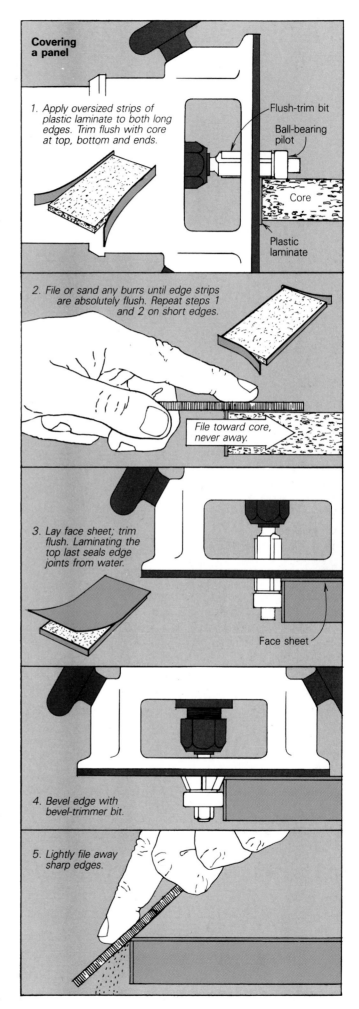

Covering a panel

1. Apply oversized strips of plastic laminate to both long edges. Trim flush with core at top, bottom and ends.

Flush-trim bit
Ball-bearing pilot
Core
Plastic laminate

2. File or sand any burrs until edge strips are absolutely flush. Repeat steps 1 and 2 on short edges.

File toward core, never away.

3. Lay face sheet; trim flush. Laminating the top last seals edge joints from water.

Face sheet

4. Bevel edge with bevel-trimmer bit.

5. Lightly file away sharp edges.

Tricks, tips, cores and new products

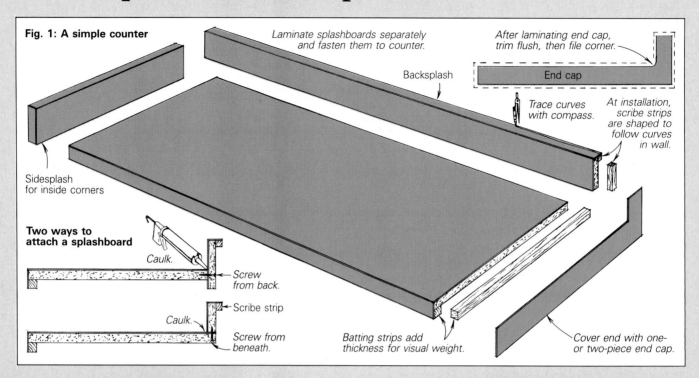

Fig. 1: A simple counter

Laminate splashboards separately and fasten them to counter.

After laminating end cap, trim flush, then file corner.

End cap

Backsplash

Trace curves with compass.

At installation, scribe strips are shaped to follow curves in wall.

Sidesplash for inside corners

Two ways to attach a splashboard

Caulk.

Screw from back.

Scribe strip

Caulk.

Screw from beneath.

Batting strips add thickness for visual weight.

Cover end with one- or two-piece end cap.

You can lay plastic laminate on almost any stable core. Solid wood, of course, moves too much, so you'll want man-made materials. For cabinet doors and drawer faces, I prefer medium-density fiberboard because it doesn't warp. Thickness can be either ⅝ in. or ¾ in. A ¾-in. door with 1/16-in. laminate on both sides turns out ⅞ in. thick, which may look a little clunky. For the cabinets themselves, I often use hardwood plywood, because it holds hinge screws better, but I wouldn't use it for any unsupported surfaces.

Countertops can be either ¾-in. plywood or fiberboard. There's a tradeoff—fiberboard is my first choice, because it's suitably ''dead'' (you don't want a counter to be resonant or springy), but it's heavy. If I'm going to have to carry a 12-ft. countertop up three flights of stairs, you can bet it'll be plywood instead. Whichever material you use, screw or glue a batting strip to the edge of your counter so that the finished edge will be 1 in. to 1½ in. thick (figure 1).

Edges can be covered with laminate or decorated with wood trim milled to any shape that suits your fancy, as in figure 2. Plastic or rubber T-molding, slipped into a kerf cut in the panel's edge, is also a good edge treatment. One source of T-molding is Outwater Plastics, 99 President St., Passaic, N.J. 07055.

I've never had any luck trying to lay new laminate over old. On one job a while ago, we tried to cover a curved surface with laminate, then cover that with another sheet of laminate that was

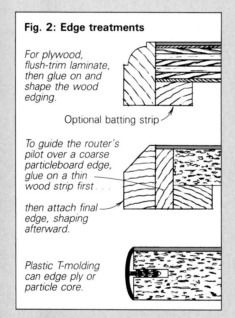

Fig. 2: Edge treatments

For plywood, flush-trim laminate, then glue on and shape the wood edging.

Optional batting strip

To guide the router's pilot over a coarse particleboard edge, glue on a thin wood strip first . . .

then attach final edge, shaping afterward.

Plastic T-molding can edge ply or particle core.

itself covered with rift-maple veneer. *Everything* delaminated. We did the whole job over, using epoxy.

Laminates make fine wall coverings, too—have you ever taken a good look at the inside of an elevator? You can bond sheets directly to sheetrock, but I generally cover both sides of ½-in. particleboard and hang these panels on Z-clips (special hardware that allows the panels to be lifted off the walls when necessary).

ColorCore is a new (albeit expensive) Formica Corp. product that's the same color all the way through. Hence there's no dark line at the joints, and a careful workman can make an apparently seamless job. But ColorCore is less forgiving

of joint irregularities, and may show contact-cement lines, too. White glue is the recommended adhesive, because it dries clear, but you have to clamp down the laminate until the glue cures. With a sharp bit, you can rout shallow decorative patterns into the surface, and, by laying different colors atop each other, bevel panel edges into multicolored stripe designs. Laminate suppliers also have a variety of other new ''designer'' products. At the rate things are developing, your shop could end up first-on-the-block without half trying.

Many types of plastic laminates can be heated and cemented around narrow curves, forming a permanent bend upon cooling. Such ''postformed'' work has been around a long time. Everybody has seen single-sheet countertops that begin with a rolled front edge which sweeps across the counter and up the splashboard. Most postforming is done in factories, but the technique is feasible for a small shop and limited production, too. The Formica Corp. will send a detailed bulletin on the process if you ask—the low-end investment in equipment is less than $400.

The Formica Corp.'s Information Center (114 Mayfield Ave., Edison, N.J. 08837) distributes numerous other technical bulletins, including a how-to guide. If you outline your project to them in a letter, they'll send relevant bulletins and color charts. Formica's technical specialist, Walter T. Davis, will give advice about tricky jobs over the phone at (513) 786-3048. —*J.G.*

countertops, you don't have to laminate both sides, but other parts, such as doors, require it or they will warp.

Spreading cement—Apply contact cement with a brush, a roller or a glue-spreader, spreading it as thinly as possible. Globs dry slowly and will cause a bump when the laminate is laid down. Take care to keep the area clean, because sawdust or chips that get caught in the glue will ruin the bond and are maddening to remove. The surface of the cement should dry evenly glossy. Edges of plywood, particleboard or fiberboard should have at least three coats, each applied after the previous coat has dried. Even on faces, it's a good idea to put a second coat in a 2-in. band around the perimeter.

For applying cement to narrow or tight areas, use a small brush with natural bristles (nylon will dissolve). It costs less to throw cheap brushes away than to buy enough solvent to clean decent ones. If you are edging a few similarly sized pieces, you can stack them and apply glue to the whole stack at once, which helps keep the faces free of cement. I've used a natural-bristle scrub brush for large areas such as countertops, but they are more easily done with a roller. Regular paint rollers will dissolve, but "high-solvent" roller sleeves, designed for spreading epoxy resins, work well. These are available wherever plastic laminates are sold. I prefer a roller with a short nap, rather than a knobby one. If you want a small roller for edges and tight spots, you can bandsaw the regular length into smaller pieces.

The cement should dry in 15 to 30 minutes, and remain ready-to-stick for a couple of hours. Don't wait too long, though, because the cement gradually loses its adhesiveness. The spread cement is ready when it is dry to the touch and has returned to room temperature. If the surface feels cool, it is still losing solvents and should be allowed to dry further.

Applying the laminate—Once the contact-cemented surfaces touch each other, they will stick, so you must be very careful to align the pieces before contact. This is relatively easy with edges and small pieces, but with larger panels it is best to lay out thin sticks—venetian-blind slats, dowels or something similar—about 12 in. apart on top of the panel, and then lay the laminate on top of them. Make sure these sticks are clean and splinter-free, because anything that gets caught underneath the laminate will cause a bump in the surface. Once the laminate has been centered over the panel, remove the sticks one at a time, consecutively, and press the laminate down. Work from one end, so as not to trap air bubbles, and progress down the length of the counter. When all the sticks are out (be sure to get them all), press the laminate down with a rubber mallet, a padded block and a hammer, or a hard roller called a J-roller—suppliers sell them.

Personally, I don't use sticks anymore. With the help of an assistant, I align one long edge and let the panel drop, an action similar to closing a book. It's a neat trick, but it requires some skill, so I wouldn't suggest it for beginners.

When making a lot of interior partitions, or a set of colored drawer bottoms, you can save a lot of trimming time by laminating an entire sheet of plastic laminate to the core material first, then tablesawing the pieces to size. To eliminate chipping while cutting, laminate only one side and run the panel through the tablesaw face-up. Then cover the other side of each piece and trim as usual. If you want to put laminate on the inside of a cabinet, be sure to do it before you assemble the cabinet. This will save you many, many hours of grief.

Moisture may cause delamination. Plan edges and joints so that water will run off, rather than into the seam. When installing a sink, most good workmen take pains to seal the core by applying a strip of laminate around the edges of the hole, in addition to caulking the rim of the sink.

Once applied, laminates can be removed, though the procedure is messy and time-consuming. Lift an edge slightly with a chisel and apply solvent. You can gradually remove the laminate without breaking it. Methyl ethyl ketone (known as MEK and sold in paint stores) will dissolve flammable cements, but it is flammable itself and it won't soften nonflammable cements; 1-1-1 trichloroethane works on both kinds of cement, and won't burn. But wear your vapor mask and gloves in any case, as both solvents are nasty. When dry, the laminate and panel can be reglued and reattached.

Trimming—Once the laminate has adhered, it must be trimmed flush with the core. The best tool is a router with a flush-trim bit, that is, a ½-in. straight carbide bit with a ball-bearing pilot on the end. This allows you to use the core itself as a guide. Don't try a bit with a steel pilot—it's guaranteed to burn the plastic surface. If you plan a lot of laminating, it's worth having a small, one-handed router called a laminate trimmer. The ease of use it affords is well worth its $100 price tag. When using a router, wear goggles or a face shield to protect your eyes from laminate chips.

To trim an edge, hold the router horizontal and guide the pilot bearing along the face of the core, keeping the router's base square against the edge. The objective is to cut the edge strip exactly even with the face, so the face sheet will overlap it without gaps. Chances are, you'll need to do some filing, because flush-trim bits often cut slightly oversize, especially if they've been sharpened more than once. File toward the core to prevent chipping. I use a smooth file for narrow edges and, when I have the room, a belt sander. You can do the entire trimming job with these tools if you don't have a router.

When routing, it's important to keep the bearing free of plastic chips and cement. WD-40 will help dissolve any glue that binds in the bearing, and a few drops of light oil will keep it rolling. If a bearing clogs tight, try soaking it in solvent to restore it. A clogged bearing will burn a ¼-in. wide swath across whatever surface it is riding on, so a little preventive maintenance is a good idea. For extra insurance on really glossy surfaces, you can run a line of masking tape for the bearing to ride on. In a pinch, you can try to clean up a burned surface with 400-grit wet-or-dry sandpaper, but it will never look the same as before, even if you lacquer it to restore the shine. It's best to replace the piece.

When all the laminating is done, clean off excess glue with MEK or lacquer thinner. The edges should be square and sharp. To give the edges a finished look, use a bevel trimmer, which is similar to a flush-trim bit, but cuts a chamfer instead of a square edge. Bevel trimmers come in various angles: 15° and 22° are standard, and even 45° can be used. The greater the angle, the more the inner layer of the laminate will show on the top surface, sometimes desirable for contrast or to make the plastic laminate look thicker. In any case, a smooth file relieves sharp edges left by the router. □

Jack Gavin is a cabinetmaker and furnituremaker in New York City.

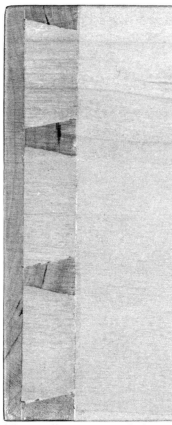

The small, conventional drawer and five shallow trays in Frid's compact, knockdown drawing table provide plenty of storage, and illustrate the basic drawermaking techniques that you can apply to any kind of furniture.

How to Make Drawers
Design for drawing table illustrates the principles

by Tage Frid

About twenty years ago, when I first started teaching at the Rhode Island School of Design, I was commissioned to make drawing tables for the school dormitories. The tables were to be plain and inexpensive, yet sturdy and able to withstand abuse. Because dormitory rooms are small, each table had to be space-efficient. This last requirement made the tables a good exercise in an important cabinetmaking skill— designing and building drawers.

When I design a piece with drawers, I first consider what will be put in them. This helps determine how I will build both the carcase (the body of the cabinet into which the drawers go) and the drawers, and of what materials. The overall size of the drawing table described in this article (see plans, p. 106), which is an improved version of the one I made twenty years ago, is based on standard sizes of drafting paper and parallel rulers. For storing big sheets of paper and finished drawings, I wanted an open compartment below the

adjustable drawing surface. For odds and ends, I added a drawer to the right of the space where your knees go. For instruments, pencils and pens, I also included some shallow trays that slide in grooves milled inside the carcase.

Once I had decided on the drawer and trays, I worked out the construction details for the carcase. There are three basic ways to make a carcase that will contain drawers: with glued-up solid wood, or with a frame-and-panel system, or with cabinet-grade plywood. I used plywood for my drawing table because it's good for knockdown joinery, and because it's simple and fast to work with. Lately, though, I've been using more and more solid wood for my furniture because I can do more with it, such as shaping, carving and bending. Of course, solid wood shrinks and swells with the seasons, so you must account for this in your drawer-hanging. A frame-and-panel carcase, with a solid or plywood panel, isolates most of the wood movement, but it limits your shaping choices, and

Photos: Roger Birn; drawings: Lee Hov

complicates the joinery and drawer-hanging.

There are several ways to hang a drawer. When I was an apprentice in Denmark, I learned the method shown in figure 1, which is the one I used for the top drawer of my drawing table and in all of my best furniture. The drawer slides in and out of the carcase on two horizontal members called runners, which fit into grooves milled in the sides of the carcase. At the front of the carcase, the drawer rests on a stretcher or a rail, which also ties together the front edges of the carcase and provides a surface to which drawer stops can be glued. For a drawer to work correctly, it must have some sort of guide to keep it from tilting down when it is pulled out. This guide, which bears against the top edges of the drawer sides, is usually called a kicker. In a chest of drawers, the bottom edge of the runner above acts as a kicker. The top drawer usually kicks against the inside of the carcase top, but in some cases (my drawing table is one) you have to install a separate kicker because the carcase doesn't have a top, or because the top is too far above the drawer to act as a kicker.

This method, called bottom-hanging (figure 1A), is good for almost any kind of furniture, whether plywood or solid. The runners are very strong and will carry the weight of a drawer filled with heavy objects. If lubricated with paraffin and made of a hardwood, such as oak or maple, the runners (and drawer sides) will last a long time. The big disadvantage is that to work right, a bottom-hung drawer must fit snugly, making it liable to stick in humid weather.

A drawer can also slide on runners that ride in grooves in the drawer sides, as in figure 1B. You don't need stretchers and kickers for each drawer, but you do need to tie a big carcase together with at least one front rail in the middle to keep the sides from bowing outward. Side-hanging is best for small, light drawers, such as in writing desks and jewelry boxes. I wouldn't use it in a chest of drawers or a kitchen cabinet, though, because the sliding surfaces are small and they would wear out pretty fast.

Some people think that metal runners (figure 1C) are used only in cheap factory furniture, but for heavy drawers, such as a desk file drawer or a kitchen-cabinet flour bin, I prefer them. Good-quality metal ball-bearing runners will support a heavier drawer than wood will, and some kinds allow the drawer to be fully extended so you can get what's in the back without removing the drawer. These runners last forever, and they never stick, no matter what the weather. Always buy your runners—or any hardware, for that matter—before you make the piece. Some types of runners require a drawer that is 1 in. narrower than the carcase opening; others need 1½-in. clearance. Nothing is more frustrating than to build a piece, only to find that the hardware you want to use won't work.

Getting started—If you want drawers that fit well, you have to take your time and make an accurate carcase. My drawing table consists of a permanently joined plywood carcase which holds the drawer and trays. To this, I attached (with knock-down fasteners) the panels that form the sides, the back, the storage compartment, and the shelf under the drawing surface. A really fine carcase should be made about ¹⁄₃₂ in. wider at the back than at the front so that the drawer action won't stiffen up from increasing friction as the drawer is pushed in. There are a couple of ways to do this. If your carcase is solid wood, you can join it up square and hand-plane a few shavings off the thickness of the back inside third of each carcase

Fig. 1: Drawer-hanging methods

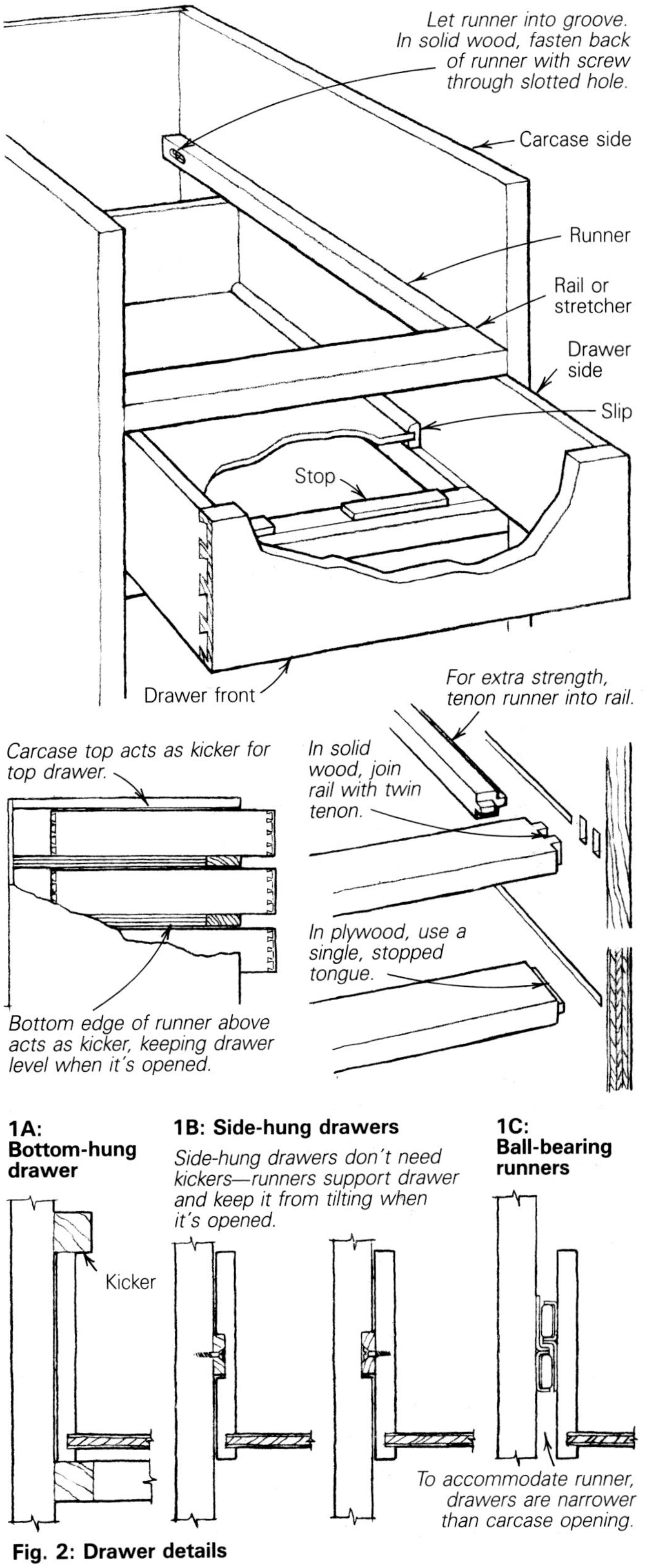

Let runner into groove. In solid wood, fasten back of runner with screw through slotted hole.

Carcase side

Runner

Rail or stretcher

Drawer side

Slip

Stop

Drawer front

For extra strength, tenon runner into rail.

Carcase top acts as kicker for top drawer.

In solid wood, join rail with twin tenon.

In plywood, use a single, stopped tongue.

Bottom edge of runner above acts as kicker, keeping drawer level when it's opened.

1A: Bottom-hung drawer

Kicker

1B: Side-hung drawers

Side-hung drawers don't need kickers—runners support drawer and keep it from tilting when it's opened.

1C: Ball-bearing runners

To accommodate runner, drawers are narrower than carcase opening.

Fig. 2: Drawer details

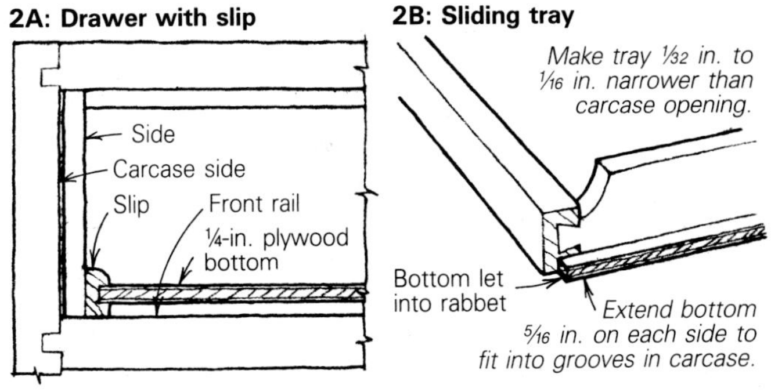

2A: Drawer with slip

Side

Carcase side

Slip Front rail

¼-in. plywood bottom

2B: Sliding tray

Make tray ¹⁄₃₂ in. to ¹⁄₁₆ in. narrower than carcase opening.

Bottom let into rabbet

Extend bottom ⁵⁄₁₆ in. on each side to fit into grooves in carcase.

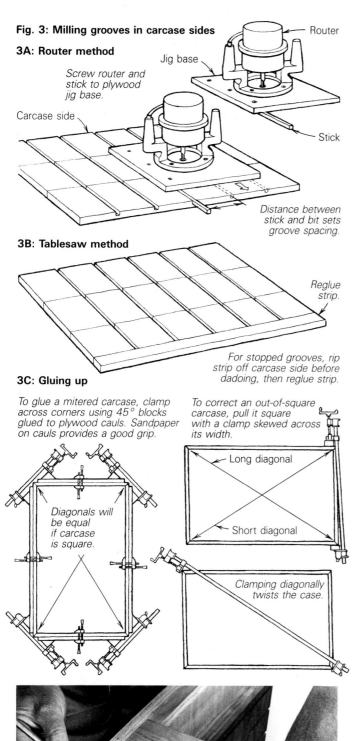

Fig. 3: Milling grooves in carcase sides

3A: Router method

Screw router and stick to plywood jig base.

Router

Jig base

Carcase side

Stick

Distance between stick and bit sets groove spacing.

3B: Tablesaw method

Reglue strip.

For stopped grooves, rip strip off carcase side before dadoing, then reglue strip.

3C: Gluing up

To glue a mitered carcase, clamp across corners using 45° blocks glued to plywood cauls. Sandpaper on cauls provides a good grip.

Diagonals will be equal if carcase is square.

To correct an out-of-square carcase, pull it square with a clamp skewed across its width.

Long diagonal

Short diagonal

Clamping diagonally twists the case.

For a perfect fit, Frid fits the drawer parts individually before he assembles them, first trimming the drawer front to a tight fit in the carcase opening. If the drawer front's length can't be scribed from inside the case, mark it directly from outside.

side before final assembly. Or, in solid wood or plywood, you can cut each end of the carcase top and bottom slightly out of square. An article in *FWW* #21, pp. 73-76, tells more about this type of carcase construction.

The drawing table has only one drawer, so I didn't bother making my carcase wider at the back. I cut the parts I needed out of a sheet of ¾-in. veneer-core cherry plywood, squaring each panel carefully and joining the carcase with tongue-and-groove joints. Where the raw edges of the plywood would be exposed, I glued on a ¼-in. thick by ⅞-in. strip of solid cherry, planing it flush with the plywood and sanding it after the glue had dried.

Next I cut the grooves for the solid-oak drawer runners and the sliding trays. This step is a critical part of making the carcase—the runners (and so the grooves) must be square to the front edges of the carcase and spaced the same distance apart on both carcase sides. Some people mount the drawer runners in a sliding dovetail joint, which is stronger. But it's a lot of extra work, and since the load is all downward, you don't really need that much strength. You could avoid grooves altogether by screwing the runners directly to the carcase, though this method isn't as accurate. For the trays, I decided to make lots of grooves relatively close together so that there would be maximum flexibility in tray arrangement.

The grooves can be crosscut with a dado blade in the tablesaw, or with a router, using the jig shown in figure 3A. I usually use the router because it's easier for an old guy like me, and if I don't want the grooves to show at the front edge of the carcase, I can stop them short. If you use the tablesaw, be sure to mill each pair of mating grooves in both carcase sides before you change the fence setting. Figure 3B shows how to stop a tablesawn groove.

If I were making a chest of drawers, I'd cut the joints for the front rails at this point. In solid wood, I'd join the rails to the sides with a twin tenon, as shown in figure 1. I usually mill the twin mortises with a router. Then, with a marking gauge, I lay out the tenons on the rail and cut them (by hand or on the tablesaw) to a tight fit. A rail can be joined to plywood with a tongue that stops short of the front edge of the carcase, so it won't be seen. For extra strength, you can tenon the runner into the back edge of the rail.

Assembling the carcase comes next. A tongue-and-grooved plywood carcase, such as my drawing table, is easy to glue up with clamps and battens. When I'm joining solid wood, I usually use dovetails or splined miters. If they fit right, dovetails don't need to be clamped at all. You just put some glue on and tap them home. Miters should be clamped across the corners, or else the pressure of the clamps might distort the case. I use the clamping fixture shown in figure 3C, and I check the carcase for square by measuring diagonally from corner to corner. If both diagonals measure the same, it's okay. Don't try to correct an out-of-square carcase by clamping the corners diagonally, or else you'll twist it. Instead, clamp across the width of the carcase, with the clamp angled slightly to pull in the long corner.

When the carcase comes out of the clamps, you can install the drawer runners. Plane or sand them smooth first, otherwise the little ripples left by machine-planing will make your drawers noisy. Because the drawing-table carcase is plywood, which won't shrink and swell, you can glue the runners right in, all the way across. If the sides of your piece are solid wood, runners should be glued only at the very front.

Fitting the drawer—Getting a wooden drawer to work like it's gliding on ball bearings is not all that difficult if you take the time to do it right. The trick is to fit the drawer *before* you make it. First, rough-mill all the drawer parts you will need. I like to use maple, oak, cherry and walnut for drawer parts. Pine and poplar are too soft. For drawer sides higher than 10 in., ½-in. Baltic birch plywood is good because it is less liable to warp. I make the sides and backs of small drawers ⅜ in. thick, and their fronts ⅝ in. thick. Larger drawers should have ½-in. sides and backs, with ¾-in. fronts.

The drawer front should be fitted first. Cut the wood to width so that it will just about go into the opening, then finish the fit with a hand plane. Now cut the front to length: Square one end (if it isn't already) and fit it into the opening, then mark the other end by scribing the back of the drawer front from inside the case. Cut it a hair long at first, then trim it to fit. If for some reason you can't reach inside, mark the length by holding the front outside the case, as shown in the photo on the facing page. The drawer front should fit so snugly that it can be just pushed in halfway. Mark and cut the drawer back exactly the same length as the front, but make the width less, to leave space for the drawer bottom to slide in and also to allow a little space to make fitting easier later on. I usually make the back about ¾ in. narrower than the front.

Fit the drawer sides the same way as you did the front, by planing the width until they will just slide in snugly. Crosscut the back ends square, then push the drawer sides back as far as you want them to go. Drawer sides should not go all the way to the back of a solid-wood carcase because when the carcase sides shrink, the drawer will pop out a little. Also, I don't like to stop a drawer against the back of the carcase unless I have to—it sounds clunky. I allow about ¼ in. between the back of the drawer and the carcase. One way to make sure the clearance is right is to place a scrap shim temporarily against the case back as you push the sides in.

When the drawer front, back and both sides have been fitted, the drawer is ready to be assembled. But before I do that, I mark the parts as shown in figure 4.

Assembling the drawer—The traditional joint for a drawer is a half-blind dovetail at the front and a through dovetail at the back. Other joints will do, but they aren't as strong. The box on p. 104 shows some examples. Some craftsmen use solid wood for drawer bottoms, but I think that ¼-in. hardwood plywood is better. It's more than strong enough and quite stable. Although it doesn't really matter, running the grain of the bottom in the same direction as that of the front looks nicest. In my best furniture, I mount the bottom in grooved strips, called drawer slips, which are glued inside each drawer after assembly, as shown in figure 5. This technique allows me to work with thin drawer sides, which are better-looking, and still leave a wide wearing surface for the drawer to slide on. To prevent the bottom from sagging in really wide drawers, use thicker plywood, or make the bottom in two pieces and support it with a rail down the middle of the drawer.

Normally, I put slips only on the sides, letting the bottom into a groove cut in the drawer front. But on my drawing table, the finger pull routed in the bottom edge of the drawer front would have exposed the groove, so I glued a slip on at the front as well. For quick drawers in kitchen cabinets, I just mill a groove directly in the drawer sides and fronts. Cut the grooves before you lay out your joints, so a groove

The drawer sides should be made equally snug, then trimmed to a length that will stop them from banging against the back of the carcase.

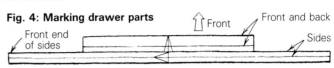

Fig. 4: Marking drawer parts

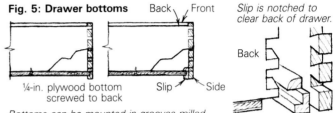

Points of triangle always face forward or upward. Put numbers on triangles to distinguish parts of multiple drawers.

Fig. 5: Drawer bottoms

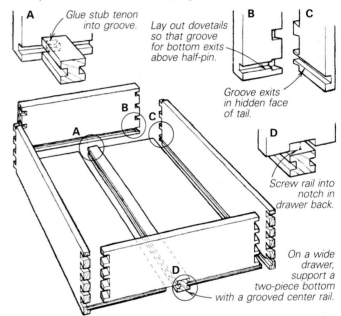

Bottoms can be mounted in grooves milled directly in the sides, or in drawer slips glued to the sides.

A finger pull that Frid routed in the drawing-table drawer front would have exposed the groove into which the plywood bottom is normally let—a problem Frid solved by gluing a slip to the front, as well as to the sides. The carcase rail, visible at the bottom of the photo, is relieved to give access to the pull.

103

Instead of dovetails...

Whenever I can, I prefer to join a drawer with handcut dovetails, half-blind at the front and through at the back. This combination of joints is mechanically strong against all the pushing and pulling that happens to a drawer, and it's quite attractive, especially if you use different colored woods for the drawer sides and front.

Other easier-to-make joints are okay for drawers, too. But remember that when a drawer is pulled out, the front-to-side joint bears most of the load, so it must be designed to resist this stress and should be strong mechanically, without relying entirely on glue. You could, for example, use dovetails at the front and a tongue-and-rabbet or a half-blind tongue-and-rabbet at the back. For quick drawers in a set of kitchen cabinets, the half-blind tongue-and-rabbet would also be okay for the drawer fronts. But if you use it, stop the drawer at the back instead of at the front, otherwise the weak short-grain of the grooved piece might crack off. Both of these joints can be

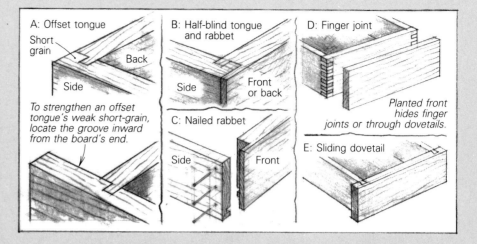

A: Offset tongue
Short grain
Back
Side
To strengthen an offset tongue's weak short-grain, locate the groove inward from the board's end.

B: Half-blind tongue and rabbet
Side
Front or back

C: Nailed rabbet
Side
Front

D: Finger joint
Planted front hides finger joints or through dovetails.

E: Sliding dovetail

made on the tablesaw. Remember to allow for them when you cut the drawer sides to exact length. A rabbet reinforced with Swedish dowels (nails) is fine for quick drawers, too.

A box or finger joint is another good drawer joint that can be cut on the tablesaw. I might use this joint for drawers in a tool chest, but I wouldn't want it in furniture because I think that the end grain of the exposed fingers is ugly. To hide the fingers, or the end grain of through dovetails used on a drawer front, you could glue on a planted front.

If a drawer is narrower than the inside of the carcase—as it would be if you were using ball-bearing runners—or if you wanted the drawer front to overhang and cover the front edges of the carcase, a sliding dovetail is a good choice for joining the drawer front to the sides. Sliding dovetails work well in both solid wood and plywood. If you set up to make this joint, you can also use it to join the back to the sides.   —T.F.

Drawer-stop ideas from three makers

Sometimes it's not practical to install a stop that works against a drawer's front, as Frid does. In this case, I stop a drawer at the back by gluing and screwing small wooden eccentrics inside the carcase, as shown in the drawing below. Before the glue dries, I rotate the eccentrics so that the drawer stops just where I want it to.
—David Hannah, Newtown, Conn.

Drawers in really well-made furniture should have outward stops, but I don't like to spend a lot of time making them. Usually, I use the method in the drawing below, which works for practically any style drawer. The stop is a small block screwed to the rail (or to the inside of the carcase top) above the drawer. As the drawer is opened, its back strikes the block and stops. So that the drawer can be inserted, the block pivots to align with a notch cut into the back. A felt pad glued to the block gives the stop a quieter action.
—Ben Mack, Mt. Tremper, N.Y.

I learned about the outward drawer stop shown below from Stephen Proctor, my teacher at the Wendell Castle workshops. It consists of a notched wooden leaf spring let into a mortise in the rail above the drawer. If you need a lot of stops, it's easy to mill the shape into a wide board, ripping the leaves off to the required width. For strength and springiness, ash is the best wood to use. Locate the stop where you want the drawer to stop, then scribe and cut the mortise. A countersunk wood screw holds the stop in place.
—Wendy Stayman, Scottsville, N.Y.

To adjust stop, rotate eccentrically mounted disc before glue sets.

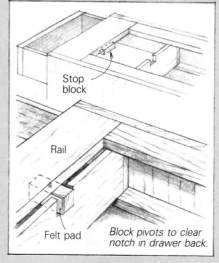

Stop block
Rail
Felt pad   Block pivots to clear notch in drawer back.

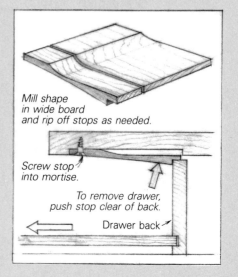

Mill shape in wide board and rip off stops as needed.

Screw stop into mortise.

To remove drawer, push stop clear of back.

Drawer back

won't come out in middle of a dovetail pin.

I had only one drawer to dovetail for my drawing table, so I did it by hand. If there are a lot of drawers to do, I use a dovetail fixture with my router, sanding or planing the inside of the drawer parts before the joints are cut. I don't dry-assemble drawer joints because if they are as tight as they should be, testing them will compress the wood fibers and the joint will be too loose later. Put just a little bit of glue on the top of the pins and front edge of the tails, and tap the joint together with a hammer. Check your drawer for square and put it on a flat bench to make sure it isn't twisted. When the glue is dry, cut the drawer slips to length and glue them in.

Next, I clean up the joints by sanding lightly with a belt sander, and planing or scraping the top and bottom edges of the sides and front. To hold the drawer for sanding, I prop it over a wide board clamped between two bench dogs, as shown in figure 6. After sanding, I try the drawer. Usually it will slide right in. I move it in and out a few times and remove it. Where the drawer binds against the runner, kicker or carcase side, there will be a shiny spot on the wood. I scrape or plane off these spots until the drawer fits perfectly.

If I'm making a drawer in January, I'll make the fit a little loose so that the drawer will still work when the wood swells up in August. Don't take too much off, or the drawer will end up too loose and will bind instead of sliding. To plane the top of a drawer, start at one end of the front and plane toward the back. When you get to the joint between the front and side, just turn the corner in one continuous motion. If you want to finish the inside of the drawer, you can do it at this point. I use two coats of 2-lb.-cut shellac. I wouldn't use oil—it smells too strong and will bleed out of the wood later.

When everything fits, slide the bottom in and fasten it with screws driven into the drawer back. To locate the drawer stops, set a marking gauge to the thickness of the drawer front and scribe a line on the top surface of the rail. Glue two 3-in. by 1-in. by ³⁄₁₆-in. blocks to the rail. Don't make the stops smaller, or someone slamming the drawer might knock them off. I don't use outward stops, but many woodworkers like them. The box on the facing page shows some good methods.

Rub paraffin on the runners, kickers, slips and inside of the carcase. Don't put any other kind of finish on the outside of a drawer or the inside of a carcase where drawers will go, unless you are using ball-bearing runners. The finish will just gum up the works and might cause the drawer to stick.

Making the trays—Making the trays is a lot easier than making the drawers. The tray parts can be kept small in dimension because the assembly is solidly glued and screwed to the plywood bottom. You don't have to fit the parts first, just cut them so that there will be ¹⁄₃₂ in. to ¹⁄₁₆ in. between the side of tray and the inside of the carcase (figure 2, p. 101). No grooves or slips are needed for the bottom, but you should let it into a rabbet milled in the tray front.

When you assemble a tray, make sure that it is square and that the bottom overhangs equally on each side. Complete the final fitting by testing the trays in the grooves and sanding the plywood lightly where necessary.

Correcting problems—Sometimes drawers won't work right, no matter how careful you are. Bowed sides are one reason. If you notice this before you assemble the drawer, position the

Fig. 6: Trimming a drawer

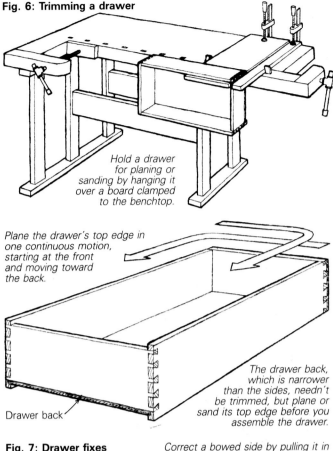

Hold a drawer for planing or sanding by hanging it over a board clamped to the benchtop.

Plane the drawer's top edge in one continuous motion, starting at the front and moving toward the back.

The drawer back, which is narrower than the sides, needn't be trimmed, but plane or sand its top edge before you assemble the drawer.

Drawer back

Fig. 7: Drawer fixes

Correct a bowed side by pulling it in with a clamp and holding it true with a small glue block.

Bowed side

Bottom

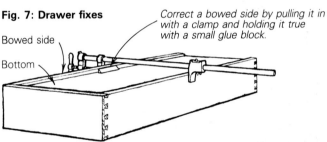

Correct twist by first kerfing the high corners to the depth of the first tail. Then insert wedges to partially flatten the drawer, planing the rest of the twist out of the bottom.

Wedge

Kerf

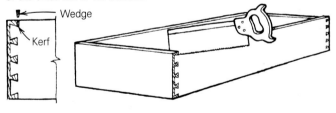

Excessively sloppy drawers can be corrected with a center guide, which fits into a track glued to the drawer bottom. Mount the guide between the front rail and a rail added to the back of the carcase.

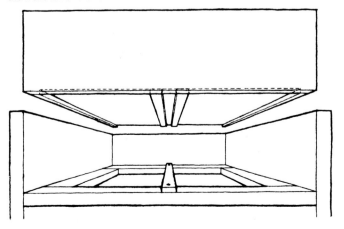

bulge of the bow to the inside of the drawer. That way, when you slide the bottom in, the side will be pushed straight. If a drawer side bows out after you put it together, pull the bow in with a clamp and hold it with a small glue block, as shown in figure 7, p. 105.

A slightly out-of-square drawer will usually be forced into true when the bottom is put in. Just make sure the bottom is truly square and fits exactly to the bottom of the grooves, and put the bottom in before you do final-fitting. A twisted drawer, which won't sit flat but teeters on two corners, is more difficult to fix, but it isn't hopeless. Take some of the twist out by driving small wedges into kerfs sawn at opposite corners in the joints between the sides and the front and

back. The kerf should go down just to the first tail of the joint. Plane the remaining twist out of the bottom edges.

A drawer that really rattles around—either because you planed too much off or because the carcase is too wide—can be fixed with a center guide, or by gluing veneer shims inside the carcase. Shims work best when the looseness is mostly at the back of the drawer. I don't like to use the center-guide method unless I have no other choice. □

Tage Frid, retired professor emeritus at the Rhode Island School of Design, is author of the three-book series Tage Frid Teaches Woodworking *(The Taunton Press). For more on drawers, see* FWW #9, pp. 49-51, and #11, pp. 50-53.

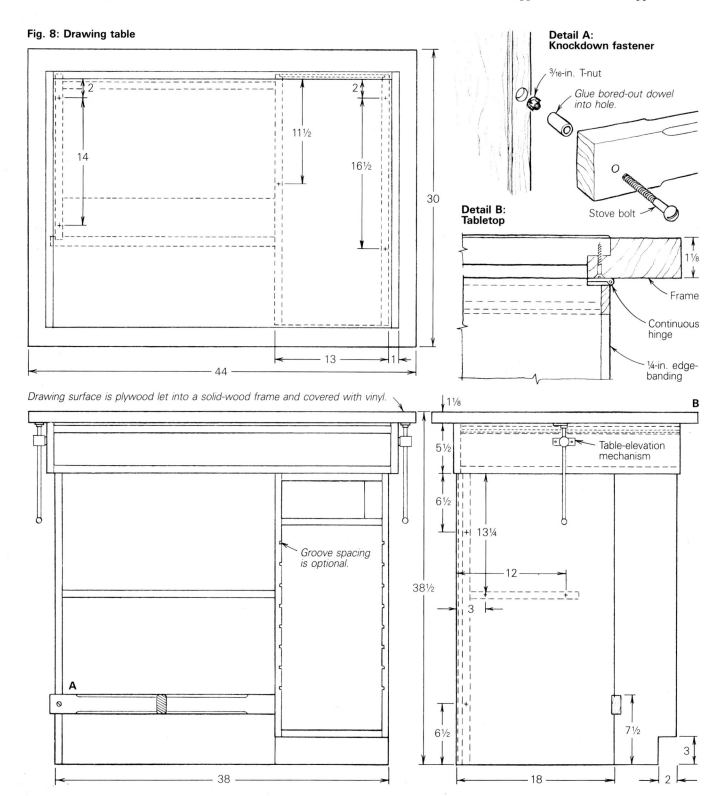

Fig. 8: Drawing table

Drawing surface is plywood let into a solid-wood frame and covered with vinyl.

Groove spacing is optional.

Detail A: Knockdown fastener

3/16-in. T-nut

Glue bored-out dowel into hole.

Stove bolt

Detail B: Tabletop

1 1/8

Frame

Continuous hinge

1/4-in. edge-banding

Table-elevation mechanism

Triangular Sensibility
Intuitive geometry makes strong designs

by John Marcoux

Polished stainless steel fasteners glisten like jewels amid the glass and streaks of color in the 'Tritut' table (honoring King Tut and the Egyptians who used triangles in their furniture), left. In workshops, Marcoux is more whimsical, using yardsticks to show how 'weak materials' make strong furniture.

Kathy Carver

I've been designing and building furniture for many years, and I sometimes found myself locked into arbitrary rules that dictate looks. Things like: Dark wood should be used for serious furniture, light wood for informal furniture; forms should be predominantly rectangular. All that was too inhibiting for me as a designer. I struggled for years to sort out a point of view that would free me up to be a more decisive, adventurous furnituremaker, one who was still able to make furniture that people would want.

Eventually I found that I liked what happened when I heeded a fundamental design rule: Form follows function. I start with common materials—dowels, nuts and bolts, rattan—and put them together so that they rely on structure as an expression of design; purpose-in-use becomes a reason for being. The small table shown above is typical of my personal solution. There's no highly figured wood added for effect, just distinctive linear patterns and geometric shapes. The table base is triangulated to make maximum use of the structural potential of its parts—thus conserving material or enabling me to build with materials I couldn't otherwise use—and to keep costs down. As I'm a natural conserver and a cost-conscious craftsman, this appeals to me.

My fascination with the triangle as a structural unit is an important part of the development of this furniture. For centuries, ancient Egyptian craftsmen used triangles in their furniture. What puzzles me is that sometime between 1500 and 1000 BC the triangle disappeared as a visible aesthetic and structural element in formal furniture (although it was still seen in rustic and wicker pieces), and rectangular forms became dominant. When I began exploring the design possibilities of triangles, I felt like a prospector who had stumbled across a rich vein in an abandoned mine.

Because triangles distribute weight in several directions, effectively neutralizing

Maple dowels are the main structural components in this weavers' bench. The triangular compartments on each side of the 31-in. high seat are for yarn and tools.

much of the force upon them, small-diameter dowels and other relatively weak materials can be used to create interlocking triangles capable of supporting a lot of weight. The triangle has another special quality: when fastened securely at its three corners, it will not change its shape as long as its joints and components remain intact. Without diagonals to brace them, rectangular constructions put under stress tend to distort into parallelograms. Any triangle, regardless of its included angles, will remain strong and rigid, so I've found that I have a lot of design freedom in creating interlocking triangles.

In any triangulated piece, the parts can be assembled in almost infinite combinations, bringing alive an aesthetic idea in which structure is also decoration. In my tables, I try to create linear and angular patterns that fascinate and delight the eye. Tops, especially those that are transparent or have ports revealing the base, must become an integral part of the table design, not just a platform set on a base. Adding mirrors and glass can create an ethereal dimension that changes with the light and with the viewer's position. When the design is right, I hope the viewer senses one of my favorite ideas: "It does what it's supposed to do with joy."

Bolted construction is a powerful asset in these tables. The legs and struts are fastened with machine bolts ⅛ in. in diam-

eter, so I'm not making holes large enough to weaken any component. To make this humdrum hardware appear gem-like and decorative, I polish faceted stainless steel cap nuts (available from Jamestown Distributors, 28 Narragansett Ave., PO Box 348, Jamestown, R.I. 02835).

In the workshops I teach, I like to introduce design ideas and the possibilities that "weak materials" offer by having people build a small table from yardsticks, like the one shown on p. 107. It's a good exercise, and you don't even need any woodworking tools. Tin snips to cut the yardsticks, a drill or a leather punch to make the holes, some wire and a pair of pliers, a screwdriver, some nuts and bolts, and a pocket knife for adding the finishing touches complete the kit. You don't need a tape measure, either—just use the markings on the yardsticks. Start with a couple of dozen yardsticks, and a few hours later you'll have a strong little table and a sense of how triangulated materials work together.

One of my simplest dowel tables, the Tri-table shown in figure 1, can support considerable weight, even though its base weighs only 14 oz. I assembled the table with 1¼-in., #4-40 stainless steel round-head machine bolts with cap nuts. I usually don't worry too much about the initial length of these bolts. After drilling through the two components to be joined,

I insert a long bolt and add a hex nut. Then I cut the bolt close to the nut with electricians' diagonal cutters, unscrew the nut (this helps fix any threads damaged by the cutters) and put on the cap nut. This way, I'm sure that the bolt won't bottom out in the cap nut before the nut can be tightened down. The Tri-table could also be lashed together with cane or rattan. I used rattan only on the top and bottom of the center-column dowels. The top is solid maple, but you could use cane or thin strips of wood in a dowel frame instead.

In constructing the table, I made two simple jigs: one to position three dowels so that I could bore and bolt them together into a triangular unit (figure 2), and one to support the base while I lashed together the center dowels of the triangular units to form a column (figure 3). To make the first jig, I drew a line representing the floor near one edge of a plywood sheet. After deciding the height and size of the tabletop, I drew its side view on the plywood. I angled a dowel between the floor line and the tabletop line until it looked right, then marked the intersections. Next I added blocks and braces to hold the other two dowels needed to build a triangle around the diagonal. I determined the length of the dowels and cut them exactly, although they could be cut after they are drilled.

The dowels should extend about ½ in. beyond the bolt holes. I center-pricked the dowels at the three points where they cross and, using a portable power drill, just eyeballed holes through the center marks. Then I sanded the dowels in a large drum sander (see pp. 110-111), and painted them three bright colors which accent the triangles of the base and create a lively pattern as the parts thread through intersections and linear crossings.

To form the base, I lashed the three triangular units together with strips cut from an inner tube. On a plywood base, I made the second jig: I drew a circle large enough to intersect the tops of the legs, divided the circumference into three equal parts, and built traps for the legs at these points. With the three legs set in the traps, I wound the center column with rattan before removing the rubber strips. To secure the rattan, I drilled a hole in one of the dowels, glued in one end of the rattan, wrapped the column, and then worked the other end back into the lashing.

While the base was still in the jig, I added ⅜-in. dowel stabiles, or braces, to keep each leg in the 120° position. Using

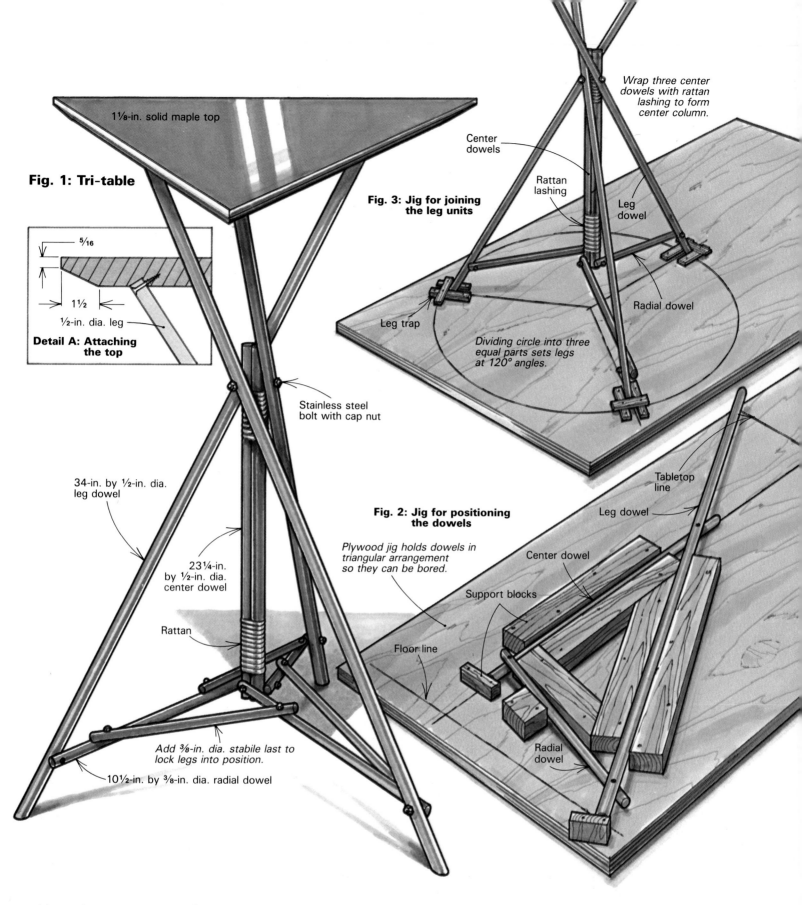

Fig. 1: Tri-table

1⅛-in. solid maple top

Detail A: Attaching the top

5/16

1½

½-in. dia. leg

34-in. by ½-in. dia. leg dowel

23¼-in. by ½-in. dia. center dowel

Rattan

Add ⅜-in. dia. stabile last to lock legs into position.

10½-in. by ⅜-in. dia. radial dowel

Stainless steel bolt with cap nut

Fig. 3: Jig for joining the leg units

Wrap three center dowels with rattan lashing to form center column.

Center dowels

Rattan lashing

Leg dowel

Leg trap

Radial dowel

Dividing circle into three equal parts sets legs at 120° angles.

Fig. 2: Jig for positioning the dowels

Plywood jig holds dowels in triangular arrangement so they can be bored.

Tabletop line

Leg dowel

Center dowel

Support blocks

Floor line

Radial dowel

rubber strips to attach the stabile to the radial dowel temporarily, I positioned it to form an attractive angle. Then I bored and bolted the stabiles and radials together, and removed the rubber strips.

Tightening the bolts and buffing the metal parts completed the base. Holes for the top are bored, as in detail A in figure 1. I left the legs square on their bottoms until after I'd assembled the table. Then I set the table on a level surface,

and cut and sanded the legs until the top was level. Alternatively, you could cut the legs at the floor line while they're still in the jig.

I liked the Tri-table so much that I've expanded the idea to make much more elaborate constructions such as chairs and dining tables. I've also developed a whole series of dual-leg tables with triangular, square or pentagonal tops.

All these tables support my long-held

and stubborn conviction that people will buy furniture that's strong, well designed and reasonably priced. Regardless of the materials used, if you combine a designer's eye with a willingness to experiment and depart from traditional woodworking themes, you can create a variety of distinctive visual effects. *(continued on next page)*

John Marcoux designs furniture in Providence, R.I.

Drawings: David Dann

Working with dowels

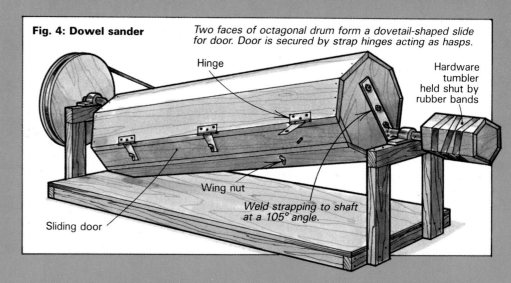

Fig. 4: Dowel sander Two faces of octagonal drum form a dovetail-shaped slide for door. Door is secured by strap hinges acting as hasps.

Hinge

Hardware tumbler held shut by rubber bands

Sliding door

Wing nut

Weld strapping to shaft at a 105° angle.

John Marcoux

I find dowels to be an efficient and economical building material that gives me a lot of freedom in developing my designs. I prefer maple dowels, if I can find them. Generally, dowels purchased from any reputable lumberyard are maple or birch. Avoid cheap imports—they're spongy and porous and they don't hold up well.

Regardless of where you buy the dowels, they'll probably be pretty rough and covered with mill marks. To avoid tedious sanding, I built an octagonal drum, 47½ in. long and 14½ in. in diameter (figure 4), that tumble-sands 30 to 50 dowels at once. I lined the drum with carpeting to cushion the dowels and to keep

the noise down, but the thing still creaks like an old wooden boat. The brackets that connect the drum to its support and drive shafts are offset, enabling the drum to move up and down along its length as it rotates. For abrasives, I cut sandpaper sheets into thin strips with tin snips. I also attached self-adhering sandpaper to each end of the drum to sand the ends of

the dowels hitting the end walls.

To use the sander, I throw in several handfuls of sandpaper strips with the dowels, turn on the motor, and work on something else for a while. Sanding time depends on how badly the dowels are marked. The drum has to turn slowly, about 25 RPM, otherwise the dowels will be tossed about too roughly and will fall

Marcoux dubbed this 18½-in. high table 'Birdfoot' because of its spindly legs. The top is bronze-colored glass.

110

Fig. 5: Marking hole centers

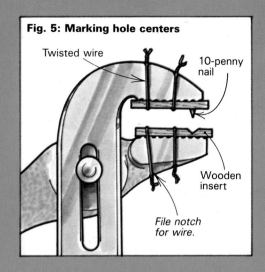

Twisted wire

10-penny nail

Wooden insert

File notch for wire.

Fig. 6: Drilling dowels

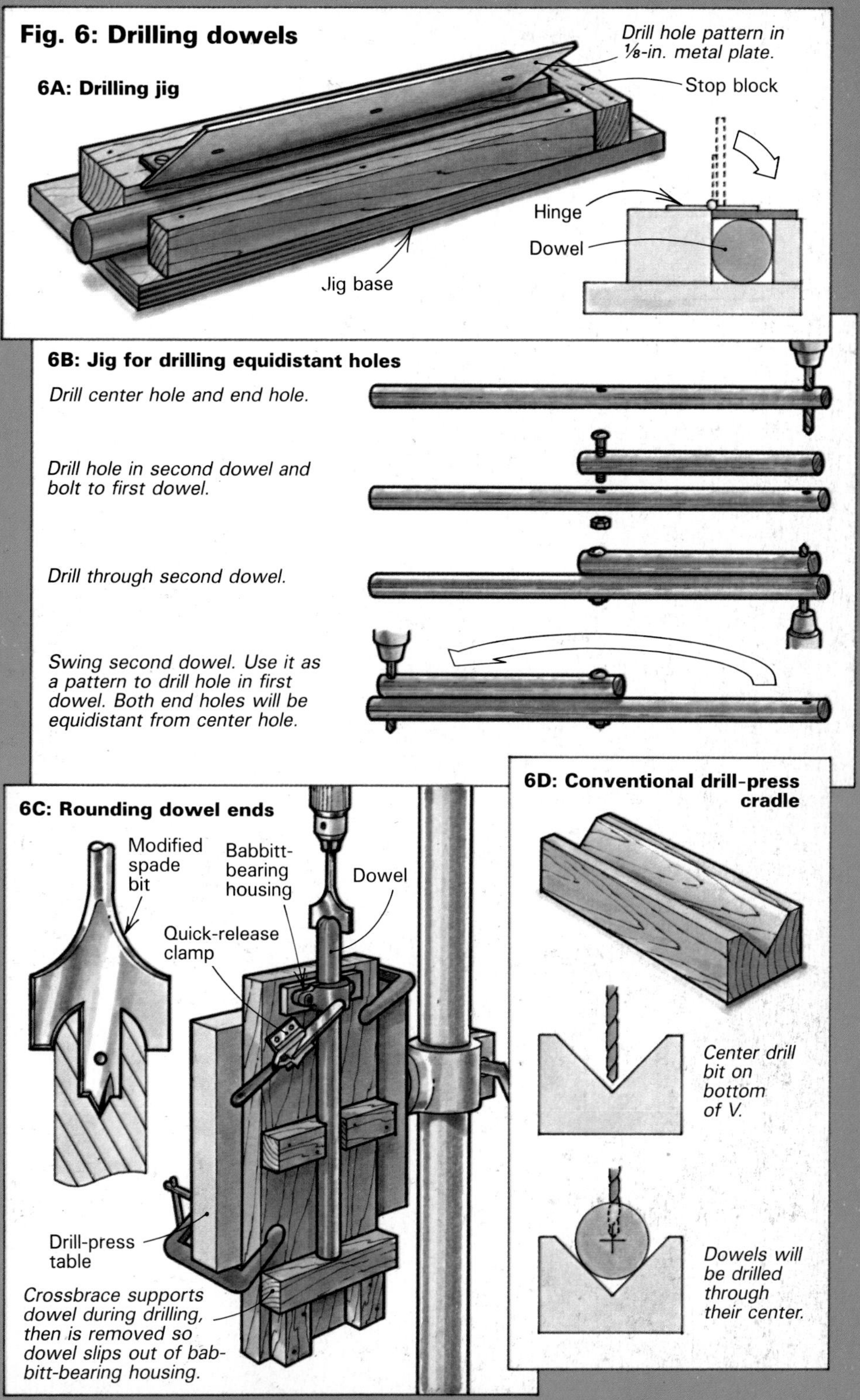

6A: Drilling jig

Drill hole pattern in ⅛-in. metal plate.

Stop block

Hinge

Dowel

Jig base

6B: Jig for drilling equidistant holes

Drill center hole and end hole.

Drill hole in second dowel and bolt to first dowel.

Drill through second dowel.

Swing second dowel. Use it as a pattern to drill hole in first dowel. Both end holes will be equidistant from center hole.

6C: Rounding dowel ends

Modified spade bit

Babbitt-bearing housing

Dowel

Quick-release clamp

Drill-press table

Crossbrace supports dowel during drilling, then is removed so dowel slips out of bab-bitt-bearing housing.

6D: Conventional drill-press cradle

Center drill bit on bottom of V.

Dowels will be drilled through their center.

from wall to wall. I also added a smaller 5½-in. dia. drum on the support-shaft end for polishing nuts and bolts and other hardware. Tumbling the metal parts with lapidary compound brings them to a bright finish. If I want to clean hardware before it's painted, I tumble the pieces for two hours with medium or fine emery-cloth strips.

When I have to drill dowels, I often use a center punch to make a starting mark and I gauge the angle of the drill by eye. You can make another good tool for marking holes from a pair of Channel Lock pliers (figure 5). In a piece of hard wood, cut a V large enough to hold a dowel and fasten the block to one jaw with wire. Drive a 10-penny common nail though another block, clip off the nail and sharpen the protruding point. Then attach that piece to the other jaw so that the nail will hit the dowel in the V-block. This tool is easy to control, and it makes a hole deep enough for you to accurately start the drill bit.

I also use a variety of blocks and jigs as drill guides. To make an accurate drilling jig for boring identical components, I simply glue two lengths of soft wood, usually about ¾ in. wide, to a base (figure 6A). The first block should be thicker than the dowels to be drilled. The second block should be ⅛ in. thinner to accommodate the thickness of the metal plate used in the jig. Drill guide holes in the metal plate at the locations you want them in the dowels. Next hinge the plate to the first block, so that the plate can be lowered over the dowel. When lowered, the plate should rest on the thinner block and lie flat over the dowel channel between the blocks. Glue the first block to the base, place the correct-size dowel next to it, push the second block lightly against the dowel, and attach the second block to the base. A stop block tacked in the dowel channel positions the dowel.

Another way to guide the bit is to fasten a predrilled dowel to a second dowel with

rubber bands and drill through the first hole to make the second. I use a similar technique (figure 6B) to drill holes that are equidistant from a center hole, as for a cross stretcher on a table.

A drill press can also be used for drilling dowels. I bolted the top half of an old babbitt-bearing housing to a wooden base so that it can be clamped down onto a dowel. The size of the housing determines the size of dowels that can be drilled; the one I use fits 1-in. dowels. After turning the drill-press table vertically (figure 6C), I

use a modified spade bit to drill and round over the end of a dowel. To shape the tops of the 1-in. legs for the Tritut table (p. 107), I ground down a 1½-in. spade bit so that it rounds over the ends of the dowel as it bores a ½-in. center hole. The center drill bit also stabilizes the outer cutters to prevent chattering which could mar the wood.

Figure 6D shows a conventional V-block cradle for steadying dowels on a drill-press table. The point of the V also helps you line up the drill bit.   —J.M.

Building Doors

Frame-and-panel makes elegant entries

by John Birchard

Michael Knouff

When the proportions are right, a traditional frame-and-panel door, like Birchard's 80-in. by 32-in. raised-panel door in cherry, is a graceful architectural element.

For a woodworker, a door is like a painter's blank canvas: a well-defined space waiting to be filled with something beautiful. Doors provide me with some of my best opportunities for creative and rewarding woodworking. Making a door for your own home is not only satisfying, it also isn't very difficult.

Doormaking is ideally suited to the small shop. I have only 500 sq. ft. of work space, but that hasn't stopped me from building as many as 12 doors at a time. I don't have room for a stroke sander or other large machines, and I get along fine without them. If time is no object, a door can be built with only hand tools and a tablesaw, but an assortment of basic power tools speeds the task and allows construction methods not possible with hand tools.

A shaper is handy for doormaking, but it isn't essential unless you're planning a production run or making doors with many panes of glass. The shaper is indispensable, however, for cope-and-stick construction (see box, p. 116).

There are two basic types of wooden doors used in residential construction: flush doors and frame-and-panel doors. Built-up flush doors can be as simple as boards joined edge to edge, with nailed-on battens for strength. The most common type of flush door, however, is the hollow-core interior door that hangs in countless tract houses. It consists of a lauan veneer over a cardboard lattice and a light wooden frame. Exterior flush doors are often a veneer skin over a solid core of boards or man-made boards. A thick solid-core door is heavy, and a big one may require strap hinges instead of butt hinges.

I prefer to make solid-wood frame-and-panel doors. Frame-and-panel construction consists of rails, stiles and muntins joined to make a frame. Grooves milled in the framework hold wooden panels in place. This construction results in a strong, du-

Fig. 1: Frame-and-panel door construction

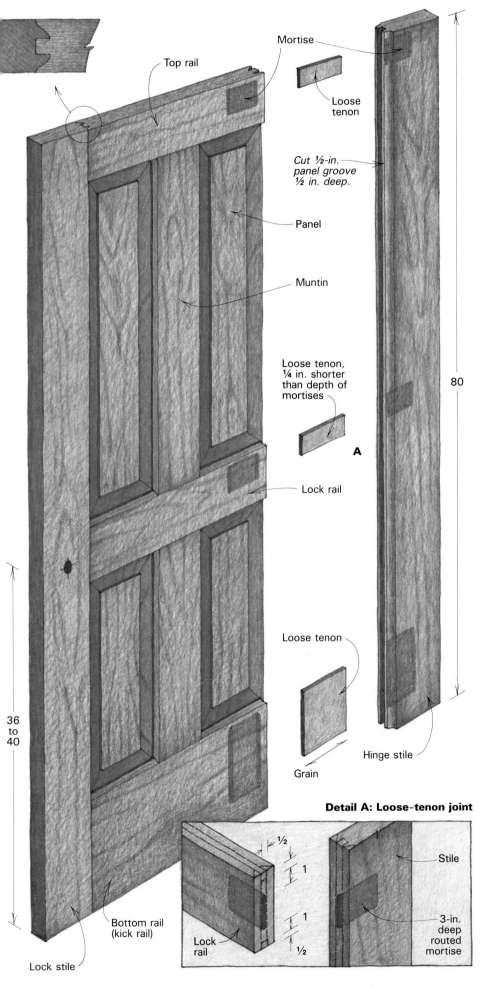

Mortise

Top rail

Loose tenon

Cut ½-in. panel groove ½ in. deep.

Panel

Muntin

Loose tenon, ¼ in. shorter than depth of mortises

A

80

Lock rail

Loose tenon

Grain

Hinge stile

36 to 40

Bottom rail (kick rail)

Lock stile

Detail A: Loose-tenon joint

½
1
1
1
½

Stile

3-in. deep routed mortise

Lock rail

rable door that's often lighter in weight than a solid-core door, and it minimizes the problems caused by wood movement that plague solid-core exterior doors. The panels in a frame-and-panel door are free to move in their grooves, and can expand and contract without affecting the overall width of the door.

There are countless variations on the basic four-panel door shown in figure 1. Changing panel proportions and varying the shape and arrangement of the framework are just the beginning. Panels can be flat, raised or carved, inlaid with other wood or with brass, or replaced by clear or stained glass. The framework can be carved or beaded—the possibilities are endless.

Design—When I design a door, I consider its size and location, the type and quality of lumber to be used, the joinery, ornamentation, and, of course, the price.

In the United States, the standard height for a residential door is 80 in., but custom doors sometimes exceed this. Exterior doors are commonly 30 in. to 36 in. wide and 1¾ in. thick. Single exterior doors wider than 42 in. present special problems because they're so heavy; for wide openings, therefore, double doors are better. Interior doors are commonly 24 in. to 32 in. wide and 1⅜ in. or 1½ in. thick.

If you're making a door for an old house, existing jambs may vary from the standards and also will probably be out of square. If the latter is the case, make the door slightly oversize and plane it to fit.

In new construction, the doors are most often made after the house has already been completely designed and framed up. If, on a lucky chance, I'm called in before the designs are final, I try to locate the exterior doors in sheltered areas. A door on the south side of a building should have a projecting roof or overhang to protect it from sun and rain. If, as is often the case, a door must be exposed to the elements, I choose a weather-resistant wood such as teak or mahogany, and employ as much glass in the design as possible. I try to design panels for an exterior door as narrow as possible. A large expanse of wood moves more with the weather and is more likely to cause problems.

I design most of my frame-and-panel doors with 5-in. or 5½-in. wide stiles. Most locksets have a 2⅜-in. or 2¾-in. backset (the measurement from the center of the doorknob to the edge of the door). So a lockset with a 2¾-in. backset will be centered in both a 5½-in. stile and the width of the lock rail, I usually make the top and lock rails the same width as the stiles. For visual weight and strength, the bottom or kick rail is usually twice as wide as the other rails.

Doorknobs should be 36 in. to 40 in. from the floor. Since I usually place the center of the lock rail 36 in. from the floor, this means boring through the lock-rail tenon. I've never had a joint fail because of this.

Good door lumber has to be straight and clear. Avoid plainsawn boards or boards with wild grain—they're more likely to cup, warp or twist. This can cause real problems in a door. Quartersawn boards are the best choice because they're more stable. I usually buy roughsawn 8/4 stock so that I can joint any small defects out of the stiles and still end up with stock 1¾ in. thick. My favorite woods are teak because of its beauty and weather-resistance, redwood because it's easy to work and inexpensive where I live, and cherry because it finishes so nicely. Walnut, mahogany and fir are also nice door woods, but harder to work. Oak is popular, but I avoid using it for exterior doors because it blackens with age.

Joinery and layout—Some type of mortise-and-tenon joint (blind, through, wedged, pinned or haunched) is best to join stiles and rails. Traditionally, rails that are wider than 8 in. or so are joined with a twin mortise-and-tenon to minimize the effects of wood movement. In a frame-and-panel door, the greatest load is concentrated on the joint between the top rail and the hinge stile, so it's particularly important to make this joint strong.

I often use cope-and-stick construction. (The molding on the frame edge is called the stick, and the process of cutting it is called sticking. Likewise, its female counterpart on the rail ends is the cope, and the process is called coping.) Since a traditional tenon will interfere with coping the rail ends on the shaper, I've developed the loose-tenon joint shown in figure 1, detail A. I think that it's at least as strong as a blind tenon, and easier to make. I sometimes use dowel joints in combination with cope-and-stick construction, but only on lightweight interior doors. I don't recommend dowel joints for exterior doors.

I'll explain how to make a cope-and-stick frame-and-panel door with the loose-tenon joint. If you don't have a shaper, you can cut the panel grooves and beading with a router. Or you can apply

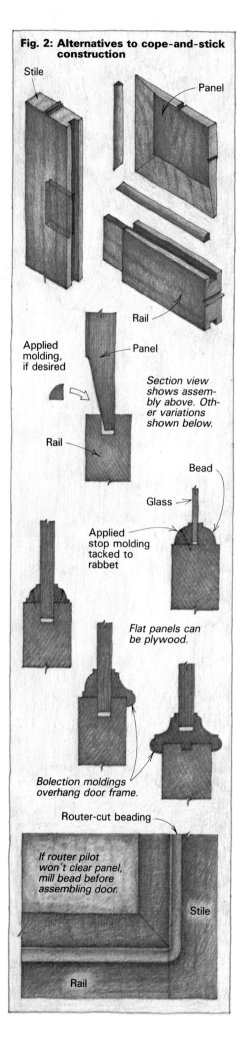

Fig. 2: Alternatives to cope-and-stick construction

Stile

Panel

Rail

Applied molding, if desired

Panel

Rail

Section view shows assembly above. Other variations shown below.

Bead

Glass

Applied stop molding tacked to rabbet

Flat panels can be plywood.

Bolection moldings overhang door frame.

Router-cut beading

If router pilot won't clear panel, mill bead before assembling door.

Stile

Rail

molding as shown in figure 2, or eliminate it altogether.

I begin by ripping the frame pieces about ½ in. wider than their finished size, then jointing one edge and one face. Next I plane all the wood to thickness, then rip to finished width. If I don't have stock wide enough for the kick rail, I glue it up. All parts must be square and straight.

The length of the rails depends on whether you cope and stick the joints or not. For example, let's take a door 36 in. wide with 5½-in. wide stiles. If I don't cope and stick, I'll cut the rails 25¼ in. long—door width minus the combined width of the stiles, plus ¼ in. For cope-and-stick construction, I add to this measurement the amount that the coping overlaps the sticking on the stiles. The extra ¼ in. makes the door 36¼ in. wide to allow for any irregularities in the jamb, and so I can clamp the door without worrying about scarring the edges. When I hang the door, I'll plane it to fit. (For traditional mortise-and-tenon joints, allow for the length of the tenons when figuring rail length.) I cut all the frame members to length with a cutoff jig on the tablesaw, using a 60- or 100-tooth carbide blade. These cuts must be perfectly square in both directions. If they're not, the joints won't be tight or the door will be twisted.

Once I've cut all the frame pieces to length, I lay out the door on my assembly table and mark where the rails join the stiles. Then I line up the stiles next to each other, inside edges up. I mark the locations of the mortises with a square and a marking gauge, centering the mortise on the stiles. I usually start the mortises about 1½ in. from the top and bottom of the door, and 1 in. from the other rail edges so the tenons won't interfere with the ½-in. deep panel grooves.

I cut the mortises with a plunge router before doing any slotting or shaping on the stile or rail edges so that there's a flat surface for the router base to slide on. Drilling a ½-in. dia. hole 3 in. deep at one end of each mortise eases the plunge of the router bit into the wood, and makes the bits last considerably longer. I cut 3-in. deep blind mortises by making several passes with a 4-in. long, ½-in. dia. spiral fluted bit, checking the router-fence adjustment often to make sure that the mortise is exactly centered in the thickness of the stile. Next I rout mortises in the rail ends, holding the pieces in the bench vise while mortising. A length of 2x6 clamped to the benchtop helps stabilize the router, and raises the work high enough off the

Plunge-routed mortises begin with a ½-in. hole drilled at one end to ease the bit's entry (above). Several passes with a ½-in. fluted router bit cut a mortise in the stile (right) and the rail end (below) for a loose tenon. A 2x6 clamped to the bench provides support for the router base.

bench so that the router fence clears the vise.

To make the loose tenons, I plane a board to ½-in. thickness, rip it to the correct width, and cut the tenons ¼ in. shorter than the total depth of both mortises. The tenons should be a friction fit in their mortises. The router-cut mortises have radiused corners, but I don't feel that it's necessary to round off the edges of the loose tenons. The gaps at the mortise ends won't affect the strength of the joint. It's also very helpful to be able to slide the rail up and down a little during assembly.

With the joints cut, I'm ready to cut the panel grooves and the decorative beading along the inner edges of the stiles, rails and muntins. For a raised panel, I usually make the grooves ½ in. wide and ½ in. deep, but for a 1¾-in. thick door, I sometimes make them ⅝ in. wide.

On the shaper, I cut the cope first on the ends of the rails and muntins. Then I cut the stick the full length of each frame member. Alternatives to coping and sticking are shown in figure 2. One of the easiest is to dry-assemble the frame, then rout

the beading around the panel openings with a pilot-bearing bit and rout the panel groove with a slotting cutter. Make sure that the bit's bearing rides on a true surface, not on the beading. The corners of a routed panel groove will have to be cleaned out with a chisel.

One nice feature of cope-and-stick joints is that the beading appears to be mitered where the stiles and rails intersect. This gives a nice sharp look to the corners, which in many designs is more appealing than the rounded corners produced by beading an assembled door with a router.

When the framework is finished, I cut the panels to size. To determine raised-panel thickness, I usually add ½ in. or more to the width of the panel groove (i.e., a ½-in. wide groove gets a panel 1 in. thick at its thickest section). To determine panel size, I dry-assemble the framework and measure from the bottoms of the panel grooves. I make the panels about ³⁄₁₆ in. smaller than this measurement to allow for cross-grain wood movement. The panels are never glued in place—

they need to float in the grooves.

I raise panels on the shaper, but this can also be done on the tablesaw or with a router (see *FWW* #23, pp. 55-58, and #44, p. 56). I sand and finish the panels completely *before* gluing the door so that I can apply finish to the edges that will be fit into the grooves. It's also a good idea to apply finish to the insides of the panel grooves, but be careful not to get any on the glue joints.

Assembly—I use plastic resin glue (urea-formaldehyde resin) on all my doors. It's water-resistant and slow to set up, which gives me more assembly time. I assemble most of my doors flat on a Formica-topped table that has access on three sides, but sometimes I clamp one stile in the bench vise and work up from there. The most important thing about assembly is to check for square and make sure that everything—especially the panels—fits perfectly before applying any glue. Be sure to put clamps on both sides of the door to keep it flat. After the glue has cured, I hand-plane the frame to flush the joints and to remove surface blemishes. Between planing and the final sanding, I trim the edges and the top of the door with either an electric hand-planer or a straight-fluted router bit like the one I use for mortising. A straightedge clamped to the door guides the router. Before trimming the top or bottom, I bevel the stile corners with a block plane so that the router or planer doesn't tear out grain at the end of the cut.

I install the top hinge 7 in. from the top of the door and the bottom hinge 11 in. from the bottom, with a middle hinge, if used, centered between the two. I cut the hinge mortises by defining each end of the mortise with a chisel cut, setting the router fence for the width of the hinge, and hogging between the chisel cuts. Then I square up the corners with a chisel.

If possible, I hang the door and do any final fitting before applying the finish. A door hung during the dry season can be expected to swell. I compensate for this by allowing a little extra clearance between the door and the jamb. Except for the hinges, I install hardware after finishing.

Finishing—Paint is the best protection for an exterior door, but it obscures the natural wood. I don't recommend straight, unthinned varnish on the surface of exterior doors because varnish degrades quickly and is difficult to renew. Straight oils aren't protective enough either. If a door is well sheltered from the sun, a finish of equal proportions of spar varnish, boiled linseed oil and mineral spirits will protect the wood if periodically renewed. Be especially sure to finish the door's top and bottom edges and any exposed end grain. For a hand-rubbed look, I flow on one coat, wait a few minutes and then wipe off the excess. Before the first coat has dried, I scrub on a second coat with 00 steel wool. After wiping off the excess, I let the finish dry overnight. I repeat this several times. This finish is easy to renew. Just flow on a new coat and wipe off the excess—the mixture soaks in where it's needed.

A properly made and properly hung door should give its maker a satisfying feeling of accomplishment, and its owners a lifetime of service.   □

John Birchard is a professional wood-worker in Mendocino, Calif. Black-and-white photos by the author. For more about doors and how to hang them, see FWW #9, p. 48; #11, pp. 74-75; and #26, pp. 56-57.

A shaper makes it simple

If you're making more than a few doors, a spindle shaper is a good investment. It can cut interlocking cope-and-stick joints which speed the making of frame-and-panel doors, give the appearance of mitered beading, and produce a stronger glue joint. And for doors with lots of sash work, a shaper is essential.

The shaper has a high-speed vertical spindle that protrudes through a hole in the middle of a table. A fence guides the stock. Cutters fit on the spindle singly, or they can be stacked in combination with spacers and bearings to make all sorts of different moldings, grooves or raised panels.

One way to tool up for a cope-and-stick joint is to buy a cope-and-stick cutter set. This is sometimes called a door-lip set, and it consists of two matching sets of cutters: one to cope the rail ends, and one to mold, or stick, the entire length of the stiles and rails. One pass mills the panel groove and beads both edges. These carbide cutter sets are convenient, but at more than $300 they're expensive.

It's cheaper to stack several high-speed steel cutters to get the profile you want. I prefer high-speed steel cutters to carbide ones because in addition to their being less expensive, I can regrind and resharpen them myself on a carborundum wheel. One of my favorite shaper cutters is the Power-matic #6178048 (available from Woodshop Specialties, Cold River Industrial Park, Quality La., Rutland, Vt. 05701). It's a reversible S-curve that can be used to stick the edges of the stiles and rails, and then flipped over to cope the rail ends. Using the Power-matic in combination with straight cutters, as shown in the drawing, I can get a panel groove on the stick or a matching stub tenon on the cope. If you use a reversible cutter, you'll need a reversing switch on your shaper so that you can flip the cutter from stick to cope cut.

As with most machines, shaper set-up is extremely important. You shouldn't alter the spindle height between cuts, or the door parts won't line up. Remember also that the stock needs to bear against the shaper fence after it's passed over the cutter as well as before. Position the fence so that some part of the original stock surface remains to bear on the fence during the last cut. If this isn't possible, you can build up the outfeed fence

Cope and stick with reversible shaper cutter

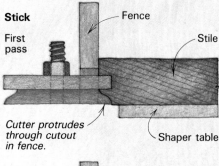

Stick

First pass

Fence

Stile

Cutter protrudes through cutout in fence.

Shaper table

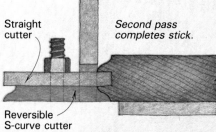

Straight cutter

Second pass completes stick.

Reversible S-curve cutter

Flip cutter and reverse shaper rotation to cut cope.

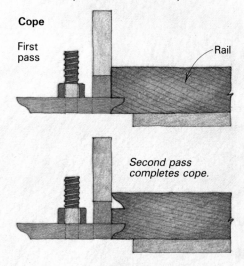

Cope

First pass

Rail

Second pass completes cope.

to contact a cut surface. The gap in the fence for the cutter can be a problem, particularly for end-grain coping on narrow pieces. To guide narrow stock past the gap, I let a piece of wood into the fence to span the gap at the height of the stub tenon.

It's easy to spend thousands of dollars on a shaper and thousands more on carbide cutters, but I didn't. For much less than the cost of one heavy-duty machine, I bought two ½-in. Sears Craftsman shapers and outfitted them with 1-HP motors and heavy-duty pulleys. These small shapers can't do everything a big machine can, but they're fine for cope-and-stick work. Having two machines cuts down on set-up time.   —J.B.

Fabric-Backed Tambours

It's not that difficult to roll your own

by Tim Daulton

There is something almost magical about a tambour, a seemingly solid row of slats that slides out of sight at the touch of a finger. Actually, a tambour is little more than a flexible sliding door, and not much harder to construct.

Like any sliding door, a tambour needs a pair of parallel tracks or grooves to guide its movement. It also needs some type of compartment, usually behind a false partition, into which the door can disappear. Both the sliding door and the tambour door open without swinging out in front of the cabinet. The tambour, however, can slip around corners to be stored out of the way, while a rigid sliding door must remain in the plane of the opening and can therefore limit the size of the compartment's opening. With tambours, you can transform curved surfaces or corners into doors, opening up numerous design possibilities.

Tambours can be designed to open either vertically or horizontally, and this versatility sometimes causes confusion when people describe tambours. A tambour that moves vertically, up and down, has horizontal slats; one that opens horizontally has vertical slats. In this article I'll describe a vertical-opening door, which has a natural counterbalance that makes it operate more smoothly than a horizontal one. In a horizontal-opening tambour, all the weight rests on the lower track, whereas the weight of a vertical-opening door is spread over two tracks. As the top slats move into the compartment, they help balance the weight of the lower slats.

The individual tambour slats can be connected with interlocked wood joints, with wires or cords (see *FWW* #48, pp. 57-58), or with a flexible backing of leather or fabric. Fabric backing is the simplest and most common method, and the one I'll use here to make a desk-top organizer (figure 1, p. 118). I prefer plain cotton canvas backing—it's durable and available in a variety of weights for different-size doors. For this small door, I used 8-oz. artists' canvas. The natural color of canvas blends with light woods, and it can easily be dyed to match darker woods. For attaching the slats to the backing, I like contact cement, since it remains flexible and any squeeze-through can readily be cleaned off the slats. Hide glue or white glue also can be used.

Any carcase or cabinet can have a tambour door, but there are some practical limitations to consider. Before you assemble the carcase, remember that you must provide a way to install the completed tambour. There are two ways to do this. One is to trap the tambour between the carcase sides as the piece is assembled. Since this method precludes removal of the door for adjustments, it's suitable for only the simplest pieces. The second method, the one I recommend, is to leave one end of the track open, usually at the back or bottom, so that the tambour can be slid in place after assembly and then closed in. This allows more careful fitting, and the door can be removed for finishing or adjustment. When designing the track, it's a good idea to consider how you're going to insert the completed tambour. In the piece shown here, the back and bottom fit into rabbets cut in the carcase sides, so it was easy to leave them both off until I had installed the tambour (figure 2, p. 119).

You must construct the carcase carefully to ensure square, parallel sides, otherwise the tambour will neither fit well nor slide smoothly. Since a tambour often occupies one or more corners of a piece, thus replacing some structural framing, you may need to include interior partitions or shelves to help hold the case together. Measure carefully to ensure that the door will clear all interior elements, as well as the back and outside panels. Also make sure that no glue gets into inaccessible sections of the track during assembly.

Before you can begin to prepare slats for the tambour, you must consider the width of the opening, which affects slat thickness, and establish the curvature of the guide track, which determines the width of the slat. Slats should be ⅜ in. to ¾ in. thick, just substantial enough to keep from flexing too much between the sides. Thin slats make the door light enough to operate easily without slamming when opened or shut. I recommend laying out the proposed track on scrap material and test-fitting slats to determine optimum slat shape and track curvature for your design, but you could simply draw the track out carefully on paper instead. Just be sure that there's enough room for the tambour to open and close completely, without coming out of its pocket. Generally, the track extends into a pocket behind a false back or interior partition so that the door's workings aren't exposed and the contents of the case don't interfere with its operation. I suggest that you build the tambour with a couple of extra slats to ensure that the door won't be too short—the excess pieces can be trimmed off before assembly if they aren't needed.

The track can be really any shape that suits your piece, although I try to avoid extremely tight circles and to keep curves as gentle as possible to reduce friction. Tighter curves demand narrower slats; the larger the track's radius, the wider the slats can be. The front edges of the slats are often beveled, chamfered or rounded so that the joints appear uniform, even around corners, and so that they won't pinch fingers and things when closing. With reverse-curve or S-shaped tracks, which bend tambours in more than one direction, slats must be beveled enough to allow the bend. The back edges of canvas-backed slats

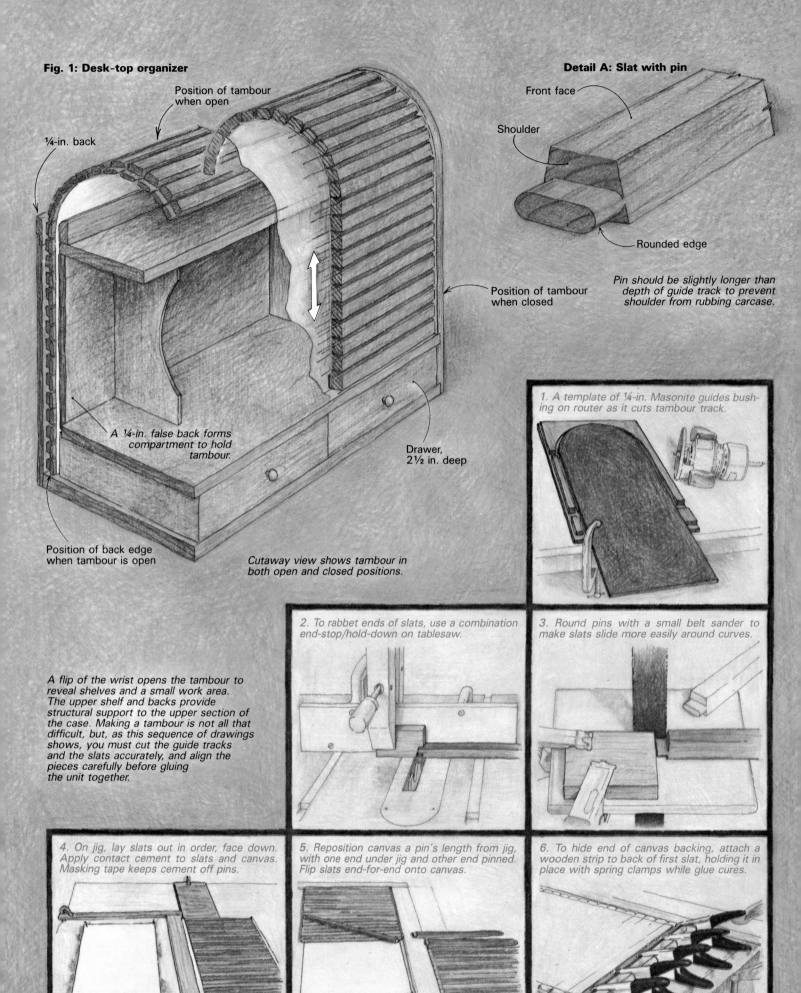

Fig. 1: Desk-top organizer

Position of tambour when open

¼-in. back

A ¼-in. false back forms compartment to hold tambour.

Position of back edge when tambour is open

Cutaway view shows tambour in both open and closed positions.

Position of tambour when closed

Drawer, 2½ in. deep

Detail A: Slat with pin

Front face

Shoulder

Rounded edge

Pin should be slightly longer than depth of guide track to prevent shoulder from rubbing carcase.

A flip of the wrist opens the tambour to reveal shelves and a small work area. The upper shelf and backs provide structural support to the upper section of the case. Making a tambour is not all that difficult, but, as this sequence of drawings shows, you must cut the guide tracks and the slats accurately, and align the pieces carefully before gluing the unit together.

1. A template of ¼-in. Masonite guides bushing on router as it cuts tambour track.

2. To rabbet ends of slats, use a combination end-stop/hold-down on tablesaw.

3. Round pins with a small belt sander to make slats slide more easily around curves.

4. On jig, lay slats out in order, face down. Apply contact cement to slats and canvas. Masking tape keeps cement off pins.

5. Reposition canvas a pin's length from jig, with one end under jig and other end pinned. Flip slats end-for-end onto canvas.

6. To hide end of canvas backing, attach a wooden strip to back of first slat, holding it in place with spring clamps while glue cures.

Drawings: Christopher Clapp

shouldn't be chamfered, as they must fit together closely at the fabric.

I cut the guide tracks using a router guided by a bushing against a shaped template (figure 1, step 1)—identical tracks can easily be cut by reversing the template on opposite sides of the carcase. To make the correct-size template, subtract the difference between the bit's radius and the bushing's outside radius from the full-size track layout. The track groove itself should be about half the thickness of the slats, usually ³⁄₁₆ in. to ³⁄₈ in., to accommodate the slat pins. Pick the closest size for which you own a router bit. A good template can be made from ¼-in. Masonite, which is smooth and dense and wears well. Cut it out carefully, and make it longer than the track will be to guide the router's entrance and exit. With a new template, I like to practice the cut a couple of times on scrap material to check the template's accuracy and to get a feel for moving the router around it smoothly. When you're satisfied with the template, attach it firmly to the top, side or bottom piece in the correct position. Tacks or screws in an inconspicuous place are more convenient than clamps. Check the alignment, and cut the first groove. Then flip the template over onto the mating piece, making sure the alignment is identical, and cut the matching track. Sand the grooves smooth with a small sanding block or folded sandpaper, and widen them slightly around any particularly tight curves to prevent binding.

Once I'm satisfied with the guide tracks, I cut the slat stock to length (I usually make extra slats to allow for defects), rip the pieces to size, and then rabbet the ends of each piece to form pins, as in figure 1, detail A. The pins should be just slightly thinner than the track groove. Rabbeting pins allows the groove to be narrower than the slat thickness and remain hidden behind a neat joint at the front face. Rabbeting the front face of the slat, so the pin is on the back half of the slat, allows you to fit the tambour flush with the face of the piece. I cut the pins on each slat on a tablesaw, using a crosscutting guide and end stop (step 2), then round their corners with a rasp or a sander so that they'll slide smoothly around corners (step 3). The pins should be slightly longer than the track is deep so that they'll bottom out, preventing the slat shoulders from rubbing against the case. The slats themselves should have a little end clearance between tracks to allow for wood movement and inconsistencies in construction. Round or bevel the long edges of the slats with a sander, router or tablesaw.

After all the tambour slats have been prepared, sand them smooth and lay them out in order, matching grain and tossing out any pieces that are seriously warped. Fasten a couple of straight boards to your work surface at right angles to form a gluing jig (step 4). Cut a length of canvas slightly narrower than the shoulder-to-shoulder width of the slats and spread contact cement over it. Lay the slats out in order, face down, next to the gluing jig and spread cement on them. Let the glue set properly, and apply a second coat if necessary. Carefully align the canvas in the jig—I clamp one end under the jig itself and tack the free end down. Now flip each slat end-for-end and press it onto the canvas, making sure it's flush and square in the jig and tight to the next slat before the glue-covered surfaces make contact (step 5). Once all the slats are stuck down, flip the completed tambour over and press the canvas down firmly onto the slats. Rub off any excess glue, trim the canvas, and you're ready to roll. I like to face the back of the first slat with a thin strip of wood to finish off the canvas edge and to reinforce the bond there (step 6). Handles or knobs can be attached now if they won't interfere with the installation of the tambour, or they can be added after the tambour is assembled.

Regardless of whether the tambour is installed as the carcase is assembled or slid into place afterward, it will probably fit tightly at first. Slide it back and forth to locate the rough spots, and carefully sand the tracks or pins until the door runs without catching anywhere. Do as much sanding and finishing as possible with the tambour out of the case, where it's easier to get at, and be careful not to saturate the fabric with finish which may stiffen or weaken it. A bit of paraffin or paste wax rubbed into the tracks after final finishing will make the door operate more smoothly, but a little friction in heavier doors is desirable since it will keep them from rolling too rapidly at the end of the track and slamming when opened or closed.

After installing the tambour and making a final check for smooth operation, add stop blocks, if necessary, to keep the tambour from sliding down too far into the hidden compartment. Close up the end of the track, and the piece is ready for final finishing.

Building a tambour may be a little trickier than fitting a hinged door or cutting straight grooves for a sliding door, but it's not really all that difficult. And the results, in space efficiency, visual appeal and design variation, can be well worth the effort. □

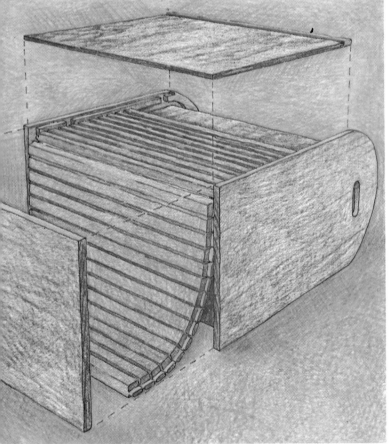

Fig. 2: Installing the tambour

Leave back and bottom off carcase until tambour has been installed. Once door is fitted properly, set the two panels into rabbets cut in carcase, then screw or tack them down.

Tim Daulton builds furniture in the woodcraft program at Arizona State University in Tempe. He recently returned from Osaka, Japan, where he studied old Japanese wood sculpture.

TURNING

Movement and Support at the Lathe
A steady hold improves your turning

by Richard Raffan

Many aspiring turners experience problems because they fail to develop basic tool control. How you hold and move your tools, even how you stand at the lathe, affects the quality of your work. A solid, vibration-free lathe is of little use if an improperly held tool chatters about on the wood. In this article, I'll cover the basics—how to support yourself, the tool and the work—which are the same for all aspects of face or center work. Practice will greatly improve your technique.

Stance—When a tool contacts a spinning block of wood, the wood exerts considerable downward pressure on the cutting edge. Think of the tool as a lever and the tool rest as a fulcrum. When force is applied on the cutting end, there is an opposite reaction at the handle end. The farther the cutting edge is from the tool rest, the greater the leverage, and the more difficult it becomes to control the tool, so keep the rest as close to the wood as practicable.

To move the tool precisely where you want it, without the wood having a say in the matter, you must get your weight behind the tool. Stand in a balanced position, feet apart. Maintain contact between your body and the machine—keep a hand on the rest and lean against the lathe bed, or keep a leg against the stand. This gives you extra support and stability, and provides a point of reference for tool movement.

Keep the tool handle tight against your body or solidly braced against your forearm. With shorter, lighter tools, keep your elbows tucked into your sides, not moving about in the air. If the handle has to leave your side, align it solidly along your forearm. Your goal is a compact stance which, when combined with a firm grip, allows you to move the tool precisely with your weight behind it. Movement comes not so much from the wrists or arms, but from the shoulders, hips and legs. If you want to move the tool edge slightly left, then the movement comes from a shift of the hip to the right rather than from a hand movement. That way your hand stays close to your side and you're more compact. If you want the tool edge to drop, raise your whole side, standing on tiptoe if necessary, to bring the handle up, with the weight of your torso and shoulders behind the tool.

Lathe height is important. Block up the lathe or stand on boards so that the lathe center is about 50mm (2 in.) above your elbow. The height of the rest in relation to center height varies from one turning situation to another, but it should be close to center. Adjust the rest for comfort and try to keep the tool near horizontal.

Holding the tool—Hold the tool with the controlling hand (right hand if you're right-handed) somewhere on its handle. I grip the handle near its ferrule, because I find this more comfortable than holding it at the end, and I can use my forearm and body along the length of the handle to stabilize the tool. Gripping the tool this way, nearer the rest, also means that when I pivot the tool, my right hand need not move in quite so large an arc as it would if it were at the end of a long handle. Hold your upper hand (left hand if you're right-handed) on the rest near the cutting edge. This hand provides fine control. You must be able to control the tool at the point where it pivots on the rest if you are to dictate the precise path of the cutting edge. You can grip the tool from either above or below. Gripping from above gives firm support when you need to move the tool sideways along the rest, and by raising a few fingers, you can direct shavings away from your face. Gripping from below allows you to clamp tool and rest together to make a solid pivot point, while permitting you to watch the edge. No matter which grip you use, the object is the same: to keep hand and tool in contact

To get the most control, Raffan leans against the lathe, tool handle solidly against his side. His left hand assumes a hand-over grip—good for lateral movement along the rest.

with the rest, and to prevent the tool from moving sideways when you don't want it to.

Don't grip the tool as though your life depended on it. Just use a light, firm grip—relaxed, but ready to tighten instantly if necessary. This will provide a kind of recoil pad so that a catch will be less disastrous. It's possible to turn while holding the tool lightly between a finger and the thumb of your right hand. You have no fine control this way, but the trick illustrates how little power is required.

As your skill develops, you'll be able to adapt these grips to suit yourself. I enjoy the control I've gained through their application—moving the edge with a little squeeze or push here and there, in conjunction with broader movement from the rest of my body.

Cutting—Begin the cut with a firm grip on the tool, and always start above the center, or axis, of the wood. Don't push the tool straight across the rest into the wood—you get better control if you tilt the edge up 10° and bring it down in an arc by slowly raising the handle (figure 1).

I have three basic rules for cutting. First, whenever possible, cut the wood with the tool moving parallel to the lathe axis. This allows you to exert pressure in a direction where it will be absorbed by the headstock or tailstock (figure 2). Put as little forward pressure as possible against the axis of the wood, to avoid chatter. A sharp tool held in the optimum position will produce a large shaving with virtually no for-

ward pressure against the wood. Experiment by rolling the tool to find this point.

Second, have the bevel of the gouge or chisel rubbing (which is impossible with any scraping technique.) This provides a secondary fulcrum and a guide to aid fine control of the tool's edge. Sometimes, when beginning a cut, this is not possible. In this case, use a firm-fulcrum grip, and move the tool into the wood through an arc. Then move the bevel so that it can rub the newly cut surface.

Third, avoid using the tools at right angles to the surface being cut. It is much more difficult to achieve flowing or straight lines this way. Hold the tool so that the edge is tangent to the work, and move the tool in the same direction as the curve (figure 3).

Learn to move the tool precisely and evenly along a definite path. Plan what you want to cut, and have a beginning, middle and end to your movements. Don't poke at the wood. Any shape poked at and messed about tends to look it, so make your cuts smooth, flowing and definite. The tool should move forward only after the wood in its path has been removed. In the hands of an expert, this becomes a rapid, flowing action.

Practice slowly. Don't try to cut too much at one go. If you push the tool in too fast, the sudden force will lead to a catch. If the tool begins to cut less efficiently or stops cutting, adjust the tool angle and roll the tool to a different position. If you push forward to find an edge, the tool will often skate over

Gripping the tool: The overhand grip, top, gives firm support when moving the tool sideways along the rest. The hand-under grip, bottom, gives good control of the tool where it pivots on the rest, and prevents the tool from moving sideways.

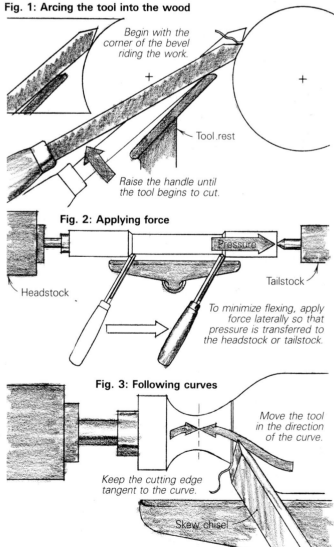

Fig. 1: Arcing the tool into the wood

Begin with the corner of the bevel riding the work.

Tool rest

Raise the handle until the tool begins to cut.

Fig. 2: Applying force

Pressure

Headstock

Tailstock

To minimize flexing, apply force laterally so that pressure is transferred to the headstock or tailstock.

Fig. 3: Following curves

Move the tool in the direction of the curve.

Keep the cutting edge tangent to the curve.

Skew chisel

Supporting the work: Any grip can be modified by extending fingers around the work to the back side to keep the wood from flexing (top left). Note how Raffan steadies his body on the lathe in the photo at left. To back up the thin wall of a bowl, above, Raffan uses his left-hand thumb to pin the tool to the rest, while the other fingers support the wood behind the cut.

the surface without cutting. The tool should never shoot forward if you lose an edge—that indicates a lack of control.

As a cut gets close to center, slow up for the last few millimeters and float the edge in gently, turning and adjusting the tool to maintain the most effective cut. Stop at dead center—don't cut below, or you risk tearing or pulling out fibers.

To improve your control, learn to stop in mid-cut. Practice easing pressure so that the edge of the tool is barely in contact with the wood. Then proceed again and stop again. Soon you should be able to remove the tool and bring it back to exactly the same position.

Practice and experience will teach you what each lathe tool can and can't do. If you have trouble, and don't know why, there are a few things to consider: First, check that the tool is sharp. If it is, but is still not cutting properly, experiment with different angles or roll the tool slightly. If this doesn't work, you may be using the wrong tool, so try another. If nothing seems to work, do some other job for a while, or go for a walk and try again later. Everyone has off days.

Supporting the wood—As you become more adventurous and turn slender pieces or bowls with thin walls, the wood will flex when a tool presses against it. If the wood flexes under power, it will vibrate, causing spiral chatter marks or worse. You'll hear a high, almost screeching sound if you're really overdoing it. You must support the wood. I always use my hand, which is far more flexible and sensitive than any mechanical support. One part supports the wood, while the other part remains in contact with the tool and rest. You can develop your own techniques, but your fingers or hand should support the wood from behind to provide counterpressure to the tool's pressure. If your hand gets hot, you're pushing too hard on the tool. Your hand should be warm, but not burning. Provide just enough support to keep the wood from flexing away from the center.

Sounds—Sounds are important in lathe work and you must learn them. Turning sounds should be a series of crescendos and decrescendos resulting from smooth, flowing cuts. Stop the lathe whenever you hear a new sound, to discover the cause. This is time-consuming at first, but you'll soon learn to recognize the basic noises—a sharp tool hisses; a dull tool makes a grinding sound. Once you hear the difference, it's easy to tell when your tool needs sharpening. With practice, you'll also be able to judge the thickness of a bowl wall, detect a loose block, or tell if you've hit a split or a knot, just by listening to the sound.

Attitude—It is worth pushing yourself. Don't be afraid to risk ruining a job with one chancey final cut. Sometimes just one more cut can make a lot of difference in the curve of a bowl. Once, when I checked the 8mm wall thickness of a large elm-burl bowl, I found it to be only 2.5mm thick near the base. I took a chance and turned the whole wall down to 2.5mm, and ended up with an even thickness—cut in one minute, not bludgeoned into submission with 20-grit abrasive in ten. That time I was successful. I've had smaller bowls shatter on me, but it is always worth the risk. Now and then you should cut bowls or boxes in half to examine the section. You can learn a great deal by doing this, and it's worth sacrificing some less-than-satisfactory pieces to help find out where you're going wrong.

As you develop your skills, beware of complacency. No matter how good you become, aspire to doing better. I find I am rarely satisfied with yesterday's masterpiece because it becomes today's run-of-the-mill. □

Richard Raffan, a professional turner who lives in Mittagong, N.S.W., Australia, regards himself as mostly self-taught. He is author of the book Turning Wood with Richard Raffan *(The Taunton Press, 1985).*

Harvesting Burls
Strange formations are turners' delight

by Mark Lindquist

Lindquist positions a gigantic yellow-birch burl in his woodlot for seasoning. Burls of this size (which can almost engulf a trunk, as on the ash tree in the inset photo) are difficult to move without the aid of professional loggers and special equipment.

Burls are perhaps the most misunderstood and mysterious material in the woodworker's realm. Most woodworkers and suppliers who use these strange, unpredictable organic formations have very little idea of how they grew or what caused them. And, although burlwood has long been prized for veneer, lumbermen and forest pathologists trying to produce straight and sound stock for the mass-production lumber industry have always regarded the burl as an enemy and a nuisance. But I find burls to be an extremely rich source of material for sculpture and turned and carved bowls, and, most importantly, an inspiration for discovering new philosophies and approaches to woodturning.

Burls are protuberances on a tree that come in all shapes and sizes. They are known colloquially as "burrs," "bumps," "knobs" or "gnarls," and scientifically as "galls." A burl may be a perfect half-sphere on the side of a tree, or look like a

Kathy Lindquist

Bill Byers

Burls come in all shapes and sizes. Shown above are burls from 16 different species, including walnut, hornbeam, ash, beech, spruce, mulberry, birch, cherry and oak. Lindquist chainsaws bowl blanks from rough burls (left), visualizing the final form inside the burl. Notice the burl's layered structure. Below, the chaotic grain of a wild-cherry, dormant-bud burl struggles with a lathe-smooth surface. Linquist's father, Melvin, turned the piece, called 'Ancient Ceremonial Form Translation,' in 1974.

Robert Aude

wreath surrounding the tree, especially if it grows leaves on short stems. Burls may be irregular, twisted and malformed; surfaces may be smooth, or rough and fissured. A burl may grow halfway around the trunk, creating a half-moon that makes a beautiful carved bowl, or along one side of a tree, or sometimes all the way up and around the entire trunk.

Burl forms offer many sculptural possibilities. Some burls are quietly round, whether shallow or deep, definitely suggesting a bowl. Others are twisted and convoluted, evoking a sense of animation. No matter how much energy shows on the outside, though, it is no clue to the incredible explosion of energy inside—a swirling, frozen pot of marbleized color, texture and structure, creating patterns too complex to understand or predict. It is one of nature's amazing mysteries—the starry galaxy within is greater than the form containing it.

A burl is not a healing over of a broken-off branch, but an irregular growth. Burls are often caused when fire, frost or something hitting the tree injures the cambium, which is the growth layer near the bark. (Interestingly, when trees are repeatedly burned on one side, they form burls on the opposite side.) Fungal or bacterial irritation of the cambium also causes burl formations, particularly the more gnarly, rough-barked ones. Some scientists suggest that a mutation or a hereditary factor, combined with environmental conditions, is responsible for burl growth. This might explain why several trees of the same species growing in a particular area (which quite likely are related) may all grow burls.

Burls generally are divided into two categories: root burls and above-ground burls. Root burls (called "crown galls" by scientists) are caused by bacteria, which possibly entered damaged areas of the tree from infected soil. These formations tend to be softer than above-ground burls because they develop within a controlled atmosphere of soil and water. Usually a large, round ball will form at the base of the trunk, and the roots will grow out of the burl.

Root burls, like above-ground burls, may occur on any tree. They form on cherry, white birch and gray birch in the East, and are extremely common in California on redwoods and manzanita. Redwood root burls may grow to be 12 ft. in diameter, nearly too big to handle. Most of the redwood "burl tables" made in California are constructed of root burls with extraordinary grain and pattern.

On the East Coast, maple and cherry commonly exhibit above-ground burls. Next in prominence is the birch family, then oak, followed by elm, beech, ash, butternut, hornbeam and poplar. Soft-wood burls are rarer, and not as interesting in grain-pattern development, nor will they take as high a polish as the hard-wood burls. California redwood and buckeye burl are exceptions, since they have magnificent grain patterns, although they do not take a high polish.

Lindquist worked the 12-in. long layered maple burl shown at left with a chainsaw, gouges, a die grinder, rifflers, rasps and foam-backed abrasive discs. Its oil finish is buffed with a tripoli/animal-fat-based compound. The piece, called 'Vessel Vessel/Arc Ark,' was made in 1978. A cherry burl yielded the 18-in. high turned bowl above. The burl contains layered and bud formations as well as bark.

An above-ground burl may grow at any height on a tree, on the trunk or on a major branch. Occasionally, more than one burl will grow on a tree, and when this occurs there are usually quite a few. The most exciting burl find is the "burl tree," a tree whose trunk has been entirely encompassed by burls growing into and around each other, forming a giant mass of burl growth and grain. Most burl trees I've found have been elm, maple or white birch.

Within the infinite variety of burl-grain development are three main classifications: annual layering, end-grain budding, and a combination of these two growth patterns. In annual layering, the burl grows in much the same pattern as the tree, though much more rapidly, adding a thicker layer than the tree, causing the bulging and swirling form of the burl. Successive layers within a burl will display inconsistencies in thickness, with thicker layers toward the center of the burl rather than nearer the supporting trunk or branch. Where the burl "hangs" from the tree, there is even apt to be a crotch-wood formation in cell growth of the burl for support.

Compared to straight-grained wood, layered-growth burls display remarkable beauty and complexity of color and configuration, yet their grain is subtle compared to that of the spectacular burls formed by the end grain of dormant buds.

Dormant-bud burls form through an explosion of early bud development that never quite makes it through the bark. All the buds shoot and clash within, causing more shoots to get started and early ones to become dormant. The buds never get past the stage of early development, growing more in width than in length, causing hard, dense wood. This type of burl is most prevalent in cherry and walnut, and also occurs in certain elm, maple, oak and white birch species.

The third classification, which I call "swirl-eye" burl, is a combination of the other two. Often these are the most complex of all burl formations, especially when the patterns are balanced. Imagine that the first two classifications were melted together, then stirred and frozen. The dormant buds, or "eyes," are mixed in with the rest of the swirly grain.

After working with hundreds of burls during the past 15 years, I know that some grain patterns frequently recur within a given species. Yet on cutting into a new burl, I can still be surprised by an entirely new configuration.

Here are a few clues about where to look for burls. Although burls may grow on trees in any terrain, usually the hilly, rocky, heavily wooded areas of mountainous regions yield the most. An individual tree may give signs of burl formation—a gradual change in bark formation, for example, or a gentle widening of the trunk, indicating that a burl is growing on the other side. If you find a burl, keep looking nearby—burled trees sometimes proliferate in certain areas.

Perhaps the most difficult problem in obtaining burls is getting permission to take them. You usually can hunt down the owner of the land on which the trees you are interested in are growing and strike some sort of agreeable deal. Often I've traded small pieces of finished work for larger burls or lots of burls.

When I find a burl in the woods, I consider its quality, its distance from a usable road, cutting problems, and what I am willing to pay. Any woodworker who has harvested a big burl far from a road will probably not do it again, remembering the pain and difficulty of that first deep-woods encounter. One solution is to cut the burl in the fall and leave it in the woods until winter, then haul it out on a toboggan pulled by a snowmobile. Purists may take exception to cutting a burl or a tree during any time other than winter. I prefer the fall, as it is the best time to find burls because the trees are shedding their leaves—it's also the nicest time to be working in the woods. After years of searching for and harvesting big burls in this old-fashioned way, I've begun to buy them from local loggers, who frequently find them and are equipped to fell them and pull them out. Town dumps are often surprising sources, as are tree-removal services and tree surgeons.

A burl can be removed either by cutting it off the tree, or by cutting down the tree and then removing the section with the burl. If possible, I prefer the former because it eliminates dealing with the branches and other wood of a downed tree. Also, the tree normally lives on after the burl is removed, often becoming healthier. Don't paint the cut—it will dry up, and the tree will gradually grow around and over the wound.

A burl is best cut close to the trunk, as nearly parallel to the trunk as possible. Deep, gouging cuts into the tree are pointless when the best use of the wood is achieved by a clean, straight cut, leaving a neat area on the tree. You will always leave some good burled wood in the tree, but the only way to get it all is to cut down the tree.

When I do cut down a tree, I try to leave a foot or so of trunk on each end of the burl so that as the log dries, checks won't telegraph into the burl. Often the burl will dry better and is less apt to check if left this way for several years.

Drying and storing burls can be as uncomplicated as piling them outdoors or as sophisticated as packing them in layers of sawdust. When cut green, burls usually are very heavy, laden with water. Some woodturners prefer to use green burls. Burls turn most easily when wet, but will warp and twist as they dry. Green burls may be stored under water over a period of time, which prevents drying. Blanketing them in wet sawdust retards checking, promoting slow, even drying.

I prefer to work dry, aged, mellow burls—checks and all. My philosophy of woodworking acknowledges the nature of the material, which is to expand and contract. I allow for the inclusion of checking within my designs, by either accepting

Tips for turning irregular pieces

by Rude Osolnik

About thirty-five years ago, I started turning irregularly shaped blocks of wood because I had a good source of supply, and because of the challenge and the distorted, discolored grain. I've turned bowls, trays and weed pots from burls and spurs (where a tree root makes the transition from horizontal to vertical), as well as from found wood—chestnut fence rails, oak wagon tongues, just about anything.

I've found that a heavy lathe is crucial when turning irregular pieces. A large, off-center blank, 3 lb. to 15 lb. out of balance, will shake a light lathe apart before the piece can be trued. A heavy bed, preferably of cast iron, will absorb the vibration. Anchoring the lathe with bolts, sandbags or heavy metal bars will also help (*FWW #25*, pp. 80-81, and #41, pp. 48-53).

I turn pieces up to 12 in. in diameter on an 800-lb. Oliver lathe. Even though the lathe is bolted to the floor, I sometimes wedge 2x4s between the bed and ceiling for extra support. For larger pieces, I use a 2,000-lb. metal-spinning lathe with a 13-in. swing over the bed.

Lathe speed is less important than the speed of the block at its periphery—the larger the diameter, the slower the speed should be. In general, I turn pieces up to 12 in. at 1200 RPM to 1800 RPM, and larger blanks at 700 RPM to 800 RPM. For blanks up to 24 in. in diameter, my big lathe turns as slowly as 150 RPM.

Before mounting an irregular turning blank on the lathe, you should trim, balance and shape the general form on the bandsaw or with a chainsaw. Bowls

Roundnose chisel and gouge

Chisel

½

¼

30°

Full-size

Round corners.

Gouge

Grind chisel back about 2 in. from cutting edge to make gouge.

and trays are best mounted on faceplates. A weed pot or other turning where only the outside is shaped can be mounted between centers.

If there is enough waste material on the blank, or if the bottom won't be seen, screw the faceplate directly to it, using long, heavy screws. If you need a backing block, attach it directly to the blank with a strong glue such as Titebond. (Paper placed in between can separate.) Make the block thick—2 in. or more—so that you can work on the bottom without interference.

You can give a faceplate-mounted, deep bowl blank added support by embedding the tailstock center in the face of the blank. If the blank is very irregular even after you've trued the outside, you can leave a column of wood in the center attached to the tailstock while you shape the inside. After the bulk of the wood

has been removed, cut off the column and finish the inside bottom surface.

I make all my turning tools, and I do most of my turning with a heavy ½-in. wide by ¼-in. deep roundnose chisel. Most people use this tool for scraping, but by grinding a long bevel on it, I can get the shearing cut usually associated with a skew chisel. The bevel, which is about 30°, rides the surface and supports the cutting edge, which can then take a smooth shaving. I also made a small, shallow gouge by grinding a groove in the top surface of a roundnose chisel, and I use it to take fine finishing cuts.

Truing up the odd shape of the rough blank is the hardest part. Once the blank has been trued and balanced on the lathe, it can be turned much like any other piece. Because of the irregular shape of the blank, the tool's cutting edge leaves and reenters the wood with every revolution of the lathe, increasing the chances of catching. Obviously, a steady tool rest and firm hand are essential.

Position the rest as close as possible to the blank. Be careful to stand to one side, out of the path of flying debris, particularly when turning burls. Remove the high spots with shallow cuts, moving the tool rest as you go to keep it close. Pay strict attention to where the edge of the work actually is. I watch the back edge where the stroboscopic effect shows the outline of the highest points most clearly.

As the tool makes more contact with the surface, you can take heavier cuts. For truing, I use a cut that is halfway between scraping and shearing. Posi-

the crack as it is, or working it open to relieve its jaggedness. I like the spontaneity of working the dry burl and being able to finish the piece, knowing it will move or shrink very little from its finished dimensions.

When I harvest burls, I usually leave them uncovered outdoors, sitting directly on the ground, for maximum exposure to the elements. Most begin staining and spalting, and I find the resulting colorations desirable. Yellow birch burls, for example, are relatively bland, but become utterly spectacular when colored or spalted.

It's a good idea to either mark the species and date of cutting on the burl, or store specific kinds of burls in separate piles so that they will all dry together. Painting of the sawn surfaces will discourage checking, but it also prolongs drying. I'd rather let the burls sit and let nature have its way. Since the grain is so twisty and gnarly, often the burls dry without checks, or with very few, which can be accepted, or cut out by dividing the burl along the cracks into smaller, usable sections.

After exposing the burls to the weather for a year or two, I move them into an open-air shed, build a lean-to over the pile using corrugated transparent roofing, or simply cover them with plastic. When the burls have sufficiently dried, they must be stored up off the ground, preferably away from sunlight. I pile them one on top of the other in my barn. Due to their various unusual shapes, this storage is awkward and cumbersome, as well as inefficient. I've built shelves and racks, but haven't solved the problem yet.

Like spalted wood, burls are abundant for those possessing the knowledge of their worth. These strange formations offer more than oddity or novelty for the woodturner, more than their hidden beauty. I find in them a profound truth, a truth about life and about the work of an artisan: in acknowledging imperfection, perfection is defined. □

Mark Lindquist turns and sculpts wood in Henniker, N.H. This article was adapted from his forthcoming book on sculpting wood, to be published by Davis Publications, Inc., 50 Portland St., Worcester, Mass. 01608.

Osolnik turns a rhododendron-burl weed pot between centers with a roundnose chisel (left). The nearly finished pot is shown above. The hole in the neck is bored after turning.

tioning the rest slightly above dead center, I angle the tool about 10° to 15° above horizontal. I don't worry about the condition of the surface until the blank is basically round. Then I re-sharpen the tool and take light, shearing cuts to get the final outside shape.

Normally I work very loosely, by feel, letting the grain pattern and shape of the block dictate the final shape, accenting areas that will enhance the finished piece. I like to leave bark on some pieces; the contrast of rough and polished textures adds character. I've even left moss in place on twig pots—the greenish color looks nice against the surrounding finished surface.

On the inside, I work from thick wood to thin—that is, from the center out—to minimize vibration in the wall. Turn the bowl wall ³⁄₁₆ in. to ¼ in. thick, then go back for the finishing touches. Check the wall thickness frequently so that you don't unintentionally cut through at an indentation.

When turning between centers, position the centers by eye and turn the blank by hand to check its balance and distance from the tool rest. After taking several initial cuts, you can reposition the centers to improve the balance of the piece, or to accent a particular grain pattern or texture.

I sand the piece on the lathe, by hand or with a disc sander. With quick-change discs and the lathe at 800 RPM, you can start with 60-grit paper—which removes torn fibers—and work through 80-, 100- and 150-grit, finishing by hand with 180-grit. Finer-grit, higher-speed sanding would burnish and polish instead of sanding. The disc will bridge gaps in the surface, so if you want to soften those, hand-sand with the lathe running slowly.

Friction and centrifugal force will dry ³⁄₁₆-in. to ¼-in. thick wet wood as you work. Start with a coarse paper—a fine grit will generate too much heat and cause checking. When you're done sanding, immediately bandsaw off the facing block so that the wood won't crack as it continues to dry. □

Rude Osolnik, retired chairman of industrial arts at Berea College, Ky., is a woodturner and turning teacher.

Turning Music Boxes

Try a different movement on your lathe

by James A. Jacobson

One of the dilemmas of the turner's craft is the persistent question: What is it for? Over the years, I'd turned innumerable round things, including dozens of boxes and containers, but most of these objects just stood around doing nothing, with no real purpose or function. The question began to nag at me. Then one day I turned a little box and fitted a music movement inside. When the tune began to play, that was answer enough for me.

I've since worked out a variety of shapes and sizes for turned musical boxes. These experiments proved so satisfying that they led me to write a book: *Woodturning Music Boxes*. In this article I'll show you the basics, including how a music movement works (see p. 132), and I'll give a list of suppliers. I'll tell you about my favorite woods, skim over the tools I like, and share some of the turning tips I've picked up. I'll also discuss a shop-made chuck that I find invaluable. Other turners, no doubt, will see ways to apply their own tricks.

Wood—It is my good fortune to live in an area of the Midwest that is endowed not only with hardwood forests, but also with numerous small sawmills, where some of the best wood for turning is almost free for the asking—those pieces that others would consider worthless. I like chaotic and unpredictable grain—sawmill cutoffs from logs, burls and spalted wood.

Some woods transmit musical vibrations better than others, amplifying the sound. Yet in my experience, any wood will make a decent music box. Oak and mahogany, for instance, are said to be poor choices, but when they are turned thin enough, I've found that they work fine. I highly recommend walnut, cherry, hard maple and Osage-orange, but other woods are worth experimenting with, too. Try whatever is in your woodpile—the turned pieces I enjoy the most are from wood that I found, lugged home, and nursed to readiness myself.

In addition to native woods, I've turned music boxes from bocote, padauk and bubinga, though mostly I use these as accent woods for designs on lids, and for decorative plugs: if I have a nice turning block that's flawed, I drill out the flaw and insert a contrasting plug before I turn the piece. Another ornamental, wood-saving trick for a block with one or two major checks is to bandsaw along the check line and glue the block back together with a contrasting piece of veneer between the two pieces.

When working out a new design, I often turn a few prototypes from glued-up construction-grade 2x4s or #3 lumber.

Tools—I prefer scraping tools because they allow me to make very light and precise cuts. This is especially important when turning the soundboard of a music box, the part to which the

music movement is attached. The soundboard should be both thin and flat. That way, it not only transmits the music to the air, but also transmits the vibrations to the sides of the turning, for more volume. Musical vibrations will also travel down the sides of a box to the surface beneath. A wooden tabletop, for instance, will amplify the sound.

For rough-turning, especially on larger blocks, I use a 1-in. roundnose scraper, pointed slightly downward. I sharpen it on a 6-in. by 48-in. belt sander with a 100- or 120-grit belt. You don't need a razor edge on a scraping tool. In fact, the edge will cut better if it has a slight burr. To prevent ruining the entire belt, which is used for other things, too, I restrict the sharpening area to a narrow strip along one edge. On smaller jobs, and for lids and insides, I usually begin with a ½-in. roundnose.

I sharpen square and skewed scrapers, which make the finishing cuts, on a regular shop grinder. For the outsides of music boxes, an extra-heavy skewed or squarenose scraper, ⅜ in. thick and 1½ in. wide, is a good tool. I like a long, heavy handle, and often make my own either from hickory or from hackberry. Hackberry, because of its interlocking grain pattern and surface texture, is a non-slip wood and very secure in the hand.

Once in a while I cut rather than scrape, using a long-and-strong ⅜-in. deep gouge. But on the kind of wood I prefer, scraping tools have advantages. A scraper is less likely to tear out unruly grain, and is ideal for truing the walls and soundboard. In addition, a scraper can very cleanly square up the narrow shoulders necessary for lids and for glass inserts.

The glass insert is a clear cover that allows you to watch the movement working yet keeps it clean. I cut my own glass inserts with a circle glass cutter, then smooth the sharp edges on the belt sander. If you'd like an insert but don't want to go to the trouble of cutting your own, you can probably find a replacement flashlight lens near enough to size to do the job. Good hardware stores usually carry them, although these days they're likely to be plastic instead of glass. No matter.

The chuck—When turning a large box, it's best to screw the blank securely to a faceplate, the way you would begin turning any heavy piece of wood. If you want to avoid screw holes in the bottom of the box, use the familiar method of gluing a piece of paper between the block and a wooden faceplate, so that the

Tunesome containers can be made of everything from Osage-orange firewood to choice padauk. The tallest music box in the photo on the facing page is 10½ in. high. The small ones, with single-tune movements, readily sell at crafts fairs for about $25.

How a music movement works

Cylinder music movements were developed by Swiss horologists (watch/clock makers) early in the 19th century. Though designers have evolved some exceedingly complex—and expensive—mechanisms, the basic principles of a music movement are easily understood (figure 1).

Each tooth on a metal comb, when plucked, vibrates and produces a musical note. The teeth are plucked by metal pins on a revolving cylinder, and the arrangement of the pins and tuning of the comb determine the tune. The cylinder is powered by a wound spring, and its speed is regulated by the air resistance of a rapidly whirling, lightweight governor called a butterfly.

In some movements, the on/off switch is merely a wire, called a stopper, that pivots into the path of the butterfly (figure 2A). This makes it simple to adapt most movements to various switches. Wires can be linked to run up through the side of the box to the lid, so the box plays when it is opened and stops when it is closed. Similarly, the stopper can run through the bottom, so the box begins to play when it is picked up. Instead of a wire, I sometimes run a small dowel through the side of the box. My usual stopper consists of a sliding cylindrical weight on a horizontal rod (figure 2B). When you tilt the box to the side, the weight slides free of the butterfly. Tilting the box the other way stops the butterfly.

Some simple movements are made without stoppers—they play until they run down—and some are cranked by hand. A slightly more complicated type of movement plays more than one tune, and usually has a built-in index stop that turns the movement off when each tune is finished (figure 3). These movements are actuated by a sliding switch, and have one clear advantage—the music begins at the start of the tune, not somewhere in the middle. Otherwise, the basic principles remain the same.

Sources: I primarily use Reuge Swiss movements, and these are readily available by mail order. Reuge catalogs its movements according to the number of teeth (the number of notes in the comb) and the number of tunes the movement will play. Reuge's 1.18 movement has 18 teeth and plays one tune. Their 2.36 has 36 teeth—allowing greater range from treble to bass—and plays two tunes. The 1.18 movement will play nearly 3½ minutes on a single winding.

Each movement type is available in a variety of melodies, and many familiar woodworking catalogs (Woodcraft and Constantine's, among others) contain a page of musical movements. In addition to the basic movements that most places sell, you can buy battery-powered movements, miniature movements, and movements with interchangeable cylinders. For the out-of-the-ordinary, try Craft Products Music Boxes, Dept. 95, 2200 Dean St., St. Charles, Ill. 60174; Klockit, Box 629, Lake Geneva, Wis. 53147; Mason & Sullivan, 586 Higgins Crowell Rd., West Yarmouth, Mass. 02673; and World of Music Boxes, 412 Main St., Avon, N.J. 07717. This last source will even make custom movements to play the tune of your choice. There's an organization for aficionados, too: The Musical Box Society International, Box 205, Rt. 3, Morgantown, Ind. 46160. —*J.A.J.*

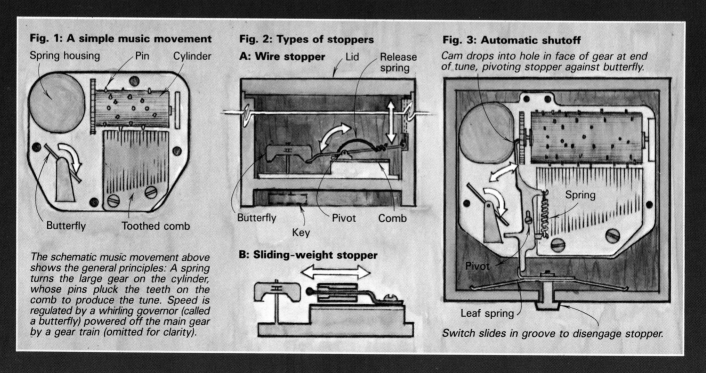

Fig. 1: A simple music movement

Spring housing · Pin · Cylinder · Butterfly · Toothed comb

The schematic music movement above shows the general principles: A spring turns the large gear on the cylinder, whose pins pluck the teeth on the comb to produce the tune. Speed is regulated by a whirling governor (called a butterfly) powered off the main gear by a gear train (omitted for clarity).

Fig. 2: Types of stoppers
A: Wire stopper — Lid · Release spring · Butterfly · Pivot · Key · Comb

B: Sliding-weight stopper

Fig. 3: Automatic shutoff
Cam drops into hole in face of gear at end of tune, pivoting stopper against butterfly.
Spring · Pivot · Leaf spring
Switch slides in groove to disengage stopper.

Drawings: Ben Thompson

block can be split off later. I bandsaw all blocks round before mounting them. When you have finished as much as you can with the blank on the faceplate, you'll have to reverse the blank so that you can turn a recess in the bottom for the music movement's winding key (and to thin out the soundboard). I've developed a screw-center chuck, shown in the drawing, that holds the box in this position. When trying the chuck, you may find that the center screw doesn't run quite true. It will seem to wobble as the lathe turns. A few gentle taps with a hammer or a wooden block, with the lathe turning, will usually put it right.

Dimensions—The dimensions of a turned music box depend on the size of the music movement. The simple box in the drawing shows the important size considerations, the turning process and some finishing touches. Other ideas can be seen in the photograph on p. 131 and are mostly self-explanatory. All you need to ensure accuracy while turning are some simple measuring tools. Inside and outside calipers and a child's compass are enough, but I like a vernier caliper as well—I usually work in millimeters, because the music movements I use are metric. In addition, I have a gauge for estimating the rounded size of a rough, irregular blank. The gauge is merely a sheet of stiff plastic with concentric circles scribed around a center hole. I position the gauge against the end of the wood, center the largest circle I can, then mark the center through the hole.

Sanding and finishing—For protection, I wear a suede glove on my left hand most of the time when I'm turning, and both gloves when sanding. I back up the sandpaper with pieces of ¼-in. foam carpet padding. These are flexible enough to follow contours smoothly, and they absorb most of the friction heat that would otherwise burn the wood. I begin with 100-grit garnet paper, except on very rough wood, where I use 60-grit. If the paper won't cut the wood fibers with the lathe turning in the usual direction, I reverse the lathe motor for a while, taking care that the faceplate doesn't start to unscrew. Next I sand with 150-grit, followed by 220- or 240-grit. It usually isn't necessary to sand the recess where the movement will be.

For a high polish, I dry-sand with 280- or 320-grit wet-or-dry paper (silicon carbide), followed by 600-grit and a final polish with 0000 steel wool.

I've done my share of shellac-polishing on the lathe, but I have a few reasons for not doing music boxes that way. First, you can't finish the entire piece at one time, because the faceplate or chuck gets in the way. Second, lathe-finishing ties up faceplates and chucks, and on occasion the lathe itself. Third, you sometimes must finish a piece as soon as you've turned it (when remounting it might cause it to go out of balance). I'd rather finish a few pieces at a time, off the lathe, at leisure.

First I apply Watco oil, sanding lightly with the grain with 600-grit wet-or-dry paper to remove the last whiskers of wood. The oil brings out the natural beauty of the wood—I never use stain. When this first coat is dry, I go on in one of two ways: I either apply two or more additional coats of Watco, or brush on a few coats of Deft lacquer, steel-wooling between coats to an even luster. In either case, a coat of paste wax, buffed or rubbed, is a good way to maintain the finish. □

James A. Jacobson, who turns wood in Collinsville, Ill., is currently working on a second book, Crafting Music Boxes. Woodturning Music Boxes *is available from Sterling Publishing Co., Two Park Ave., New York, N.Y. 10016.*

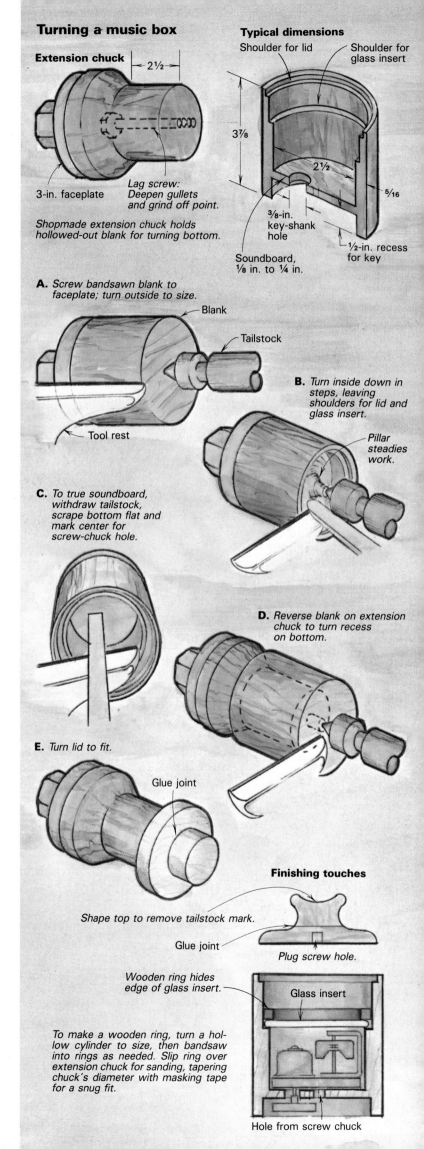

Turning a music box

Extension chuck

3-in. faceplate

Lag screw: Deepen gullets and grind off point.

Shopmade extension chuck holds hollowed-out blank for turning bottom.

Typical dimensions

Shoulder for lid

Shoulder for glass insert

3⅞

2½

⅜-in. key-shank hole

Soundboard, ⅛ in. to ¼ in.

5/16

½-in. recess for key

A. Screw bandsawn blank to faceplate; turn outside to size.

Blank

Tailstock

Tool rest

B. Turn inside down in steps, leaving shoulders for lid and glass insert.

Pillar steadies work.

C. To true soundboard, withdraw tailstock, scrape bottom flat and mark center for screw-chuck hole.

D. Reverse blank on extension chuck to turn recess on bottom.

E. Turn lid to fit.

Glue joint

Finishing touches

Shape top to remove tailstock mark.

Glue joint

Plug screw hole.

Wooden ring hides edge of glass insert.

Glass insert

To make a wooden ring, turn a hollow cylinder to size, then bandsaw into rings as needed. Slip ring over extension chuck for sanding, tapering chuck's diameter with masking tape for a snug fit.

Hole from screw chuck

If you plan ahead and have a thick enough blank, you can turn a bowl bottom of any shape without leaving a clue as to how it was attached to the lathe. The photo above shows the secret: grip the bowl via a small wooden plug, which you saw off after shaping.

The Bottom Line for Turned Bowls
Versatile chucking plug permits a variety of designs

by Wendell Smith

A woodturner can often improve a bowl just by realizing that its bottom is as important to its design as its rim or its overall shape. You may neglect the bottom, but if you submit a piece to a juried exhibition, you can be sure the judges won't. The best bowls don't reveal how they were attached to the lathe. But chucking procedures can interfere with good bowl design. The trick is to make the design you want, while leaving no trace of the method.

The simplest method of chucking is to screw the bowl bottom to a faceplate, but then the finished bottom must be at least as thick as the length of the screws penetrating into the wood. Unless you want a thick bottom and plugged screw holes, a more refined method is needed.

Other chucking methods can impose restrictions. Turning a recess into the bowl bottom for an expanding-collet chuck requires that you design a bowl with a rimmed bottom. If you turn a male plug on the bottom to fit some type of ring chuck, you'll have a footed bowl. On the other hand, facing off the bottom so that it is flat and can be attached to a scrap block with double-sided tape or with glue and paper does lead to a flat bottom.

For green wood, I use a simple on-the-lathe method that lets me prepare and finish bottoms of any thickness, and have them flat or smoothly curved (with a slight flat spot to stand on), rimmed or footed, while maintaining complete freedom of design. This technique requires starting with wood thick enough to turn a ½-in. by 3-in. plug on the bowl bottom, using the plug to hold the wood on the lathe, and then removing the plug to finish up.

The plug is helpful when turning green bowls because the blank is solidly attached to a faceplate. You cannot use the glue-and-paper method because the glue will not stick to the wet wood. Balance is important with green stock because of its weight, and with the subsequently dried bowls because of their eccentricity.

For chucking dry wood, which is often not thick enough to allow for a chucking plug, I usually use glue and paper to fix the blank to a scrap block that is screwed to the faceplate. This requires a clean-up procedure based on a simple off-the-lathe hand-scraping method (bottom right photo, p. 136).

The photographs illustrate my finishing method for re-

Flat Curved Rimmed Footed

moving the chucking plug from the base of an otherwise finished bowl about 5 in. high and 10 in. in diameter. This bowl was rough-turned green by first screwing a 3-in. face-plate to what would become the open (top) side of the blank, using ¾-in. #12 flat-head wood screws. With the faceplate mounted on the lathe, the bottom can be faced off with a deep-fluted gouge. Then, with the tool rest slightly below the center of the blank, use a parting tool to make a ½-in. deep shearing cut about 1½ in. from the blank's center. It is important to hold the parting-tool handle low when doing this, so the tool cuts, not scrapes. If your design calls for a footed bowl, cut deeper to leave a longer plug. With a gouge, shape the outside of the bowl to a rough form from the rim to the parting-tool groove. After the outside has been roughed out, remove the faceplate from the top of the blank and screw it to the plug. Although the bowl blank may not be perfectly recentered, it's unnecessary to true up the outside until the wood has dried. The inside of the bowl is turned using conventional methods. The photo sequence shows how to remove the plug, picking up after the bowl has been dried, re-turned and sanded.

1. The tailstock ring center holds the bowl, finish-sanded except for the chucking plug on its base, against a pressure plate made from a 1-in. by 13-in. hardwood disc. A groove in the plate holds the bowl's rim in place. Make a new groove for each size bowl, using a parting tool to size the groove until the rim of the bowl bears on either its inside edge or its outside edge. Now push the bowl onto the plate and bring the tailstock in. Before locking the tailstock, however, crank the ram far enough out to leave room for a small tool rest. At this point, any type of foot can be turned on the bowl. Here I chose a smooth, footless finish.

3. After reducing the plug to a ¾-in. diameter, smooth and flatten the bowl bottom using a straight-across or right-skew scraper, followed by sanding. Then, with the tool rest parallel to the lathe axis, use a thin parting tool to make a shearing cut about 1/16 in. from the bowl's base. Before cutting deeply, widen the cut slightly on the right. Keep the cut wider than the tool as you cut into the plug, to reduce resistance to cutting and to keep from breaking the bridge. I find it best to rotate the parting tool slightly clockwise and counterclockwise while cutting, as though cutting a small bead. The small 1/16-in. platform of waste wood left between the base of the bowl and the bridge prevents the parting tool from tearing wood fibers on the bowl bottom.

2. With a parting tool or a beading tool, make 1/16-in. to 1/8-in. shearing cuts until the 3-in. plug is reduced to ¾ in. in diameter. Don't use too much force on the tool, or the bowl will slip. If the wood has a fancy figure, put the tool rest perpendicular to the lathe axis, then scrape away the plug with a small round-nose tool. A deep gouge could be used if the tool rest were lowered.

4. With the lathe off, I use a Japanese *dozuki* saw to cut the small bridge between the bowl and the plug. Before sawing, pull the tailstock ram back slightly to take pressure off the bridge. The masking tape protects the bowl bottom from the saw. For a full view of the work at this stage, see p. 134.

For a full view of the work at this stage, see p. 134.

5. Place the bowl rim-down in a right-angle stop-block jig as shown at right and remove whatever waste remains by slicing cross-grain with a bench chisel, held bevel-up. The tape prevents the chisel from damaging the finished base. Finally, scrape the center of the base with the grain, then hand-sand.

Glue-and-paper chucks—To remove a glue-and-paper chucking block, place the completed bowl face-down on a towel and tap in an old plane blade, bevel-up. Insert the blade between the two bottom plies of the plywood, rather than between the block and the bowl, to prevent damage. Lift the blade end to lever off most of the block. The remaining waste can be pared off with a bench chisel, used bevel-up.

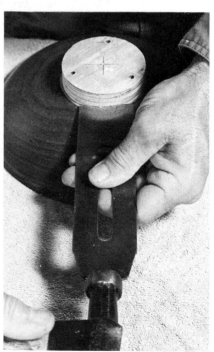

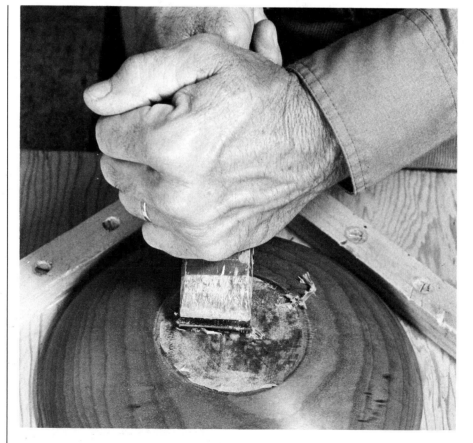

Remove the final traces of the glue-and-paper joint with a 1½-in. paint scraper, then follow up with sandpaper. The secret to using these scrapers is to leave a burr on the cutting edge when sharpening it on a grinder. □

Wendell Smith, who lives in Fairport, N.Y., is a chemist in the Kodak Research Labs. Photos by the author.

Chatterwork

*A risky path
to a faceted finish*

by Stephen Paulsen

For the past six years, I've been perfecting a technique for decorating small spindle turnings with three-dimensional surface texture. I call it chatterwork. It's an efficient way of producing mandala-like patterns that resemble those cut on a 19th-century Holtzapffel lathe, or the meticulously carved surfaces of David Pye's turned containers on the back cover of *FWW* #13. Chatterwork can be done on any lathe, and takes minutes instead of hours, although it looks as if a lot more time was involved. Since this technique also cuts sanding time, it's economically feasible for production turning.

While I can imagine many applications for chatterwork, from drawer pulls to dowel caps and decorative inlays, I use it mostly on the stoppers for my glass-lined wooden scent bottles. Hard, heavy, dense woods—ebony, brazilwood, rosewood and African blackwood—are best for chatterwork because they hold the sharpest detail.

You may already have inadvertently

***Chatterwork graces the lids and
insides of Paulsen's tiny boxes,
and the spired stoppers of his
glass-lined wooden scent bottles.***

Photos this page: White Light

A light shearing cut with the skew (**A**) creates a spiral flute pattern on the pointed finial (**B**).

The edge and corner of a parting tool makes concentric circles of chatterwork (**C**).

A skew decorates the spherical barrel of the stopper (**D**).

Burnishing with a pointed stick of the same wood species as the spindle (**E**) polishes and highlights the pattern.

produced crude chatterwork on your own turnings. Here's how it happens: A slender spindle can flex as it spins, and tool pressure pushes it into an elliptical rather than circular path around its axis. At high speed, the flexing wood vibrates against the tool's edge, which leaves marks on the surface of the wood. Chatter can also be caused by a tool that's dull or held at the wrong angle, but this type of blemish hardly leaves a decorative surface.

I control chatter by carefully reducing the diameter of the spindle so it can flex easily, then I delicately manipulate the work with a razor-sharp tool to make it chatter. Chatterwork is workmanship of extreme risk—I'm practically daring the spindle to break, and often it obliges. Little explosions of exotic wood, pieces and splinters flying, are part and parcel of the technique. Needless to say, eye protection is essential.

I work on a small Duro lathe equipped with a ¾-in. Jacobs chuck on the headstock spindle. For most of my turning, I use a ½-in. skew, and a ½-in. wide parting tool ⅛ in. thick. I also make small parting tools out of ¼-in. square steel key stock (normally used for keying pulleys to motor shafts). I only use a tool for a few quick cuts before regrinding, so the key stock holds an edge long enough to suit me. My homemade parting tools are designed to cut a very small amount of material at a time, to minimize resistance between tool and work. I rarely use these special parting tools for the actual chattering procedure.

Nothing affects final results more than tool sharpness. I grind all my tools to one of two basic angles: 60° for parting tools and 75° for skews. I keep a two-wheel grinder next to the lathe, with the parting-tool angle set on one wheel and the skew angle on the other. Because I resharpen so often, I don't have time to reset tool rests. I prefer a fresh razor burr straight from the medium wheel, so I never hone or whet a tool by hand.

Good light is essential for proper reading of the chattered surface, so my lathe sits under a combination of fluorescent and incandescent lights, including a flex-arm desk lamp on the ways. Behind the lathe, I've tacked a Masonite panel, painted white to reflect light on the spindle.

Here's how I begin a stopper. From a 7-in. long, 1-in. square blank mounted between centers, I rough out four stoppers without cutting them apart. For a headstock center, I clamp a pointed ¼-in. dia. steel dowel in the chuck. With the tailstock tightened enough for the steel dowel to drive the spindle, I turn a ½-in. dia. tenon on the tailstock end of the piece. Then I flip the stock end-for-end, and clamp the tenon in the chuck. After roughing out four stoppers, I part through the spindle. This leaves one stopper attached to the tenon in the chuck, and the other three, each with its own tenon, on the rest of the blank, which I set aside.

Before removing too much material near the headstock, I turn the stopper to its final shape. Since there's no tailstock support, the piece is already somewhat flexible and beginning to chatter, particularly at the unsupported end. In fact, the form and the finished texture are occurring simultaneously because I'm often producing a changing progression of chattered surfaces as I'm turning the shape. Each moment, the changing texture of the piece suggests changes in my original design. Does a dramatic development in the texture merit a revision of form? When has each section of the turning reached its ideal state? There's an interesting tension as the work develops.

When I'm satisfied with the shape, I sand the areas that won't have decoration. I don't cover an entire piece with chatterwork—it looks best when contrasted next to a smooth surface. I sand as little as possible. Preserving the sharp edges of a turning gives a vitality that's lost in a heavily sanded piece.

Here I'll explain three chatterwork patterns I use on a stopper. Experience has taught me what patterns I'm likely to get with, say, the edge of a skew or the corner of a parting tool, but there are lots of variables and I'm often surprised by the results. Experimentation is the only way to learn what patterns are possible.

For chatterwork, I run the lathe between 1400 RPM and 2200 RPM. Since the stopper spindle is already very thin near the pointed finial, there is usually plenty of flex there. I make a light shearing cut with the edge of a sharp skew—just one quick pass—along the conical profile. This makes a nice spiraling flute pattern. If the tool bites too deeply, the work will explode into useless fragments. After each cut, I turn off the lathe and inspect the work. If the first attempt doesn't yield a pleasing surface, I try another cut. This time I'll force a slightly greater flex by applying light downward pressure on the spindle as the cut progresses. If I'm still not getting enough flex, I use a parting tool to reduce the diameter of the stopper slightly on the headstock side of the finial.

I decorate the stopper's disc with a series of concentric circles of radial flutes (or facets). With the edge and corner of a sharp parting tool, I begin at the center of the disc where the finial emerges, and lay in concentric circular ridges. Slight pressure toward the headstock deflects the spindle and initiates the chatter as I cut each circle. Again, each cut takes only a few seconds, and I stop the lathe after every cut or two to inspect the work. During these pauses I regrind the cutting edge—at least every fourth or fifth cut. I keep the ring-chatter cuts shallow, and always plan enough thickness to the disc to allow me to shear off the chattered surface and begin a second or even third series of chatter cuts if I'm not satisfied. Often I have to reduce the thickness of the spindle to give more flex. Fluted rings are fairly easy. You should be able to cut them on the first or second try.

On the spherical barrel, I make a pattern that resembles the texture of beaten metal. I get this effect by making a smooth cut with a sharp skew just as if I were reducing the diameter. Since the stem diameter was reduced after the shape was completed, the skew now chatters over the surface instead of reducing the diameter. The chatter is shallow, but noticeable. With one pass down the headstock side of the barrel and a mirror-image pass down the tailstock side, amazing patterns can emerge.

After I've chattered a surface, I burnish it before going on to the next one. This accentuates the texture, polishes the high points, and reveals any errors. My burnisher is simply a ¼-in. square stick, 12 in. to 18 in. long, of the same species as the spindle being burnished. I sharpen each end to a point. (The ends are quickly blunted, so it's handy to have several burnishers sharpened in advance before each turning session.) One pass over the spinning chatterwork does it.

When I'm finished, I examine the piece for flaws, moving the light around the work to highlight the surface. Sometimes light sanding is necessary. Then I apply Watco with cheesecloth or other lint-free fabric while the stopper is still on the lathe, and I polish with a clean, dry cloth. I part the piece at the stem and set it aside. When the finish is dry, I buff the stopper on a linen wheel or wool bonnet lightly dressed with pure carnauba wax. □

_____

Stephen Paulsen earns his living producing scent bottles, jewelry boxes and small containers in Goleta, Calif.

WOOD

Quartersawn Lumber

The quality's in the cutting

by Sam Talarico

A quartersawn board is special. Dimensionally stabler than a board sawn any other way, it won't cup as it dries, and as the seasons change, it won't move very much in width. This stability makes quartersawn boards ideal for drawer sides, tabletops, frame rails and stiles—wherever cross-grain movement or cupping could be a problem. Because their surfaces wear more evenly than those of plainsawn, or flatsawn, boards, quartersawn boards are often used for flooring. When quartersawn some hardwood species, such as the oaks, also reveal spectacular, shimmering flake figure scattered across the grain.

If quartersawn lumber is so attractive and well behaved, why saw any other way? Economics. Quartersawing yields fewer clear, knot-free boards than does plainsawing, and it isn't practical for small-diameter logs. For these reasons, most commercial sawmills don't do it. It's also a time-consuming and fairly wasteful way to cut up a log.

Quartersawn lumber owes both its dimensional stability and its subdued figure to the orientation of the annual rings. Figure 1 shows the difference between a plainsawn board and a quartersawn board. A plainsawn board is a tangential slice from a log. The board's face is more or less tangent to the annual rings, which form ellipses or parabolas on the surface. Theoretically, the ideal quartersawn board is a radial slice. The annual rings are perpendicular to the face, and their edges form parallel lines on the surface. (In commercial practice, any board with rings 60° to 90° to the surface is considered quartersawn.) Because wood moves roughly twice as much tangentially to the rings as it does radially (this ratio varies with the species), the plainsawn board moves more in width, the quartersawn more in thickness.

A tree's rays radiate from the heart like the spokes of a wheel. In quartersawing, the sawblade cuts roughly parallel to the rays. Severed rays show on the board's surface as the flake I described earlier, which is also called "ray fleck." In species where the rays are small, this may hardly be noticeable. Hardwood species with very large rays produce the best flake. Mahogany is good, but in Pennsylvania, where I live, white oak is the best, with red oak and sycamore close behind.

Alternative methods of quartersawing are shown in figure 2, along with the conventional method shown in figure 3. The log is first quartered, then the boards are sawn from the quarter. This method is a compromise. For each board to be the ideal—a true radial slice—the log quarter would have to be repositioned after each cut, which would be a slow and costly procedure. Boards quartersawn the conventional way are close to being true radial slices, and there's no need to turn the log after each cut. This system produces narrow boards with tapered edges, but the widest boards are the most perfectly quartered— the rings are closest to 90° to the surface.

Sawing "through and through," or flitchsawing, produces a few boards near the center of the log that contain the pith. On either side of the pith, the rings are almost 90° to the board's surface. If you rip one of these boards through the pith, you'll have two quartersawn boards. Even though they weren't sawn from a quartered log, these boards are radial slices and therefore quartersawn.

When the growth rings are cut at an angle too far off the radial, the boards are referred to as riftsawn. The rings are less than 60° but greater than 30° to the board's surface. The figure is still straight, but since the cut isn't parallel to the rays, the flake is less pronounced. Riftsawn flake is sometimes called "comb figure."

When you shop for quartersawn hardwood, don't expect to find a wide choice of species. Mostly you'll find red and white oak from about 4/4 to 8/4 in thickness. Widths of 4 in. to 6 in. are

This white-oak log shows a fine example of the cross-grain flake that quartersawing produces in species with large rays. The flake comes from slicing the rays longitudinally.

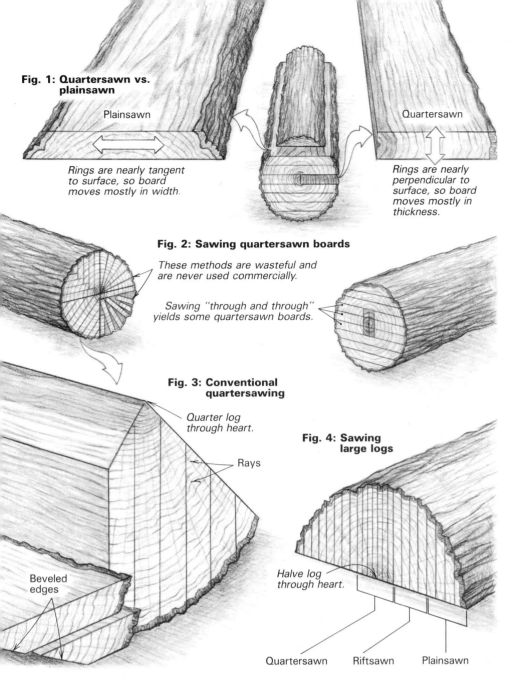

Fig. 1: Quartersawn vs. plainsawn

Plainsawn

Quartersawn

Rings are nearly tangent to surface, so board moves mostly in width.

Rings are nearly perpendicular to surface, so board moves mostly in thickness.

Fig. 2: Sawing quartersawn boards

These methods are wasteful and are never used commercially.

Sawing "through and through" yields some quartersawn boards.

Fig. 3: Conventional quartersawing

Quarter log through heart.

Rays

Beveled edges

Fig. 4: Sawing large logs

Halve log through heart.

Quartersawn   Riftsawn   Plainsawn

A large bandmill can handle bigger logs than can a circular sawmill. Even so, the buttress of this 46-in. dia. log had to be trimmed with a chainsaw to fit.

average. You'll also find that dealers' policies vary greatly. Many hardwood dealers sell quartersawn boards for 20% to 75% more than plainsawn boards of the same species. Sometimes the highly flaked boards are sorted out and sold at a premium. On the other hand, some sellers don't even offer quartersawn as a separate grade, and won't charge extra for the quartersawn boards mixed in with the plainsawn boards. (There usually are some in any pile. Look on the end of the board for rings at 60° to 90° to the faces.) Some dealers will let you pick out the boards you want, some won't; but don't expect anyone to move a ton of lumber so you can pick out one board. In my experience, some lumberyards' quartersawn grade is a mixture of about two-thirds riftsawn boards and one-third quartersawn. Quartersawn softwoods are more standardized. Most places you can ask for "vertical-grain" or "edge-grain" Douglas fir or southern yellow pine. Expect

to pay a lot more for this grade.

A few lumber businesses, like mine, specialize in quartersawn hardwood. I find that the biggest demand is for boards with lots of flake, so I saw primarily to get the best figure. I saw my best logs on the bandmill at C.F. Martin & Co. in Nazareth, Pa., shown in the photo above. The blade makes a narrow kerf, which allows me to cut thin boards without much waste. On the bandmill, I rarely quartersaw oak or sycamore thicker than 5/4—the more boards I get out of a log, the more surfaces there are to showcase the flake. When I'm using a circular mill, however, the ¼-in. to ⅜-in. kerf of the blade turns a lot of potential boards into sawdust. So instead of wasting all that wood sawing thin boards, I saw thick boards and resaw them later on a bandsaw to expose the flake.

If you want to have your own logs quartersawn at a local sawmill, there are a few things to consider before you talk to

the sawyer. Sawyers at small mills may not be familiar with quartersawing, so be prepared to explain what you want. Quartersawing small logs produces very narrow boards, so I recommend cutting only butt logs (from the bottom of the tree) with a minimum small-end diameter of 20 in. Butt logs contain the highest-quality boards and yield the best flake. Very large logs are unwieldy, though, and most sawmills aren't able to cut them. If I have a log that's too large for the mill, I rip it into manageable halves with a chainsaw, then saw it as in figure 4. Technically, this is not quartersawing, but like the "through and through" sawing method in figure 2, it produces quite a few quartersawn boards in addition to riftsawn and plainsawn boards. It saves the time (and expense) involved in quartering a very large log. When halving or quartering a log, always locate the heart on both ends, snap a line, then rip through the center of the heart.

Quartersawn lumber takes longer to dry than does plainsawn. Because of the orientation of the rings, moisture is released from the edges rather than from the face of the board. Before drying, I number the boards in the order in which they came off the log. This enables me to bookmatch boards to make a wider panel.

Because quartersawn lumber is more expensive, some people might consider it a luxury. True, you wouldn't buy it for building sawhorses. But, like a good wine, it's well worth the price for a special occasion. □

Sam Talarico is a lumber dealer, woodworker and winemaker in Mohnton, Pa. Photos by the author.

Drawing: Lee Hov

Purchased in sheets and worked with unpretentious joinery, plywood lends itself to straightforward furniture projects such as this child's loft bed, plans for which appear on pp. 148-149.

Plywood Basics
The ideal material for box furniture

by Ann Taylor

If you want to store something, put it in a box. If you want to store something in particular, turn the box up on one of its ends and fit it with shelves, dividers, drawers and/or doors. The basic box is basic furniture. It can stand on its own as a bookcase, hang on the wall as a cabinet, line up in rows as a wall system, or stretch out into a loft bed with plenty of room for storage. For fast, easy construction, nothing beats a box: it's simply four panels joined at the corners, with a back added on for strength or for appearance. And it can be built, without apology, out of plywood.

Cabinet-grade hardwood plywood is the perfect material for furniture-box construction. It's sold in 4x8 sheets, so you can simply cut box parts from a sheet, without having to mill and glue up as with solid wood. Because it's made up of a stack of thin veneers, plywood doesn't swell and shrink with seasonal moisture changes. This makes for some interesting design possibilities. You can, for example, decorate the end of a plywood panel with a contrasting wood without fear of the cross-grain construction cracking. I've found plywood to be economical, too. Even at a cost of between $20 and $100 per sheet, depending on grade and species, it's less expensive than hardwood bought for $3 and more a board foot.

Designing with plywood—Because plywood comes in big sheets, there's a temptation to build hulking, ill-proportioned monoliths that fill every inch of the available space, or use up every bit of the plywood purchased. Just because all the space under the stairs could be filled with plywood boxes doesn't mean it should be. I plan my furniture-boxes by first measuring the space they will occupy, then making a scale elevation drawing, which helps me visualize how my design will fit in with the rest of the room's furniture and architectural elements. If the drawing doesn't tell me enough, I make a scale mockup out of cardboard.

A box with classic proportions has a short-side to long-side ratio of 5:8. Adhering to this so-called golden mean is likely to produce a well-proportioned box, but you must also consider real-world dimensions: the room where your boxes will live, and the doorways and staircases through which you'll have to maneuver them. If the boxes must contain specific things, measure these objects, make allowances for clearance, and keep the numbers in front of you as you plan. Multi-box furniture—such as a wall system—compounds the design decisions. What are the best dimensions for each box? How many boxes should there be? Working out the relationships on graph paper, I try to size the boxes so that they'll work in many different configurations, thus increasing the versatility of my designs.

Plywood is marginally more rigid along the grain of the face veneer than across it, but decisions about grain direction still can be more aesthetic than structural—a plywood shelf will bear the same weight regardless of grain direction. Grain does affect the visual size of a box, though. If you run the grain in a box's sides horizontally, the box will look shorter. Drawer fronts with vertical grain look deeper. This is most noticeable with oak and other vividly figured woods.

Plywood will sag if it must span too great a distance, vertical or horizontal. Besides drooping shelves, this also causes the sides of tall carcases to bow outward under their own weight, making it impossible to fit them with smooth-working doors and drawers. For ¾-in. plywood, I've found that 36 in. is the maximum horizontal span unless support is provided by a vertical divider or a face frame. For storing heavy objects, such as big books, 30 in. is better. The long sides of a tall bookcase can span 48 in. or so; if taller, the sides should be tied together with a horizontal member.

After I've designed and drawn the boxes, I make a cutting list that names each part, its thickness, width and length. The length is always along the grain, the width always across. To reduce waste, it's sometimes helpful to draw each piece to scale on graph paper, and after drawing an arrow to indicate grain direction, to cut out the panels and arrange them on a rectangle scaled to represent a 4x8 sheet. Once you have determined how to cut the plywood, decide which cut to make first and mark it with a numbered arrow, indicating grain direction, on the drawing. Then label each piece as you cut it.

Cutting and joining—Plywood rips cleanly along the grain, but the face veneer of the sheet splinters when crosscut. Minimize the damage by using a good-quality plywood-cutting blade. On my 10-in. tablesaw, I prefer a 40-tooth carbide-tipped blade with a triple-chip tooth pattern. The 100-tooth steel blades sold in most hardware stores will work, though, if kept very sharp. Get in the habit of positioning what will be the show side of your plywood up when you tablesaw; that way, any splintering will be hidden later. If you're using a radial-arm saw or a portable circular saw, position the good side down. A strip of masking tape applied along the line of cut before sawing will also reduce chipping. Since my basement shop is cramped, I usually have the lumberyard make

Taylor crosscuts panels on her Sears tablesaw, using a shopmade cutoff box. For larger cuts, she feeds sheets against a Biesemeyer fence, which permits cuts to the center of an 8-ft. sheet.

the first rip cut. I ask them to allow at least ¼ in. extra, and then I square the panel on my tablesaw, using the factory edge against the fence.

It makes sense to rough-rip full sheets first, cutting the panels about ⅛ in. oversize, then trimming them to the final size when they're smaller and more manageable. For accuracy, trim all panels of the same width at the same rip-fence setting. Since most box parts are too large to saw with the tablesaw's miter gauge, I use a homemade cutoff box to trim them square. Panels that are too cumbersome to tablesaw can be cut with a portable circular saw or a saber saw guided against a wooden fence clamped to the work. Clean up any ragged edges by cutting the panel a bit oversize and trimming cleanly to the line with a router guided against the wooden fence.

The parts of a basic plywood box can be joined in many ways, ranging from a simple nailed butt joint to dowel or plate joinery. I use four joints for plywood: the rabbet-and-groove (offset tongue), double rabbet, tongue-and-groove, and rabbet—all cut on my tablesaw with a sharp dado

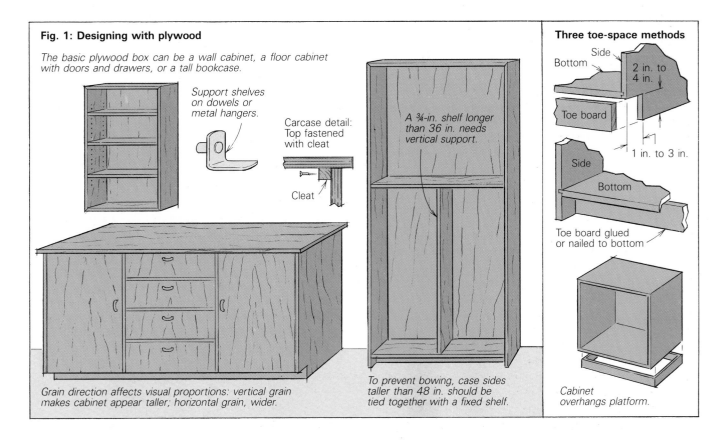

Fig. 1: Designing with plywood

The basic plywood box can be a wall cabinet, a floor cabinet with doors and drawers, or a tall bookcase.

Support shelves on dowels or metal hangers.

Carcase detail: Top fastened with cleat

Cleat

A ¾-in. shelf longer than 36 in. needs vertical support.

Grain direction affects visual proportions: vertical grain makes cabinet appear taller; horizontal grain, wider.

To prevent bowing, case sides taller than 48 in. should be tied together with a fixed shelf.

Three toe-space methods

Side
Bottom
2 in. to 4 in.
Toe board
1 in. to 3 in.
Side
Bottom
Toe board glued or nailed to bottom
Cabinet overhangs platform.

How to buy hardwood plywood

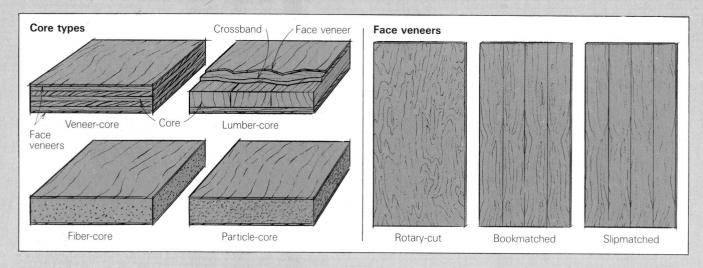

Core types — Crossband / Face veneer — Veneer-core / Core / Lumber-core — Face veneers / Fiber-core / Particle-core

Face veneers — Rotary-cut / Bookmatched / Slipmatched

Most local lumberyards sell a big selection of fir structural plywoods and paneling, but far fewer stock cabinet-grade plywoods. You may have to look around to find what you need. Yards that support busy millwork and cabinet shops, because they use hardwood plywood, are a good place to start. These yards usually keep a good supply on hand, and they're familiar with the hardwood-plywood grading system, if what you want needs to be special-ordered. In most cities, a check of the "Plywood & Veneers" heading in the Yellow Pages will turn up wholesale suppliers. Wholesalers won't always sell small quantities to amateurs, but it doesn't hurt to ask. At worst, they'll refer you to a well-stocked retailer, or to one who can order for you.

Hardwood plywoods are graded by the quality of their face or surface veneers and by the way these veneers are arranged on one of four kinds of cores, as shown in the drawing. The chart shows the six veneer grades. Typically, one side of a sheet will be premium or A grade, the other side will be a lower grade; thus a sheet might be graded A-1, A-2, and so on. Most suppliers stock grades A-1 through A-3, and will also have on hand something that they call "shop grade." This grade, which doesn't appear in the official rule book, refers to seconds, or sheets that have been damaged in transit or storage. Defects in these sheets are often hardly noticeable, and the lower price makes this grade a good buy.

In addition to the letter-number grade, a sheet will be identified by how the face veneer is cut and laid. Rotary-cut veneer is peeled off the log in one big sheet and glued to the core. It's usu-ally cheaper, but the figure tends to be pronounced. Plain-sliced (also called flat-cut) veneer is usually bookmatched or slipmatched and has a more subdued (and usually more interesting) figure.

Face veneers of any grade or type can be applied to a veneer, lumber, fiber or particle core. Veneer is the most common core and consists of an odd number of veneer sheets or plies, frequently fir or a cheaper hardwood, built up to the required thickness. The face veneers are then glued on top. Veneer-core plywood may contain interply voids, but these usually don't cause much of a problem. Lumber-core—strips of a solid, stable lumber such as mahogany glued up into a large sheet and veneered over—is the most expensive, but the nicest to work with. Fiber-core, similar to Masonite, is made up from sawmill waste ground to a powdery consistency and pressed into sheet form. Particle-core is similar, but is made of larger fibers.

Which grade and core should you buy? That depends on what you're building. Mostly I make children's furniture, so I buy shop-grade (A-1 or A-2 seconds) ¾-in. veneer-core oak and birch. This grade is also excellent for kitchen cabinets and wall units. If I were investing more time in a piece of furniture, I might consider an A-1 lumber-core plywood.

Another thing to keep in mind when buying is that wholesale plywood prices, like lumber prices, are commonly given in dollars per thousand square feet. So if you ask the price on A-2 rotary-cut oak, for example, the salesman might quote $1,380. To find the per-sheet price, move the decimal point three places to the left and multiply by 32, the number of square feet in a 4x8 sheet. In this case, the price is $1.38 per square foot, or $44.16 per sheet. —A.T.

HARDWOOD PLYWOOD GRADES

A Premium grade	Whether veneer is one piece (rotary-cut) or several (plain-sliced), it's free of defects and discoloration. If the veneer is sliced, the grain is bookmatched or slipmatched for figure and color.
1 Good grade	Face veneers are smooth and tight, but, if sliced, may not be figure- or color-matched.
2 Sound grade	Face veneers are smooth and tight, but not matched for color or figure. Sound knots up to ¾ in. and discoloration are allowed.
3 Utility grade	Veneer can have tight knots up to 1 in., discoloration and slight splits.
4 Backing grade	Open splits and knots up to 3 in. are allowed in face veneer This grade is rarely found in off-the-shelf plywood.
SP Specialty grade	Custom-made to buyer requirements. Most architectural paneling is of this grade.

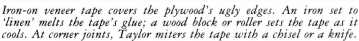
Iron-on veneer tape covers the plywood's ugly edges. An iron set to 'linen' melts the tape's glue; a wood block or roller sets the tape as it cools. At corner joints, Taylor miters the tape with a chisel or a knife.

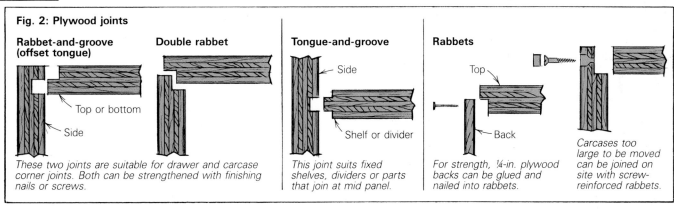

Fig. 2: Plywood joints

Rabbet-and-groove (offset tongue)

Top or bottom

Side

These two joints are suitable for drawer and carcase corner joints. Both can be strengthened with finishing nails or screws.

Double rabbet

Tongue-and-groove

Side

Shelf or divider

This joint suits fixed shelves, dividers or parts that join at mid panel.

Rabbets

Top

Back

For strength, ¼-in. plywood backs can be glued and nailed into rabbets.

Carcases too large to be moved can be joined on site with screw-reinforced rabbets.

set. Figure 2 shows which joint is used where. A box with four flush corners, for example, might hang on the wall, or sit on the floor atop a platform that forms a toe space. I join flush corners with a rabbet-and-groove or, if the box is large and must be delivered knocked down, with a rabbet that I screw together on site. Pilot holes will prevent screws from splitting the plies, and if the screws show, they should be counterbored and plugged. I use No. 8 or No. 6, 1½-in. wood or drywall screws to join ¾-in. plywood. The bed project illustrated on pp. 148-149 shows another knockdown joint.

For fixed shelves and dividers where the end of one plywood panel joins the face of another, use either a tongue-and-groove or a rabbet-and-groove. Brace a box against racking by adding a back. I find that ¼-in. plywood glued and nailed into a rabbet milled into the back edges of the box is fine for this purpose. Make the rabbet for the back the last joint cut, however, since it determines which panels become the left, right, top and bottom of a carcase. And in case of splintering or cutting errors, you can put mistakes at the back of the box.

As a rule of thumb for ¾-in. plywood, I make grooves ⅜ in. wide and ⅜ in. deep. I size the tongues accordingly, but leave a 1/64-in. space between the groove bottom and the end of the tongue for glue clearance. To prevent chipping, I cut cross-grain dadoes in two steps. First, I set up the dado blades and rip fence, and lower the blades so that they just cut through the face veneer. Then I raise them and mill the cut to final depth. Before I pass good plywood through a setup, I always

try it first with scraps of the same stock that I'll be using. A test tongue should be deliberately too thick to fit the groove so that you can raise the blade in tiny increments until it fits exactly, or it can be trimmed by hand with a plane.

Adjustable shelves can be supported by ¼-in. dowels tapped into ⅜-in. deep holes bored into the case sides before the box is assembled. I space shelf-pin holes about 1 in. apart, and locate them about 1½ in. in from the back and front edges of the case. Be very accurate in laying out these holes, else the shelf will teeter when it's installed. A template of ¼-in. Masonite pegboard will ensure consistent hole location. To keep the drill bit from wandering out of line, I dimple each hole with an awl and use a brad-point drill bit in a Portalign tool. Make sure the bit has a depth stop to keep you from drilling through the plywood. Another way to support shelves is with metal or plastic shelf standards let into grooves milled in the case sides, or with steel shelf hangers that plug into ¼-in. holes.

Gluing up—To check the accuracy of the joinery, assemble the box without glue. Examine each joint, and trim away tight spots and ridges with a chisel or a plane. Fix a sloppy-fitting joint by gluing a strip of veneer to the tongue, sanding it smooth after the glue has dried. Since plywood faces are easily marred by clamps, and because there's no other way to apply pressure to a long joint in the middle of a big box, I use 2x4 cauls for each assembly job. If you plane the edge of

Plans for a child's loft bed

Like all the furniture I build for children, this loft bed is durable enough for the small child who plays under the desk and runs his toy cars along the shelves, but spacious enough for the older child whose stereo sound system spreads over the desk behind his computer. And because the bed is up high in a box, it doesn't need to be made each morning. The project was designed for a six-year-old whose room in the family's newly restored Victorian house had a high ceiling but no closet and only one wall long enough for a bed.

The bed consists of four basic boxes—one each for the bed, storage cabinet, desk and bookcase. All but one are made of ¾-in. shop-grade veneer-core birch plywood. To keep the size down, I used a 30-in. wide cot mattress (no box springs) rather than a standard twin-size mattress. Whichever you use, measure it before you begin cutting. Drawers are made of ⅝-in. fir plywood, to keep costs down, but if you prefer, use hardwood plywood. The desk top can be hardwood plywood, let into a rabbet, instead of laminate-covered fir plywood.

The drawing shows a refined version of the piece shown in the photo on p. 144, so it differs in some details. For extra strength, for example, the stretcher connects the center of the leg support to the storage cabinet, instead of fastening at its back edge. The desk can be longer or shorter to suit the child's room, or to more economically use what plywood you have available.   —A.T.

CUTTING LIST

Amt.	Description*	L x W	Amt.	Description*	L x W
Storage cabinet			*Bed box*		
2	Cabinet sides	60 x 32	2	Bed sides	78 x 12
1	Cabinet top	31¼ x 31¾	2	Bed ends	31¼ x 12
1	Fixed shelf	31¼ x 31¾	1	Bed bottom	77¼ x 31¼
1	Cabinet bottom	31¼ x 31¾		(¼-in. fir plywood)	
1	Toe board	30½ x 2	5	Bed supports	30½
1	Cabinet back	60 x 31¼		(fir 2x4)	
	(¼-in. fir plywood)		2	Mattress boards	76⅜ x 15⅛
2	Cabinet doors	18¼ x 14¾		(½-in. fir plywood)	
2	Door pulls	18¼ x 1½			
	(¾-in. solid birch)		*Desk box*		
1	Top drawer false front	30⅜ x 4½	1	Desk top	72¼ x 29¾
3	Middle drawer	30⅜ x 7		(⅝-in. fir plywood)	
	false fronts		1	Top surface	73 x 30½
1	Bottom drawer	30⅜ x 8½		(plastic laminate)	
	false front		2	Long sides	73 x 3
5	Drawer pulls	30⅜ x 1½	2	Ends	29¾ x 3
	(¾-in. solid birch)		4	Desk crossmembers	29 x 2⅜
5	Drawer bottoms	29⅝ x 21⅝		(¾-in. pine)	
	(¼-in. fir plywood)		2	Leg uprights	27⅜ x 3
10	Drawer runners	31 x ⁵⁄₁₆		(¾-in. solid birch)	
	(¾-in. hardwood)		2	Leg crossmembers	29 x 3
				(¾-in. solid birch)	
			1	Stretcher	72¼ x 3
Drawer parts listed below are ⅝-in. fir plywood:				(1-in. solid birch)	
1	Top drawer front	29⅝ x 4½			
3	Middle drawer fronts	29⅝ x 7	*Bookcase box*		
1	Bottom drawer front	29⅝ x 8½	1	Front side	60 x 12
2	Top drawer sides	22 x 4½		(¾-in. solid birch)	
6	Middle drawer sides	22 x 7	1	Back side	60 x 12
2	Bottom drawer sides	22 x 8½	1	Bottom	31¼ x 12
1	Top drawer back	29⅝ x 4	1	Top	31¼ x 12
3	Middle drawer backs	29⅝ x 6½	4	Toe boards	30½ x 2
1	Bottom drawer back	29⅝ x 8	2	Adjustable shelves	30½ x 11⅞
			1	Fixed shelf	31¾ x 12
			3	Bookstops	30½ x 1½
				(¾-in. solid birch)	
			1	Roll of iron-on plywood edge tape	

Parts are ¾-in. birch plywood, except where noted. Dimensions allow for joints.

each caul slightly convex, it will bear down harder on the middle of the joint, pushing the joint home more effectively.

Once the box is dry-assembled, check it for square by measuring diagonally from corner to corner. Both diagonals should measure exactly the same, but for practical purposes a ¹⁄₁₆-in. tolerance is good enough. Another way to check for square is with an accurate framing square, but it isn't as reliable, especially if the box parts bow a bit under clamp pressure. Correct small out-of-square errors by adjusting the clamps; if this won't work, disassemble and check each panel for square.

Before gluing up, sand the box parts with at least 100-grit, finer if you want. Be careful when sanding plywood, particularly with a belt sander. It's surprisingly easy to sand right through the face veneer, resulting in a blemish that's impossible to repair. If the wood appears to darken, the sander is going through the veneer into the next veneer layer. I finish after assembly, but some woodworkers finish before, so that glue squeeze-out won't stick. Don't dribble finish into the joints, however, or the glue won't hold. Let squeeze-out dry completely, then slice it off with a sharp chisel, scraper or razor

blade. Wiping the glue, even with a damp cloth, will only force it into the grain, where it will show up when you finish.

Before the glue is dry, I attach the back, which helps square the box. If the back won't be seen, as in a chest of drawers, make it out of ¼-in. Masonite or fir plywood. Open bookcases and cabinets should be backed in plywood that has the same face veneer as the rest of the box. In either case, size the back so that it fits snugly into the rabbets. Don't measure between the rabbets—the clamps may have bowed the carcase in a little, and your measurement will give you a back that's too small. I put a light bead of glue in the rabbet, and nail the back in with 1-in. ring-shank paneling nails, first on one side and then along the top or bottom. If the sides bow, pull them in gently with a pipe clamp before nailing.

Finishing up—There are two ways to hide the ugly exposed edge of plywood: by edgebanding it with thin strips of wood before assembly, or by covering it with iron-on veneer tape or a solid-wood face frame after the cabinet is put together. Some people argue that edgebanding is more durable and a

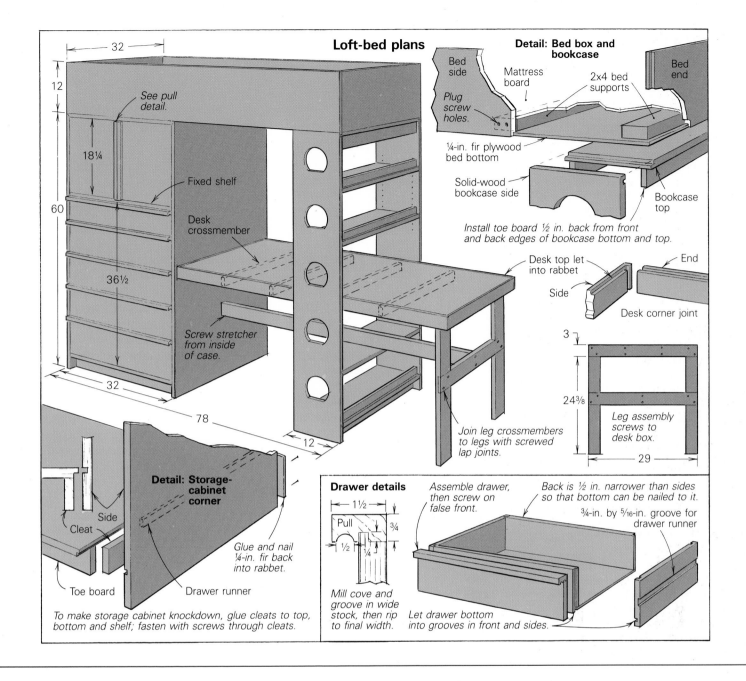

Loft-bed plans

32

12

See pull detail.

18¼

Fixed shelf

60

Desk crossmember

36½

Screw stretcher from inside of case.

32

78

12

Detail: Bed box and bookcase

Bed side

Mattress board

2x4 bed supports

Bed end

Plug screw holes.

¼-in. fir plywood bed bottom

Solid-wood bookcase side

Bookcase top

Install toe board ½ in. back from front and back edges of bookcase bottom and top.

Desk top let into rabbet

End

Side

Desk corner joint

3

24⅜

Leg assembly screws to desk box.

29

Join leg crossmembers to legs with screwed lap joints.

Detail: Storage-cabinet corner

Side

Cleat

Toe board

Glue and nail ¼-in. fir back into rabbet.

Drawer runner

To make storage cabinet knockdown, glue cleats to top, bottom and shelf; fasten with screws through cleats.

Drawer details

1½

Pull

¾

½

¼

Mill cove and groove in wide stock, then rip to final width.

Assemble drawer, then screw on false front.

Back is ½ in. narrower than sides so that bottom can be nailed to it.

¾-in. by 5/16-in. groove for drawer runner

Let drawer bottom into grooves in front and sides.

face frame stronger. While this may be true, I find iron-on veneer tape faster and a lot easier to handle. Bought in 250-ft. rolls (from The Woodworkers' Store, 21801 Industrial Blvd., Rogers, Minn. 55374, or from some lumberyards), it costs about 15¢ per linear foot. You can cut it with scissors and apply it with an ordinary household iron. If incorrectly positioned, the tape can be reheated and moved.

To apply the tape, cut a strip about ¼ in. longer than you need and iron it in place with the iron set on "linen." While the tape is hot and the glue melted, press it down with a block of scrapwood; the pressure of the iron alone is not always sufficient to set the tape. Even though plywood corner joints are rabbet-and-groove, the veneer tape looks best if it's mitered at the corner (photo, p. 147). These miters can be cut with a 1-in. chisel, but a straightedge and X-acto knife makes a neater cut. With two layers of tape overlapping at the corner, I place a straightedge diagonally from the outside corner to the inside, then knife through both thicknesses of veneer at once. Reheat the tape, then pull the joint tight and press down. Since the tape is 13/16 in. wide, I trim it flush with a

chisel, and then sand the outside of the box with 100-grit and finer belts. I round the taped edges and corners slightly with 120-grit sandpaper. This helps bond the tape to the edge, and prevents it and the face veneer from being snagged and chipped.

A completed box can be fitted with drawers or doors using the construction methods shown in the drawings above. You can buy metal drawer slides or make your own out of hardwood. Doors can be hung on butt or knife pivot hinges, or on the adjustable concealed hinges described in *FWW* #43, p. 59.

Plywood boxes can be finished with just about any wood finish, or even covered with plastic laminate. A clear, fast-drying finish such as shellac or lacquer, or an oil finish is the easiest to apply. If the box is stained, discolorations from glue and uneven sanding, and ripples and other imperfections in the plywood will become more obvious, as will variations in grain. Paint will hide all these and any mistakes that you've had to fill or patch. □

Ann Taylor makes furniture in Winnetka, Ill. Photos by the author.

Black Walnut Woes

A tree-grower learns from the roots up

by John R. Harwood

Like most woodworkers, I admit an emotional attachment to trees. When I decided to plant black walnut trees in an abandoned field on our property in Upstate New York, I understood that their lumber wasn't likely to ever find its way onto my workbench. Yet I wished to replace some of the trees cut, often before their time, to meet the demand for lumber that I was helping to place upon the forests. I chose walnut for its uncommon beauty and outstanding workability, as well as for the scarcity of this valuable species in our area. Needless to say, I did not know what I was getting into. Stick a bunch of seedlings into the ground and sit back and watch them grow, right? Not quite! I found that if you sit back after planting hardwoods, you won't have much to watch grow except weeds.

I began in the winter of 1976 by placing an order with Van's Pines, in West Olive, Mich., for 100 black walnut

A woodworkers' rite of spring: the black walnut tree beginning to bloom.

bare-rooted seedlings, 3 ft. to 4 ft. tall. For the remainder of the winter I read anything I could find about tree-planting in general or walnuts in particular, and I also enrolled in courses in environmental science and forestry. Most of the literature I found was directed toward establishing conifer stands. The little bit of available material about walnut plantations presumed machinery far superior to my lawn tractor, and manpower greater than my two hands. I found that I would have to learn as I went along.

Spring came, and with it two parcels—a long, soft one containing the seedlings, and the other, which looked like a manual jack-hammer, my dibble bar. A dibble bar is a planting tool used for conifers, but ignorance, if not bliss, is at least a postponement of unhappiness. I decided to plant that day since the weather was gray and drizzly—the seedlings would not dry out as they were being handled and the trees would not need immediate watering. I sloshed my way up to the "plantation" site, with visions of walnut trees dancing in my head.

Ceremoniously, I extracted the first seedling for planting, only to find that its taproot was a good 4 in. longer than the spade on the dibble bar. The ground was so saturated, however, that I was able to force the bar far enough down to place the root without breaking it. Fortunately, the average root on the remaining seedlings was only slightly longer than the spade. As I untangled the bundle, the quantity of seedlings seemed to grow, as did the effort required to plant each of them. I began to wonder why I had ordered so many. The final count was 112 walnut seedlings standing proud, albeit in crooked rows, at a spacing of 8 ft. by 8 ft., or two big steps and one little one—a rather small plantation of less than 6,000 sq. ft., barely an eighth of an acre. Though my goal was 10 acres of walnuts, I proudly gazed upon my modest accomplishment, then headed home for a hot bath and some muscle liniment.

Two weeks later the still-dormant walnuts could barely be seen through the lush growth of spring grasses. By midsummer the seedlings showed signs of transplant shock, insect damage, and stress from competition. I mounted furious warfare against the weeds. Somewhere between blisters and backaches, I decided that a gasoline-powered weed whacker was just what I needed, only to learn that this monster does a fine job of gashing the tender bark off of seedlings when its operator grows weary. The insects had already eaten most of the sickly leaves, so pesticides seemed of no use at this point.

I could see that my simplistic approach to planting hardwoods was futile, so I began to plan the next spring's endeavor with a little more forethought. I continued my part-time

Drawings: Christopher Clapp

studies. I met with the regional state forester. Meanwhile, to my amazement, most of my bedraggled walnuts set healthy winter buds, and were obviously interested in surviving. I ordered another 200 seedlings.

As spring drew near, I finalized my plans. I would again plant in wet weather, and this time I would discourage the weeds by scarifying the soil around each hole with a shovel. I would drop a timed-release fertilizer tablet into each hole, and I was prepared to apply insecticide at the first sign of damage. I theorized that the dibble-bar method might cause trapped air around the bottom of long taproots, so I had ordered smaller planting stock. I had also ordered 50 black alders to intermix as trainers: alders grow faster than walnuts, encouraging the slower-growing trees to head straight up for light and not branch out too much. When the alders began to suppress the more valuable walnuts, I would thin them out for firewood. I was becoming a more sophisticated tree-planter.

As I trudged through my plantation that spring, I discovered that deer and rabbits love healthy walnut buds—only two trees, fortuitously planted within a blackberry bramble, had escaped the forage. Discouraged, I nevertheless resolved to stick to my plans, and I set to work. After several hours of back-breaking scarifying, though, I gladly dropped that idea. It was all for the best: by midsummer no difference could be detected between the seedlings whose sod I had scarified and those I had not. By then the alders had all perished, presumably due to root damage. Their roots are really too crooked and multi-branched for dibble-bar planting.

Things looked pretty bad at that point, but I was due for a little beginner's luck. While contemplating the relative costs and benefits of fencing the whole plantation versus constantly spraying various animal repellents, I decided to salvage some old 4-ft. welded-wire fencing. I had only enough to make six 3-ft. dia. cages, but at least I would be able to protect the

In a nutshell

by Charles Leik

My father has spent his life farming within sight of where he was born in central Michigan 78 years ago. Over the years he has planted acres of corn, wheat and beans, but nothing has given him as much pleasure as growing trees. His stands have included tens of thousands of pine planted in the poorer soil and more severe winter climate a short distance to the north, yet his greatest satisfaction comes from the one hundred black walnut trees surrounding the farmstead in Portland. As a youngster, I learned real patience picking out nut meats over the kitchen table on wintry Sunday afternoons—but the black walnut was a delicacy well worth the effort. Now, with Dad's careful attention, each year these trees progress a bit more toward the quality veneer logs that my children will harvest toward the middle of the next century.

Black walnut (*Juglans nigra*) develops best on deep, moderately well-drained, nearly neutral soils that are generally moist and fertile. It is native to the area from the East Coast to the Missouri Valley and from the Southern Appalachians to the Canadian border. Dad's walnut plantings are on the northern fringe of their natural habitat, and growth is considerably slower than, say, in the Shenandoah Valley of Virginia. Slower growth isn't all bad, though, as the most desirable veneer patterns result from the smaller annual rings of trees from north of the Ohio Valley. It isn't unknown for unscrupulous sellers to truck southern logs to northern locations and represent them as locally grown.

Dad dates his interest in growing walnuts from the Depression era, when he shucked walnuts from trees growing wild in fencerows and sold the nuts for a dollar a bushel in Detroit. He planted his first trees from nuts in 1929. These trees are now 50 ft. tall and 19 in. in diameter at breast height (DBH). In late autumn of 1968, Dad made preparations for his largest planting. After shucking the nuts, he placed them in a leaf-lined pit, where they would be kept moist but would not freeze. He planted these nuts the following spring. In some cases germination was delayed quite a while, as seedlings continued to appear for several springs. Before long, the stand was so thick that many trees had to be transplanted. After 15 growing seasons, these trees averaged 32 ft. in height and over 8 in. DBH.

A danger of planting nuts instead of seedlings is that squirrels and chipmunks may mistake them for a winter food cache. Some foresters recommend burying the nuts in a perforated tin can, which deters animals while allowing the nuts to germinate. Tin cans (don't use aluminum cans) soon rust away, posing no problem for a growing seedling.

Dad's goal is to produce 16-ft. logs, so he approaches training and pruning with considerable thought. He trims the branches as high as possible without shocking the tree by taking off too many in a season. Trees planted in open country will usually fork, and then Dad has to decide which branch should be lopped off and which can be trained as a new leader. He studies the alternatives like a gem cutter, solicits opinions from visitors, and by fall has generally made his decisions for pruning.

After a new leader has been established, or when a tree leans away from the prevailing westerlies, a guy rope is necessary to encourage straightness. At first Dad installed a taut rope between the limb and a stake, but in high winds either the tree or the rope was liable to snap. Now he runs the ground end of the rope through a pulley-type device and attaches a weight to the end. This allows the tree to flex in a wind, yet continuously tugs the tree or branch in the desired direction.

If a tree does break off, or has undesirable characteristics, Dad cuts it off at ground level. A 4-ft. to 5-ft. leader usually comes back the first year. Without such drastic cutting, the stub would just send out bushy branches, which would make the tree useless for lumber.

Now that the 1969 planting is well along, Dad has started a new enterprise. My brother and I bought a small farm several years ago that has eight acres of small hardwoods, many of them walnuts. Dad is trimming these trees and eliminating less valuable species that compete for sunlight and moisture. This approach to walnut-growing gives him a 10- to 20-year head start by utilizing already thriving trees.

Walnut-growing is not a short-term proposition, but Dad gets satisfaction from the thought that his efforts will allow those not yet born the opportunity to make fine furniture from this premium lumber. □

Charles Leik is a banker and woodworker who lives in Great Falls, Va.

best-looking survivors from the first year's planting. I secured each cage with two 5-ft. long stakes woven through the fencing. Then in July I discovered that several seedlings I had written off had resprouted from the root, and were growing at a rate far greater than those with original stems. I thought I was finally on to something.

I was not positive the cages would provide total protection. They were also expensive, averaging $6 per cage plus the stakes and the time required. Then, too, I had to consider the risk of rot in stems resprouting so near the ground, especially with dense grass maintaining a moist environment. The books emphasized the grave importance of avoiding all injuries to the bark, since a walnut tree with heart rot is of no value. I would just have to wait and see. Perhaps it was cabin fever that drove me to complete madness—that winter I ordered 400 new seedlings.

As to why my lunacy doubled every year I cannot say; perhaps I hoped to overwhelm the odds. I decided to drop the dibble-bar method. Though no walnut mortality could be attributed to its use, no tree had gotten off to a good start being forced into such a small hole. I rented a hand-operated, gas-driven post-hole digger and purchased several cubic yards of weed-free topsoil.

Planting day arrived and the weather was beautiful, 70°F with bright sun and a steady breeze. Perfect for the friend I had persuaded to help me, but bad for the seedlings. The weatherman had promised rain, so I had made no provision

A 4-ft. wire cage protects a young seedling from animal forage.

for carrying enough water up to the field to give the seedlings a good soaking. The post-hole digger, which I was to operate, was like a lawn mower connected to a 6-in. auger drill by a flexible shaft—a real torture machine. My companion was to fill each hole with a tree and soil brought up in a small cart, towed by the lawn tractor, from where the truck had dumped it. Somehow, we managed to plant all 400 seedlings. The rain clouds I had been watching as the sun set dropped a foot of snow that night, and the temperature dropped 50°F. Nature's watering remained frozen above the ground long enough to either kill or hopelessly weaken most of the trees within a week.

•   •   •

Each of the past four springs, I have ritually planted about 100 trees, though I've concentrated on species with a greater chance of success, such as spruce and larch, plus small numbers of birch and oak. Because it takes so long for a particular acre to grow quality cabinet lumber, I've made an experimental planting of 30 Japanese larches, as a cash crop, intermixed with 10 black cherries.

I have by no means forsaken the walnuts, or hardwood reforestation in general, and have continued to care for the trees that have survived. The only trees that have had a predictable chance have been those placed in cages, so I dutifully purchase several rolls of fencing each year and delegate its use as best as possible. I have managed to cage, and in some cases cut back and resprout, more than 50 of the trees in the walnut plantation. Two years ago I begrudgingly applied simizene, a pre-emergence herbicide, around some. With one application, second- and third-year seedlings grew above their cages that year, and out of the reach of the insects in the surrounding high grass the following. All of the first six trees caged were treated, and they are now true saplings, beyond the possibility of deer and rabbit browse, so I've moved their cages on to other needy recipients. The trees without cages resemble gnarled bushes.

This year I have the inclination to plant walnuts again—no, not 800, but maybe 25. Last spring I sprouted nuts collected from local trees, and knowing that the parents had good growth habits and were well adapted to our climate gives me confidence. But I will not be tempted to plant more than I can care for. With a garden tiller on the tractor, I'll be able to loosen the soil and subdue competition without much effort. I'll consider one application of herbicide next spring, if called for based on the competition present late this summer. If planted and cared for properly, walnuts can grow 3 ft. or more a year, allowing the cages to be reused after three or four years. Once the trees are out of the cages, I have only to worry about insect infestation and disease, winter die-back, and storm damage. I have learned a lot, and I have gained a great sense of satisfaction from helping the trees grow. □

John Harwood, a designer and woodworker, operates Grassy Lane Studios in Cazenovia, N.Y. For more on how to grow black walnut trees, read Nut Tree Culture in North America *edited by Richard A. Jaynes (Northern Nut Growers Association, Broken Arrow Rd., Hamden, Conn. 06518),* Black Walnut for Profit *by Bruce Thompson (Graphic Publishing Co., Inc., Lake Mills, Iowa 50450), and* Black Walnut as a Crop *(publication #S/N 001-001-00403-1, available from the U.S. Government Printing Office, Washington, D.C. 20402).*

The Great American Pines

Forty species yield three distinct families of cabinet woods

by Jon W. Arno

The newspaper ad might read: "Common pine shelving boards, only 59¢ a board foot!" So the weekend woodworker, on his precious hobby budget, hustles off to load up. With just 100 bd. ft. of that affordable pine, he might reproduce that beautiful 17th-century New England china cupboard he's admired in the local museum.

Yet when the reproduction is finally done, something just isn't quite right. The joinery is accurate, the antique finish genuine, the hardware hand-forged. Nevertheless, there is something unmistakably 20th-century about the piece.

Our craftsman resigns himself to the apparent fact that it simply takes a couple of centuries for pine to develop its mellow, pumpkin-orange patina. The truth is, this particular pine lumber is never going to mellow, not in a thousand years. Why? Because pine isn't just pine. That bargain wood was a western yellow pine, probably *Pinus ponderosa,* while the Colonial original was almost certainly made of a decidedly different species: *Pinus strobus,* or eastern white pine. Both woods have a distinctly individual character. To a reproduction cabinetmaker, their lumber is not interchangeable.

The genus *Pinus* of the botanical family *Pinaceae* contains more than ninety species worldwide, several of which are among the most important in the timber and paper industries. The range of the pines is restricted to the Northern Hemisphere, except for one species that strays below the equator in Indonesia. As with fine hardwoods, North America is especially blessed with pines. Half of our 40 native pine species are important timber producers, and some have become major reforestation species, growing now where no true pine had grown before.

In Colonial days, the East Coast pines fit nicely into three basic groups. In the North were a "soft" (white pine), a "hard" (pitch pine), and an "intermediate" (red pine) which was very like Scotch pine, the wood that European cabinetmakers call "deal." In the South, the many kinds of pines were all very hard. In comparison with soft white pine, whose uniform texture works easily, some of the southern yellow pines have earlywood as soft as basswood, while the latewood within the same annual ring is as hard as rosewood. The southern yellow pines are therefore difficult to work, and have a showier grain pattern than the softer pines, especially when stained.

Throughout the Colonies, the hard pines provided building timbers, tough construction lumber and wear-proof floors. For furniture, the northern cabinetmakers favored the bland, easier-working white pine, but the southern cabinetmakers utilized the harder wood of the local trees. For this reason, museum curators today routinely find drawer runners and sides of southern Colonial furniture to be in good condition still, while in northern furniture the same parts have mostly worn out.

As local lumber stands were exhausted, loggers moved west and discovered other species of pine: two soft pines (western white pine and sugar pine), and a number of western yellow pines, the most important of which are much softer and more workable than the southern yellows. At the very least, today's cabinetmaker ought learn how to distinguish between the white pines as a group, the southern yellow pines, and the western yellow pines. Amateur lumberjacks might note that with one or two minor exceptions, the soft pines have needles growing in bunches of five, while the harder pines have them in bunches of two or three. The chart on p. 154 compares pines within each of the three groups and shows macrophotographs of typical species.

Keep in mind that pine furniture has always been decidedly local in character. The Europeans made Scotch pine tables, New Englanders made white pine chests, and southern farmers built yellow pine cupboards with flashy grain. In the television show *Bonanza,* Ben Cartwright's furniture would have been of pure ponderosa pine. Country-style pine furniture was originally made of whatever pine grew in the particular geographic area.

The white pines—If you like traditional American furniture and want your projects to be "authentic," your first choice will naturally be eastern white pine. This is the "pumpkin pine" of early New England, so called because of the rich, golden-orange patina it develops with age. It's also the tree that Paul Bunyan harvested as he made his way from pinery to pinery along our northern border. The lumberjacks called it cork pine because its extremely low density caused it to ride high in the river as the logs were floated to the sawmill. For the cabinetmaker, this low density means that the wood is soft, easily worked, and lightweight. Wood from the white pine group is, in general, less dense than that of the species in the other groups. It is also not as resinous and has less contrast between earlywood and latewood. Thus the white pines cut more predictably, and can be finished to a mellower, more uniform tone.

The woods of eastern white pine and western white pine are so similar that I doubt whether a Colonial cabinetmaker could have told one from the other. The sapwood of both trees is light cream, almost white, in color, with the heartwood ranging from yellow to light orange-tan. Idaho has been the primary producer of western white pine, and the term "Idaho white pine" or the initials "IWP" stamped on a board identify one of America's finest softwoods.

Unless historical authenticity is important, however, I'd most likely choose the third major member of the group, sugar pine, for the primary wood in a furniture project. It has outstanding working characteristics (though it mars quite easily) and great stability, and it is available in large, wide, blemish-free boards—volumetrically, sugar pine is the largest true pine in the world. The wood is extremely consistent in

THE THREE GROUPS OF PINE LUMBER

Group A: White pines

Prime lumber from trees in this group is soft, light, easily worked, and commonly available in lumberyards. As shown in the 10X end-grain macrophotograph at right, *Pinus strobus* (eastern white pine), which is typical of trees in this group, has a gradual transition from earlywood to latewood within each growth ring, and an evenness of cell-wall thickness throughout, which means that earlywood and latewood have similar densities. These characteristics make for good woodworking and staining properties.

BOTANICAL NAME	COMMON NAME(S)	RANGE	PROPERTIES OF THE WOOD
P. strobus	Eastern white pine, northern white pine, cork pine, Weymouth pine.	Northeastern United States and eastern Canada, Appalachians south to Georgia.	Creamy white wood with yellow to orange-tan heartwood; traditional pine of Colonial New England. Average specific gravity 0.34.
P. monticola	Western white pine, Idaho white pine.	Western Montana, Idaho, into Washington and Oregon.	Virtually identical to eastern white pine. Specific gravity 0.35.
P. lambertiana	Sugar pine.	Oregon, northern and eastern California.	Creamy tan color, prominent "fleck" marks; available in large, clear stock; excellent carving wood. Specific gravity 0.34.

Severe growing conditions make the woods of the following western trees extremely variable: Limber pine, *P. flexilis;* whitebark pine, *P. albicaulis;* the pinyon pines (four or more species and hybrids); bristlecone pine, *P. aristata;* and foxtail pine, *P. balfouriana.*

Group B: Southern yellow pines

Woods in this group vary according to growing conditions, but latewood is predictably very hard and sometimes wide, while earlywood is soft, making for hard-to-work woods with racy grain patterns. Wood is resinous, dense, strong. Not generally a cabinet-quality wood, except for period furniture that demands it and for a long-lasting secondary wood. Makes good pressure-treated decking. The 10X macrophotograph of *P. echinata* (shortleaf pine), typical of the southern yellow pine group, shows wide, dense latewood, abrupt transition between earlywood and latewood within each growth ring, and extreme differences in wall thickness between earlywood and latewood.

P. palustris	Longleaf pine.	Southeastern and Gulf coastal plain.	Hard; yellow to orange-brown color; very resinous. Specific gravity 0.54.
P. echinata	Shortleaf pine.	From Texas to Georgia, and from Kentucky to northern Florida.	Similar to longleaf; slightly less dense. Specific gravity 0.47.
P. taeda	Loblolly pine.	Similar to shortleaf, except more southerly.	Same as shortleaf. Specific gravity 0.47.
P. elliottii	Slash pine.	Florida, southern Georgia and Gulf coastal plain.	Much like longleaf pine; one of the denser southern yellow pines. Specific gravity 0.54.

Minor species include Virginia pine, or Jersey pine, *P. virginiana,* specific gravity 0.45; pond pine, *P. serotina,* specific gravity 0.51; pitch pine, *P. rigida,* specific gravity 0.47; spruce pine (cedar pine, poor pine), *P. glabra,* specific gravity 0.41; sand pine, *P. clausa,* specific gravity 0.46; and Table Mountain pine, *P. pungens,* specific gravity 0.46, not abundant.

Group C: Western yellow pines

Woods in this group are slightly denser and more yellow than the white pines, but are lighter, less resinous and more workable than the southern yellow pines. *P. ponderosa,* shown at 10X in the macrophotograph at right, is typical of the pines in this group. Transition from earlywood to latewood is abrupt, yet latewood is not as wide or hard as in the southern yellow pines. Wood works well, holds crisp edges. Stain accentuates grain pattern. Dimpled grain common. Commonly seen in lumberyards as moldings and trim. The minor species listed are of little importance as timber producers due to their limited range and/or poor quality.

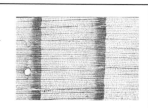

P. ponderosa	Ponderosa pine.	Inter Rocky Mountain region from Mexico to Canada, northern California and Oregon.	Best cabinet wood of the yellow pines. Specific gravity 0.38.
P. jeffreyi	Jeffrey pine.	Northern and eastern California, southeastern Oregon.	Virtually the same as ponderosa and marketed with it as "ponderosa" pine.
P. contorta	Lodgepole pine.	Northern Rockies, eastern California, Pacific Northwest.	Usually knottier than ponderosa or Jeffrey. Specific gravity 0.38.

Among the minor species are Torrey pine, *P. torreyana;* Monterey pine, *P. radiata;* Digger pine, *P. sabiniana;* and knobcone pine, *P. attenuata.* These may be available locally to western woodworkers. Some may be cut and shipped with the major species, especially in the lower grades and/or as dimension lumber.

The following species are not western trees, but are included in this group because of their wood's working characteristics:

P. banksiana	Jack pine.	Eastern Canada, northern Great Lakes states, New York and New England.	Wood most resembles lodgepole pine; knotty; light in color; wide sapwood; coarse-grained, may have dimpled grain. Specific gravity 0.40.
P. resinosa	Red pine, Norway pine.	Northeastern and Great Lakes states, eastern Canada.	Midway between the southern and western yellow pines in density; creamy white to yellow sapwood, orange to brown heartwood; less grainy and resinous than southern pines, but not as soft and workable as western yellow pines. Specific gravity 0.41.

Photos: John Limbach, Ripon Microslides

texture and a creamy light tan or beige in color, with a distinctive pattern in the grain caused by its characteristic resin canals. While all pines have numerous, fairly large resin canals (when compared to larch, spruce and Douglas fir), no other pine displays them so plentifully and prominently. This gives sugar pine the most distinctive—some think it beautiful—appearance of the white pines.

Several other western species—including limber pine, bristlecone pine and the pinyon pines—are listed in the chart as part of the white pine group, but their gnarly, short growth habit limits their value as lumber.

Southern yellow pines—These trees are hard, strong, dense and resinous, and a major source of paper pulp, plywood and construction timber. On the basis of commercial value and volume, the southern yellows are our most important pines, but very little lumber from this group finds a place in my shop. The trees produce a large band of latewood during the growing season, and they exhibit an abrupt transition between earlywood and latewood, with enormous contrast in density between the two zones. The knots are virtually impervious to stain. I don't like southern yellow pine, and much prefer to work with wood from either of the other two groups, yet I understand how southern yellow could be close to a period cabinetmaker's heart.

In reproducing a period piece in southern yellow pine, you would be better off trusting your eyes than relying on the differences listed in the chart. Woods from this group may be quite variable, but this seems less a matter of species than of growing conditions. Trees seeded on abandoned plantation lands grow faster than those that struggle up in mature forests. Producing broader annual rings and wider sapwood, the wood of these fast-growing trees may be considerably less dense than that of the typical southern yellow pine.

Western yellow pines—Most of the western yellow pines are less dense and resinous than the southern yellow pines. For a cabinetmaker, western yellows are a fine secondary wood, and some have novel grain patterns that can be attractive as a primary wood as well.

Ponderosa pine is one of the largest and most plentiful of the pines, which explains its ready availability and moderate price in lumberyards throughout the country. Unfortunately, it is not a rapid grower in the somewhat arid habitats of its range, and the day may come when this close-grained wood is no longer plentiful enough to hold its place as America's general-purpose, low-cost timber.

Ponderosa is only about 10% denser than the white pines, and therefore only a little harder, yet it is still undeniably a yellow pine in most ways. Just take the description of the southern pines and tone it down to the point where the wood's personality becomes amenable. The annual rings, for instance, are distinct and sometimes very showy, but there is less contrast in hardness between earlywood and latewood. Ponderosa has very narrow latewood, and the old-growth timber, with its narrow growth rings, can look surprisingly even-grained. The wood is superb for millwork: it machines beautifully and holds crisp edges.

Lodgepole pine is similar to ponderosa in color and density, but usually has smaller knots and many more of them. This species yields far less lumber per log than ponderosa. Growing in dense stands, the trees look like telephone poles with crowns of short needles, two to the bunch.

The ponderosa and lodgepole pines often exhibit a dimpled grain pattern. If you split a piece of the wood with an ax, small bumps on one side will be matched by dimples on the other. This abnormality, almost "normal" in these two pines, is caused by resin blisters in the inner bark which distort the cambium layer. The pattern is sometimes visible on the surface of plainsawn boards, and when the surface is tight enough to finish smoothly, it can resemble bird's-eye maple.

Northern yellow pines—Woodworkers may want to distinguish the northern yellow pines, species with which the first New England Colonists were familiar. Although two of these trees have working characteristics that assign them to groups we've already considered, the third, red pine, has qualities that help put all three groups in perspective.

Pitch pine is used primarily for pulp and only occasionally for lumber, although it was an important Colonial species before the stands were razed. Its wood resembles that of the southern yellow pines in color, resin content and hardness, and the lumber trade treats it as a "minor species" of the southern yellow pines. With a specific gravity of 0.47, it is by far the densest of the pines native to the northeastern United States.

Jack pine is a Canadian spillover invading the northern Great Lakes states and parts of New York and New England. It is a small tree which quickly seeds on burned-over land but is eventually displaced by more dominant species. Its wood—weak with wide sapwood, light in color, excessively knotty and somewhat coarse in texture—is something like inferior lodgepole pine, but jack pine seldom grows as straight. Like lodgepole, it sometimes has dimpled grain. In Canada, where their ranges overlap, these two trees will produce natural hybrids.

Red pine, the dominant yellow pine of the northeast, is a massive and beautiful tree. Legend has it that its other common name, Norway pine, stems from Norway, Maine, and has nothing to do with Scandinavia. In any event, it is definitely a native Northern American species. The wood of red pine falls somewhere between the western and southern yellow pines in most characteristics. It is slightly heavier than ponderosa, but substantially lighter than the southern yellow pines. The contrast between earlywood and latewood is more pronounced than in the western yellow pines, but substantially more gradual than in its southern cousins. Like the western yellow pines, its sapwood is light enough in color to resemble the white pines; its heartwood, however, is often a bright orange-brown. If carefully selected, the dark orange heartwood of red pine can be substituted for deal (Scotch pine) in the reproduction of European furniture designs.

Arbitrarily, I've assigned red pine to the western yellow pines in the chart, where it shows up as one of the worst cabinet woods. If I'd put it in with the southern yellow pines, however, it would be a star. So understand what your project requires and pick the group before you try to pick a species. And keep in mind that any wood comes in several grades—no woodworker should buy materials blindly. Yet getting to know the pines is an adventure no woodworker, and certainly no American woodworker, should miss. □

Jon Arno is an amateur woodworker in Brookfield, Wis. He wrote about elm in FWW #25, pp. 86-87, *and about the poplars in* #41, pp. 62-64.

A Dehumidifier Kiln

Home-dried lumber with no frills

by Donald Klimesh

For the past few years, I've been drying my own lumber in a kiln that I designed and built around a 22-pint/day Montgomery Ward dehumidifier. It will dry 300 bd. ft. of lumber in 8-ft. lengths, at a cost of about 10¢/bd. ft. for electricity. The dehumidifier cost me about $170, and the rest of the materials for the kiln totaled another $75.

The skeleton of my kiln is a wood frame of 1x6s covered with 4-mil clear plastic sheet, overlapped at the seams, and attached to the frame with wood strips and staples. I covered the plastic with 3½-in. fiberglass insulation. Don't fasten the insulation to the lid, because the insulation's removability is part of the kiln's temperature control. The dehumidifier sits inside, with its drain hose passing through a hole in the plastic and emptying into a catch pan outside the kiln. The water that collects here must be weighed daily to monitor the operation of the kiln. There is also a small electric fan inside, which runs continuously to circulate the air. I used a fan from an old appliance, but a small household fan would work fine.

The lumber to be dried is loaded on 4x4 supports, which for 1-in. lumber should be spaced no more than 2 ft. apart. To prevent the end grain from drying faster than the side grain—the main cause of checking—I liberally coat the ends of the boards with oil-based enamel paint. I use ¾-in. stickers to separate the layers of boards and to allow air to circulate. Space the stickers about 18 in. to 20 in. apart, and keep them one above another to minimize kinking.

It's easy to dry wood, but it's relatively difficult to end up with useful lumber. The first time I used my kiln, I ran the dehumidifier full-tilt. The wood dried much too quickly. The boards bent badly when ripped, and many were filled with internal checks, a defect called honeycombing. I've since overcome these problems with controlled drying and conditioning.

Wood will gain or lose moisture depending on the relative humidity of the air that surrounds it. As long as the relative humidity remains the same, a piece of wood will eventually reach a point where it neither gains nor loses moisture. The moisture that remains in the wood when it has reached this balance with the air is called its equilibrium moisture content, or EMC (*FWW* #39, pp. 92-95). I operate my kiln until the wood reaches an MC of approximately 7%.

To measure the relative humidity inside the kiln, I use a wet- and dry-bulb hygrometer (available from Edmund Scientific Co., 101 E. Gloucester Pike, Barrington, N.J. 08007). It consists of a standard thermometer mounted side by side on the same base with a wet-bulb thermometer which has a cloth wick fitted over the bulb. The other end of the wick dips into a small reservoir, which I fill with distilled water to prevent mineral buildup and to ensure accurate readings. The hygrometer hangs inside the kiln, and I cut a hole in the fiberglass so that I can read it through the plastic. I cover this window with a piece of insulation when I'm not reading the hygrometer, so that condensation won't fog up the plastic.

To determine the equilibrium moisture content, you need to know the relative humidity, but since the EMC is a more useful number to me than the RH, I've eliminated the need for calculations by making a chart that gives me the potential EMC of the wood directly from the wet- and dry-bulb readings. Just remember that the hygrometer actually measures the condition of the *air* inside the kiln, not of the lumber. It takes some time at any given relative humidity for the wood to reach the EMC shown on the chart—how long depends on the species and thickness of the wood. To lessen drying time and minimize degrade, you should air-dry dead-green lumber to below its fiber saturation point (25% to 30%

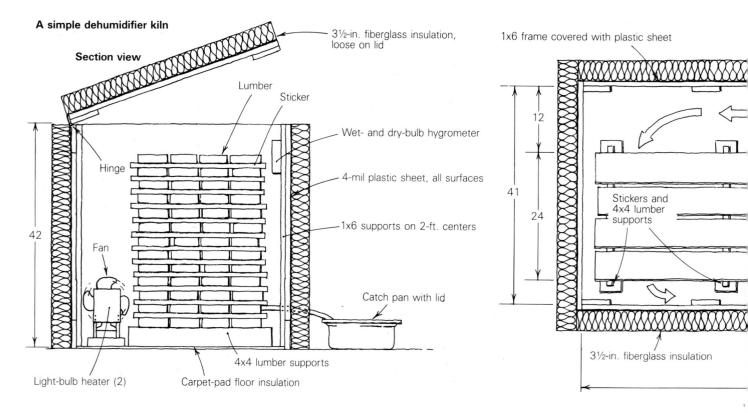

A simple dehumidifier kiln

Section view

3½-in. fiberglass insulation, loose on lid

1x6 frame covered with plastic sheet

Lumber

Sticker

Wet- and dry-bulb hygrometer

4-mil plastic sheet, all surfaces

1x6 supports on 2-ft. centers

Hinge

12

41

24

Stickers and 4x4 lumber supports

42

Fan

Catch pan with lid

3½-in. fiberglass insulation

Light-bulb heater (2)

4x4 lumber supports

Carpet-pad floor insulation

Photo: Jack Glaser; drawing: Ken Daniel

moisture content) before kilning it. An article in *FWW #33*, pp. 88-89, explains how.

To keep track of the drying process, I use a data sheet with the following headings: date, time, wet-bulb temperature, dry-bulb temperature, EMC, total weight of water collected, and rate of drying as measured by pounds of water per day. I start a fresh load with the humidistat control on the dehumidifier set about one-quarter of the maximum dry setting. Then I monitor the drying rate by daily weighing the water that collects in the catch pan, and I compare this to the maximum allowable weight of water listed in my drying schedule. If the daily catch of water exceeds the maximum recommended in the drying schedule, the wood is drying too fast, and I turn the humidistat down. If the catch is less than half the amount listed in the drying schedule, I turn the control up to speed the drying rate. Keep the catch pan covered, or else water will evaporate and weights will be inaccurate.

I maintain the kiln temperature at 105°F to 115°F throughout the drying cycle. Higher temperatures would speed drying, but might also harm the dehumidifier. In commercial kilns, dry-bulb temperatures go as high as 180°F, but these kilns must dry wood quickly to make a profit. I don't have to rush.

I can control the temperature in three ways: by changing the humidistat setting, by removing the insulation cover on the lid, or by adding auxiliary heat. Although the main function of the humidistat is to control the relative humidity inside the kiln, the dehumidifier motor also produces heat. If the temperature exceeds 115°F, I remove insulation from the lid to cool it down. If the temperature is below 105°F and the lid is totally covered, I add heat by turning on one or both of the two shielded light-bulb heaters (detail A, below).

The lumber is dry enough for me when, with hygrometer readings of 7% EMC, the daily catch of water amounts to 0.2 lb./100 sq. ft. (not bd. ft.) of lumber, which indicates a moisture content of approximately 7%. You can measure the moisture content of the wood itself to be sure, but if you

Controlling the kiln

Regulate drying by monitoring EMC, *which is indicated by the point at which the diagonal lines in the* EMC *chart intersect the wet- and dry-bulb temperatures. Find this* EMC *in the left-hand column of the drying schedule. The right-hand column shows the maximum weight of water you can remove (per 100 sq. ft. of lumber) without degrade.* Turn down the humidistat if you get more; turn it up if you get less than half.*

* These figures derive from experimentation, and your results may differ.

Equilibrium moisture content (EMC)

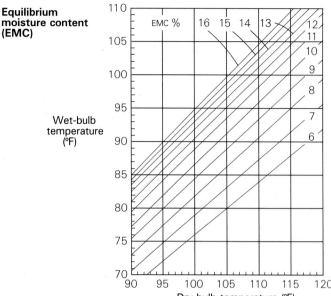

Drying schedule

Equilibrium moisture content (EMC) from chart above	Maximum water collected per day per 100 sq. ft. of lumber	
16% and above	11.0 lb./day	
15	8.0 lb./day	
14	7.0 lb./day	Note:
13	6.0 lb./day	100 bd. ft. of
12	5.0 lb./day	1-in. lumber = 100 sq. ft.
11	4.5 lb./day	
10	4.0 lb./day	100 bd. ft. of
9	3.0 lb./day	2-in. lumber = 50 sq. ft.
8	2.0 lb./day	
7†	2.0 lb./day	

† *When water yield is less than 0.2 lb./100 sq. ft., lumber has reached approximately 7% moisture content.*

Top view

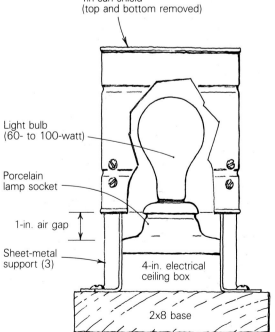

Light-bulb heaters *(see detail A)*

Continuously running fan

Airflow

Dehumidifier

Hygrometer

Hygrometer viewing port

Catch pan

Drain hose

120

Detail A: Auxiliary light-bulb heater

Tin-can shield (top and bottom removed)

Light bulb (60- to 100-watt)

Porcelain lamp socket

1-in. air gap

Sheet-metal support (3)

4-in. electrical ceiling box

2x8 base

don't have a moisture meter, you'll have to sacrifice part of a board. Here's how: Crosscut a strip 1 in. wide about 1 ft. in from the end of a board. Weigh this section on any sensitive scale—a gram scale, beam balance, food-portion scale or postage scale—anything that will give you an accurate reading in small increments. Write down the weight. Now bake the piece of wood in a 225°F oven for several hours to drive off all moisture. Weigh this dried piece and subtract its weight from the wet weight, to find out how much water it contained. Now divide the weight of the water by the oven-dry weight of the wood, multiply by 100 (move the decimal two places to the right), put a percent sign (%) after this figure, and you have the moisture content. But even if you've reached 7% MC, your wood isn't ready to use yet.

As lumber dries, it develops residual compression stresses in the outer fibers. This condition is called casehardening, a misnomer since the "case" is not really harder than the inside. It is most noticeable when you're resawing or ripping boards. Even if the board being cut is dry and straight, a casehardened board will bend when it is cut, sometimes severely. Commercial kilns solve the casehardening problem by adding a step called conditioning. Steam is introduced into the kiln to add moisture, which swells the outer fibers and causes them to yield, so they will be under less stress when they are redried. I also condition my dried lumber, but my process is less sophisticated. After the boards are dry, I remove them from the kiln and spray both sides of each board with warm water from a garden hose. Then I immediately restack the lumber in the kiln and redry, following the drying schedule.

The final drying step is called equalizing. When the lumber has dried again after conditioning (less than 0.2 lb. of water per day per 100 sq. ft. with hygrometer readings of 7% EMC, which is approximately 7% MC), I continue to operate the kiln for one week for each inch of lumber thickness, with the auxiliary heater lamps turned off. By this time I'm usually tired of the daily chore of weighing the water, so I just let the dehumidifier run with the humidistat set to give approximately 7% EMC, as measured by the hygrometer.

How long does it take? A batch of 320 bd. ft. of green, 1-in. red oak took me 60 days—46 days to dry and another 14 days for conditioning and equalizing. A total of 563 lb. of water was removed during the drying process. Drying time varies for different species, and thicker lumber takes longer.

So far, I've used the kiln and my drying schedule to dry oak, white pine, maple and cherry. While it may seem that the process is time-consuming, it takes only a few minutes each day to weigh the water, read the thermometers and occasionally adjust the humidistat. □

Donald Klimesh, of Birmingham, Mich., is an amateur woodworker and an engineer with Ford Motor Co. For more information on drying, read Dry Kiln Handbook *by J.L. Bachrich, published by H.A. Simons (International) Ltd., 425 Carrall St., Vancouver, B.C. V6B 2J6.*

Don't let that dry look fool you

Wood is only as dry as the air that surrounds it, and once dried it doesn't necessarily stay that way. Instead, wood always seeks a moisture equilibrium with its environment.

No matter how long wood has been seasoned, whether or not it has been kiln-dried, lumber still contains some water. This is called its moisture content (MC), and is usually expressed as a percent. The moisture content changes as the relative humidity (RH) of the air around the wood changes.

An example: Two identical boards of, say, white oak are kiln-dried to a moisture content of 7%. One is shipped to the Northeast, where the relative humidity outdoors averages 75% year round. The other goes to the Southwest, where the relative humidity averages 38%.

In the 75% RH of the Northeast, the board picks up moisture from the air and eventually reaches a moisture content of 14%, where it stops absorbing moisture and stabilizes. The board has now reached the equilibrium moisture content (EMC) for that relative humidity, and will hold at 14% as long as the relative humidity stays at 75%.

In the Southwest, at 38% RH, the board loses moisture to the air until its moisture content stabilizes at about 6%. This board also has reached the EMC for

that relative humidity.

When the relative humidity of the air changes, the moisture content of the wood changes, until it reaches a new equilibrium moisture content.

Wood should be dried to a moisture content close to the EMC it will reach in the environment in which it will be used. In the Northeastern winter, in a heated, non-humidified room, the relative humidity might average 25% or less. Wood exposed to this low RH would reach equilibrium around 5% moisture content. In summer, when windows are open, inside humidity levels are close to those outside.

Why is all this important? Because wood expands across the grain when the moisture content increases, and shrinks across the grain when the moisture content decreases. Furniture must be designed to allow for this movement.

Here are some terms woodworkers should know:

Moisture content (MC): The ratio (expressed as a percentage) of the weight of water in a piece of wood to the weight of the wood when it has been completely dried in an oven. To calculate, subtract the dry weight from the wet

Klimesh loads his kiln with green, 2-in. pine boards.

weight, and divide the result by the dry weight, as in the equation:

$$MC = \frac{W_{wet} - W_{oven-dry}}{W_{oven-dry}} \times 100$$

Relative humidity (RH): The ratio (expressed as a percentage) of the amount of water vapor in the air to the maximum amount the air could hold at a given temperature. Saturated air is said to be at 100% RH.

Fiber saturation point (FSP): The moisture content (which varies with the species) where all water has evaporated from the cell cavities, but the cell walls are still saturated. Wood shrinkage occurs only when the cell walls begin to dry. —*D.K.*

Bluestain fungi

I have several hundred bd. ft. of 3-in. and 4-in. thick bass-wood which someone stacked, just after it was sawn, without stickering the pile. The wood developed what looks like a blue mold or mildew, which goes all through the timber. The wood doesn't appear to be structurally affected.

I intend to use the wood solely for decorative decoy carving. Should I invest any time working with this wood, or should I just feed it to my stove this winter? Would high humidity reactivate the mildew spores and cause future weakness to develop? —Jim Smith, Minneapolis, Minn.

R. Bruce Hoadley replies: Your sample of basswood has a moderate infestation of bluestain fungi, a common sapstain "discoloration." Once the wood is dry, the fungi's progress will be arrested and no further development will occur. Since this type of fungus merely lives in the wood, but causes no cell breakdown, the wood should be perfectly fit for use in decorative decoys. A good base coat of paint should hide the streaks of discoloration. I doubt if a carved decorative decoy will ever be subjected to a high enough humidity to reactivate the fungi. [R. Bruce Hoadley is professor of wood technology at the University of Massachusetts at Amherst.]

Identifying oak

I have trouble differentiating between English brown oak (Quercus robur) and American white oak (Quercus alba) in some 17th-century furniture. Both types seem to be equally dark. Is there a way to identify these two oaks by looking at the end grain with a 10X magnifying glass?
—Herbert W. Berry, Syracuse, N.Y.

Regis B. Miller replies: Sorry, no. The many species of oak throughout the world can be separated into three distinct groups fairly easily: the red oaks, the white oaks, and the live oaks. The red oaks and white oaks are ring-porous; the live oaks are diffuse-porous. To distinguish between the red and white oaks, you must look at the end grain with a 10X to 20X hand lens. The key character is the latewood pores. In red oaks they are distinct, thick-walled and solitary, whereas in white oaks they are barely visible, thin-walled and not solitary. Also, white oaks have tyloses, red don't. With a hand lens, or even a light microscope, that's about as far as you can go.

Since English brown oak and American white oak are both in the white oak group, there is no positive way to separate them. It is true that the heartwood color of English brown oak is different from that of American white oak, but the variation within each species is too great for you to be absolutely sure of the identification.
[Regis B. Miller is project leader at the Center for Wood Anatomy Research in Madison, Wis.]

Allergy symptoms

How long will it take for the allergy-type symptoms of a "mahogany cough" to disappear following cessation of exposure? Also, how can you tell if the charcoal filter in a respirator is no longer working? I'm told that painters can tell because they start to smell the fumes again, but some woods have little or no odor when they're being cut.
—Audrey M. Johnson, Oakdale, Calif.

George Mustoe replies: The respiratory symptoms caused by allergic reactions to wood dust usually clear up within a few days once contact with the irritant has ceased. The severity of the symptoms depends on the length of exposure, the amount of dust inhaled, and the individual's sensitivity to the material. After repeated contact, the intensity of the allergic response is liable to increase and the symptoms become worse.

With freshly milled lumber, irritation may come from volatile oils, but in most cases problems arise from exposure to dust. A good dust mask offers adequate protection. A cartridge-type respirator isn't necessary in this case.

You can test the effectiveness of a toxic-vapor respirator by sniffing an open container of acetone, lacquer thinner or other smelly solvent. If the fumes permeate into the mask, either the filter is worn out, the mask leaks around the wearer's face, or the intake or exhaust ports are stuck open.
[George Mustoe, a geochemistry research technician in Bellingham, Wash., wrote about respiratory hazards in *FWW* #41.]

Magnolia wood

During a recent excursion into our woodlot, I found a tree that I believe is mountain magnolia. What can you tell me about this wood? —Mike Mease, Port Matilda, Pa.

R. Bruce Hoadley replies: *Magnolia acuminata* is most commonly called cucumbertree, or simply cucumber. It's a straight-grained, fairly heavy (0.44 to 0.46 specific gravity), diffuse-porous wood with white sapwood and greenish heartwood. It's a good choice for a secondary furniture wood. Commercially the lumber is often mixed with and sold as yellow-poplar (tuliptree), which it closely resembles, although cucumber's sapwood is somewhat lighter in color. Another difference: The band of marginal, or terminal, parenchyma (the small cells that appear as a line separating the annual rings) is sometimes more distinct on cucumbertree, giving the tangential surfaces a somewhat more visible growth-ring figure.
[R. Bruce Hoadley is professor of wood technology at the University of Massachusetts at Amherst.]

Importing wood

I enjoyed reading "The Trade in Exotic Hardwoods" in FWW #38. The last sentence in this article states, "Shops using large quantities of rare woods might even find it worthwhile to import their own wood, rather than buying it on the domestic market." Someday I may want to import my own wood. Can you buy wood that has been kiln-dried? Any information on importing from abroad, especially Brazil, would be most helpful. —Andrew Brennan, Westlake Village, Calif.

Paul McClure replies: Importing wood may seem to be a money-saving venture, but it can be quite the opposite. Buying "sight unseen" lumber is a risky business. There are the obvious problems of language, and massive amounts of paperwork and red tape. You will be tying up your money for as long as a year while the lumber is logged, milled, partially air-dried, bundled, and loaded aboard a ship.

Most countries, including Brazil, require a minimum order of 5 cubic meters (2,120 bd. ft.). Find a trustworthy lumber supplier and try to meet in person, if possible, before starting negotiations. It is essential that you order "first European quality lumber" if you expect good, usable stock. Once your lumber has been shipped, you'll need a port broker in the United States. It's the broker's job to handle all the necessary paperwork in this country, and to forward your lumber to a drying kiln. Almost all imported woods are kiln-dried in this country because fuel in Third World lumber-producing countries is expensive. Besides, the lumber would only pick up moisture during its ocean voyage.

You can inspect the lumber once it arrives on the dock, to make sure it's the grade, size, quantity and species that you ordered. If it's not, however, you're out of luck.

A friend of mine ordered African padauk, 6 in. and wider in 6-ft. lengths, and inspected it on the Ivory Coast dock before it was loaded on the ship. The shipment of padauk that arrived in New Orleans, however, consisted of 6-ft. and 10-ft. 1x3s. It seems that his wood had been switched with another load of padauk for a flooring mill in Italy.
[Paul McClure is a dealer in exotic woods in Tempe, Ariz.]

FINISHING AND GLUE

Water-Gilding

How to match the golden age's incomparable shine

by Nancy Russo

This girandole from about 1820, designed by H.H. Richardson, holds candles that reflect light into the room and bathe its own water-gilt profusion with dancing beams.

Period furnituremakers who don't work with gold are missing out on some of the most passionate furniture ever made. It's true that gold leaf, misused, can be garish. But at its best, burnished gold has visual qualities that pull a design together, bringing order to elements that, finished in another way, would be incomprehensible. A woodworker, furniture designer or frame maker today can incorporate bright or antiqued gold into his work in much the same way that he might use inlaying, marquetry or carving.

There are two fundamentally different ways to apply gold leaf, and each has its place. Water-gilding was once the principal method for ornamenting objects of real value—panel paintings, clocks, furniture, architectural members, and picture and mirror frames. It was used as far back as ancient Egypt and has remained virtually unchanged since the Middle Ages. Water-gilding is crucial to many period styles, but it has become obscure in the last eighty years or so. Few people outside the trade recognize a water-gilt surface, much less understand how it's done.

Nowadays, oil-gilding (*FWW* #36, pp. 77-79) is much more common. It is an ancient and durable method of attaching leaf to wood, glass, metal or just about any surface that can be made nonporous with a sealer. The leaf, either real gold or imitation, is pressed onto a coat of high-quality varnish that has been allowed to dry to a particular tack. Today, oil-gilding with 23-karat gold leaf is used primarily for outdoor work, from signs to state capitol domes. Because gold does not tarnish, the surface can be left unsealed, and the shine will last as long as the support and varnish remain intact. Most picture-frame moldings are oil-gilded these days, too, but with aluminum leaf or gold-colored "metal leaf" which is then distressed and antiqued with glazes. Oil-gilding is quick, and if you use imitation leaf, it's relatively cheap.

Water-gilding, in contrast, is rare to-

162

Leaf can be cut on a leather pad with a smooth-edged knife, whose handle here rests on some sheets of rabbit-skin glue. Also shown are agate burnishers, boxes of leaf, and a pestle for grinding lump clay, a piece of which sits at the back of the pad.

day, partly due to the cost of gold but also because of the time and labor involved. The leaf is laid on a many-layered ground of gesso and clay, both with hide glue as a binder. Then the surface—actually the ground itself, under the gold—can be polished by rubbing it with an agate burnisher. The tops of moldings and carvings can be burnished to a mirror-like reflection, and the hollows left with a matte, metallic luster, creating an incomparable richness of surface.

Antique water-gilt items slowly dull with age, mostly from environmental pollution, which eventually becomes difficult if not impossible to remove. These pieces were rarely protected with a finish and can be ruined by water, a fate many have suffered from careless cleaning. In many cases, although the gold is gone, the surface beneath may be reactivated and gilded again. But gesso that's been exposed to dampness for any length of time decomposes, softens irreparably, and must be replaced.

Small repairs are best done by patching. My feeling about complete re-gilding of antiques is, don't if you don't have to, but if you do, stick to the original gilding technique and burnishing patterns, and don't artificially age or "antique." The gold will mellow in its own time, whereas the various finishes used in antiquing are apt to change rapidly, drastically altering the effect.

Materials and tools—Today, most gold leaf is machine-beaten to a thinness of 0.00003 in., thinner than any piece of paper. If laid on a dry surface, a sheet of gold will sail off with the slightest puff of air. If crumbled in the hand, it disintegrates and all but disappears. Machine-beaten leaf is four times thinner than its medieval counterpart, and so thin that it is virtually transparent, which allows any color beneath it to shine through, especially when the gold has been partly worn through. Oil-gilded surfaces, toned to imitate this effect, never have the brilliance and depth of a burnished surface.

Pure gold is called 24K (karat). Gold leaf, which is 23K, is alloyed with 1K silver or copper, or a combination of the two. The other metals color the gold slightly warmer or cooler.

The standard leaf today is 3⅜ in. square and comes in "books" containing 25 leaves. There are 20 books to a pack, the wholesale unit, enough for an experienced gilder to cover 30 sq. ft. One manufacturer, M. Swift and Sons, 10 Love La., Hartford, Conn. 06141, currently charges about $275 per pack.

The two main types of gold leaf are loose leaf and patent leaf. Loose leaf is sold in two commercial grades: surface gold and glass gold. Surface gold may have small holes or imperfections, but these will be backed up in the book by a smaller piece of leaf for patching the

gaps. Glass gold has no irregularities, because patches would show through when gilding on glass. Patent, or transfer, gold is leaf slightly adhered to a piece of tissue in the book. The tissue extends beyond the edges of the gold, so you can pick up each leaf by hand, which is especially helpful when gilding outside on a windy day.

Silver leaf is about three times thicker than gold leaf. Many Victorian picture frames were leafed with silver, then sealed with an alcohol-based, transparent, amber-colored lacquer to make them look like gold. In most cases, the silver has begun to tarnish—black spots can be seen beneath the gold lacquer. Some Victorian frames were deliberately tarnished in decorative patterns before being gold-lacquered.

"Dutch metal" refers to what is now called gold "metal leaf." It is made of copper and zinc, and is larger than gold leaf and thick enough to handle. The same is true of aluminum leaf, which came into use in the 19th century.

Because of the increasing thinness of gold leaf, by the 17th century a tool was needed to handle loose leaf, and the gilders' tip came into use. It's a wide, flat brush of badger or squirrel hair, 2 in. long, with a cardboard handle. The tip transfers the gold from the book to a pad or directly to the work. The gilder rubs the tip over her hair or face to collect a minute amount of oil (not to

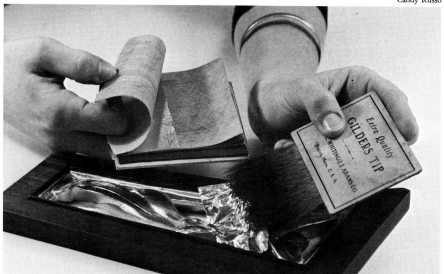

Candy Russo

The gilders' tip picks up and transfers the gold from its padded book. A beginner may instead opt to use 'patent gold' (where each leaf comes lightly adhered to a sheet of paper), or to press waxed paper over the leaf for easier handling. The piece here, part of a table by Sam Bush, is shown as it would look being patched after burnishing.

create static, as is sometimes thought), and the oil provides just enough stick for the gold leaf to adhere to the tip for transferring.

If a full sheet of gold is not needed, it can be cut to size with a gilders' knife. The knife is not sharp and has no rough edges to catch and tear the gold. Gold leaf can be cut and transferred directly from the book with the aid of a piece of cardboard for stiffening and a piece of leather padding inserted between the last two pages, as shown in the photo above.

After the gold has been laid and the proper amount of time has elapsed, the gold can be burnished. The burnishers used today are made of polished agate fitted into a ferrule with a paintbrush-type handle. The common agate has a slightly crooked shape and a smooth, rounded point. This shape is in imitation of a dog's tooth, such as those used by Renaissance gilders, and remains the most practical for all-around use.

Procedure—The wood to be water-gilded is first sanded to remove sharp edges and corners, and then many coats of gesso are applied, forming a "bed" for the gold. Gesso is a mixture of whiting (calcium carbonate, ground very fine and washed) and rabbit-skin glue, with the consistency of heavy cream. It is kept hot to maintain brushability, because rabbit-skin glue congeals just like other hot hide glues when cooled to room temperature. Usually six or seven coats of gesso are sufficient, especially if the wood is a fine-textured one such as poplar or basswood. The gesso and its

application are extremely important for a good gild and burnish.

You can either use a pre-mixed, packaged gesso, or make it from scratch. The packaged type, Grumbacher's Dry Ground Gesso, is a mixture of whiting and glue pellets. For large jobs, it's cheaper to make your own gesso: Mix 1 oz. by weight of rabbit-skin glue to 4 fl. oz. of water. Allow the glue to completely swell and soften at room temperature, which can take from 15 minutes to several hours, depending on its particle size. Sift 3 to 4 cups of whiting through a wire strainer. Measure 4 fl. oz. of water into a metal container, and slowly add the sifted whiting until the mixture mounds on the spoon and begins to look just slightly less smooth and glossy. To make sure that the whiting is completely absorbed, I shake it into the can from a spoon, slowly, until the water won't absorb any more, then I add more, stirring out any lumps, until the mixture mounds. Heat the glue mixture in a double boiler over low heat until it melts. Add 3 fl. oz. of the melted glue all at once to the whiting mixture. Using a good brush with no loose hairs, slowly stir from the bottom in one direction until the gesso is well mixed.

Both kinds of gesso will keep for a few weeks if refrigerated, but will gradually break down. If the gesso begins to look a little watery on top, it may be too soft to use. Don't take chances with gesso. If in doubt, make a new batch.

For use, heat the gesso in a double

boiler, adding a few drops of water each time you heat it to compensate for evaporation. Overheating, either too often or too hot, can break down the glue and can also cause pinholes, the bane of a gilder's existence. If pinholes develop in the first full-strength coat of gesso, they will telegraph through the successive coats, and even the top coat of clay will have pinholes. To avoid them, work in a warm, dry room and keep the gesso from cooling in the pot as you work. If small bubbles develop while you're making the gesso, and some always do, agitate the container, letting them rise to the surface. Then when the gesso cools and skins over, just peel off the skin. You can also add a wetting agent, such as oxgall (available from an art supply store), which will help the bubbles rise to the surface. If in the end your final dry coat of gesso shows pinholes, try wetting your finger and rubbing over the gesso until the sludge fills the holes.

After the gesso is heated, apply it first as a primer coat. Dilute the gesso to half strength with water, brush it on and let it dry. The first full-strength coat is scrubbed on quickly for good adhesion, especially important if the wood is open-textured. A good-quality, ¾-in. wide, square-end sable brush is the right choice for all stages of gilding. Wet the brush with water and squeeze it dry, then apply the gesso, working quickly and with the brush fairly well loaded. Avoid over-brushing, or the surface will become lumpy. Each coat can be applied as soon as the previous coat has dulled, until you've built up the thickness to as much as 1/16 in.

When the gesso is dry, surface it absolutely smooth with sandpaper, either wet or dry, or scrapers. I usually start with 320-grit aluminum oxide paper and work down to as fine a paper as necessary to eliminate all sandpaper marks without actually putting a polish on the gessoed surface, because if this happens, the clay will resist bonding to the gesso. It's important not to sand the gesso into sharp edges or corners which could be knocked off or chipped. Shallow, ornamental carving can be done with regular carving tools after final-sanding. Gesso carves crisply and cleanly.

Next comes the gilders' clay. This is the red coating sometimes seen peeking through worn gold leaf. It's a very fine-textured, unctuous material that takes a polish when rubbed with the agate burnisher. Red clay looks best under gold leaf when rub-through antiquing effects are used. Blue-gray, white, black and yellow clays are also common, the color of the clay affecting the tone—warm or cool—of the final gold finish. Dark clays are used under silver leaf, while yellow clay helps to hide breaks in the gold in the matte areas. Commonly, the whole object will be given several coats of ochre clay over the gesso, then the areas to be burnished will be given a few additional coats of red clay or dark gray clay.

Clay is sold in solid lump form from Europe, or as a thick pre-ground paste packed in small jars. Gilders' clay formulas are a closely guarded secret of the makers. Modern gilders' clay probably contains some additives such as glycerin, whiting and dyes, which are meant to extend and improve the clay.

The clay must be ground in water to a smooth-as-silk consistency, rabbit-skin glue (or gelatin) and water added, and several coats of the mixture brushed over the surfaced gesso. The recipe I use makes about ¼ cup. I like to make only as much as I need for a given job. If you are working with lump clay, first grind it to a powder. I have a piece of fine steel screen, which I bought at a hardware store, stapled over a deep wooden box. Holding the clay as if I were grating cheese, I rub it over the screen to pulverize it. Grate about two rounded tablespoons' worth, put it into a clean metal container, such as a tuna can, then add water to form a paste. Now strain the clay to remove any grit. I force it through an extremely fine piece of brass mesh soldered onto a copper cylinder; some people use several layers of fine nylon stocking. Jarred clays, which you might expect to be grit-free, are sometimes not. At best, gritty clay will make the gold less bright. At worst, grit can ruin your burnisher and cause it to scratch the gold on future jobs. After straining, add water, stirring with a pointed sable brush until the clay mixture is thin enough to drop off the brush one drop at a time. Before the mixture reaches this point, it will be necessary to add the water very slowly, drop by drop, or the clay will be too thin.

Now make up the rabbit-skin glue, using the same proportions as for gesso. Melt the glue in a double boiler and add it to the clay/water mixture by dribbling it down the side of the can in a thin, steady stream, stirring all the time. Almost immediately, the clay will begin to clabber, or curdle. Sometimes it suddenly gets quite thick, almost stiff, and other times a slight thickening is barely discernible. Keep adding the glue steadily. Just after the clabbering stage, the clay will begin to thin out again. You want to bring it back to the point where it drops off the brush one drop at a time. As the glue is added, the clay goes through these stages very quickly, from thin to clabber to thin again, so go slowly and carefully.

To be on the safe side, I always test each batch of clay on a gessoed sample piece. Apply a little clay, leaf over it, and test how it burnishes. After testing the clay, brush it on the surfaced gesso. Several coats are needed before the clay looks opaque and covers the gesso completely. Keep the clay warm while you work, as you did for the gesso, and try not to let it pool in the hollows, or pinholes may develop.

The clay mixture has very little body, and even five or six coats will not hide defects in the gesso. The clay should not need to be surfaced, but if you notice any grittiness when it has dried, you can smooth it with a worn piece of 400-grit or 600-grit sandpaper and polish out with a piece of linen or a white Scotch-Brite scrubbing pad. Avoid steel wool—it leaves particles behind, and some brands are protected from rusting with oil, which can ruin the clay surface.

Now the gold leaf can be applied. The clay surface where the first pieces of gold leaf are to be laid is first flooded with a solution of water and alcohol. This activates the glue in the clay, creating adhesion. The proportion of alcohol doesn't matter too much. I use about 1 part methyl alcohol to 3 parts water. When gilding with silver leaf, which is heavier than gold, or if the leaf didn't adhere perfectly on the test piece, I add a tiny pea-sized piece of rabbit-skin glue to the solution. Be careful, though—too much glue will dull the burnish.

Really flood the surface, because the layers of gesso and clay will absorb the water like a sponge. If the clay looks dull instead of wet and shiny, the gold will not stick. Using the gilders' tip, quickly pick up the gold and with a smooth motion transfer it to the work. I rub a dab of Chapstick on my wrist and pass the tip over it occasionally so that the gold will adhere. You'll find that using the gilders' tip takes a little practice. The larger the pieces of gold need-

ed, the more practice it takes to lift and transfer the leaf smoothly, without the gold folding up before it reaches the surface. Don't be intimidated by the fact that it is gold and is so fragile. A few wasted pieces amount to only a few cents, and you will waste some. After most of the water has been absorbed and the gold flattens out, tamp it down lightly with cotton and lay the next few pieces, overlapping the edges slightly.

When the whole piece has been gilded in this manner, the matte areas are burnished with cotton to ensure good contact and to bring up a rich luster. The "skewings," loose pieces of gold at the overlaps, come off at the same time. With a clean piece of cotton, lightly rub over the gold in a circular motion, applying more pressure as the skewings are removed. The gold will look like solid, polished metal. This is a matte gild.

Highlights can now be burnished mirror-bright. The areas to be burnished should not be bone-dry, but they shouldn't be too damp, or the burnisher will tear through the gold. Glide the burnisher back and forth over the gold, and if everything is just the way it should be, you'll find you can apply quite a bit of pressure. Burnishing is one of the craftsman's real rewards for preparation of the ground. The Latin word *brunir,* from which "burnish" is derived, means brown, and aptly describes the gold as it changes from a pale color to dark, metallic reflections. The burnisher presses folds and overlaps into each other; these double-thick areas appear as more solid areas in worn, antique pieces.

The whole job can now be left as is, antiqued, or given a protective finish. Any finish will dull the gold, and for this reason many old pieces were never sealed at all. Nitrocellulose lacquer, sprayed or brushed, dulls the gold less than other finishes. Orange shellac is often used instead, to warm the color. Don't worry if the finish coat blooms (whitens slightly) as you apply it. It will dry bright and clear. □

Nancy Russo has been gilding and restoring since 1971, and now has her own shop, Gold Leaf Restorations, in Portland, Ore. Gilding materials can be obtained from H. Behlen & Bros. (call 518-843-1380 for a local distributor); from Art Essentials, Box 260, Monsey, N.Y. 10952; and from sign painters' suppliers and good local art-supply stores.

Glues for Woodworking
Synthetics solve some problems, pose new ones

by George Mustoe

Adhesives have changed enormously since the days when artisans prepared their own crude glues from meat scraps or milk curds. Twentieth-century chemistry has given us hundreds of new synthetic adhesives, some of which are of interest to the woodworker. Generally these adhesives—epoxies, cyanoacrylates, hot-melt glues and contact cements—are far more expensive than the hide glues, polyvinyl acetates and water-resistant glues that I discussed in a previous article in *FWW* #43, although they aren't necessarily more effective. In the small woodshop, cost alone limits use of most of these glues to special jobs.

Epoxy resins—Although epoxies are among the more expensive adhesives, their physical properties—high strength, low shrinkage, transparency, insolubility, and ability to bond to a diverse array of materials—make them ideal for certain applications. The extreme strength of epoxy is seldom essential in joining wood to wood, but it makes it possible to bond wood to glass or to metal. Cured epoxy machines well, and its dimensional stability makes it an excellent choice for filling gaps and mending holes.

All epoxies are two-part systems: a resin, and a liquid catalyst or hardener. They harden by chemical reaction between the two components, not by solvent evaporation. The glue is activated by mixing the resin and hardener together, usually in equal proportions. Changing the resin/hardener proportion affects the properties of the cured epoxy: slightly increasing the hardener by up to 10% makes the bond more flexible, while increasing the resin by up to 10% makes the bond more brittle. Using a larger proportion of either component weakens the bond.

Curing time for epoxies varies according to temperature. Epoxies generally require temperatures of 65°F or higher to set, although special formulas have been developed for use at lower temperatures. Heating the joint to 100°F to 150°F speeds the setting rate, but also increases the health risk: the vapors from hot epoxy are very toxic. Viscosity drops dramatically at higher temperatures, causing the epoxy to flow out of the joint onto other areas of the work. Whatever the temperature, uncured epoxy is toxic, and repeated skin contact can provoke allergic reactions in some people. Acetone is recommended for cleaning up uncured epoxy, but denatured alcohol works just as well and is less flammable.

Epoxies come in a variety of different types. "Quick-set" or "5-minute" epoxies are convenient where you need a strong, fast-setting bond, but their brief pot life can be frustrating if your assembly takes longer than you expected. They also have less strength and water-resistance than conventional epoxy. Hand-moldable sticks of epoxy putty are easy to mix, and work well as a filler. Opaque "filled epoxies" contain suspended solids such as clay or powdered metal to provide increased strength, higher viscosity or other desired proper-

ties. Filled epoxies have a putty-like consistency that makes them perfect for filling large voids or repairing surface dents, but they have a limited shelf life because the filler eventually settles out of suspension. Vigorous stirring will sometimes restore old stock to a usable condition. When clear epoxy resin gets old, it may become thick and granular (some preparations have recommended shelf lives of only 6 to 12 months), but warming the container to about 100°F in a hot water bath will return the epoxy to its original state.

Many retail brands of clear epoxy are bought in bulk from the manufacturer and repackaged into small containers. There isn't much difference between brands, and you can save money by purchasing epoxy in larger quantities. One ounce of epoxy in a tube costs about $2.25, but Sig Model Airplane Epoxy, an excellent transparent glue found in hobby stores, costs about $7.50 for 12 ounces. Though epoxy manufacturers won't often sell bulk quantities directly to the public, they'll usually provide technical assistance and lists of local distributors. Armstrong Products Company, PO Box 647, Warsaw, Ind. 46580, makes a clear all-purpose epoxy called A-271 resin, a "quick-set" resin called A-36, and several other types. Devcon Corporation, 30 Endicott St., Danvers, Mass. 01923, also distributes epoxy in bulk. As another example of the money you can save by buying in quantity, Devcon 210 epoxy costs $2 an ounce in hardware stores, but about 62¢ an ounce in gallon lots.

Several epoxies have been marketed specifically for woodworkers by Industrial Formulators of Canada, Ltd. Their G-1 epoxy is a general-purpose clear resin; G-2 is recommended for oily and acidic woods such as teak and oak. Cold Cure is meant for use at temperatures as low as 35°F, Five Cure sets in 15 minutes or less at temperatures above 40°F, and Sun Cure is a low-viscosity laminating resin. You can mail-order these epoxies from Flounder Bay Boat Lumber, 3rd and "O" Ave., Anacortes, Wash. 98221.

An extensive line of epoxies, additives and dispensing pumps is sold by Gougeon Brothers, Inc., 706 Martin St., Bay City, Mich. 48706, under the trademark West System. Developed for boatbuilding, the Gougeon system uses epoxies both as adhesives and as saturation coatings to prevent transfer of moisture and improve dimensional stability.

Polyester resins—If you want to reinforce wood with fiberglass cloth, your best choice is epoxy resin, but because of epoxy's high cost, polyester resin is commonly used instead. It is also less toxic and much cheaper. Like epoxies, polyester resins are two-part systems: a low-viscosity liquid which hardens when a small amount of catalyst is added. Although polyester resin performs well for reinforcing fiberglass, it lacks sufficient wetting ability to bind to wood fibers. It will adhere to wood only if the solidified resin can interlock with surface irregularities. You can get an adequate bond if you roughen

166

Adhesive Selection Guide

Adhesive	Application characteristics	Properties after curing	Recommended uses
Epoxy Armstrong A-271, Cold Cure, Devcon 210, Five Cure, Industrial Formulators' G-1 and G-2, Sig Model Airplane Epoxy, Sun Cure, West System	Moderate viscosity, decreasing greatly at warm temperatures, min. curing temp. 65°F**, excellent gap-filling ability, two-part system, liquid and vapors are toxic, may cause skin irritation	Highly transparent, waterproof, bonds to many materials, sands and machines well	Marine and outdoor use, excellent for bonding nonporous materials
Cyanoacrylate Devcon Zip Grip 10, Duro Super Glue, Eastman 910, Elmer's Wonder Bond, Hot Stuff, Krazy Glue, Scotchweld CA-3	Very fast bonding***, very low viscosity, min. curing temp. 60°F, poor gap-filling ability, odor may be irritating, bonding may be inhibited by oil or acidic residues, excess is very difficult to clean up	Highly transparent, very water-resistant	Small repairs, modelmaking, bonding nonporous materials
Hot-melt stick Bostik Thermogrip, Swingline Fix Stix	Sets almost instantly, high viscosity, excellent gap-filling ability, does not penetrate well, difficult to apply over large areas, nontoxic, glue gun needed	Neutral opaque color, moderate strength, remains slightly flexible, cannot be sanded, softens when heated	Furniture repairs, small projects such as toys, construction of jigs and patterns
Hot-melt sheet	Instant bonding, applied with hot iron, poor gap-filling ability		Veneering
Contact cement, solvent-based Weldwood Contact Cement, Wilhold Contact Cement	Instant bonding, min. curing temp. 70°F, poor gap-filling ability, highly toxic, very flammable, difficult to clean up	Low strength, creeps under load	Bonding plastic laminates to plywood, not recommended for veneering, though it is widely used for this purpose
Contact cement, water-based (latex)* Elmer's Cabinet Maker's Contact Cement, Weldwood Acrylic Latex Contact Cement	Instant bonding, min. curing temp. 65°F, poor gap-filling ability, low toxicity, easy to clean up, "open time" must be carefully monitored according to label directions	Very low strength, water-resistant, creeps under load	Recommended when limited ventilation conditions prevent using solvent-type cement

> * Water-based adhesive may cause warping of veneer or thin panels.
> ** May be rapidly heat-cured at 100°F to 150°F.
> *** Surface activator speeds set.

the surface with a rasp or coarse sandpaper. Brush the catalyst-activated resin over the wood and allow it to soak in thoroughly. Before it begins to set, apply glass cloth and brush another coat of activated resin over the cloth.

Unlike epoxy, polyester resin shrinks considerably after curing, and it may remain slightly tacky long after solidification. To produce a smooth surface finish, polyester finishing resins sometimes contain emulsified wax which floats to the surface as the resin cures.

You may be able to save up to 50% by purchasing polyester resin and fiberglass cloth from a local business that uses them. Boatyards are usually willing to sell a gallon or two of resin from their 55-gallon drums at minimal mark-up. These industrial-grade resins are sometimes slightly red or purple in color, compared to the water-clear retail resins. You can color clear polyester resin by adding pigments specially made for this purpose.

Cyanoacrylate glues—No adhesive has received more attention in the last few years than cyanoacrylate, commonly known as "superglue." Rumors abound, but cyanoacrylate is not made from barnacles as stated in an earlier article that appeared in *FWW*. Nor is it new—the first cyanoacrylate adhesive, Eastman 910, was discovered by accident during a test

of the light-refracting properties of a new organic compound when a drop was placed between glass prisms and they stuck fast. The glue was patented and first marketed in 1958, and industry has been using it ever since.

Cyanoacrylate will bond most plastics and rubber, and is good for gluing rubber to wood or to metal. Higher-viscosity formulas are sold for use on wood and other porous materials. Elmer's Wonder Bond Plus and Krazy Glue for Wood and Leather are two brands available in small retail packages. As most users have discovered, cyanoacrylate also has a remarkable ability to bond skin. Glue distributors now sell solvents to dissolve unwanted bonds, although acetone and nail polish remover are somewhat helpful for this purpose.

Cyanoacrylate provides a very water-resistant, but not completely waterproof, bond. Prolonged immersion in water eventually weakens the joint. This adhesive will also resist most organic solvents.

Cyanoacrylate glue is most useful in modelmaking, musical instrument building and other small-scale applications. Its main advantage is its extremely rapid set—3M's Scotchweld CA-3, for example, sets in about 30 seconds. You can reduce this setting time to as little as one second by brushing on 3M's Scotchweld Surface Activator for Cyanoacrylate Adhesives before you apply the glue. Moisture will also speed curing, but on wet surfaces the glue will leave chalky stains. I sometimes use the moisture of my breath to humidify small parts before gluing. The strength of the cyanoacrylate bond continues to increase slowly during the first 48 hours.

Shelf life of most cyanoacrylates is about 6 to 12 months—the glue thickens as it gets old—but storing the adhesive in the refrigerator will prolong its useful life. Since moisture speeds the setting time, however, allow the container to warm up to room temperature before you open it, or condensation in the bottle will offset the advantage of refrigeration.

Early cyanoacrylates did not work well on wood or other porous materials because the glue's viscosity is extremely low: the glue soaked into the surfaces, producing a starved joint. This same property, though, allows the adhesive to penetrate hairline cracks. Cyanoacrylate dripped into a ragged break will reinforce the fracture, and it can strengthen joints already glued with another adhesive that have loosened slightly if it is dripped along the existing glueline. You can repair a large gap by packing it with baking soda, then dripping glue on, which turns the powder into a hard, white filler. To fill a small crack or hole, put a few drops of glue in the crack, then sand immediately with wet-or-dry sandpaper before the glue sets. The wood dust mixes with the glue to form a hard filler that matches the color of the wood. This works best on dark woods; on light-colored woods the patch will be slightly darker than the surrounding wood. On thin stock, it's a good idea to put a piece of masking tape on the back of the crack, to keep the glue from sticking to the bench.

Cyanoacrylates do not set as quickly if there is acid present in the joint. If you're gluing an acidic wood such as oak, you'll get better results if you prepare the surfaces by brushing on a surface activator. These activators are mildly basic and neutralize the acid.

Cyanoacrylate is the most expensive adhesive generally available. Like epoxy, most brands are purchased in bulk and repackaged for retail sale, but you can save by buying in larger quantities. C.F. Martin Co. (of guitar fame), 510 Sycamore St., Nazareth, Pa. 18064, sells 3M Scotchweld CA-3 in 1-oz. containers for $12, Scotchweld Surface Activator for $8, or a kit consisting of two ounces of CA-3 and one container of surface activator for $25. Although there isn't much difference in glue quality between brands, there is a difference between the containers the glue is packaged in. Some styles clog before the adhesive is gone, when glue solidifies near the tip. Polyethylene dropper bottles are less likely to clog than metal squeeze tubes or rigid plastic containers. It helps to clear the nozzle by squeezing a little air out of the upright container before closing it.

Hot-melt glues—Synthetic hot-melt glues are easy to apply and they set up quickly. Most are made of polyamide resins which melt at around 400°F. Hot-melts are widely used in industry, where their quick set is an advantage on assembly lines. Their good gap-filling properties make them ideal for repairing worn, sloppy joints in old furniture. Hot-melts form thicker gluelines than most other adhesives, and have relatively low strength and poor penetrating ability. They're good for temporary jigs or tack-on fastenings, where extreme strength is not required. They're also well suited for joints that may need to be disassembled, but the heat necessary to break the glue bond may also damage the surrounding finish. Hot-melts develop 90% of their final bond strength within 60 sec-

onds. The glue remains somewhat flexible and does not sand well. When the glue has cooled, excess can be removed with a sharp blade.

Hot-melt sticks are sold for use in an electric glue gun. Manufacturers make several grades that cool at different rates. Those sold in retail stores allow you only about 10 seconds to assemble parts, but you can increase open time slightly by preheating the parts. Hot-melts are also sold in thin sheets for veneering (available from Woodcraft Supply). You can use an ordinary household iron to provide heat, then weight or clamp the veneer until the glue has cooled.

Contact cements—Contact cements are rubber-based (usually neoprene) liquids that dry by solvent evaporation. They are used most often to bond high-pressure plastic laminates, such as Formica, to plywood or particleboard, without the need for clamps or prolonged pressure. Contact cements are sometimes used to attach veneers, but the glue bond can fail in spots because of seasonal moisture changes in the veneer, causing bumps in the veneered surface or separation at the edges.

There are two types of contact cements: solvent-based and water-based. Solvent-based cements, most of which are extremely flammable, dry in about 5 to 10 minutes. The nonflammable solvent-based cements are made with chlorinated hydrocarbons, and their vapors are toxic. These vapors are not trapped by an organic-vapor respirator, so you should use adequate ventilation with this and any solvent-based adhesive. Water-based contact cements are nontoxic and nonflammable, but they take longer to dry—about 20 minutes to an hour before parts can be assembled. The uncured adhesive is water-soluble, so you can clean your tools in water if the glue hasn't dried. Water-based contact cement provides better coverage than the solvent-based type, but it should not be used on metallic surfaces.

Contact cements are heat-resistant and water-resistant, although adhesive strength is low and the pliable glue film is likely to creep under load. Both types can be applied by brush, roller or spray. Apply adhesive to both surfaces to be mated and assemble when dry, but be sure that the parts are properly aligned. Adjustment is impossible once the two surfaces contact. Go over the glued surface with a roller to ensure an even bond.

"Construction adhesive" is a thick mastic used by carpenters to fasten flooring or wall paneling. As yet, it has not been widely used in other areas of woodworking.

A few other adhesives that may have limited use in woodworking are the acrylic cements, most commonly encountered as pressure-sensitive contact adhesives. Liquid acrylics are also used in some linoleum cements and other mastics. "Anaerobic adhesives" remain liquid when exposed to air and solidify when deprived of oxygen. The Loctite Corporation markets a variety of anaerobic adhesives which are widely used for securing nuts, bolts and threaded studs. Because of its high porosity, however, wood contains too much oxygen to allow anaerobic adhesives to set. □

George Mustoe is a geochemistry research technician at Western Washington University in Bellingham, Wash. He wrote about respiratory hazards in FWW #41 and about making cross-country skis in issue #31. For more on woodworking glues, see "Which Glue Do You Use?" in issue #43.

Varnish Finish That's Rubbed On

Sanding is the way to a glass-smooth surface

by Joe Thomas

When I first started working wood, I read a lot about finishing. The more I read, the more confused I got. There are literally hundreds of stains, dyes, varnishes and fillers around—some soluble in water, some in alcohol, others in oil. It seems to me, you ought to have fun working with wood without having to build a chemical processing plant. So I experimented and developed my own finishing method using paste rubbing stains and varnishes. I'm sure it's not the most sophisticated in the world, but if you follow my procedure, you'll get a silky smooth, alcohol- and water-resistant finish.

The secret to good finishing is to prepare the wood properly by careful sanding. Actually, wood preparation should begin even before you reach the sanding stage. I carefully choose the wood for a piece I'm building. I love distinctive grain and knots, so I try to use them to good advantage. If you prefer clear wood, work around the defects, or position them where you won't have to give them extra sanding later. If possible, don't use wood with planer snipes—ugly gouges caused by improperly adjusted planers. Even if sanded smooth, the glazed wood of a snipe will sometimes show as a streak. Another way to save sanding time is to chisel off the glue squeezed out of joints instead of wiping it off with a damp rag, which just smears it around. Let the glue set for about half an hour, until it's rubbery, and it will slice right off with a sharp chisel.

You will need a good-quality finishing sander. I have a Rockwell orbital that isn't made anymore, but of the half-dozen other sanders I've tried, I think the Black & Decker #7430 (which takes a third of a sheet of sandpaper) and the Makita block sander (a quarter of a sheet) are both good buys. Whichever sander you use, cut a stack of sheets to fit it at one time, so you won't have to stop sanding in the middle of a project to cut more paper. For inside curves, tight spots and end grain, I have a drum sander that fits my ¼-in. portable drill and accepts small sheets of regular sandpaper instead of sleeves. I got it from Singley Specialty Co. Inc., PO Box 5087, Greensboro, N.C. 27403.

Before I begin sanding, I clear my bench of all tools—if you drop a sanded piece on a sharp tool, the small nick that results will look like the Grand Canyon when you stain. I start orbital-sanding with 180-grit aluminum oxide paper until all the scratches and tool marks are gone. To check for missed blemishes, I view the wood obliquely, with the light in front of me. If none are visible, I give the piece a thorough once-over with 220-grit. What do I mean by thorough? It's no 15-minute ordeal. If you're working a 5-in. by 12-in. piece with 220-grit, for example, you ought to see the surface improve after 30 seconds to one minute of sanding. More sanding at that grit won't give you a smoother surface. Switch to a finer grit. Once you learn to find flaws by viewing the wood correctly, you'll know when to stop. If you're progressing too slowly, start with 120- or 150-grit, working up to 220. If you must, use a belt sander to smooth large flaws, but never use a belt coarser than 100-grit.

Now I'm ready to raise the grain for the first time. Raising the grain causes loose wood fibers to stick up from the surface of the wood so that they can be removed with steel wool. Dampen an old washcloth—not dripping but wet—and wipe the wood surface with it. After the wood dries, the surface will feel fuzzy. Now with a loose ball of 0000 steel wool, take a swipe over the wood in each direction. The wool will hook the loose wood fibers and pull them free. Vacuum away any strands of loose steel wool that may remain.

With a fresh piece of 220-grit on your sander, sand the surface again, checking for defects as before. Repeat the grain-raising process, hit the piece again with steel wool, vacuum, then switch to sanding with 320-grit paper. At this point, I protect the wood from marring with an old towel on my bench. By now, the wood should feel smooth as glass. Give it a quick polishing with 600-grit wet-or-dry paper and then wipe off the sanding dust with a tack rag, a sticky cleaning cloth sold by paint stores.

Next comes the exciting part: staining and finishing. I don't always stain, though. If the wood is already the color I want, I just go ahead and finish it. When I do stain, I prefer oil paste wiping stains. The Bartley Collection Ltd., 121 Schelter Rd., Prairie View, Ill. 60069, is one good source for these stains. I've been happy with the finish I get without using any of the paste wood fillers that are on the market, but I don't see why they wouldn't work.

I use the stain right out of the can. Spoon a few blobs into an aluminum pie tin, dip a terry cloth pad into it, and rub the stain firmly and briskly into the wood, going with the grain. When you run out of the small amount of stain on the pad, briskly polish the stained area with a larger piece of terry cloth. Now go back for more stain, blending it into the already stained area and polishing again. Continue this way until you're done, allowing the work to dry for 24 hours.

I use either of two kinds of varnish: the paste varnish sold by Bartley, or McCloskey antique polyurethane. Both are rubbed on and polished just like the stain. If you prefer the McCloskey, or any other store-bought polyurethane, thin it 1:1 with mineral spirits. Apply four or five light coats, allowing 24 hours' drying between. Don't try to get away with one or two thick coats, or you'll wind up with a blotchy, ugly film that you'll just have to sand off.

When the final coat has dried, polish it with 600-grit wet-or-dry paper lubricated with mineral spirits. Wrap the paper around a scrap-wood block and wet the grit with spirits, dribbling a few drops on the varnished wood while you're at it. Now begin sanding, with the grain. On the first pass, you'll feel the paper sort of bumping along the relatively rough varnished surface. On the second or third pass, it will feel like a vacuum is sticking the paper to the surface. At that point, quit. You're done. Buff the surface with a soft, dry rag, and sit back and admire the beautiful finish you've created. □

Joe Thomas works wood in Tucker, Ga. He published his own book about finishing called Silky, Sensuous Wood Finishing *($13, 61 pp.), which is available from him at PO Box 1158, Lilburn, Ga. 30247.*

Gleaming ebony piano finishes, traditionally achieved by patient polishing of many coats of black nitrocellulose lacquer, can be ruined if the wood's figure telegraphs through the film. Before he lacquered the piano pictured here, Steinert masked the wood grain with smoothly sanded coats of polyester surfacer.

That Piano Finish
Modern method makes opaque lacquer gleam

by Donald M. Steinert

For sheer elegance, few wood finishes approach the black-lacquered gleam of an ebony-finish grand piano. As many contemporary furnituremakers are discovering, however, there's really no reason why such a finish should be limited to pianos, or to one color. Opaque lacquers are sold in many colors which, if polished to a glowing sheen, can impart a vitality to wooden objects that clear finishes can't match.

Traditional piano finishes consist of many coats of nitrocellulose lacquer painstakingly built up over a carefully filled and sanded wood surface. Brought to a high gloss by hours of polishing, such a finish is more time-consuming than difficult to achieve. In the interest of expediency, some modern piano-

makers, particularly in Europe and Japan, have turned to clear and colored polyester finishes. This material dries and builds faster than lacquer, so fewer coats are needed. It also forms a harder, stabler surface that masks wood figure, keeping it from telegraphing through the top coats.

Polyester finishing requires equipment that is impractical for the small shop, so I've experimented with a polyester/nitrocellulose finish. My method combines the stability and surface-smoothing qualities of polyester with the workability of nitrocellulose lacquer. While not easy, especially for the beginner, this technique can be mastered by anyone willing to take the time to experiment.

Preparing the surface—The success of any lacquer finish, opaque or clear, depends on the smoothness and stability of the surface to which it is applied. Mahogany is traditionally the favored wood of pianomakers because it is fine-textured and relatively stable, so the lacquer film is less likely to stretch and crack as the wood swells and shrinks with the seasons. Maple, poplar and most cabinet plywoods are also excellent for lacquering. Oak, fir and pine are poor choices.

Even a mild-figured wood such as mahogany has open-pored grain which must be filled before lacquering. Paste wood-fillers and/or sanding sealers are usually used for this purpose, but I've had better luck with my polyester system. Paste filler, a fine silica powder suspended in an oil vehicle, is messy to apply. Unless you allow plenty of drying time, at least several days, the oil may react with the lacquer, possibly dimpling the lacquer film later. Though easier to work with, lacquer sanding sealers are formulated to be readily sandable, which makes them brittle and prone to cracking.

The polyester filler I use is Prestec 2090 gray sanding surfacer, and it's available in quantities as small as one quart from Simtec, 1188 North Grove, Bldgs. K&L, Anaheim, Calif. 92806. Prestec also comes in white and black. Like the fiberglass compounds to which it is related, Prestec is a two-part system: a viscous resin, and a methyl ethyl ketone peroxide (MEKP) hardening catalyst which you buy separately from a body-shop supply house. The hardener may be sold under different brand names, so just ask for MEKP polyester catalyst. Prestec is about 97% solids, so one coat of polyester is about equal in thickness to six or seven coats of lacquer. It adheres well to wood, cures in one to 24 hours, and is fairly elastic, thus it serves as an effective intermediary between the wood and the nitrocellulose lacquer that goes over it.

Prestec 2090 must be sprayed, and it's only fair to point out that this material is demanding and somewhat hazardous to handle. MEKP is toxic and extremely flammable. A drop of it accidentally splashed into an eye can blind you, so wear proper eye protection. Work in a well-ventilated shop, or outside if the weather is warm and dry. Wear an organic vapor mask when mixing and spraying, and a dust nuisance mask when sanding the dry film. (For an article on respiratory protective equipment, see *FWW* #41, pp. 36-39.)

The biggest disadvantage of polyester is its limited pot life. The resin will set up in 20 to 40 minutes, and if it hardens before you've emptied and cleaned your spray gun, the gun will be ruined. Mix only as much resin as you will be able to spray within the pot life.

To prepare a surface for polyester, sand it to at least 100-grit or finer. Knots, gouges and other defects should be filled with automotive body compound, then sanded flush. I don't use plastic wood fillers because they usually shrink. Unless you're ready to clean up a major mess, don't spray polyester over an old finish. The old finish will soften and you'll have a hard film floating on jelly. Strip off the old coating, sand well, and dust the surface with a lacquer-thinner-dampened rag, allowing 24 hours for drying.

Prestec should be mixed according to the directions on the can. For safety, I add the catalyst with a laboratory pipette (photo, above right). Thinned to the appropriate viscosity with acetone, polyester is actually easier to spray than lacquer. With the compressor's air regulator at about 40 PSI, I hold the gun 8 in. to 16 in. from the work, applying a mist coat first, followed by a heavier hiding coat 3 to 5 minutes later.

Polyester catalyst is toxic and extremely flammable. To avoid splashing it, Steinert adds it to the resin with a glass pipette, available from laboratory supply houses.

You don't have to wait until one coat cures before applying the next. Keep building the film until it's as thick as you want. Open-pored woods will require a thicker coat than will closed-grain ones.

Polyester takes longer to surface-dry than lacquer does, and it will collect dust. But that doesn't matter because it will be thoroughly sanded before the top coats go on. Depending on how much catalyst you add and on the temperature and humidity, Prestec will dry in about 45 minutes. I usually allow 8 hours of air-curing before sanding. Small objects can be force-dried in an oven set at 110°F to 150°F. If you try this, let the polyester air-dry for a while first to avoid blistering.

Spraying the top coats—Sand the hardened polyester with open-coat garnet paper, starting with 100-grit and finishing with 220, without skipping any grits. Sand by hand or with a straight-line power sander. But don't use an orbital sander—the swirls will telegraph. Don't rush sanding, either; the smoother you get the polyester, the smoother the lacquer coats will be. If you decide to sand finer than 220-grit, switch to silicon carbide paper. I vacuum the dust between grits, then wipe the surface with a naphtha-dampened rag.

Of all the materials suitable for opaque finishes—lacquer, enamel, polyurethane and even colored polyester—I think nitrocellulose lacquer is the most practical because it's a solvent-release finish, which means its volatile solvents evaporate to leave behind a film of coalesced nitrocellulose particles. Each successive coat softens the previous one, so, in effect, multiple coats of lacquer blend into one integrated coat, with none of the intercoat adhesion problems often encountered with polymerizing finishes (such as polyurethane or epoxy), which dry irreversibly by molecular cross-linking. Lacquer films remain dissolvable indefinitely, so scratches and sand-throughs are easily repaired, and refinishing can be done at any time, even if the cured lacquer needs to be stripped off.

Opaque lacquers are sold in hundreds of types, colors and

gloss ranges. In ten years of experimenting, I've found that the nitrocellulose lacquers developed for the automotive industry are tougher and polish out better than those formulated for wood, though both types have essentially the same working properties. Also, colored automotive lacquer is easier to buy because it's sold or can be ordered by any local autobody supply house, as can most of the materials and tools I've mentioned. If you can't buy opaque lacquer locally, try my supplier: Bay City Paint Company, 2279 Market St., San Francisco, Calif. 94103. Bay City will custom-mix colors to match your sample, in quantities as small as one quart. You can fine-tune the color by adding universal colorants.

Though some craftspeople prefer the acrylic lacquers that industry is increasingly using (see box, below), I don't much care for them. Acrylic lacquer builds faster by virtue of its higher solids content, but I've had trouble getting it to adhere to wood and it's not compatible with polyester. It neither flows out as well as nitrocellulose nor polishes as nicely when dry.

I start top-coating with four double coats of lacquer, sprayed on at 40 PSI to 50 PSI with the gun 8 in. to 12 in. from the work. A double coat is just that—two coats sprayed one right after the other without allowing the initial concentration of solvent to evaporate or "flash," which it will do in 5 to 10 minutes in moderate weather. Lacquer has flashed when you can run the back of your hand over it lightly without sticking. Between double coats, I do wait for the flash, during which time some dust always gets into the film, creating nibs which must be sanded out later.

You may be tempted to spray the lacquer at a thicker viscosity, hoping to build the film faster. But solvents are trapped by a thick, wet coat, causing the film to shrink unevenly into a crazed or checked surface. On the other hand, the lacquer will run on vertical surfaces if it's too thin. Experiment to find the right viscosity. To avoid fisheyes—small,

circular flaws where the lacquer won't adhere due to minute surface contamination—I add Du Pont fisheye eliminator to the lacquer. By the way, polyester filler can also fisheye. Prevent it with Simtec's eliminator, which is called B-32.

After spraying four double coats, forget about the project for at least 24 hours. Fooling around with the finish at this point will compound any problems, or cause new ones. If the first four coats dry trouble-free, dry-sand with 400-grit silicon carbide paper to knock off the dust nibs. Major imperfections, such as drools, runs and sags, should be wet-sanded out by hand with naphtha or mineral spirits as the lubricant. Clean the surface with a fresh naphtha-soaked rag, let it dry, and then spray four more double coats, exactly as before.

Let the lacquer dry for at least two weeks at 65°F to 70°F before polishing it. A month would be even better.

Final-sanding and polishing—Wet-sand the cured lacquer with 400-grit silicon carbide using either naphtha or a half-and-half mixture of paraffin oil and mineral spirits as the lubricant. Don't lubricate with water, though. If you accidentally sand through to bare wood, water will raise the grain. On small pieces, hand-sand, backing your paper with a felt or cork block. Sand a larger piece, such as a piano, with a pneumatic straight-line power sander. *Never* wet-sand with an electric power sander—the risk of shock or fire is too great. I used to be miserly with costly silicon carbide paper. I've since learned that using dull paper is slow, and it will never leave the uniformly smooth surface that fresh, sharp paper will.

Sanding through the top coats at the arrises—the line where two surfaces meet at an exterior angle—may be unavoidable. I minimize this problem by "banding" or spraying a heavier build along the edges. Where sand-throughs do occur, repair the damage by thinning a teaspoon of lacquer to brushing consistency, then laying a thin bead of the lacquer on the bare

---

Colorful finishes with acrylic lacquer

by George Morris

Fast and richly colored opaque finishes are easily achieved by spraying clear nitrocellulose lacquer over acrylic-lacquer color base coats. I combine these two very different materials for two reasons. First, colored acrylic lacquers are readily available in any quantity at automotive supply stores in my area, while opaque nitrocellulose lacquers are much harder to find. Second, acrylic lacquer dries to a hard film much more slowly than does nitrocellulose, remaining tender and imprintable for as long as two to three weeks after spraying. A clear top coat of fast-drying nitrocellulose solves this problem.

Since opaque color is the desired end, you can skip the otherwise necessary step of using paste wood-filler by choosing a dense, nonporous wood or plywood for the lacquered object. I prepare wood for colored lacquer just as I would for clear lacquer, smoothing surface irregularities with a scraper, followed by sanding with a felt or wood block wrapped in 120-grit, then 220-grit.

Using an alcohol-based aniline dye, I stain the wood to match the color of the acrylic lacquer I'll be using. Dyeing the wood has two advantages: it makes strong colors more achievable with only two or three color coats, and the inevitable dings and dents are less noticeable. Avoid water-based dyes because they raise the grain. I let the dye dry for 5 minutes, and then with a soft cloth I clean off the powdery residue left behind before proceeding with the color coats.

I spray on two coats of acrylic, waiting 10 minutes between coats. Before each coat flashes, I check for flaws by examining the wet film in oblique light, and I correct them right away, knocking down runs and sags with a finger or a brush before the film sets any further.

Sanding them out later is as messy as sanding slightly wet paint.

I wait an hour, and then spray on three coats of clear nitrocellulose lacquer, allowing an hour between coats. After the initial three clear coats have dried overnight, I sand with 320-grit stearated paper to level the surface. Then I clean the surface with a tack rag, and spray three or four more coats of clear lacquer to complete the job. It's best to wait a few days before wet-sanding, using water as a lubricant, with 600-grit wet-or-dry paper. I follow this with a final buff with McGuire's Machine Glaze Nos. 1 and 3 or equivalent polishing compounds for high gloss, or 0000 steel wool for a satin finish. □

George Morris teaches guitarmaking at The Vermont Instrument Workshop in Post Mills, Vt. He wrote about lacquering in FWW #31, pp. 90-94.

Sand-throughs at the arrises may be unavoidable. Fix them by painting a bead of lacquer over the exposed area. As the bead dries, it will shrink into an invisible repair.

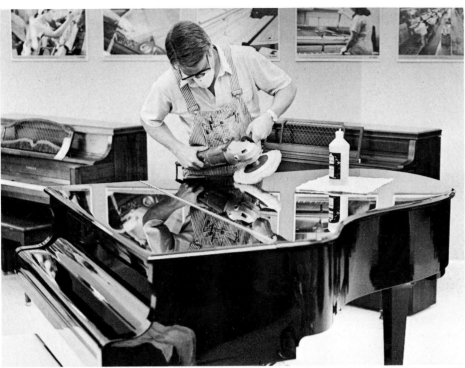

Steinert polishes built-up lacquer by hand or with an automotive lamb's-wool bonnet. He starts with medium-grade compound, finishing with a fine-grit called swirl-mark eliminator.

spots with the edge, not the tip, of a ¼-in. wide sable artists' brush (photo, above left). As the lacquer dries, the bead will shrink flat, making the fix virtually invisible. If you accidentally sand through to the polyester on a flat surface, scuff the area with 600-grit paper and spray on several thin coats of lacquer. Let the repaired surface dry thoroughly and pick up where you left off. You can accelerate drying with a heat lamp, but be careful; the lacquer will blister if you get it too hot.

Once the entire piece has been wet-sanded, clean it up with a soft, naphtha-dampened rag. Check for flaws, then wet-sand again, this time with 600-grit paper. When you complete this step, the lacquer should be dull but absolutely smooth and delightful to touch.

I let the lacquer dry for 24 hours before beginning to polish it with any one of a range of auto polishing compounds made by Du Pont, Ditzler or 3M. Small objects are best polished by hand, but for large surfaces I use a Bosch rotary buffer with a lamb's-wool bonnet, cleaning it often with a tool sold for this purpose. Any buffer will do, except high-speed body grinders, whose friction is likely to heat and soften the lacquer. For hand-polishing, I use old diapers.

For both power- and hand-polishing, three grades of compound will be adequate: a medium-duty rubbing compound and two finer compounds. Start with the medium compound. If you're hand-polishing, smear a ribbon of compound on the surface and rub in a straight-line motion, with the grain. Bear down hard when you begin, and try to overcome the natural tendency to polish in an arc. As the compound dries and the shine begins to show, reduce pressure to a light buffing. Repeat this procedure with the fine compound.

Follow the same steps if you machine-buff. Be careful, though; if you park the buffer in one place or push down too hard, the lacquer will heat up and wrinkle or "orange peel" slightly. If this happens, stop polishing, let the surface cool, then resume with a gentler action. A bad burn will have to be

wet-sanded and/or sprayed again.

Hand-polishing leaves streaks in the surface; the power buffer leaves minute swirls. Both kinds of marks can be removed with a very fine compound commonly called swirl-mark eliminator (photo, above right), which can be hand- or power-buffed.

By now, you should have a brilliant, mirror-smooth surface. All that remains is to blow off the compound residue with compressed air and give the piece a light dusting with a tack cloth. I use a toothpick to get compound out of the nooks and crevices. To enhance the depth of the sheen, some piano finishers spray on a clear lacquer top coat after polishing. But I've found that this is just another opportunity for dust to collect, and a clear finish over a colored one is harder to repair.

Fresh lacquer needs more babying than do other finishes. I caution my customers not to place heavy objects such as lamps or vases on a new lacquer finish for at least two to three months, to avoid imprinting. For periodic polishing and dusting, I use swirl-mark eliminator or automotive waxes and polishes. Furniture care products that contain silicon, Johnson's Pledge for example, will likely turn hazy a day or two after application. Never dust a lacquer finish with a dry cloth, regardless of how soft it is.

I've found that producing a polished lacquer finish is a very physical, almost athletic activity which demands patient practice, not to mention the ability to survive a fair number of setbacks, to get right. Try it first on scrap plywood or on an unimportant piece. Once you've developed a feel for the materials and tools—particularly the spray gun—I'm sure you'll be amazed with the classy, colorful surfaces you'll be able to produce. □

Donald Steinert, of Grants Pass, Ore., restores and refinishes pianos, furniture and Rolls-Royce woodwork. He wrote about his work in FWW #32, p. 42.

Clearing the Air

A low-tech way to ventilate the small shop

by David W. Carnell

Airborne wood dust and toxic finishing vapors are less visible shop hazards than the snarling machines that can devour a finger. These substances are easily overlooked, yet they pose an equally serious health risk. They're dangerous to breathe, but it often takes years for the damage to show. If conditions are wrong, they might also cause an explosion.

Shop ventilation is the obvious solution to the dust and vapor problem. A good system should change the air often enough to dilute airborne-contamination concentrations to safe levels, leave as few stagnant areas as possible, and carry contaminated air away from workers to an exhaust fan. This kind of ventilation system, if set up effectively, minimizes the need for uncomfortable respirators.

The ideal air-cleaning system is actually several systems: local collection at each dust-producing machine, local exhaust fans in finishing and sanding areas, and a general exhaust setup to remove the dust and vapors that elude the other systems. The expense of the ideal system, however, forces most of us to compromise.

In a small shop where operations vary throughout the day, a general exhaust system is a good all-purpose solution. You don't need to spend a fortune on fancy equipment to get an effective general exhaust system. It can be as simple as an exhaust fan at one end of the shop and an air intake at the other.

Fans are rated by how much air they move, in cubic feet per minute (CFM). Here's how to find the size fan you'll need: Divide the shop volume (length times width times height equals volume in cubic feet) by 6 to find the fan rating in CFM required for 10 changes per hour; divide by 3 for 20 changes. For example, a shop with a volume of 1200 cu. ft. needs a fan rated at 200 CFM for 10 changes per hour, at 400 CFM for 20 changes per hour.

You can buy a commercially made industrial-size exhaust fan. Or you can hold down cost by using a window fan or a bathroom or kitchen exhaust fan instead. Since these are powered by shaded-pole motors that don't have brushes or internal switches, they don't produce sparks that could ignite fumes.

Window fans are good if they exhaust directly to the outside and move enough air to provide 10 to 20 air changes per hour for your shop. Bathroom and kitchen exhaust fans can feed into ducts to the outside that are up to 10 ft. long, but if you must use a longer duct, you'll need a centrifugal blower that develops enough power to overcome the pressure drop in the duct. These centrifugal blowers are often available from mail-order surplus houses at less than the retail price. A duct should be at least as large as the discharge opening on the blower. The duct should also be as straight as possible, since every bend will increase the pressure drop, and reduce the efficiency of the blower. The blower from a hot-air furnace or a central air conditioner (typically, 750-CFM to 1,000-CFM) can ventilate larger shops. Check heating and ventilation contractors for low-cost blowers from junked equipment.

Another requisite is an air intake large enough to supply the air that the exhaust fan is supposed to move. In its simplest form, this can be a hole in the wall, covered with a furnace or air-conditioner filter to keep outside dust from entering the shop. In most climates, though, incoming air must be heated in the winter. An electric space heater placed in the intake airstream will help some. Commercial air makeup units are available, but they're expensive: $500 to $700 for shops under 1,000 cu. ft. These draw outside air over a self-contained heating element before blowing it into the room. The type most practical for a small shop has electric-resistance heat, but gas- or oil-fired units are also made. If your shop is connected to a house that has steam or hot-water heat, you could place a radiator or a convector over the air intake. If you don't want to buy a heater, you can reduce the amount of heat you lose by running the exhaust fan only occasionally, when you're actually producing dust or vapors.

For thorough ventilation, it's best to make the air flow through the long dimension of the shop, so place the exhaust fan and the air intake at opposite ends of the shop, or at opposite corners of the long diagonal, as shown in figure 1. The exhaust fan should be located high in the shop wall; the air intake, low.

Check your ventilation system with a homemade smoke generator: Put two small plastic or paper cups side by side in a holder that can be moved around the shop without spilling, like the one shown in figure 2. Put two tablespoons of household ammonia in one cup, and the same amount of concentrated hydrochloric acid in the other. Swimming-pool supply houses and chemical supply houses sell concentrated hydrochloric acid (36% to 38%). Be careful, though. This acid is dangerous to handle, and eye protection is a must. Don't allow the ammonia and the acid to come in contact with one another, or they will react violently. The fumes coming from the two cups, however, will react to form voluminous white clouds of ammonium chloride that will show you how the air is flowing. Testing the airflow produced by your ventilation system is the only real check of how well it performs, so run the shop equipment and move about to simulate working in the shop. You may have to relocate your dust- and vapor-producing operations so that the contaminated air will be drawn away from the worker, toward the exhaust fan. When you're done testing, dispose of the ammonia and the acid separately, before they have a chance to spill or to eat through the cups. I suggest that you flush them separately down the toilet, or pour them separately down the drain, running lots of water after disposing of each.

Flammable dusts and vapors can, and do, create potentially explosive atmospheres in industrial operations. But it's unlikely that home workshops or small woodworking shops could develop the conditions required for such large-scale, room-sized explosions—you'd be driven out by the irritation

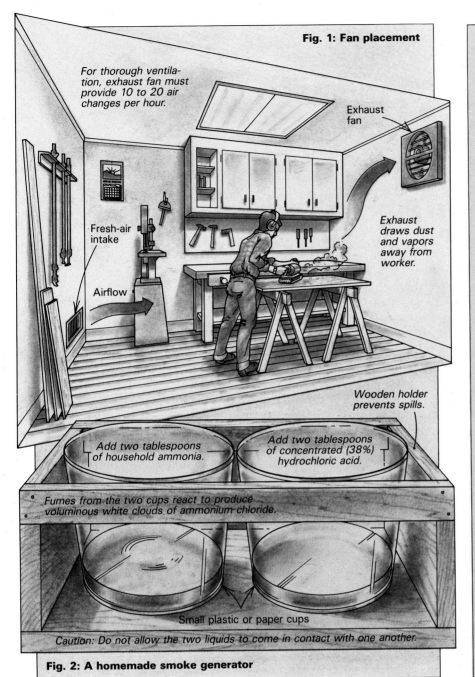

Fig. 1: Fan placement

For thorough ventilation, exhaust fan must provide 10 to 20 air changes per hour.

Exhaust fan

Exhaust draws dust and vapors away from worker.

Fresh-air intake

Airflow

Wooden holder prevents spills.

Add two tablespoons of household ammonia.

Add two tablespoons of concentrated (38%) hydrochloric acid.

Fumes from the two cups react to produce voluminous white clouds of ammonium chloride.

Small plastic or paper cups

Caution: Do not allow the two liquids to come in contact with one another.

Fig. 2: A homemade smoke generator

Sources of supply

Exhaust fans: McKilligan Industrial & Supply Corp., 435 Main St., Johnson City, N.Y. 13790; and Brodhead-Garrett Co., 4560 E. 71st St., Cleveland, Ohio 44105.
Centrifugal blowers and electronic cooling fans: Surplus Center, 1000-1015 West "O" St., PO Box 82209, Lincoln, Neb. 68501.
Flexible hose for ducts: Abbeon Cal, Inc., 123 Gray Ave., Santa Barbara, Calif. 93101.
Electric, gas-, or oil-fired air makeup units: Air Economy Corp., PO Box 29, Flemington, N.J. 08822.
Electronic air cleaners: There are two general types of units. *Electrostatic precipitators* contain a blower that draws dust-laden air over a high-voltage grid, where dust particles receive an electrical charge. When the charged particles pass over a collection plate with the opposite charge, they stick fast. Clean air blows out the other end of the unit. Units that are large enough for woodshop applications cost $2,000 and up. These are available from United Air Specialists, 4440 Creek Rd., Cincinnati, Ohio 45242; and Paxton/Patterson, 5719 W. 65th St., Chicago, Ill. 60638.

Negative-ion generators disperse negative ions into the air. The ions impart a negative charge to airborne dust particles, and the charged particles fall to the floor, where they can be swept up. ESI/APSEE units cost $595 and up, and are available from Electron Sciences, Inc., 3916 Riley St., San Diego, Calif. 92110.

before concentrations got that high. Flammable concentrations of vapors are 20 to 100 times higher (depending on the chemical) than the permissible exposure limits set by OSHA. The really fine dust from sanding operations is the only shop dust capable of forming an explosive mixture in air, but it has to be present at a concentration of 1 gram per cubic foot. It would take almost 2 gallons of airborne dust to reach that concentration in a 10-ft. by 20-ft. by 8-ft. shop.

It is possible, however, to have localized explosions. The many fires caused by solvent-based adhesives (such as contact cement), flammable finishes, or gasoline used indoors for cleaning (which is extremely dangerous) are examples of localized flammable vapor concentrations. Because the vapors are heavier than air, they collect near the floor, and they can be ignited by any spark or flame. Most gas-fired furnaces and water heaters have pilot lights that burn continuously, and these are especially likely ignition sources because the small draft through them draws the flammable mixture along the floor and ignites it. These pilots are also out of sight and easy

to overlook. Frequently, the vapors flash back to the solvent container and set it afire, too. Oil burners, sparking electric motors, lit cigarettes, even static electricity can ignite the vapors. Tool and machinery motors are all spark producers, as are most switches, except the mercury type. But none of these presents any hazard in a shop with good housekeeping and adequate ventilation.

Dust accumulation on shop motors that is dislodged when the motor is sparking can ignite and flash, so it's a good idea to regularly vacuum motors. If you dispose of sawdust by tossing it into a shop stove, you're inviting a violent combustion. It's better to put the sawdust in the trash can, or use it to mulch the garden. □

David W. Carnell is a chemical engineer, now retired, and an amateur woodworker. He lives in Wilmington, N.C. For more on chip and dust collection, see FWW #12, pp. 76-78, and #25, pp. 58-59. For information on respiratory hazards, see #41, pp. 36-39.

The restored dressing table.

The Finish Crack'd
Conservator's fix for a fractured film

by Gregory J. Landrey

What a face lift does for an aging movie star, finish restoration can do for a piece of furniture. In my work as a conservator at the Winterthur Museum, I use a variety of restoration methods on many period pieces. But the technique I'll describe here will work just as well on grandma's favorite dresser as on a collector's treasure.

When the 200-year-old mahogany dressing table shown above arrived in my shop this past summer, it had an extremely degraded varnish finish, exhibiting the yellowing, crazing and film shrinkage that can occur with time. Since the crackle pattern (a result of oxidation and subsequent contraction of the finish layer) extended through only the top part of the film, we decided that the finish was restorable. Crazing generally doesn't develop with thin-film finishes, such as French-polished or contemporary oil finishes, but it's fairly common with the thick, hard, resinous films characteristic of period varnishes and modern shellacs, lacquers and polyurethanes. The method I used to restore the table's finish—cleaning the film, abrading off the degraded portion, and polishing the remaining finish—is an acceptable conservation procedure because it preserves the original finish, leaving the patina of the wood undisturbed. The same process can be used on any reasonably thick finish in need of cosmetic repair.

Several factors contribute to finish deterioration: chemical instability, solvent loss, humidity, temperature, wear and tear, poor care, and, perhaps most damaging, exposure to light. Both natural and artificial light accelerate finish breakdown, which is why valuable furniture should be displayed in areas with moderate light levels, out of direct sunlight.

In dealing with an eroded finish, you have two choices: strip off the old finish and apply a new one, or repair the existing film. If a significant amount of the finish is gone, extremely discolored or seriously water-damaged, refinishing is probably called for. But, when possible, conservators prefer to save the old finish, doing only what is necessary to repair any damage and to retard further deterioration. The objective is not to make the piece look brand-new, but to let it age comfortably, preserving the whispered history of days gone by. This requires a fair amount of patience and even more finesse, but in most cases it takes less time, space and money than complete refinishing would.

Types of finishes—To determine the best way to repair a damaged finish, be it period or modern, you must first consider the original finishing materials and the finisher's intent. Through the centuries, a great many finishes have been concocted to enhance the beauty of wood, and to protect it from the ravages of moisture, sunlight, insects, and everyday wear. The earliest finishes in America were oils such as linseed, poppyseed and walnut, and waxes such as beeswax. These did little to protect the furniture, however, and often dulled its appearance. On period furniture—furniture built prior to 1830 and the advent of commercially available finishing products—three major types of finishes were commonly used: fixed-oil varnishes, spirit varnishes and essential-oil varnishes. Eighteenth-century cabinetmakers most often applied some type of fixed-oil varnish, consisting of a drying oil, usually boiled linseed, and a resin, such as copal, sandarac or amber. In the 19th century, spirit varnishes were more widely used, with alcohol as the common vehicle, and sandarac, copal, mastic or shellac the usual resin. An inexpensive essential-oil varnish, actually a type of spirit varnish, consisted of turpentine and rosin, a pine resin also known as colophony. Applying a spirit varnish over a previous, sometimes incom-patible, finish was also common practice.

What effect were these early finish chemists after? According to Isaac Byington, a late-18th-century carpenter/cabinetmaker from Bristol, Connecticut, the ideal was "a varnish which stands water and shines like glass." In stylish homes, illuminated only by candlelight and subjected to constant fireplace soot, a high-gloss furniture finish was highly desirable.

Most of today's finishes can be divided into two types: solvent-release and reactive. Shellac, nitrocellulose lacquer and some acrylics fit into the solvent-release group. The reactive finishes are drying oils, such as tung and boiled linseed, and polymerizing varnishes, such as alkyd resin and polyurethane. For conservation purposes—the touch-up of finish losses on period pieces, for example—solvent-release finishes are preferred because they retain solubility and are therefore reversible. This reversibility is important in restoration work, since due to inevitable degradation, further repair may later be necessary. Chemically reactive finishes polymerize, making them difficult to remove.

In addition to these various finish formulas, many cleaners and polishes have been devised over the years to keep furniture glowing—everything from linseed oil and beeswax to a whole range of commercial polishes and waxes. Finishes still degrade, however. In fact, polishes that don't provide a good moisture barrier or that chemically bond to the finish can even accelerate degradation.

Finish identification—With such a variety of possible surface films, the first step in restoration is to determine the type of finish on the piece, since this will limit what cleaners can be used. I begin with a visual inspection, looking obliquely at the surface in good light to detect scratches, variations in color, and changes in gloss

Photos: Herbert Crossan, courtesy of the Henry Francis du Pont Winterthur Museum

indicating worn areas. For the dressing table, examining the broken film under the microscope (a 15X hand lens works fine, too) gave me an idea of the thickness of the film and the extent of the crazing. The pattern of the cracks can give clues, too. The regular fissures in the table's finish suggested a spirit varnish. Lacquer, on the other hand, breaks down in irregular fissures or long, rectangular checks; shellac, in an island configuration. I also found an earlier finish (later identified as an oil varnish) on the drawer lips, indicating that the thick spirit varnish had been applied well after the table was built. In addition, I knew that the piece had been polished yearly with linseed oil during its first eight years at Winterthur.

At Winterthur, we sometimes have our analytical laboratory test samples of an unknown finish by infrared spectrometry or other related techniques. On this piece, the accumulation of varnish, oil, dirt and cleaning solvents, coupled with ultraviolet disintegration, made lab analysis difficult. Despite these problems, Dr. George Reilly, head of Winterthur's analytical lab, compared the finish with known samples and determined that it contained a damar or mastic resin, commonly used in varnish for oil paintings.

Even if you don't have access to a lab, you can still do some simple testing to identify a finish. The strategy I often find most helpful is to test a small, inconspicuous area of the finish with progressively

stronger solvents. This may reveal more about the class of finish, and can also tell you what solvents are safe to use in cleaning (safe for the finish, not for you—be sure to wear gloves and a vapor mask). On the table, I began with a cotton swab dampened with reagent ethyl alcohol. Gentle rubbing succeeded in softening the film, confirming that it was a spirit varnish. A weak hydrocarbon such as mineral spirits will soften or dissolve many turpentine- or petroleum-distillate-based finishes such as fresh damar, wax and some oil finishes. Lacquer thinner will dissolve a nitrocellulose film. Strong halogens such as methylene chloride will soften many oils, alkyd resins and polyurethanes. If you can't dissolve the film, it's likely that it is an extremely oxidized, chemically reactive film.

Obviously, if your goal is to completely strip a finish, this solvent-testing will tell you what will work. And if you're debating whether to completely refinish or not, you might first want to try either of two processes some restorers have experimented with: reapplication or amalgamation. In reapplication, the piece is washed down with the weakest solvent that will remove the finish, and the solution is collected and then reapplied. In amalgamation, a badly crazed finish is softened with the appropriate solvent, then moved around with a pad or brush to level the film. The trouble with both methods is that you succeed only in "turning over" the finish, introducing contaminants to the wood and disturbing the patina. Because not all the solvent evaporates, you're also liable to end up with a softer finish. In addition, you'll still have a chemically degraded film. I've rarely seen either procedure done satisfactorily, even on inexpensive furniture, and I certainly wouldn't try either on a valuable piece.

Cleaning—Once you've identified the degraded finish, the next step is to clean it. This is a four-part process: touch-up of areas that have lost finish entirely, removal of dirt, reduction of the crazed portion, and rubout of the remaining finish.

To protect bare wood from the water and solvents used later on, scratches or nicks in the finish must be sealed. Because they're reversible, shellac and nitrocellulose lacquer are commonly used for touch-up. For period pieces, I prefer shellac, as it closely approximates a spirit-varnish finish; on a contemporary piece, I'll often use brushing lacquer instead. I touched up scratches on the dressing table with a thin coat of 2-lb.-cut clear shellac applied

with a fine-tip artists' brush. Often a repaired scratch will appear too light after the entire surface has been cleaned and polished with wax. When this happens, I remove the polish in that area and apply a second coat of shellac toned with an alcohol-soluble stain, or with artists' dry-earth pigments if opacity is desired. When matching the color, it's better to err on the dark side, as the eye will pass over such a mark more readily than over a light one.

Surface dirt can consist of dust, fibers, soot, salt, fungi and grease. Besides muddying appearance, dirt attracts moisture that will increase oxidation and mold growth. Thus for aesthetics as well as long-term preservation of the furniture, dirt must be removed. I first vacuumed the table to pick up loose particles, then lifted most of the dirt with a cotton pad dampened with a 5% solution of mild soap and water (I use Vulpex soap, available from Conservation Materials Ltd., Box 2884, 340 Freeport Blvd., Sparks, Nev. 89431). It's best to work on a small section at a time, allowing it to air-dry thoroughly.

Usually you'll need an organic solvent to soften or remove old polishes such as linseed oil and beeswax. Mineral spirits will remove most waxes and some oils, and I gave the table a thorough rubdown with Stoddard solvent, an odorless mineral spirit (also available from Conservation Materials Ltd.). A word of caution: Again, knowing the composition of the finish is important—*don't* use min-

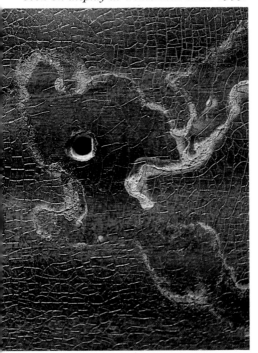

Close-up of the table's finish, before restoration. Built around 1750, the piece had been on display at Winterthur since 1959.

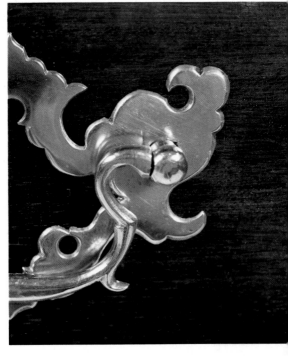

With careful cleaning, abrasion and polishing, Landrey restored the finish to period condition in less than forty hours.

eral spirits for cleaning an oil finish.

If the finish isn't badly crazed, you can skip the remaining cleaning steps and go straight to polishing. The dressing table, however, required the full treatment.

Because the crackle pattern extended only about halfway through the finish film, I could abrade off most of the degraded portion without disturbing the rest. On the flat surfaces, I used 320A- to 400A-rated wet-or-dry silicon carbide abrasive paper, dusting some fine pumice between the dry paper and the finish to reduce the paper's harshness. It takes a patient hand to keep from going through the finish, but not all the crazing needs to be removed, just enough so that the remaining finish reflects light more evenly. As you go along, look for accumulation of

sanding dust and pumice in the film's cracks: when most of the crazing has been eliminated, the dust won't have a place to collect. To prevent damage along the edges, I made a sanding block from a piece of pine with rounded corners, to which I glued ⅛-in. cotton padding. Then I rubbed down the curved areas of the legs, drawer moldings and top edges with 0000 steel wool.

To reproduce the high-gloss finish popular on such high-style pieces, I finished up by rubbing out the surface with rottenstone, a fine abrasive favored by 18th-century finishers, using mineral spirits as a lubricant. (I don't use the traditional oil lubrication for rottenstone because I prefer not to risk leaving any oil behind when restoring this type of finish.) A final rubbing with a

cotton pad dampened with mineral spirits removed the residual rottenstone.

Polishing—After cleaning, all that remains is to polish the piece to brighten the finish and to protect the rubbed-out surface. There's an assortment of commercially available polishes to pick from.

Linseed oil, though popular, is not a good choice. Even a thin film of linseed oil will darken with age and attract dust, particularly in crevices. It's not a good moisture barrier either, and it polymerizes fully, becoming extremely difficult to remove if necessary later. Lemon oil, an innocuous non-drying oil, will saturate the color of the piece but do little to protect it. It too is a dust magnet. Tung oil, although sometimes a highly desirable finish, presents some problems as a polish. Pure tung oil lacks the luster and gloss a high-style period piece should have, and like linseed oil, it will bond to the finish and become quite difficult to remove. Watco oil, which contains a significant amount of linseed oil, won't penetrate an existing finish film sufficiently to dry thoroughly to a hard, protective layer.

Carnauba and microcrystalline paste waxes are, in my opinion, the best polishes. Chemically inert, they're compatible with most finishes, and they're effective moisture barriers. Buffed to a hard, dry film, they won't trap dust. Although a wax may whiten when subjected to excessive heat or moisture, it can easily be removed with mineral spirits and a new coat applied.

I most often use brown Behlen Bros. Blue Label paste wax or Renaissance microcrystalline wax (available from Garrett Wade and Conservation Materials, respectively). Because of the relatively dark finish on this dressing table, I chose the brown wax, applying it sparingly with flannel cloths and buffing it out. Sometimes it's also necessary to use a stiff brush on some sections to work the wax into the remaining irregularities in the film. It takes a fair amount of elbow grease to get an even luster, but the wax will last, and with proper care the restored finish shouldn't need any additional cleaning or polishing for years to come. □

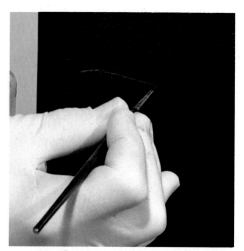

To protect bare wood from cleaning solvents, Landrey first touched up scratches with shellac (above left). Then he removed surface dirt with soap and water (above right), and gently abraded with silicon carbide paper, used with a padded block (below).

Greg Landrey is an associate furniture conservator at Winterthur Museum in Winterthur, Del. This article was prepared with the assistance of Michael Palmer, wood anatomist at Winterthur. For more on period finishes, see FWW #33, pp. 71-75, and #35, pp. 54-57; for contemporary finishing, see #17, pp. 72-75.

Water-Based Varnishes
How they compare to the old favorites

by Don Newell

Though you might not have heard of water-based "latex" varnishes, they've been around for about ten years. But they've been easy to overlook because they haven't been advertised very much. I decided to find out if these finishes are good enough to use on a valuable piece of furniture, and, if so, why I should choose one instead of a tried and true conventional varnish. I did some experimenting with different brands to see how well they performed.

Why make a water-based varnish? Two reasons: Brushes clean up in soap and water, as long as the varnish hasn't hardened; and, unlike conventional solvent-based varnishes, water-based materials don't pollute the air with hydrocarbons as they dry. Because these water-based formulas contain negligible amounts of organic solvents, they provide an alternative for woodworkers concerned about exposure to toxic conventional finishes (*FWW* #41, pp. 36-38).

The water-based clan are not varnishes in the traditional sense. With conventional varnishes, after most of the solvent has evaporated, the film begins to harden by first absorbing oxygen (a process called oxidation), then polymerizing: the molecules cross-link to form a hard film that, once dry, is no longer soluble in the original solvent. In contrast, water-based varnishes consist of a solution of film-forming polymers (usually acrylic resins) dispersed in a carrying medium of water. When the water evaporates, the dispersed polymer particles coalesce to form a coherent, protective acrylic film—much the same way that PVA glues cure.

Water-based latex varnishes, as a group, are still evolving. Some have come and gone, while others are still available. Both Valspar and PPG Industries, for example, marketed water-based products in the mid 1970s, but eventually withdrew them because they didn't perform well.

I bought a can of every brand of clear water-based varnish I could lay my hands on, which amounted to five: Sears Interior Latex Varnish, Deft Interior Acrylic Wood Armor, Flecto Varathane Ultra Plastic Finish, Fuller O'Brien Pen-Chrome Super-V Varnish, and Benjamin Moore VaquaKleer. As a benchmark for comparison, I used ZAR Antique Polyurethane Varnish, which is a conventional polyurethane. In general, the price of water-based varnishes is somewhat higher than that of regular varnishes.

All the water-based clears I tested contained about the same percentage of solids, a level considerably below that of their conventional counterparts. And all carried virtually the same directions on the can labels, such as the need to use nylon-bristle brushes or short-hair rollers to apply the material. Although the labels don't mention it, some manufacturers recommend spraying as an alternative to brushing.

I applied two coats of each brand on pine, walnut and mahogany boards, allowing the first coat to dry overnight before laying on the second. I tried to duplicate the brushing of an actual piece of cabinetry by applying the varnishes to both

Each brand of water-based varnish tested had its own brushing characteristics. Some were watery, others were much like regular varnish. Brushing all five brands on the same board allowed Newell to compare the quality of the films side-by-side.

horizontal and vertical surfaces. It was under these real working conditions that I discovered the vast difference in workability between the brands. The Sears Latex and Deft Wood Armor were so thin-bodied that they brushed on like water, though they stayed on the surface with little apparent absorption into the wood. The Flecto Varathane, Pen-Chrome Super-V and VaquaKleer were thicker in consistency, and could be applied in much heavier brush coats, more like regular solvent-based varnish. Before attempting to do serious work with either of the runny varnishes (Sears Latex and Deft Wood Armor), it's a good idea to get the feel of them first. Initially, I found myself trying to load on too much varnish in an attempt to produce a decent film thickness. This was a mistake: heavily applied, the thin varnishes ran and sagged on vertical surfaces. When brushing these thin-bodied latexes, it's best to err on the skimpy side, applying several thin coats (allowing drying time in between) instead of one heavy coat.

Because of the lower solids content, you'll need about two coats of any of the clear latexes to equal the dry-film thickness of a single coat of regular varnish. Since water evaporates more slowly than volatile lacquer thinners, water-based materials don't quickly "flash" as lacquers do. But compared to regular varnishes, the clear latexes do dry quickly. The brands I tested dried to the touch in about one hour. With most, a second coat can be applied after two to three hours, though the first coat will still be somewhat soft. Thus, you can apply two coats in the time that it takes to apply and let harden one coat of solvent-based varnish.

These latex finishes contain about 70% water, and I discovered that every brand raised the grain severely when the first coat was applied. After this coat had hardened, I scuff-sanded the raised grain with 400-grit. No further grain-raising occurred with subsequent coats. Since wood finishers often deliberately raise the grain and sand off any whiskers before finishing (*FWW* #16, pp. 69-71), I don't consider this to be a negative factor.

According to the manufacturers of some of the varnishes, a water-based acrylic clear will not completely cure in less than two weeks. For the finisher's purposes, however, overnight is dry enough for doing about anything you want with the finish. After eight hours, I could wet-sand most of the films with 400-grit paper in the same manner as I would with a conventional varnish after it had dried overnight. I tried both water and mineral spirits as a sanding lubricant, with equal results. After wiping off the sanding slurry, I polished with a fine, white automotive polishing compound, and most of the finishes polished out well. None of the labels mentioned this technique, but I recommend at least wet-sanding to remove brush marks and dust specks.

Though all the varnishes except the Flecto Varathane contain acrylic-resin polymers—the Varathane is an oil-modified, water-soluble polyurethane—I found that each brand has its own characteristics.

Sears Interior Latex Varnish: Thin and watery when applied, this product dried to a hard, even film with few brush marks. The dry film, however, was dead flat in appearance and hid much of the wood's figure. Polishing removed the brush marks, but didn't do anything to help the lackluster surface tone. I wouldn't recommend this one.

Deft Interior Acrylic Wood Armor: Another extremely thin, runny material, this finish produced a film that showed brush marks, and that was uneven and wrinkled where heavily applied. These surface flaws were too deep to sand out. Thus, I found Wood Armor's performance unsatisfactory.

After I reported the test results on off-the-shelf Wood Armor to Deft, they sent samples of a new, experimental Wood Armor, in both glossy and satin finishes. The experimental Wood Armor brushed well (though Deft recommends the use of a foam-brush applicator, which I didn't try) and built an excellent film. It dried without wrinkling, and the finish had a first-rate appearance. Sanding and polishing removed tiny imperfections, but dulled the gloss. Deft won't specify a date, but if and when this new varnish becomes available, it will be one of the best of the water-based latexes.

Flecto Varathane Ultra Plastic Finish: This product is a water-soluble form of polyurethane which brushed and handled much like a conventional varnish. Flow was good, with almost no brush strokes in the dry film. While this varnish eventually dried to a very hard film, complete curing required several days instead of the average overnight drying time. When I checked with Flecto, they told me that the particular lot I had purchased was quite moisture-sensitive, resulting in a prolonged drying time. A newer lot presently on the market apparently doesn't have this problem.

Fuller O'Brien Pen-Chrome Super-V Varnish: This finish, which contains some polyurethane in addition to acrylic resin, appears to have everything going for it. It brushed like a conventional varnish, leaving only a few brush marks, and had a good film build. It wet-sanded and polished as well as the ZAR polyurethane varnish I used as a standard. Of the varnishes tested, this was my favorite.

Benjamin Moore VaquaKleer: This material brushed very easily, appeared to produce excellent film build, and gave good flow with few apparent brush marks. Drying time seemed a bit longer than that needed for the other acrylic materials, especially the Pen-Chrome Super-V and the experimental Wood Armor.

. . .

In general, except for the flat-drying Sears Latex and the wrinkle-prone Wood Armor, the water-based varnishes I tested performed satisfactorily. After final-polishing, it was impossible to distinguish the better ones from a conventional varnish finish. They also seem about as tough as ordinary varnish, and I believe they'll hold up as well. I found that scratches could be easily touched up.

To test durability, I applied a drop of ethyl alcohol to the hardened film, to simulate a spilled alcoholic drink. A distinctive ring remained on every one of the water-based finishes after the alcohol had evaporated, though the Flecto Varathane was less severely marked than the others. I also tested all the finishes by leaving a wet glass full of water on the surface for five hours. Each finish exhibited some whitening and dulling, especially under the outer rim of the glass. After the glass was removed and the film allowed to dry overnight, however, all the finishes returned to a nearly normal appearance, but the ring mark was still clearly visible.

I didn't conduct any heat-resistance tests, but acrylic resin is thermoplastic, and these finishes probably won't resist marking from a hot pan or cup as well as a conventional varnish will.

Because these products contain such a high percentage of water, I ran a separate set of tests to measure how much water actually remained in the wood after the finish had dried. The results showed that the application of a water-based varnish increased the wood's moisture content less than 1%. As these finishes introduce a lot of water into the wood surface when first applied, however, I don't recommend that you use them on veneer or on very wide, thin boards—the wood is liable to warp.

Despite the excellent results I got with the Fuller O'Brien Pen-Chrome Super-V, for serious finishing work I still prefer conventional lacquer or varnish. As a group, the old standards offer a wider choice of properties (e.g., the chemical resistance of polyurethane). From a performance standpoint, there isn't anything that the water-based varnishes can do better, except keep hydrocarbons out of the air. □

Don Newell is a finishes chemist and consultant who lives in Farmington, Mich. Photo by the author.

Repairing shellac finishes

I have an Ingraham shelf clock that is finished with a heavily applied black finish. Wood alcohol and lacquer thinner both soften it. I'd like to repair small areas of the finish that are damaged, but in the past I've had problems matching thick finishes like these. What materials and techniques should I use? —Bob Stillman, Coeur d'Alene, Idaho

Gregory J. Landrey replies: Your 19th-century Ingraham clock, built in Bristol, Conn., most likely has a shellac finish that's turned dark over the years. To blend in the damaged areas, try a shellac colored with an aniline dye. If the old finish is opaque, a ground pigment like lampblack may give the right effect. You'll have to experiment to get the right color. (Dry fresco colors are available from Wood Finishing Supply Co., Inc., 1267 Mary Dr., Macedon, N.Y. 14502.) Apply the tinted shellac at a consistency no less than a 2-lb.-cut (a proportion based on mixing 2 lb. of shellac flakes to a gallon of alcohol) with a fine-tipped brush. It will take a number of applications to raise the damaged area just slightly above the level of the surrounding finish, so be patient. After you've built up enough shellac and allowed it to dry, you'll have to level the repair with the surrounding finish. The easiest way is to rub with 00 or 000 steel wool wrapped around the tip of a cotton swab. [Greg Landrey is an associate furniture conservator at Winterthur Museum in Winterthur, Del.]

Removing an oil finish

Several years ago, I finished an oak coffee table with Minwax Antique Oil. Since then, the table has been cleaned with furniture oil or a mixture of turpentine and linseed oil. This finish isn't tough enough to hold up under the abuse the table is subjected to, and I want to refinish with polyurethane. What can I use to remove all traces of the oil finish? —John O'Leary, Northport, N.Y.

Jim Cummins replies: Stripping your table may not be your best option. Minwax Antique Oil has several advantages, in my opinion, over polyurethane, and I'd suggest that you give it another chance. For one thing, I think it looks better—more like wood than slick plastic. For another, you can repair an oil finish easily just by rubbing on more oil, whereas polyurethane doesn't adhere well to itself. You've just been treating your oil finish wrong since you first applied it: Furniture polishes, which are simply non-drying oils that impart a temporary gloss, won't help the finish. And the turpentine/linseed mixture is so much lighter-bodied than the Minwax—and takes so much longer to dry—that it won't do much good either.

Instead, if you finish a table with three or four very thin coats of Antique Oil and refresh it with a thin coat whenever it shows wear, you'll probably be well pleased. For scratches, you can sand the old finish around the scratch to a feather edge and apply more oil—it will blend right in. For routine maintenance, rub on a fresh coat every few months. This will clean superficial grim off the surface, and should make the finish last indefinitely. Two-year-old oil can look fresh as new, but two-year-old polyurethane will show every scar. [Jim Cummins is an associate editor at *Fine Woodworking*.]

Cratered finish

I'm having problems refinishing a tabletop. I removed the original finish with Hope's Furniture Refinisher and then applied a polyurethane finish, but it cratered in small spots. I removed the polyurethane finish with Formby's Paint Remover, sanded the top down to bare wood, and restained it. Next I applied Deft. This finish also cratered. Can you help? —R. William Furman, Ft. Collins, Colo.

Don Newell replies: At some time, silicone must have been applied to the tabletop—perhaps in a polish. Silicone is very tenacious stuff, and solvents and removers tend to spread it around rather than remove it. These craters, called "fisheyes," happen when silicone prevents the finish from adhering.

Wet 400-grit wet-or-dry sandpaper with mineral spirits, and sand down to bare wood. Dry the wood and wipe off all the sanding dust. If you're going to restain, do it now. Next, brush on a very thin coat of shellac, thinned three parts denatured alcohol to one part shellac. Don't build up a thick layer. Let this dry, and apply Deft normally. You should not have cratering this time. To be absolutely sure, I'd add a small amount of fisheye remover (available from Constantine) to the Deft; it's an additive designed to eliminate fisheyes caused by silicone and other impurities.
[Don Newell, of Farmington, Mich., is a former paint and varnish chemist.]

Satin piano finish

We spray lots of ebony piano finishes in our shop. We use a black nitrocellulose lacquer, and have no problems until the final rubout. We wet-sand the lacquer with a pneumatic straight-line sander and 400-grit paper lubricated with mineral spirits. Next, we rub with 0000 steel wool that's been unraveled and stretched across a short, narrow board; the board has a felt pad tacked to it so the steel wool stays flat against the finish. This rubout results in an even-looking satin finish, but instead of deep black, it has a gray look, most noticeable toward the edges of the lids. We suspect that this is caused by the refraction of light in the fine grooves left by the sandpaper.

We've tried all kinds of rubbing compounds and oils, to no avail. Some even highlight the sandpaper scratches. Are we missing some mysterious step in our procedure? —John Minor, Champaign, Ill.

Donald M. Steinert replies: It may comfort you to know that your problems creating a satin-ebony finish are quite common.

Visit a piano dealer to see what kind of finishes the factories are producing on new pianos. Make a point to see satin-ebony grands by Steinway, and by Yamaha or another Japanese manufacturer. You'll see that the "gray look" is common to both. You're correct that this is caused by light bouncing off the minute scratches left by both the abrasive paper and the steel wool.

You'll notice that the scratches on the Yamaha are almost perfectly straight, parallel and uninterrupted. The final rubout on a Yamaha piano is done by machine, with the entire lid passing on a belt under a roller that rubs out the full width in one pass. The Steinway finish probably looks more like yours because it's rubbed out by hand. The exaggeration near the edges happens when you reverse direction as you rub. Obviously, the individual particles on the abrasive paper or the individual strands of steel wool don't stay exactly in the same grooves. Instead, tiny "hooks" are created near the edge of the lid at the point of reversal.

Try rubbing the lacquer with silicon carbide paper only. Mineral spirits will work fine as a sanding lubricant, but a mix of paraffin oil and mineral spirits is even better. This method will remove more lacquer than will steel wool, so apply additional coats before sanding.

Wet-sand with 400-grit until the surface is smooth, flat and uniform. Then wet-sand with 600-grit at right angles to the 400-grit scratches until these are gone—a process called cross-sanding. Next, wet-sand with 1200-grit at right angles to the 600-grit scratches until they disappear (3M "ultra-fine" paper in grits from 1200 to 1500 can be special-ordered by an automotive paint supply house). Voila! You should have a superior satin finish.
[Donald Steinert, who lives in Grants Pass, Ore., wrote about piano finishing in *FWW* #44.]

THINGS TO MAKE

Wooden Puzzles
Easy to make, but tough to solve

by Stewart T. Coffin

Many years ago, while engaged in the home enterprise of making canoe paddles, I found myself with the problem of what to do with piles of odd-shaped wood scraps. What emerged from this (with some help from my three children) was an intriguing little puzzle of 12 notched sticks. This in turn led to other ideas for new and unusual geometric puzzles—some 70-odd at the latest count—which soon grew into a thriving family business. Recently, with my labor force gone thither and shop space crowded out by other projects, I've been encouraging others to try their hand at this fascinating craft. This article should be enough to get any woodworker started—those who become addicted will find more of the same in my book, *Puzzle Craft.*

Puzzles don't have to be especially complicated or difficult to make to be absorbing. We found that the one that consistently brought the most amusement at craft fairs was our buttonhole puzzle, also known as the "idiot stick." (We used to make them from scraps of exotic wood, but a popsicle stick would do instead.) It's no more than a short length of hardwood with a loop of string that's just slightly too short to pass over the end of the stick. It ties through a buttonhole, just like a price tag, and the idea is to get it off in one piece. I know of a few of these sticks that are still attached to the same jacket or

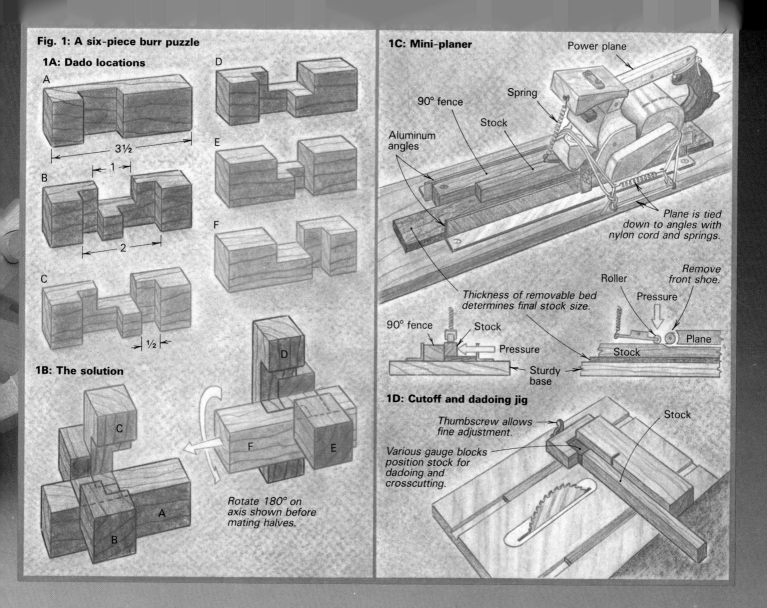

Fig. 1: A six-piece burr puzzle

1A: Dado locations

A

3½

1

B

2

C

½

1B: The solution

C

D

F

E

A

B

Rotate 180° on
axis shown before
mating halves.

D

E

F

1C: Mini-planer

Power plane

90° fence

Spring

Stock

Aluminum
angles

Plane is tied
down to angles with
nylon cord and springs.

Remove
front shoe.

Roller

Pressure

Thickness of removable bed
determines final stock size.

90° fence

Stock

Pressure

Plane

Stock

Sturdy
base

1D: Cutoff and dadoing jig

Thumbscrew allows
fine adjustment.

Stock

Various gauge blocks
position stock for
dadoing and
crosscutting.

sweater we put them on ten years ago, but whether the clothing's owners are still working out the solution or not, I can't say. (I have to admit that the first time somebody tied one on me, I had to cut the cord.) For readers who find such teasers more frustrating than interesting, the solution is given at the end of this article.

Some of my puzzles have been licensed to manufacturers, but most were engineered so I could make them in limited production in my small shop. I started with only an 8-in. tablesaw and a belt sander. Later I found a thickness planer to be indispensable, but because of the small scale of the work, I made mine from a portable power plane mounted over a fixed bed, as shown in figure 1C. Eventually I added two more tablesaws—one just for ripping and one for making notches—and, finally, a bandsaw.

Among all interlocking puzzles, the six-piece burr (the center puzzle on the facing page) is one of the most ancient. Many people are apt to dismiss it on sight as being too trivial, but while some variations of the burr puzzle have numerous solutions and are therefore fairly easy to solve, others such as the one shown in figure 1, which has just one solution, can be quite taxing.

When making a burr, as with most other puzzles, the woodworking is simple and straightforward, but all cuts must be extremely accurate or the puzzle will be sloppy. To check measurements, you'll want at the very least a good set of vernier calipers, or, better yet, a micrometer. Keep in mind that wood shrinks

and swells with changes in humidity. Don't aim for too tight a fit on a dry winter day or the puzzle will lock solid in summer. Saws must be set up square and true and kept very sharp—a hollow-ground (no-set) plywood blade will do fine.

Domestic woods such as cherry, walnut and white oak can be used, but my preference is Honduras mahogany because it's more stable. Among the more exotic tropical woods, Brazilian rosewood is my first choice.

Thickness the sticks to exactly 1 in. square. I first rip the stock to 1¹⁄₁₆ in. square. To bring the sticks down to final dimension, I set the planer to skim off the sawmarks on two adjacent faces, then reset it to final size and skim the other two.

Next I cut the sticks to their 3½-in. finished length. I never mark sizes on the stock, because that would be a time-wasting and inaccurate step when such close tolerances are required. Instead, I rely on a jig to ensure accuracy and speed. The setup shown in figure 1D holds the stick exactly square to the blade, and positions it to length by means of a removable gauge block. The same setup, with different gauge blocks, ensures that the notches are in the right place. I cut them with a dado set shimmed out with paper to 0.002 in. oversize.

When I've cut the pieces, I test the fit and give them a very light sanding to ease the corners, making the parts much more inviting to handle. To keep the appearance crisp, I lightly chamfer the ends of the sticks with a flat file. Then I dunk each piece

185

Coffin's 'Octahedral Cluster' puzzle, apart and assembled. The basic 12-sided block is made on the tablesaw jig shown below.

in thinned lacquer and immediately wipe it off with a clean rag. With oily woods such as rosewood, no lacquer is necessary.

The burr puzzle is an *orthogonal* puzzle—its geometry is based on the cube. Another sort of puzzle is the *rhombic-dodecahedral* type ("R-D," for short), whose geometry is based on a figure with 12 sides. The jig shown in the photo below easily makes 12-sided blocks. It's simply a V-cradle set at 45° to the sawblade. Place a 1½-in. square stick in the cradle, with its end against the stop at the far end of the V. Push the jig

This V-cradle jig makes solid 12-sided blocks as described in the text. Such blocks can be glued together to make the author's 'Octahedral Cluster' puzzle, shown at the top of the page. The clamp is necessary only for the final cut.

through the sawblade, rotating the stick after each pass, to cut off its four corners. Then advance the stick by means of a gauge block. (The length of the block depends partly on the width of your sawblade's kerf—try 2⁵⁄₁₆ in., and adjust to suit.) Cut about halfway through the stick from all four sides; at the last cut, a 12-sided block will result. Then trim the stick's corners, advance it with another gauge block and repeat the process.

You can glue these little rhombic dodecahedrons together to make various puzzles, such as my "Octahedral Cluster," shown in the photos above. But even if you don't plan to ever make the cluster, the little blocks make good Christmas-stocking stuffers, and are pretty to have around. I used to sell them for 35¢ each, and there's a man up in Toronto who's bought about a thousand of them. I'm not sure why.

Some of the corner-waste pieces from those blocks led to another puzzle: When my children were quite small, they used to spend hours in my shop, gluing together scraps to make "puzzles" for their friends. One time, daughter Abbie, merrily gluing corner scraps in different ways, chanced on a fascinating arrangement. As shown in the photo at the top of the facing page, the puzzle has mirror-image halves of six sides each, which fit together to make an R-D, obviously with no difficulty whatsoever. Taking it apart, however, is another matter. Most people will grasp randomly with the thumb and forefinger of each hand and pull. But the puzzle will never come apart that way, because you're always grasping both pieces in each hand. Only by an unnatural three-finger grip with each hand can the puzzle be disassembled. If made carefully, the planes of dissection are practically invisible. My kids made and sold these for a few years at $3 apiece for large ones and $1 for little ones. They used to

The mirror-image halves of 'Pennyhedron' easily slide together to form a hollow rhombic dodecahedron, but getting them apart again requires a three-finger grip that takes most people a while to figure out. Figure 2 shows how to make the puzzle.

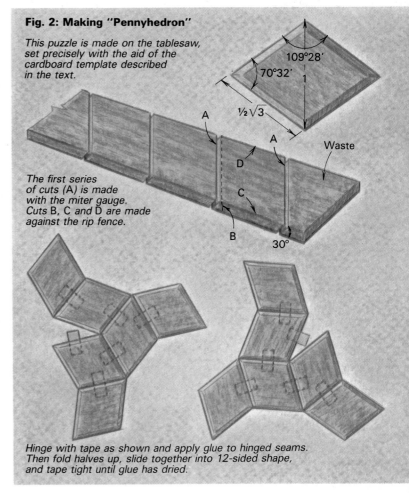

Fig. 2: Making "Pennyhedron"

This puzzle is made on the tablesaw, set precisely with the aid of the cardboard template described in the text.

109°28'
70°32'
½√3
Waste

The first series of cuts (A) is made with the miter gauge. Cuts B, C and D are made against the rip fence.

A
A
D
C
B
30°

Hinge with tape as shown and apply glue to hinged seams. Then fold halves up, slide together into 12-sided shape, and tape tight until glue has dried.

put a penny inside, and therefore named it "Pennyhedron." I think we ran out of scraps and they got interested in other things at about the same time, so production ceased.

"Pennyhedron," which consists of 12 identical rhombic panels, is not difficult to make. Prepare a strip of ¼-in. lauan plywood (or other wood of uniform thickness) about 2½ in. wide and 3 ft. long. You will crosscut this strip at a slight angle—as shown in figure 2—into 12 pieces with the sawblade tilted to 30° and the miter gauge adjusted to the correct angle. This yields one good diagonal cut (A) on each piece. The drawing shows the work as done on a saw whose blade tilts to the right; if your saw tilts to the left, your workpiece will be the mirror image of mine. The other three cuts are simply made against the rip fence as described below. The exact profile of each finished side is shown in figure 2.

It's impossible to set the miter gauge by measuring the angles, but a large-scale cardboard template will do the job. Make a triangle with a baseline of 24 in., and two other equal sides of $20\frac{25}{32}$ in., as near as you can measure. These are the proportions of half the shape, with the baseline equal to the short diagonal of the piece (the ratio is $1:\frac{1}{2}\sqrt{3}$). To set the miter gauge, raise the blade to full height, press one of the short sides of the template against it, and adjust the miter gauge so it aligns with the other short side of the template. Then tilt the sawblade to 30°, lower it to a safe height and make the first series of cuts, a little farther apart than the strip is wide. Next set the rip fence to a little less than the width of the strip (with the blade tilting *away* from the fence, of course, so as not to trap the work) and run the good diagonal cut against the fence to cut the second diagonal. Then cut the other two sides with the same setting.

At craft fairs, we found that people frequently asked what age group a particular puzzle was suited for. This opened the door for one of our favorite tricks: My youngest daughter, Margie, then about seven or eight, would be mingling with the crowd. I would take our most complicated-looking puzzle apart and say, "Anyone who can put this together can take it away." Most adults hung back in fear of embarrassment, leaving an opportunity for Margie to emerge from the crowd, quickly assemble the puzzle, tuck it under her arm and smugly walk away. The crowd always realized that the joke was on them. Children of that age learn very quickly, which leads me to one final tale.

I had licensed one of my designs to a manufacturer, who in turn had contracted with a factory to mold 20,000 of them in plastic. Production was no problem, but the factory couldn't find anyone to put the pieces together for packaging, and was about to jam up solid with puzzle parts. So I made a deal with them and told them to ship the pieces to my factory. My "factory" turned out to be some picnic tables set up on the lawn, and the work force consisted of all the kids in the neighborhood. They all learned quickly, and not one dropped out, especially when I paid them 2¢ per puzzle assembled. The youngest worker was six years old. We finished the job in ten days. □

Stewart Coffin first wrote on wooden puzzles in FWW *#17, and is now making canoes and puzzling out designs for ultralight paddles.* Puzzle Craft *is available from him at 79 Old Sudbury Rd., Lincoln, Mass. 01773, for $10. To put the buttonhole puzzle on, pull the fabric through the loop of string until the far end of the stick can slip through the buttonhole. Then pull the stick until the string tightens. Reverse the steps to remove it.*

Hepplewhite Chest of Drawers
Delicate inlay fans life into a traditional piece

by Carlyle Lynch

An aura of mystery cloaks this beautiful chest: where was it made and by whom? Adding to its charm is the delicate string inlay and fan, shown full-size at top of page.

At an antiques show, a small mahogany Hepplewhite chest with a delicate fan inlay beckoned me. The owners let me measure and draw it, but we haven't been able to learn much more about this beautiful unsigned piece, except that it came from an old home in Fauquier County, the heart of Virginia's horse country.

The owners presume that the chest was made nearby in the old port city of Alexandria. Overland transport of heavy lumber was so difficult two hundred years ago that most mahogany furniture was built in coastal areas. The chest's secondary wood is white pine, but that's no clue to its origin, since cabinetmakers in both New England and Virginia used white pine extensively as a secondary wood, and northerners shipped a great deal of mahogany furniture to wealthy southern farmers. If the secondary wood were yellow pine, you could reliably classify the piece as a southern antique.

The construction techniques shown on p. 190 are typical of those used by 18th-century cabinetmakers. On the original chest, ⅛-in. thick mahogany strips hide the rail housings in the solid-mahogany sides, and similar strips face the white-pine drawer rails. The apron and the edge of the solid-pine base also are veneered. A white string inlay highlights the solid-wood top and the drawer fronts. A narrow diamond-pattern inlay band runs around the front and sides just below the level of the chest base. To reproduce the piece, you could use solid wood throughout, except for the apron, where veneer and a marquetry

fan are more appropriate.

The original top, a single piece of ⅜-in. mahogany, is so thin that I wonder if the maker resawed a board to get the same beautiful grain for a second chest. The top appears to be glued all around. Because any seasonal wood movement in the thin top is in the same direction as in the sides, the top is still tight and without cracks, nearly two hundred years after it was made.

The fan inlay is a most appealing feature of this chest. Today you can buy a pre-cut veneer fan, patch it into a mahogany veneer sheet and apply the sheet to the apron, as if you were gluing down a marquetry picture. Readers wishing to reproduce the original authentically, however, will probably prefer to make their own ⅛-in. thick veneer, and their own fan, as discussed below. In this method, the apron blank is first veneered with mahogany, then a recess is carved in it to accept the lighter-colored pieces of the fan. Before you start on the inlay, cut the veneered apron to size, but don't scroll-saw it to shape yet. Wait until the inlay has been done. That way you can saw the apron to match the bottom curve of the inlay.

If you cut your own fan, make an exact copy of the inlay from thin cardboard before making one from wood. Start with a piece of cardboard slightly larger than the fan. That way, as you cut out the individual leaves, you'll be making the fan-shaped cutout you'll need later for a fitting template. If you want to make an elliptical fan like the original, you can trace the photo

Photos: top, Richard Aufenger; bottom, author

on the facing page and transfer it to the cardboard. Here I'll make a slightly different, circular inlay. Either way, after you make the template, cut out the eight leaves with a sharp knife.

Next, using a sharp pencil, trace each leaf pattern onto ⅛-in. thick maple. As much as possible, avoid short cross-grain near the narrow ends of the leaves. Saw the leaves out with a jewelers' saw, fine scroll saw or coping saw. Cut on the waste side of the pencil lines, then plane and file the edges down to the lines and fit the pieces into the cardboard template.

Once the leaves fit snugly in the template, they must be individually shaded by scorching in hot sand. When making the fan inlay for this article, I used only about three tablespoons of fine white sand in a small metal plate, but you might find it easier to control the temperature with about an inch of sand in a pan. Put the container on a hot plate set on medium until the sand is hot. Before risking the real leaves, experiment on scrap pieces to determine how long each must be heated. Grip each one with tweezers and dip its edge in the sand. For a start, try about five seconds; you may have to adjust the temperature. On the original, the tone gradually lightens across the leaf, giving the fan a real three-dimensional look. Don't overdo it, or you'll char the pieces.

While the shaded pieces are cooling, use the template to trace the fan shape on a 2-in. wide piece of brown-paper packing tape. The tape should be cut the same size as or slightly smaller than the template; any overhang will just get in your way. Now fit the maple back into the template and tape the leaves together. Lift the inlay out as a unit, sandwich it between two pieces of wood that can be clamped in a vise, and file the fan's back edge to a slight bevel to ensure a tight fit.

Clamp the beveled fan in position on the apron and carefully pencil a line around it. Remove the fan and use a ⅜-in. gouge to carve a recess about ³⁄₃₂ in. deep within the outline, then flatten the bottom with a hand router plane. Cut the recess shallow enough to leave the fan about ¹⁄₃₂ in. proud of the apron surface. Dry-fit the inlay and pare the recess outline for a snug fit. Next spread yellow glue over the recess bottom, drop the entire inlay as a unit into the indentation, put a smooth piece of wood between the inlay and a clamp, and press the fan into place. Immediately remove the clamp and block, and wipe off excess glue with a damp rag. The inlay should be stuck firmly enough to stay put while you sand off the tape. A little more sanding will create enough dust to fill any small spaces between the leaves. To ensure that the fan is down, cover the inlay with waxed paper, replace the wood block, and reclamp the assembly until dry.

Rabbet the top edge of the apron with a router, saw or shaper to take the ³⁄₁₆-in. wide diamond inlay band. The apron now requires a narrow, curved groove for the maple stringing, and similar grooves are needed on the top and the drawer fronts. I prefer to cut straight grooves by hand with a homemade scratch stock similar to the one discussed below, but for cutting curved grooves, a small router, such as a Dremel hand tool with its router attachment, is faster.

If you don't want to use a router—and I didn't until recently when I was given a Dremel tool and discovered how handy it can be—all the inlaying can be done with a small homemade scratch stock, as shown at right above. I used it with a pivot for cutting the circular-arc inlay, and clamped a wooden fence to the beam for cutting straight grooves. To make the cutter, use a 100-grit aluminum oxide wheel to grind a piece of hand hacksaw blade. No bevel is needed; the sides should be ground square with the face. To use the tool, hold it firmly near the blade and lean it a little toward the direction you are moving

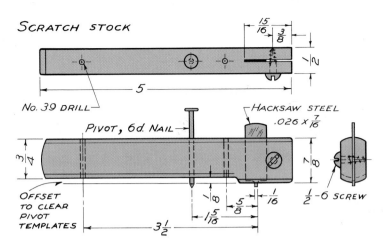

it. Use a light scraping pressure, working first in one direction and then in the other.

To cut a ¹⁄₁₆-in. circular inlay groove under the fan, clamp a piece of wood to the apron edge, mark on it the center for the 3½-in. radius arc and punch a small hole there. The hole will anchor the scratch-stock pivot or the Dremel pivot guide. After the groove is cut, soften the string inlay in boiling water so it can be bent around the curve. I recommend that you use commercially available ¹⁄₁₆-in. by ¹⁄₁₆-in. sawn maple inlay—it's easier to bend than the ¹⁄₂₈-in. by ¹⁄₁₆-in. types, which are cut from veneer and tend to flip over on edge when bent. I used maple stringing because it's more readily available than the holly used on the original chest. If you don't want to buy inlay, you could saw your own with a fine-tooth plywood blade. Once the inlay is soft enough to bend, apply a thin coat of yellow glue to the bottom and sides of the groove, and press the inlay in with the face of a hammer. When the glue has dried, sand all the inlay flush with the apron surface.

Next cut the inlay grooves for the top and the drawer fronts. Whether you use a scratch stock or a Dremel tool, cut the straight grooves first. Then by starting the cutter in the groove, you can work around the curves without chipping any corners. To do the curves, I recommend clamping the piece to the workbench and using homemade metal templates, shown below, to protect the wood and to anchor the guide pivot of the Dremel or scratch stock. Set the pivot in the indentation punched in the metal template and place the cutter bit in the end of a straight groove to start. Then pivot the cutter to the end of the next straight groove. When inlaying the top and drawers, apply glue to the groove and press in long, straight pieces wherever possi-

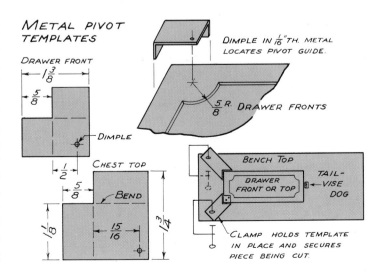

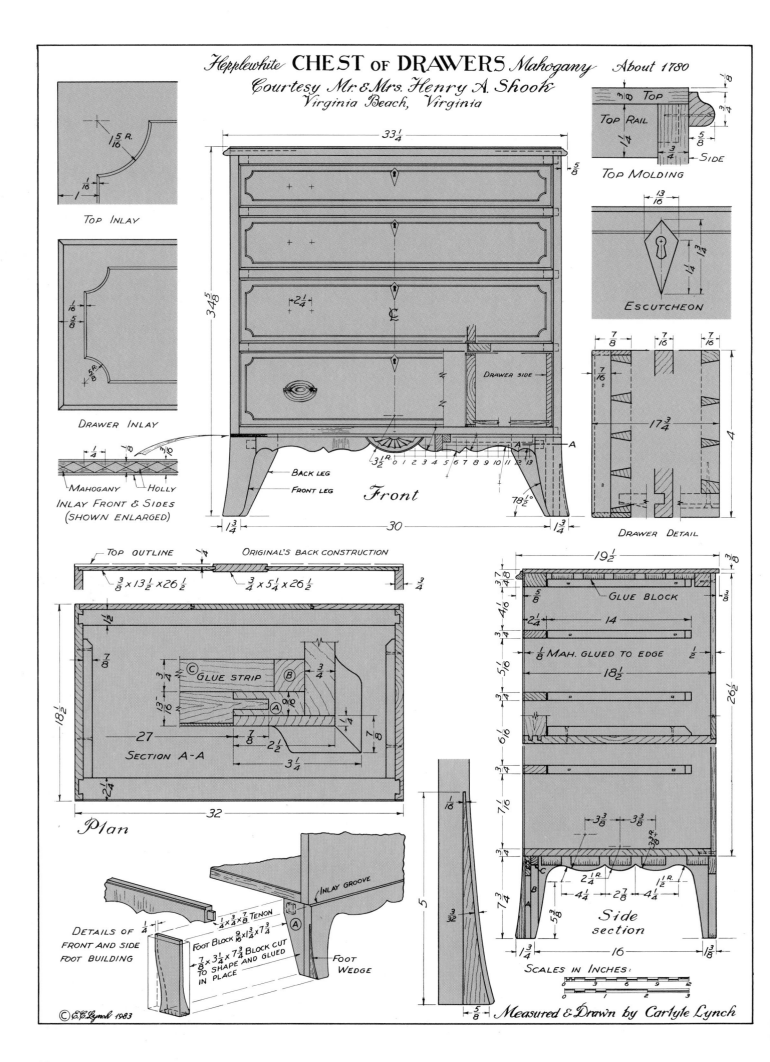

Hepplewhite CHEST OF DRAWERS *Mahogany About 1780*

Courtesy Mr. & Mrs. Henry A. Shook
Virginia Beach, Virginia

TOP INLAY

DRAWER INLAY

MAHOGANY — HOLLY
INLAY FRONT & SIDES
(SHOWN ENLARGED)

Front

BACK LEG
FRONT LEG

DRAWER SIDE

TOP MOLDING

TOP RAIL
TOP
SIDE

ESCUTCHEON

DRAWER DETAIL

TOP OUTLINE

ORIGINAL'S BACK CONSTRUCTION

GLUE STRIP

SECTION A-A

Plan

DETAILS OF
FRONT AND SIDE
FOOT BUILDING

INLAY GROOVE

TENON

FOOT BLOCK
BLOCK CUT
TO SHAPE AND GLUED
IN PLACE

FOOT
WEDGE

GLUE BLOCK

MAH. GLUED TO EDGE

Side
section

SCALES IN INCHES:

Measured & Drawn by Carlyle Lynch

190

ble. To join pieces at the corners, put a piece of tape across the groove where the joint will be and cross the inlay strips over it, so they're held out of the glued groove. Cut a miter through both strips with a sharp knife and remove the tape. The joint will be tight when the pieces are forced into the groove.

Regardless of whether you buy pre-cut inlay or make your own, be careful when applying finishes. Much of the beauty of the original chest is due to the clear, unstained dark mahogany, which is enhanced by the white inlay and brightly polished hardware. The types of mahogany available today, however, usually need to be stained as well as filled in the finishing process, and there's a danger of staining the inlay out of existence. Although it may sound tedious, an easy way to protect the white areas is to take a tiny watercolor brush and apply enough white shellac to seal the inlay before you stain the chest.

If you reproduce the piece from my drawing, note that the top rails are dovetailed into the sides, while blind mortises with twin tenons are used on the lower rails. If you prefer, you can dovetail all the drawer rails. Also, cut a housed dovetail joint so that you can slide the bottom in from the back. Notch the bottom's front corners to hide the joints.

The feet can be made in two ways. Foot pieces with a concave taper can be glued into recesses cut into the sides, then the front of the foot assembly covered with a shaped piece. On the sides, if you want to shape the legs without interrupting the grain pattern, glue flaired wedges into kerfs sawn in the side feet. Since a 10-in. tablesaw can cut only 3-in. deep kerfs, cut the space for the wedges in two steps, beginning with a tablesaw and finishing up with a handsaw. To be safe, make the tablesaw cuts clear across the sides while they're square. Bandsaw the

sides to the scroll pattern to make it easier to handsaw the remaining 2 in. of the 5-in. deep kerf. I find that two handsaws clamped together will make a kerf as wide as that of a 10-in. combination blade. Drive in the glue-coated wedges after soaking the area with hot wet towels for 10 minutes, and clamp.

The drawer fronts listed in the bill of materials are $\frac{5}{16}$ in. narrower, top to bottom, than the opening, allowing $\frac{1}{4}$ in. for the cock beading and $\frac{1}{16}$-in. vertical play. Mahogany is stable in humid conditions, but $\frac{3}{32}$-in. to $\frac{1}{8}$-in. vertical play may be needed in some regions. It's better to be generous in allowing for vertical play, rather than trying to shave down a cock-beaded drawer. Drawer runners are strips fastened to the sides with two nails each. Don't secure them more firmly than that, or the sides may eventually split from wood movement.

The back shown here is made of tongue-and-grooved vertical boards. The original chest's back has two thin boards that fit into grooves cut in the edges of a thicker, center support. Nails hold the thin boards in rabbets in the chest sides, to the top rail, and to the edge of the bottom. □

Carlyle Lynch, a designer, cabinetmaker and retired teacher, lives in Broadway, Va. Drawings by the author. Lynch's plans for a Queen Anne highboy appeared in FWW #42, *and others of his drawings are available from Garrett Wade, Lee Valley Tools Ltd., and Woodcraft Supply. Constantine's (2050 Eastchester Rd., Bronx, N.Y. 10461) stocks fans, escutcheons and inlay borders suitable for the chest shown here. Manhattan Supply Corp. (151 Sunnyside Blvd., Plainview, N.Y. 11803) has $\frac{1}{16}$-in. end-mill router bits with $\frac{1}{8}$-in. shanks. For more on inlay, see* FWW #27, pp. 44-55.

BILL OF MATERIALS			Dimensions				Dimensions
Amt. Description		Wood	T x W x L	Amt. Description		Wood	T x W x L
Case:				**Drawers******:**			
1	Top	mahogany	$\frac{3}{8}$ x 18$\frac{7}{8}$ x 32	1	Front	mahogany	$\frac{7}{8}$ x 3$\frac{3}{4}$ x 30$\frac{7}{16}$
1	Top molding	mahogany	$\frac{5}{8}$ x $\frac{3}{4}$ x 34	1	Back	pine	$\frac{7}{16}$ x 3$\frac{3}{16}$ x 30$\frac{7}{16}$
2	Top moldings	mahogany	$\frac{5}{8}$ x $\frac{3}{4}$ x 20	2	Sides	pine	$\frac{7}{16}$ x 4 x 17$\frac{5}{16}$
2	Sides	mahogany	$\frac{3}{4}$ x 18$\frac{1}{2}$ x 34$\frac{1}{4}$	1	Front	mahogany	$\frac{7}{8}$ x 4$\frac{3}{4}$ x 30$\frac{7}{16}$
1	Bottom	pine	$\frac{3}{4}$ x 18 x 30$\frac{1}{2}$ s/s	1	Back	pine	$\frac{7}{16}$ x 4$\frac{3}{16}$ x 30$\frac{7}{16}$
3	Drawer rails	pine	$\frac{3}{4}$ x 2$\frac{1}{4}$* x 30$\frac{1}{2}$ s/s	2	Sides	pine	$\frac{7}{16}$ x 5 x 17$\frac{5}{16}$
1	Top rail	pine	1$\frac{1}{4}$ x 2$\frac{1}{4}$* x 30$\frac{1}{2}$ s/s	1	Front	mahogany	$\frac{7}{8}$ x 5$\frac{3}{4}$ x 30$\frac{7}{16}$
1	Top back rail	pine	1$\frac{1}{4}$ x 1$\frac{1}{2}$ x 30$\frac{1}{2}$ s/s	1	Back	pine	$\frac{7}{16}$ x 5$\frac{3}{16}$ x 30$\frac{7}{16}$
6	Drawer runners	pine	$\frac{3}{4}$ x $\frac{7}{8}$ x 14	2	Sides	pine	$\frac{7}{16}$ x 6 x 17$\frac{5}{16}$
2	Kickers	pine	$\frac{3}{4}$ x $\frac{7}{8}$ x 14	1	Front	mahogany	$\frac{7}{8}$ x 6$\frac{3}{4}$ x 30$\frac{7}{16}$
1	Back (tongue-and-grooved boards)	pine	$\frac{1}{2}$ x 31$\frac{1}{4}$ x 26$\frac{1}{2}$	1	Back	pine	$\frac{7}{16}$ x 6$\frac{3}{16}$ x 30$\frac{7}{16}$
				2	Sides	pine	$\frac{7}{16}$ x 7 x 17$\frac{5}{16}$
1	Apron	pine	$\frac{3}{4}$* x 1$\frac{7}{8}$ x 27	4	Bottoms ($\frac{1}{4}$-in. plywood can also be used)	pine	$\frac{3}{8}$ x 17$\frac{1}{4}$ x 29$\frac{3}{4}$
2	Front feet	mahogany	$\frac{7}{8}$ x 3$\frac{1}{4}$ x 7$\frac{3}{4}$				
2	Front foot blocks	pine	$\frac{9}{16}$ x 1$\frac{3}{4}$ x 7$\frac{3}{4}$	8	Cock beading	mahogany	$\frac{1}{8}$ x 1 x 30$\frac{7}{16}$
2	Apron and foot glue blocks (makes two pairs)	pine	$\frac{3}{4}$ x $\frac{3}{4}$ x 29	2	Cock beading	mahogany	$\frac{1}{8}$ x $\frac{1}{2}$ x 24
				Inlay:			
4	End foot wedges	mahogany	$\frac{5}{8}$ x 2 x 5	12	String inlay	maple	$\frac{1}{16}$ x $\frac{1}{16}$ x 36
2	Back feet	pine	$\frac{3}{4}$ x 4$\frac{3}{8}$ x 7$\frac{3}{4}$	1	Fan inlay (makes eight leaves)	maple	$\frac{1}{8}$ x 1$\frac{1}{2}$ x 5$\frac{1}{2}$
				4	Escutcheons	maple	$\frac{1}{8}$ x $\frac{13}{16}$ x 1$\frac{3}{4}$
				3	Base diamond inlay band		$\frac{3}{16}$ x $\frac{3}{24}$ x 36

Hardware: Eight brass pulls, 2$\frac{1}{4}$-in. bore, similar to D-3 or D-5 from Ball and Ball, 463 West Lincoln Hwy., Exton, Pa. 19341; four drawer locks with barrel keys, $\frac{7}{8}$-in. selvage to key pin.

s/s = shoulder-to-shoulder. Allow $\frac{1}{2}$ in. to 1 in. extra length for each tenon or dovetail.
 * Veneered
 ** Dimensions include $\frac{1}{16}$-in. vertical allowance for humidity changes.

How to Make a Wooden Flute

Lathe-boring long holes, and keeping them centered

by Whittaker Freegard

My first attempt at making a flute was a turned piece of pine, bored with a brace and bit. It didn't work. The next time, I drilled the tube with spade bits in a Jacobs chuck in the lathe. The flute could be played, but my processes were slow and uncertain, and the results sometimes unpredictable.

Over the years, I've improved my techniques, and learned enough about the precise anatomy of flutes to make one with precision and within a reasonable amount of time. Basically, a blank is rough-turned round, the inner diameter is bored, then the blank is mounted on a wooden mandrel for turning the tube to its final diameter. This ensures that the bore is exactly centered, one of the most important details in flute making. Length, finger-hole location and wall thickness all must be in balance for a successful instrument. I rely heavily on lathe accessories to make my flutes, but you don't actually need all the equipment I have to make a single flute; I've outlined some alternatives on p. 194. If you would like to increase the versatility of your lathe for such projects as tall lamps, drilled-out containers, and even a little metalworking, however, the bits and chucks I talk about here are a worthwhile investment. Mine paid for themselves a long time ago.

Preparing the blank—The flute shown here has a detachable head joint and is tuned to a G-major scale. If you want another pitch or a different sound qual-

Whittaker Freegard has made flutes under the shop name of Garett Alden for ten years in Mendocino County, Calif., and Eureka Springs, Ark.

Fig. 1: Measurements for a six-hole flute

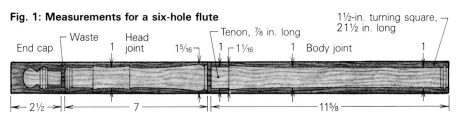

Cut the flute blank with minimal waste between sections to ensure matching grain. Dimensions are important if the flute is to play in tune.

ity, you can experiment with other dimensions. Generally, large or long bores produce lower tones; narrower and shorter bores, higher ones. Thick walls give a richer but less responsive sound; thin walls, a thinner, breathier tone.

The denser and more resinous a wood, the fuller and richer the tone. My consistent favorite is cocobolo, although many exotic and domestic hardwoods produce excellent tones. In general, select a wood with as closed grain as possible, but avoid rock maple. It is exasperatingly hard on shell augers, and unless sealed with epoxy, it has a dry, thin tone. My favorite native hardwoods are black walnut and cherry, especially when the wood is burled or compressed. I buy 6/4 or 8/4 lumber and bandsaw the planks into 1½-in. turning squares. To allow for the jointed flute's body tenon, and the end cap for the head joint, I cut each blank to 21½ in., making sure that the blank is free of checks.

Measuring as shown in figure 1, I cut the body, head joint and end cap to length, and mark the top and bottom ends of each piece. The figure pattern will appear different when the square is rounded, and it's all too easy to end up with mismatched sections.

I use a spur center in the headstock to mount the head joint and body section

in the lathe. To reduce vibration, I round each blank with a large gouge, then I use a wide cut-off tool to make a 1-in. long tenon on the tailstock end, so it will slide snugly into my shopmade ball-bearing hollow tailstock, shown in figure 3. The drill bits pass through the center of this hollow tailstock to bore out the instrument. Then I cut a ½-in. long step in the headstock end to fit a 3-jaw chuck. I cut this step larger than the final flute diameter, because the full length of the blank is needed.

Boring out—At this point, the lathe changes from a turning tool to a boring tool. As shown in figure 3, lathes can bore from either end. Boring each section of a flute to final diameter is best done in three steps, beginning with a short pilot hole. In the second step, a hand-held bit extends the pilot through the blank, and the third step expands the center hole to its full diameter. To begin the pilot hole, as shown in figure 3A, I hold the work in a 3-jaw chuck and support the tailstock end in the ball-bearing hollow tailstock. I mount a ½-in. twist bit in a Jacobs chuck in the tailstock. The hollow tailstock must be adjusted so that the bit lines up exactly with the center of the blank. With the work turning at the lathe's slowest

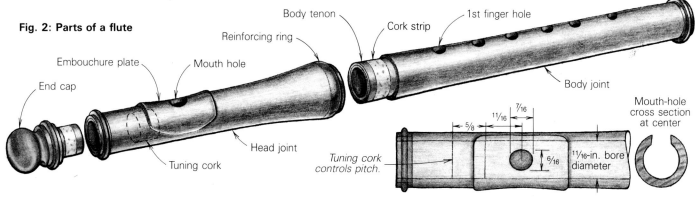

Fig. 2: Parts of a flute

End cap

Embouchure plate · Mouth hole

Reinforcing ring

Body tenon

Cork strip

1st finger hole

Body joint

Head joint

Tuning cork

Tuning cork controls pitch.

⁷⁄₁₆

¹¹⁄₁₆

⁵⁄₈

⁶⁄₁₆

¹¹⁄₁₆-in. bore diameter

Mouth-hole cross section at center

Fig. 3: Three setups for boring on the lathe

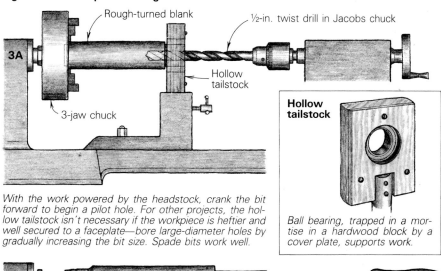

Rough-turned blank

½-in. twist drill in Jacobs chuck

3A

3-jaw chuck

Hollow tailstock

Hollow tailstock

Ball bearing, trapped in a mortise in a hardwood block by a cover plate, supports work.

With the work powered by the headstock, crank the bit forward to begin a pilot hole. For other projects, the hollow tailstock isn't necessary if the workpiece is heftier and well secured to a faceplate—bore large-diameter holes by gradually increasing the bit size. Spade bits work well.

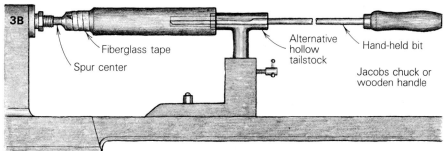

3B

Fiberglass tape

Spur center

Alternative hollow tailstock

Hand-held bit

Jacobs chuck or wooden handle

*Bore a full-length pilot hole with a hand-held shell auger. The author uses the chuck and tailstock shown in step **A**, but the setup shown in **B** will work too (see box, p. 66). As explained in the main text, full diameter is next bored with a hand-held Planetor bit, following the pilot hole.*

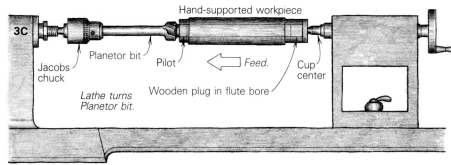

Hand-supported workpiece

3C

Jacobs chuck

Planetor bit

Pilot

Feed.

Cup center

Lathe turns Planetor bit.

Wooden plug in flute bore

To slightly enlarge the bore to accept the body tenon, fit a Planetor bit with a pilot that matches the bore diameter, then crank the work forward into the bit's cutting spurs. A piloted spade bit will also enlarge holes, but may split thin-walled turnings.

Bored and turned on the lathe, this 19-in. rosewood flute (left) has ends and center joint reinforced by rings of water buffalo horn. To make a flute, a ½-in. dia. pilot hole is first bored with the 30-in. long shell auger (bottom), which cuts into end grain without wandering. The Planetor bit (center) follows the pilot hole by means of a shopmade center insert, a wooden or metal plug turned to fit the pilot hole. The coiled spring ejects chips. Both bits are hand-held and fed into the work as it turns.

speed, about 750 RPM, I crank the tailstock forward to drill a 2-in. deep hole. The rigidity of the tailstock ensures that the hole starts straight. Then I remove the tailstock from the lathe bed.

To bore the full length, I use two specialized bits, shown in the photo at the bottom of these pages. Unless the wood grain is particularly uneven, a shell auger will bore a long, straight hole without wandering. Once started into the pilot hole, it cuts on-center, aligning itself with the stationary centerpoint of the turning work. As shown in figure 3B, the bit is held freehand, not in the tailstock chuck, and is pushed into the work in short steps. Feeding the bit into the wood by hand is a great pleasure, and not nearly as difficult as it may sound. Withdraw the bit from time to time to clear the chips, and be careful that you don't get the bit so hot that its cutting edge loses its temper. This full-length hole is the pilot for the final bore.

To bore to full diameter, I use an ¹¹⁄₁₆-in. Planetor bit, which has an 18-in. shank and a coiled chip ejector. My model is an older one, but you can still get the equivalent from the source listed at the end of this article. The Planetor bit is also hand-held, but for a better grip I tighten it into a Jacobs chuck. This completes the boring in the body joint, but the head joint still requires a socket to accept the tenon on the body.

To make the socket, I bore from the headstock end, as shown in figure 3C. I remove the 3-jaw chuck and install a ½-in. Jacobs chuck, fitted with a short 1-in. Planetor bit with an ¹¹⁄₁₆-in. pilot center. I remove the hollow tailstock and remount the regular tailstock, fitted with a cup center. To center the flute blank on the tailstock, I push a hardwood plug into the end of the bore. The tailstock should be adjusted so that the blank is supported by the Planetor bit's pilot, but not pressed against the cutting spurs. With the lathe at its slowest speed, I support the blank with my left hand and slowly turn the tailstock crank to push the blank ⅞ in. into the bit. This completes the head-joint boring.

Turning the outside on a mandrel—
To turn the outside of the flute, I support the blank on a mandrel, a rod that extends through the blank and projects an inch or more at each end. I make mandrels from birch dowels, turning them down until they make a snug sliding fit in the bore. Better a little loose than too tight, so occasionally I use some thin paper or wooden shims between the mandrel and the blank, taking care that the mandrel is centered in the bore.

To help protect the ends of the flute from splitting, you may want to add reinforcing rings, which also provide a visual transition between the sections. I used water buffalo horn on the flute shown here, but rings can also be made from brass tubing, soldered silver sheet, or cow horn. To make them from brass tubing, mount the tube on a mandrel on the lathe, and with a jewelers' saw, saw off as many rings as you need. Rings should be put onto the blanks before the outside profile is turned. Cut a seat into the blank to fit the inner diameter of the ring, apply some glue, and

tap the ring into place. Horn rings are fitted oversize, then turned down at the same time as the blank.

Turn the tenon on the body so that it makes a good sliding fit in the head-joint socket. To ensure an airtight seal, I glue a ½-in. wide strip of cork in a shallow groove around the tenon. Bevel one end of the cork strip so that the joint overlaps, apply yellow glue, and clamp with a rubber band. When the glue is dry, carefully sand the strip down while the body is turning. When checking the fit, apply a little cork grease (available from any music store) for lubrication. Otherwise, the fit will end up too loose.

Next I turn the outside profile of the flute. Pay careful attention to the diameters in figure 1, because they determine final wall thickness. If you'd like a raised mouthpiece, called an embouchure plate, which some people feel makes a flute easier to play, turn the area oversize and carve away the unwanted wood by hand before sanding. Sand and polish the flute with progressively finer grades of paper, finishing with a worn 600-grit. Final polishing is done with the grain, with the motor off. After I have polished the flute sections, I make the end cap, a short section that slides snugly into the top end of the

Fig 4: Drilling guide

Measurements from bottom end to center of:		Approx. dia. after shaping and tuning
Mouth hole	15 14/32	oval
6th finger hole	8 31/32	6/16
5th finger hole	7 22/32	5/16
4th finger hole	6 16/32	5/16
3rd finger hole	5 5/32	4/16
2nd finger hole	4 6/32	6/16
1st finger hole	2 23/32	5/16

head joint. It, too, has a cork inlay, and can be topped off by turning a short ornamental end. All of the sections can now be put together. Remember to use a liberal amount of cork grease, and don't force the fit, or the socket may split. If the socket is too tight, carefully sand or file the cork.

The holes—Measuring as shown in figure 4, and keeping the mouth hole and finger holes in a straight line, mark and indent the center of each hole. To prevent tearout, insert a softwood dowel in the bore before you drill. To drill the mouth hole, support the head joint in a V-block or a handscrew on the drill-press table, and use a ⅜-in. brad-point bit. To ensure that the hole will be in the right place, align the point of the bit with the mark on the blank, and clamp things down before you drill. Change to a ¼-in. bit and drill the finger holes.

I undercut and shape the mouth hole with round files and narrow knife blades. Figure 2 on p. 193 shows a typical cross-section at the center of the hole. I prefer an oval mouth hole, but its shape has been a subject of debate throughout the flute's history. Most mouth holes are undercut on the edge against which your airstream is directed, although the amount of undercutting is again a matter of preference. I feel that too little angle rather than too much is better, to achieve maximum control and flexibility in playing. The finger holes, too, will require undercutting and enlarging for the flute to play in tune.

After the holes are drilled, sand the bore. I slit a dowel, slip the edge of a sandpaper strip into it and wrap the paper around the dowel. You can use the sanding rod manually or chucked in the lathe headstock, using progressively finer grits to produce a smooth bore.

Next make the tuning cork, which blocks the tube just above the mouth hole and controls the pitch. First, run a

Some low-tech boring setups

The simplest hollow tailstock consists of a copper-pipe T-fitting, as shown in figure 3B on p. 193, supported by the toolrest base. To make the blank fit it, bore a shallow seating hole, the outer diameter of the pipe, in the end of the blank, using a spade bit. An electric drill will be accurate enough. Lubricate the seat with spray silicone once in a while as it turns. Silicone will penetrate the wood and interfere with any finish you apply, so to prevent problems, cut off the end of the blank after boring. Chances are that the first couple of inches of the bore will be enlarged because of the number of times you have to remove and reinsert the bit, so you should plan some extra length to be cut off anyway.

The copper won't be stiff enough to hold the blank firmly against a spur center in the headstock, but if you rough-turn the end round and tape it to the headstock with fiberglass tape, the setup will work without a 3-jaw chuck.

Extra-long twist bits (bellhangers' bits) are no substitute for a shell auger.

Twist bits wander when boring end grain, and you will scrap a lot of blanks before you get a straight hole. Twist drills can enlarge a pilot hole, however, working up bit by bit until the bore is full-size. A series of larger and larger spade bits with extensions could also be used. Extend a spade bit for light-duty boring by lapping and silver-soldering it to ¼-in. steel rod stock. This modified spade bit has the advantage of being able to bore a long hole without clogging on its own chips, which twist bits invariably do. Clamp vise-grips to the end of the rod as a handle, and mark any long bit so that you don't bore too far. There's nothing quite like the sound of a shell auger jamming into the spur center—expensive "music."

Another way, adequate for shorter holes, calls for spade bits in a Jacobs chuck in the headstock. Leave the blank square. Clamp blocks to the tool rest to form a support track that will let you move the work into the bit by advancing the tailstock.   —W.F.

Playing the flute

Some people produce a sound the first time they try, others may have to practice for days. Blowing across, not into, the mouth hole (as in blowing across a bottle top) causes the stream of air to be split by the opposite edge of the hole, creating the tone. By slightly rolling the mouth hole toward or away from your lips, you can hear the tone become clearer, then fade. Aim the airstream carefully, and use the least amount of air that will produce a strong, clear tone.

When you can confidently produce a tone, try playing a scale. Be sure the pads of your fingers completely cover the finger holes. The fingering chart shows a major scale as Do, Re, Mi, with sharps and flats between. Another way to play sharps and flats is by covering only half of the finger hole. The second octave is fingered the same, but with more air pressure. You can add color and variety by rolling or sliding your fingers off a hole, a more advanced technique that allows you to subtly change the pitch of any note.   —W.F.

Freegard and wife, Nanita, show correct hand and mouth positions for flute-playing.

Fig. 5: Fingering chart, chromatic scale

		Do	Re		Mi	Fa		Sol		La		Ti	Do
Left hand	1st finger	●	●	●	●	●	●	●	●	●	●	○	○	○
	2nd finger	●	●	●	●	●	●	●	●	○	○	●	○	●
	3rd finger	●	●	●	●	●	●	○	○	●	○	○	○	●
Right hand	1st finger	●	●	●	●	●	●	○	●	○	○	○	○	●
	2nd finger	●	●	●	○	○	○	○	○	○	●	○	●	●
	3rd finger	●	◐	○	●	○	○	○	○	○	●	○	○	●

pencil point around the top inside edge of the bore, and then press the head joint against the end of a ⅝-in. long piece of bottle cork. The graphite will leave a mark of the bore's diameter. With a knife, shave the cork around the pencil line, test it for fit, then push it into place, ¹¹⁄₁₆ in. from the center of the mouth hole. Once the cork is in place, you should be able to get a clean, flute-like tone by blowing across the mouth hole. The tone will be much improved when you oil the flute—use a light, non-toxic oil (such as mineral oil or safflower oil), and be sure to wipe off all the excess, so that there is no oil buildup.

The tuning process may sound mysterious and complicated, but it is neither if done methodically. We have deliberately drilled undersized holes, because it's best to tune each note by enlarging the hole, rather than by constricting it by adding substances such as beeswax.

It may take some practice to produce a clear, reliable tone, necessary for tuning your instrument. Refer to the playing instructions in the box above, and if you are still uncertain, enlist the aid of a flute-playing friend. If you can't hear when the flute is in tune, try playing the scale along with a well-tuned piano, another instrument or an electronic tuner.

With all of the sections together, the tonic note (all six finger holes covered), G in this case, should be in tune, while the finger holes will sound flat in various degrees. If the tonic note itself is flat, you can sharpen it by flaring the end of the tube up to the first finger hole. If the note is sharp, pull out the tenon a little. Start the finger-hole tuning at the bottom hole (A) and slowly work your way up the scale, playing back and forth to recheck previous tuning. In the first octave, enlarge the diameter of each hole to sharpen the pitch. Undercutting the inside edge of a hole will also sharpen the pitch, and help the response of a sluggish note, but this is best saved for tuning the second octave. As a tuning overview, leave the third hole from the bottom (C) small. The two holes you will have to enlarge the most are the second finger holes on both hands—B on the right hand, E on the left.

Tuning the two octaves together is called the fine-tuning, and is done completely with undercutting after the first octave is in tune. Undercutting the upper edge of a hole raises the pitch for the first and second octaves; undercutting the lower edge raises the pitch in the second octave, and has only a very slight effect in the first octave. This is especially helpful since the second octave tends to be flatter in general than the first. If

you remove too much wood, add a little beeswax. Heat the tip of a nail, melt a drop of wax with it, and transfer the wax to the rim of the hole.

Lightly oil the wood once or twice a year so it doesn't dry out, and try to keep the flute from extremes of temperature and humidity. After playing, gently swab the moisture from the bore. If you leave the flute assembled for too long a period, the tenon cork may become compressed, loosening the fit. A remedy is to dampen the cork and heat it briefly with a match, but be careful not to scorch it.   □

Sources

Shell augers: Woodcraft Supply, 41 Atlantic Ave., PO Box 4000, Woburn, Mass. 01888. About $30.

Planetor bits: Rule Industries, Cape Ann Industrial Park, Gloucester, Mass. 01930, (617) 281-0440. Catalog PB-83.
  Bore—P-69L (12-in. shaft with chip ejector), ¹¹⁄₁₆-in. dia., $22.50; 5½-in. shank extension XJ-55, $5.75.
  Socket—P-100 (1-in. dia. bit), $12.75; 3½-in. shank SB-35, $5.35.

Sheet cork: International Violin Company, Ltd., 4026 West Belvedere Ave., Baltimore, Md. 21215.

Water buffalo horn: Don Kostecki, 6245 N. Fairfield, Chicago, Ill. 60659.

Plans for a High-Chair/Rocker
Two chairs for the price of one

by R.W. Swinyard

"Dad, will you make us a high chair for Aimee?"

A few months after the birth of my first grandchild, my daughter, Linda, made that request in a phone call from Maryland. What proud grandparent would be able to refuse? This maple high-chair/rocker is the result. I built two bases, one for the high chair and another for the rocker, so Aimee will get a few more years' use out of the piece. When either base is detached from the seat, the chair fits easily into the backseat of a small car.

In this article, I'll tell how I use an auxiliary tilted table on my drill press to angle the holes so that all the chair's parts go together. I always test-assemble the parts as I go. Each part in a chair affects the next, and going piece-by-piece gives me a chance to make small changes if necessary.

The auxiliary table is a ramp that tilts the part being drilled to the correct angle. Mine, shown in figure 2 on the facing page, is a piece of plywood about 8 in. by 10 in. I tilt it simply by tacking plywood shims to its back edge. To check the angle, I line up the auxiliary table's centerline under the bit and aim it at the center of the drill-press column. Then I set a T-bevel between the centerline and the column, and verify the angle with a protractor. The various angles at which to tilt the table are shown in the drawings.

Many of the holes are at compound angles, that is, they appear to lean in two directions, one from the front view, the other from the side. I drill such holes in two ways. The cleats at the top of the rocker base illustrate one way. As shown at right, the rocker legs radiate from the cleats at 13° in side view and at 11° in front view. I raise the auxiliary table to the 13° angle by tacking shims under it at the back, then I block up one side of the table to 11°, the second angle. This tilts the workpiece in two directions at once. A second way—which I use to drill the holes in the seat for the back corner

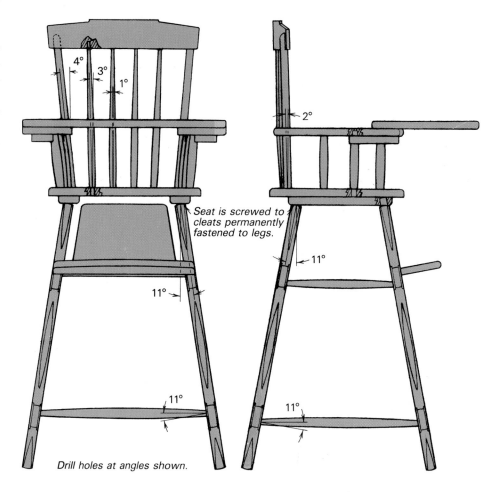

Fig. 1: High chair converts to rocker

The same seat can be screwed to two different bases to extend the life of the chair.

Seat is screwed to cleats permanently fastened to legs.

Drill holes at angles shown.

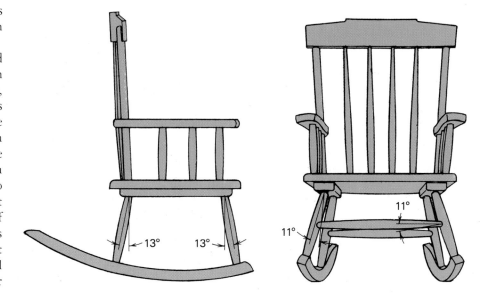

posts—is to determine the axis line along which the "compound angles" actually become a single angle (for more on axis lines, see pp. 74-79). In the finished chair seat, for instance, the back corner posts show a 4° tilt in front view and a 2° tilt in side view. You can get the posts to align with these angles by drilling a 6° hole as shown in figure 2. The axis line is shown as line A on the seat plan in figure 3.

An axis line, whether it be the angled line on the seat or merely the centerline of the part itself—as when drilling the legs—must point in the same direction as the table's centerline, or the angle will not be correct. As an aid in positioning the workpiece, line up the auxiliary table's centerline directly under the bit and point it at the center of the drill-press column. Then when you position the axis line on the workpiece under the bit and point it at the column, the part will be positioned correctly.

Some parts can lie flat on the auxiliary table when being drilled, but others will need extra support. The chair's crest rail can be braced against a block to keep it steady. Round parts, such as the rocker legs, ought to be clamped in a handscrew, and so should the rockers themselves. Spade bits work fine for the through holes, and machine-spur bits or Forstner bits are good for the blind ones.

First lay out the seat as in the drawing and drill the back corner post holes. Next turn the corner posts to the size shown in figure 7 on p. 199, which contains dimensions for most of the other chair turnings as well. The two crucial diameters are the ¾-in. tenon for the seat and the ⅞-in. diameter that fits the hole in the armrest. One way to size tenons is to caliper the diameter of the drill bit that will cut the mortise, then use the calipers to check the size of the tenon while it's still on the lathe. Some experimentation will show you the tolerances you should allow with your particular set of bits. Aim for a snug not a force fit. Set the posts in the seat and make the armrest blanks (oversize for the time being: ¾x3x14½), but don't drill the other holes in the seat yet.

For each armrest to fit over its corner post, the hole in it must be drilled at the correct angle and orientation. In your mind's eye, slide the armrest down the post until it lies flat on the seat and parallel to the seat's edge. Notice that the

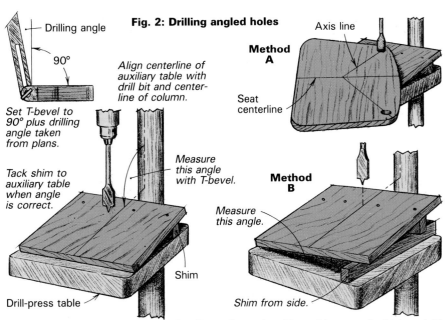

Fig. 2: Drilling angled holes

Drilling angle
90°

Set T-bevel to 90° plus drilling angle taken from plans.

Align centerline of auxiliary table with drill bit and centerline of column.

Tack shim to auxiliary table when angle is correct.

Measure this angle with T-bevel.

Drill-press table

Shim

Axis line

Method A

Seat centerline

Method B

Measure this angle.

Shim from side.

When the plans call for a single angle, shim a plywood auxiliary table as required (above left). Compound angles can be drilled in two ways. **Method A:** A single 6° hole drilled on the axis line (line A in the seat plan below) yields an approximate tilt of 2° in side view and 4° in front view. **Method B:** First shim the table up to one angle, then shim the side to the other.

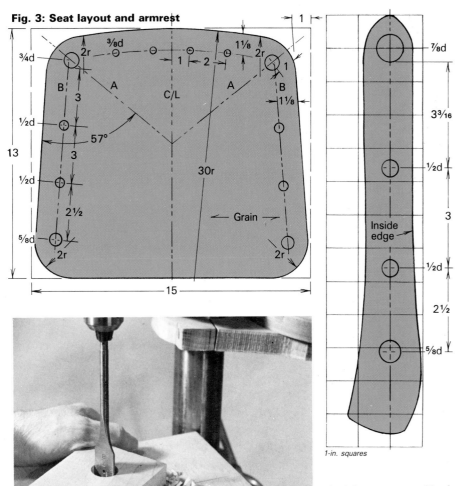

Fig. 3: Seat layout and armrest

At left, an armrest blank is drilled to fit over its corner post, as explained in the text. Imagine that the seat blank is still on the auxiliary table, with its axis line over the table's centerline. The armrest must be aligned with the seat's edge, radiating out at the 57° angle shown in figure 3.

197

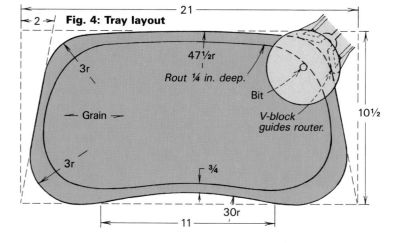

Fig. 4: Tray layout

21
2
47½r
Rout ¼ in. deep.
3r
Grain
Bit
V-block guides router.
10½
3r
¾
11
30r

Cut the tray to shape, then rout the dish's outline with a core-box bit, guiding the router with a V-block as shown in figure 4. Next rout out the center with a straight bit (photo above), leaving bridges to support the router. Then chisel these away and sand.

hole in the armrest lines up exactly with the angle of the hole in the seat. Now imagine that the seat is still on the auxiliary table, and that you have just drilled the corner post hole. If you were to raise the quill and lay the armrest blank in position flat on the seat, you could drill the hole. But this would risk damaging the seat beneath if anything shifted. So instead, you can mark the correct position for the arm on the auxiliary table, and drill the hole as shown in the photo on p. 197.

To determine where to mark the correct position for the armrest on the table, refer to the seat plan in figure 3. There is a 57° angle marked between the axis line on the seat and the centerline of the armrest. When the back corner post hole was being drilled, the axis line on the seat was directly over the centerline of the auxiliary table. The armrest's centerline must therefore be turned 57° from the auxiliary table's centerline when you drill the hole.

Also, as you slide the armrest up and down the post, the higher it is, the farther it moves back in relation to the seat. Consider the arm spindles. I've designed them to be perpendicular to the seat in side view, as shown in figure 1, not to tilt back the way the back corner posts do. I therefore had to compensate for the armrest's backward displacement by offsetting the arm spindle holes farther forward from the corner post hole in the armrest than they are in the seat. I made a trial assembly and found that the offset, measured along the centerline of the armrest, was ³⁄₁₆ in., and this is the amount shown in figure 3.

Next verify the angle for the arm

The armrests slip into blocks glued to the bottom of the tray and are locked by clamping levers (photo above, plan below). The legs (bottom of page) are sawn square and centered in the lathe. After the tenon at the tailstock end has been turned, the leg is removed and its corners rounded with the router. Back in the lathe, each leg is then turned to the shape shown, with 'squares' where the rung mortises will be drilled.

Fig. 5: Tray clamp and crest rail

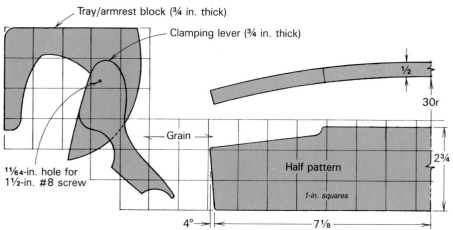

Tray/armrest block (¾ in. thick)
Clamping lever (¾ in. thick)
½
30r
Grain
2¾
Half pattern
1-in. squares
¹¹⁄₆₄-in. hole for 1½-in. #8 screw
4°
7⅛

Fig. 6: High-chair legs and footrest

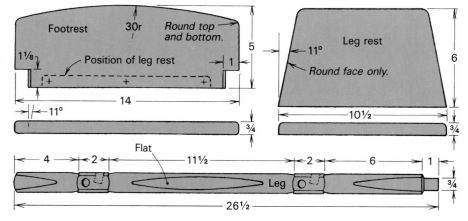

Footrest
30r
Round top and bottom.
1⅛
Position of leg rest
1
5
Leg rest
11°
Round face only.
6
14
11°
10½
¾
¾
Flat
4
2
11½
2
6
1
Leg
¾
26½

198

spindle holes. I used a T-bevel, with its handle perpendicular to line B in figure 3, to check that the angle of slant of the corner post in that plane was the 4° the drawing indicated it should be. It was, so I shimmed the auxiliary table to suit, drilling all holes in both arm-rests to a depth of ⅝ in. Then I drilled the matching holes through the seat.

I bandsawed the curves on both arm-rests according to the pattern in figure 3. Figure 5 and the bottom photo on the facing page show how the tray bottom locks into the front end of the armrest.

To drill the seat for the back center spindles, first shim the auxiliary table to 2°, the backward tilt of the spindles, then block it up to the necessary side angles, which are shown in figure 1. The crest-rail blank should be tilted only toward the sides of the chair when you're drilling the holes in it, so it will follow the 2° backward tilt of the corner posts.

I test-assembled everything, sanded away all machine marks, rounded the edges with the router where appropriate, and plugged the screw heads. Then I made the tray as shown in figure 4 and the photo at the top of the facing page, and I turned the legs as illustrated in figure 6. I made the footrest and the leg rest to the shapes shown.

For the final base assembly, I attached the footrest and the lower front rung to the legs first, so I could drive the screws holding the footrest with a brace and screwdriver bit. I assembled the back next, then the sides, using web clamps to hold the frame together while the glue dried, and checking for square-ness with a framing square.

Keep in mind that the chair seat will be screwed to the tops of the cleats. During glue-up, be sure that the top surface of both cleats lies in the same flat plane. You can check this by laying a pair of straightedges from cleat to cleat and sighting along them, then working the cleats into proper alignment. The same concern applies to the rocker base.

When all was done, I applied two coats of urethane varnish to the chair, the base and the rocker, and gave the tray three coats of Constantine's Bowl Seal.

There's one necessary item not shown in the drawings—a safety strap that's fastened under the seat. □

R.W. Swinyard is a retired industrial arts teacher from Kinderhook, N.Y. Photos by the author.

Fig. 7: Rockers, spindles, cleats and rungs

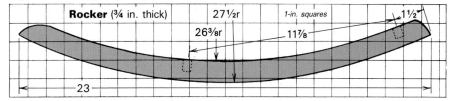

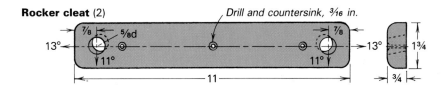

Rocker-base turnings

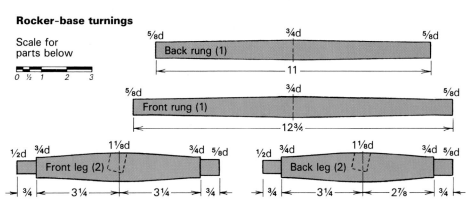

Rocker cleat (2)   *Drill and countersink, 3/16 in.*

Chair-seat turnings

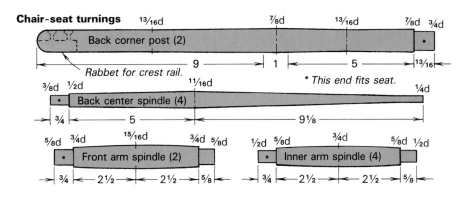

High-chair cleat (2)   *Drill and countersink, 3/16 in.*

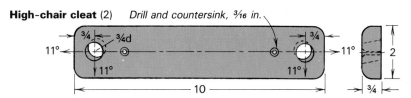

High-chair rungs

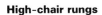

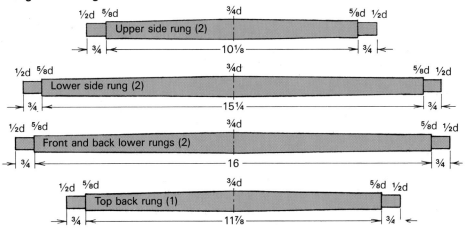

Inventing the Coffee Table

Antique tray generates a mahogany "reproduction"

by Eugene Landon

Though I am committed to producing exact American reproductions, I'm sometimes required to make a furniture form that simply did not exist in the 18th century. Recently a client approached me with a mahogany tray, a family heirloom, and asked if somehow it could be used to make a coffee table that would blend with her 18th-century home and other period furniture.

More than likely, the tray was not meant originally to be used as a service tray: it has through dovetails at the corners, and the practice in the 18th century was to hide the joinery. Perhaps it might have been a linen tray from inside a cabinet, where it would have been out of sight behind the doors. The tray's dimensions dictated the size of the tabletop. I stepped the rails back from that, made them 2½ in. deep, a typical size, and chose a table height of 17 in., which would match the usual height for a chair seat.

Despite the fact that there was no original to copy, I still like to call this table a reproduction, because I made it the same way a cabinetmaker would have made it then. The top, for instance, is held on with glue blocks all around. Admittedly, it may split; a lot of tops secured in this manner did, and a lot of them didn't. As far as I'm concerned, it would be nice if it did split, because it then would look old and would be a better match for the tray itself, which is split in two places. For me, doing the job right means doing it the way it would have been done originally—that's implicit in the definition of the word "reproduction." An "adaptation" is something entirely different, where one can certainly try to improve on the old methods and designs. I'm not saying you'll succeed, but you can try. Just remember that for anything you gain, there is something you can lose.

The drawback in making a tray table this long is that its tray is a bit unwieldy to carry through standard doorways. The table's size, however, is properly proportioned to go with most period sofas, and I wouldn't make it too much shorter, because it will lose some of its presence. I also recommend that you retain the lower side on the front of the tray. It gives the table an orientation, thereby adding to its character.

I'd build this table out of mahogany, walnut or cherry, since those were the woods most often used in the 18th century. Even a nice piece of curly maple could be another possibility. There are other options as well. The legs are straight Chippendale, but they could have fretwork knee blocks and other fancy decoration. The stretchers could be more elaborate and pierced, and the rails could be pierced and gadrooned, too. To focus attention on my client's antique tray, I wanted the emphasis placed on it rather than on the table. I guess you could call the effect "country high style."

When building the tray, you can make through dovetails or blind ones, whichever you prefer. For the handle cutouts, drill pairs of large holes, cut between them with a fretsaw, then round all the edges. I attached the bottom with counter-sunk flathead screws, just as the original bottom was attached with handmade ones.

For the table itself, I first cut the leg blanks and the mortises. When laying out the mortises, plan for a shoulder at the top of the rail so that the leg has some strength. The sides also should have shoulders, but you don't need one at the bottom. After making the mortises, I chamfered the inner corners of the legs. Next, I planed the flutes in the legs with an old wooden fluting plane, but you could make them with a router, drill press, tablesaw or carving tools. I like the plane because it always leaves a slight irregularity. This is very difficult to see straight-on, but if you look down the length of the leg, you will be able to spot a little wander. If the legs are too perfect, they won't look right, lacking that very subtle 18th-century character. The same goes for all of the table's rounded edges. It is best to plane them by hand, and where the plane won't reach, pare them with a chisel.

When making the rails, miter the ends of the tenons so that each has the greatest possible purchase to the mortise, but don't allow the tenons to butt against each other. You have to leave some room so that the leg can shrink without splitting.

To make the joint in the middle of the stretchers, I scribed the lines with a knife, cut inside them with a fine-tooth tenon saw, then pared with a chisel to the final fit. Notice how the overlap is offset to leave plenty of material in one stretcher for strength. Cut the tenon shoulders to match the chamfer angle on the legs. Make the tenons a little bit short at first, to establish the angle, then pare the shoulders back to fit.

I left the tray its natural color after stripping and cleaning it, and I stained the rest of the table to match by rubbing in stains and dry powders. The finish is shellac, rubbed on with a rag and some linseed oil—the usual French polish. There was a big dark stain in the center of the tray—a typical sign of an old accident, old age, so I left it. Sometimes I'll add black streaks and marks to pieces, but nothing that would be too noticeable. When I make a reproduction, I expect that my client will be able to set it down in the middle of a room full of 18th-century furniture and have it disappear. This takes a little work. I have a friend who wanted to learn woodworking. So I got him into my shop every Friday from four in the afternoon until about eleven, and we each made identical pie safes. Finally the pieces were done, and it came time to do the antiquing. I handed him a chain and said, "Go to it," and he handed it right back and said, "You first, I can't bear it." So I started beating up my cabinet, then I kicked it across the room until I could hear it crack. I said, "Now we're getting there . . ." And pretty soon he got the idea. You can use your own judgment, but remember that many old pieces have led a hard life, and look it. □

Gene Landon makes and restores period furniture in Montoursville, Pa. He wrote about tall-case clocks in FWW #26.

Mahogany table with tray

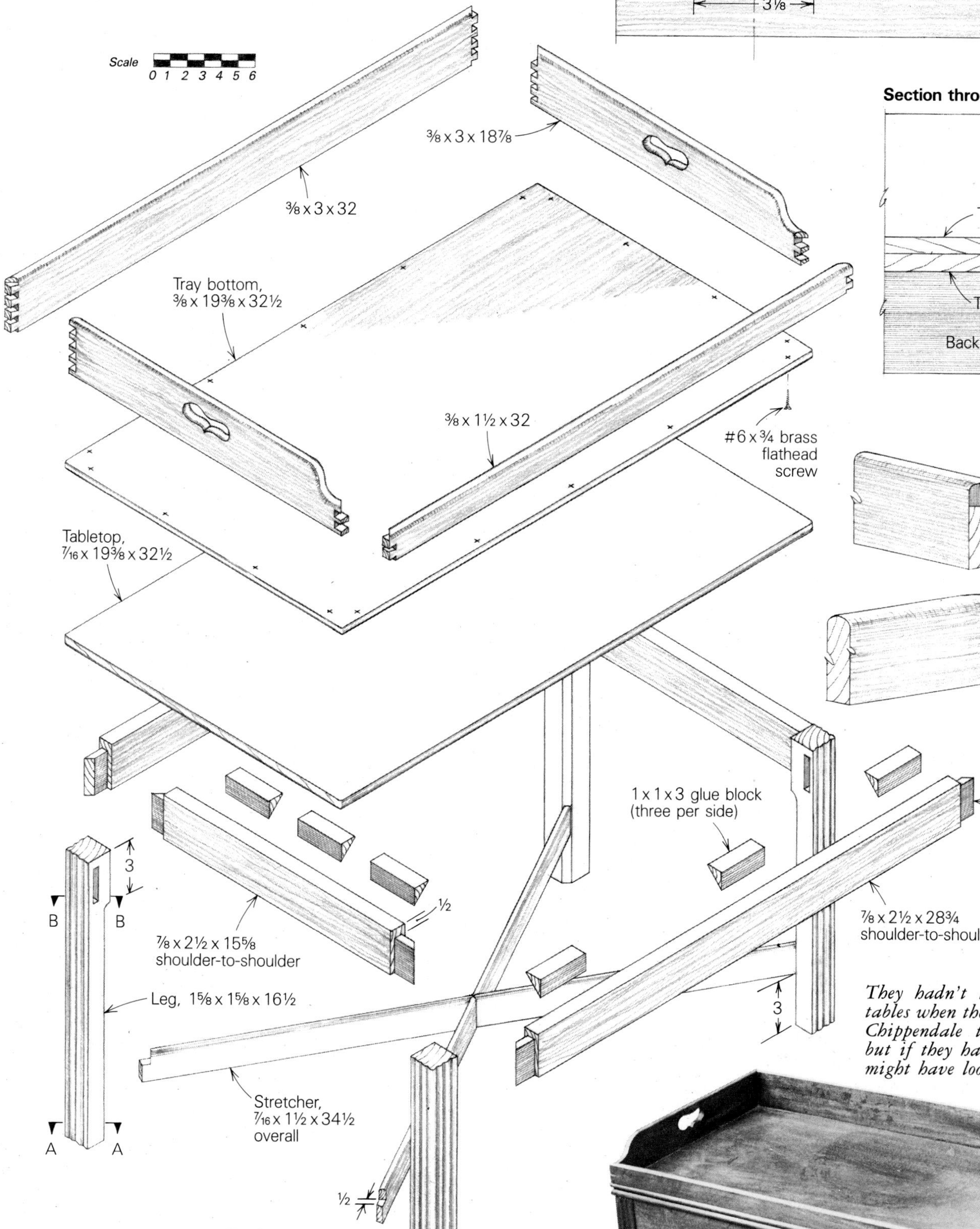

Scale
0 1 2 3 4 5 6
⅜ x 3 x 32
⅜ x 3 x 18⅞
Tray bottom,
⅜ x 19⅜ x 32½
⅜ x 1½ x 32
#6 x ¾ brass
flathead
screw
Tabletop,
7⁄16 x 19⅜ x 32½
1 x 1 x 3 glue block
(three per side)
1¼-in. tenon
3
B
B
½
⅞ x 2½ x 15⅝
shoulder-to-shoulder
⅞ x 2½ x 28¾
shoulder-to-shoulder
Leg, 1⅝ x 1⅝ x 16½
3
Stretcher,
7⁄16 x 1½ x 34½
overall
A
A
½

Detail of tray end

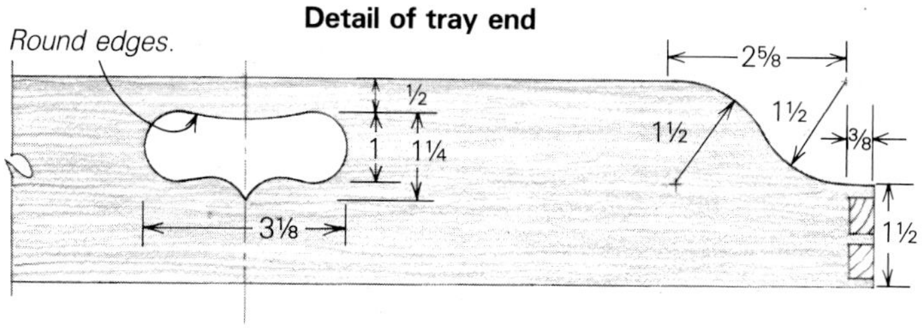

Round edges.
½
1
1¼
3⅛
2⅝
1½
1½
⅜
1½

Section through tray and table

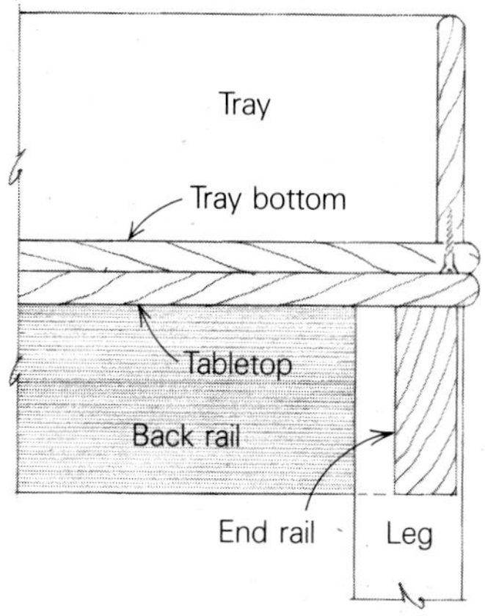

Tray
Tray bottom
Tabletop
Back rail
End rail
Leg

Detail of stretcher center joint

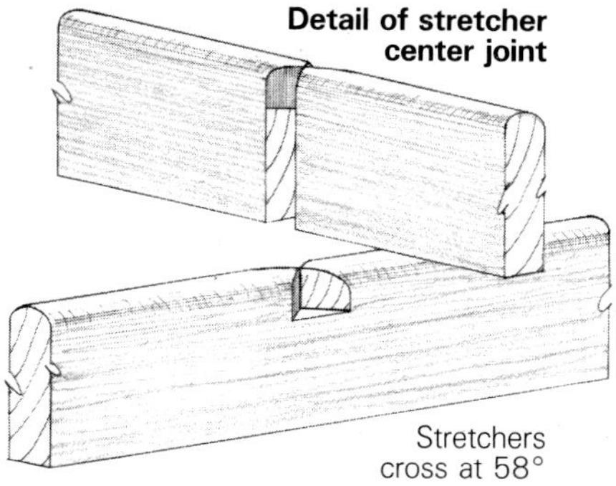

Stretchers
cross at 58°

Section A–A

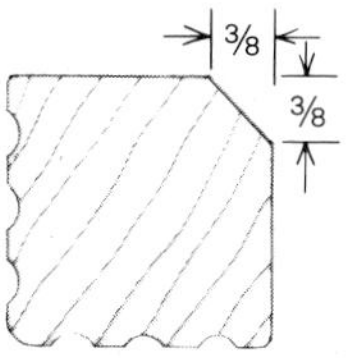

⅜
⅜

Section B–B

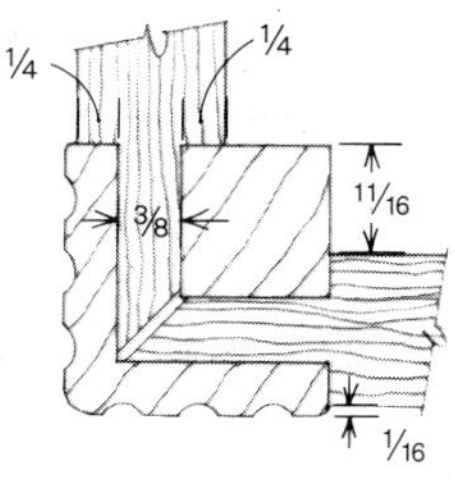

¼
¼
⅜
11⁄16
1⁄16

They hadn't thought of coffee tables when the tray half of this Chippendale table was made, but if they had, the table part might have looked like this.

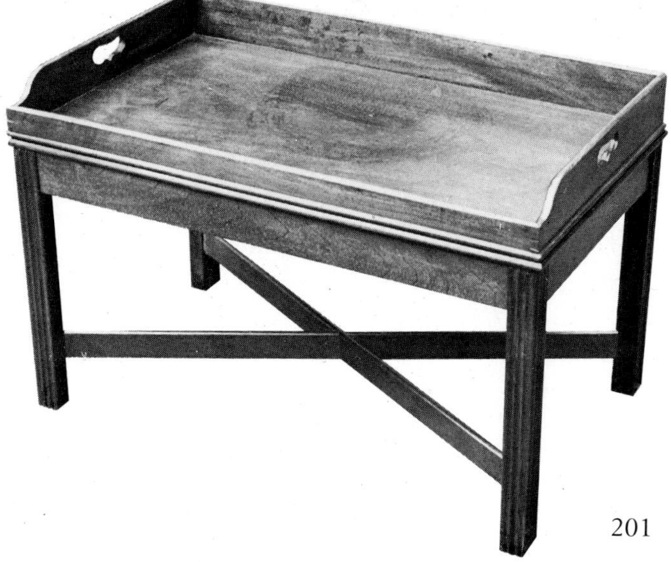

Drawing: Louis M. Bassler

Chippendale Sofa

Templates for the basic frame, and some design options

by Norman L. Vandal

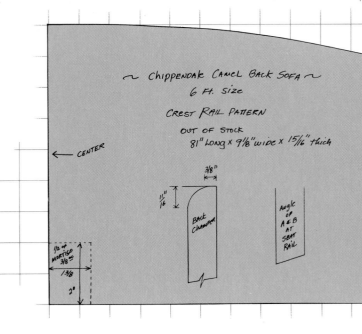

CHIPPENDALE CAMEL BACK SOFA
6 FT. SIZE
CREST RAIL PATTERN
OUT OF STOCK
81" LONG X 9⅛" WIDE X 1⁵⁄₁₆" thick

Any professional woodworker has to keep an eye on the market. Over the years I've earned a living making things that simply weren't available anywhere else, everything from period architectural components to period planes for restorers who wanted to stick their own moldings.

Many of my furniture customers come to me because of the double jeopardy of buying antiques: originals are not only very high in price, they may also be in very poor condition. In January 1983, for instance, a Philadelphia camelback sofa sold at Christie's, New York, for the record price of $264,000, even though it had some serious problems—amputated leg bottoms had been pieced in, the rear legs had been cut off and refastened, and the stretchers had been replaced. Keeping all this in mind, I thought it a good idea to add a camelback sofa to my designs.

I wanted to stay faithful to the lines and solid joinery of the originals, so I studied Chippendale sofas in museums and period-furniture books. Surprisingly, my best source turned out to be copies of *The Magazine Antiques.* Dealers like to sell furniture stripped of its upholstery to ensure buyers that it's original, and many of the ads showed the entire frame and the joinery. I saw that period cabinetmakers varied the shape of the legs, front seat rail and crest rail without changing the shape of the basic frame much. I figured that I could do the same for my customers, and build a good frame to sell for a little over a thousand dollars, which compares favorably in price with factory "reproductions," and, in my opinion, greatly surpasses them in quality.

Templates and variations—Joinery details are shown on the facing page. Sofas are not as difficult to make as they may

look. Unlike upholstered chair seats, which are always trapezoidal, sofa seats are rectangular. Thus a measured drawing of the frame's end view shows many parts in true dimension. With these parts as a starting point, I worked out a reliable set of templates, shown throughout this article, for the angled parts. The templates take care of the tricky problems, ensuring that everything will go together and stand square.

When building a sofa, you first make the end frames, which include the legs, end rails and side stretchers. Then you connect these with the seat rails, center and frame stretchers, and back frame, and finally you add the arms. In period sofas, there are variations in the arm roll and its supports, and I selected the system I felt worked best. The templates given here are for a New England style sofa with Marlborough legs, which can be blocked or left plain. Straight-leg sofas were the most numerous, exemplifying the Chinese influence in the Chippendale style. Yet the molded leg and the cabriole leg shown on p. 207 work just as well. For the Philadelphia look, as shown at left, the variations are simple: Marlborough legs, peaks on each side of the crest, and a serpentine front seat rail. You'll also find templates for the crest rail, vertical arm supports, and upholsterers' bar (the upright member underneath the arm at the back—it gives the upholsterer a surface around which to pull and tack the material).

Scale up the templates to full size, either by following the grid lines or by photo-enlarging them. I made the templates from heavy cardboard so I could cut them out and trace the parts directly from them. As you can see in the drawings, on my templates I've carefully laid out mortise and tenon dimensions and other useful information.

You don't need templates for the front and rear seat rails—just mark them out

Adapting the basic templates yields this Philadelphia-style sofa with serpentine front.

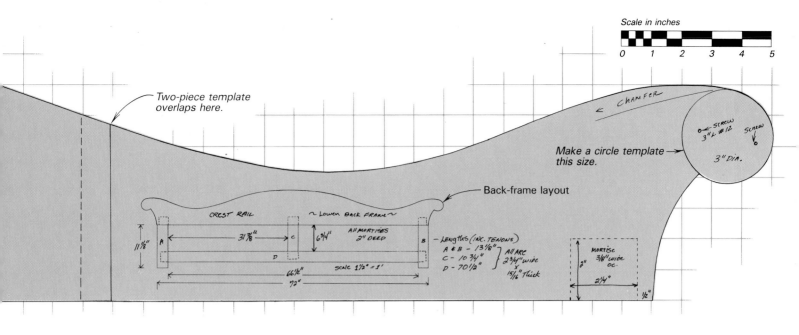

Two-piece template overlaps here.

Scale in inches
0 1 2 3 4 5

← CHAMFER

Make a circle template this size.

← SCREW 3"L. #12 SCREW
3" DIA.

Back-frame layout

CREST RAIL   ~ LOWER BACK FRAME ~

11⅛"

A   31⅞"   C   6¾"   ALL MORTISES 2" DEEP   B

D

66½"

72"   Scale 1½" = 1'

— LENGTHS (INC. TENONS)
A & B – 13⅛"
C – 10¾"   } ALL ARE
D – 70½"   2¾" WIDE × 15/16" THICK

MORTISE 3/8" WIDE O.C.

2"   2¼"   ½"

directly on the stock. (If you plan a serpentine front seat rail, of course, you'll have to work out a full-scale top-view template for the curve.) The center legs, front and back, fall exactly in the middle of the rails. As shown in the photo on p. 205, the front seat rail is one piece; the rear seat rail is two pieces, each tenoned into the back center leg, which needs to be full length to support the center of the back. In addition to the low stretcher between the center legs, an upper stretcher prevents the frame itself from spreading. This frame stretcher (which will be hidden by the upholstery) is tenoned off-center into the seat rails, so as not to weaken the legs. Locate it toward the bottom of the rails, where it will not interfere with the setting of upholstery springs. Original sofas didn't have springs, just webbing, but your upholsterer may suggest that the modern method is better. For more on upholstery and whether to agree with your upholsterer or not, see p. 206.

The tenons on the side stretchers have only one shoulder, at the outside. I make the center stretcher the same way, and offset the mortises in the center legs so the stretcher will be centered.

Materials—Most of the frame will be hidden by upholstery, and period cabinet-makers knew this full well. Legs, which showed, were top-grade wood. Mahogany predominated in Philadelphia; cherry was peculiar to Connecticut. Walnut was used in high-style pieces from all areas, and you'll find that the finest sofas, with formal Marlborough legs or ball-and-claw feet, are always mahogany or walnut. But secondary woods are another matter. I've seen seat frames made of maple and oak, and even chestnut in some New England examples. The back frames are usually of a softer wood, sometimes pine, although yellow-poplar or basswood holds the

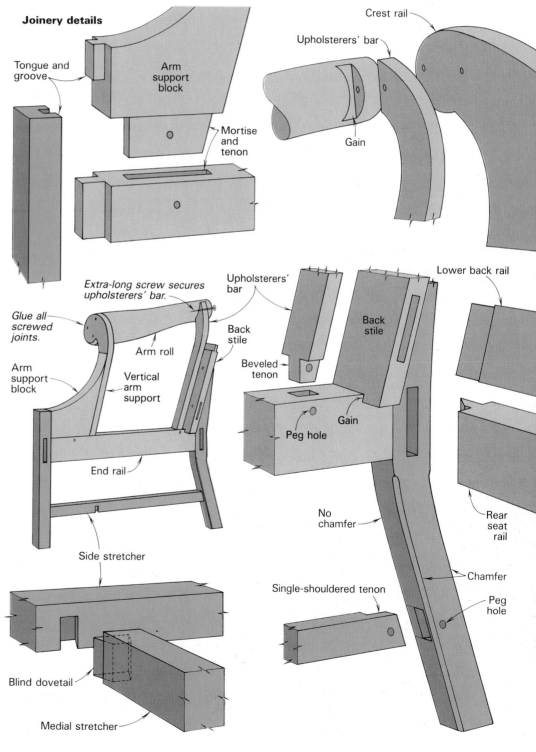

Joinery details

Tongue and groove

Arm support block

Mortise and tenon

Crest rail

Upholsterers' bar

Gain

Extra-long screw secures upholsterers' bar.

Glue all screwed joints.

Arm roll

Arm support block

Vertical arm support

End rail

Side stretcher

Blind dovetail

Medial stretcher

Upholsterers' bar

Back stile

Beveled tenon

Peg hole

Gain

No chamfer

Single-shouldered tenon

Lower back rail

Back stile

Rear seat rail

Chamfer

Peg hole

tacking better. If you can find it, soft maple is an excellent wood for the frame. Whatever you use, test some scraps, and avoid any wood you can't easily drive a tack into, or one that won't hold it well.

Arm rolls are always a soft wood, and pine or poplar is suitable. The vertical arm supports should be hardwood, but avoid woods such as oak or ash because they may split when the upholstery is tacked on. Curly maple would be my first choice here (somebody once suggested plywood, but it doesn't hold upholstery tacks well).

Construction—Many of my construction notes are shown on the templates, but here are some additional hints.

The tablesaw jigs shown in the photos below will help when cutting the back legs to shape. They ensure that the legs will match each other exactly and that the straight sections will be true.

Begin construction with the end frames. Before test-assembling them, cut all the joints shown on the end-rail and leg tem-

plates, and shape the legs and side stretchers. Then permanently assemble the end frames. The arm rolls, their support blocks and the vertical uprights will all be added later. Secure the tenons with pegs.

Trial-assemble the end frames to the front and rear seat rails and the center parts. Do any fitting of the joints now, making sure that the tenon shoulders are square and the mortises true. This will ensure that the frame assembles squarely when you're gluing up. Muster all your speed and dexterity and glue up the frame. I don't install the medial stretcher yet, but measure it off the frame and slip it up into the other stretchers from below as one of the last steps in construction (it has dovetails at each

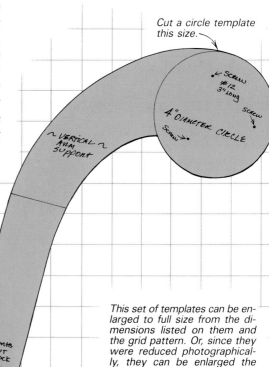

Cut a circle template this size.

SCREW #12 3" LONG

4" DIAMETER CIRCLE

SCREW

SCREW

~VERTICAL ARM SUPPORT~

This set of templates can be enlarged to full size from the dimensions listed on them and the grid pattern. Or, since they were reduced photographically, they can be enlarged the same way by a stat camera. Make them of heavy cardboard, add joinery details, and trace them directly on the stock.

Other dimensions:

Rear seat rails:
stock, 35⁷/₁₆ x 3 x 1³/₄; 33³/₈, shoulder-to-shoulder; tenons, ⁷/₈ long at center leg (butt), 1³/₁₆ long at end legs (mitered).

Front seat rail:
stock, 71¹/₈ x 3 x 1³/₄; 68¹/₂, shoulder-to-shoulder; tenons, 1³/₁₆ long (mitered); center-leg mortise, 1³/₄ long, ⁵/₈ wide (through, centered).

Center and side stretchers:
stock, 24¹³/₁₆ x 1¹/₄ x ¹⁵/₁₆; 22¹³/₁₆, from shoulder to long point of rear shoulder.

Medial stretcher:
stock, 72 x 1¹/₄ x ¹⁵/₁₆; scribe to fit.

Frame stretcher:
stock, 24 x 1³/₄ x 1¹/₂; scribe to fit during trial assembly.

Leg template also shows top of leg and mortises.

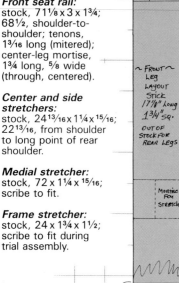

1¹/₂"

GROOVED
For arm support BLOCK
⁵/₈"

Mortise For Seat Rails ⁵/₈" wide 1³/₁₆" DEEP ON CENTER

~FRONT~ Leg Layout Stick 17⁷/₈" Long 1³/₄" SQ. OUT OF STOCK FOR REAR Legs

Mortise For Stretch.

TENON LAYOUT SEAT RAILS
TENONS ON CENTER
⁵/₈" 1³/₁₆"

~ARM SUPPORT~ BLOCK
two out of stock 1³/₄" thick 7" wide 20" long

TENON SHOULDER

~TENON~ 5/8" thick 4" Long 2" wide

TONGUE
REMOVE
REMOVE
90°

LOCATED ON CENTER OF 1³/₄ STOCK

two supports cut out of stock 21" long 8¹/₂" wide ⁷/₁₆" Thick

FRONT
Side VIEW

1³/₁₆" | 1³/₈" | 4"
TENON (FRONT LEG) SHOULDER
ARM SUPPORT Block MORTISE ⁵/₈" wide OR IN 1³/₄" RAIL
2"

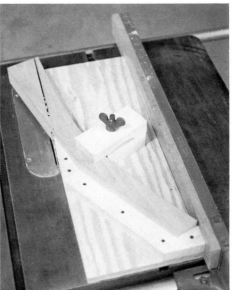

Tablesaw jigs position each rear leg exactly the same, ensuring that the frame will stand square.

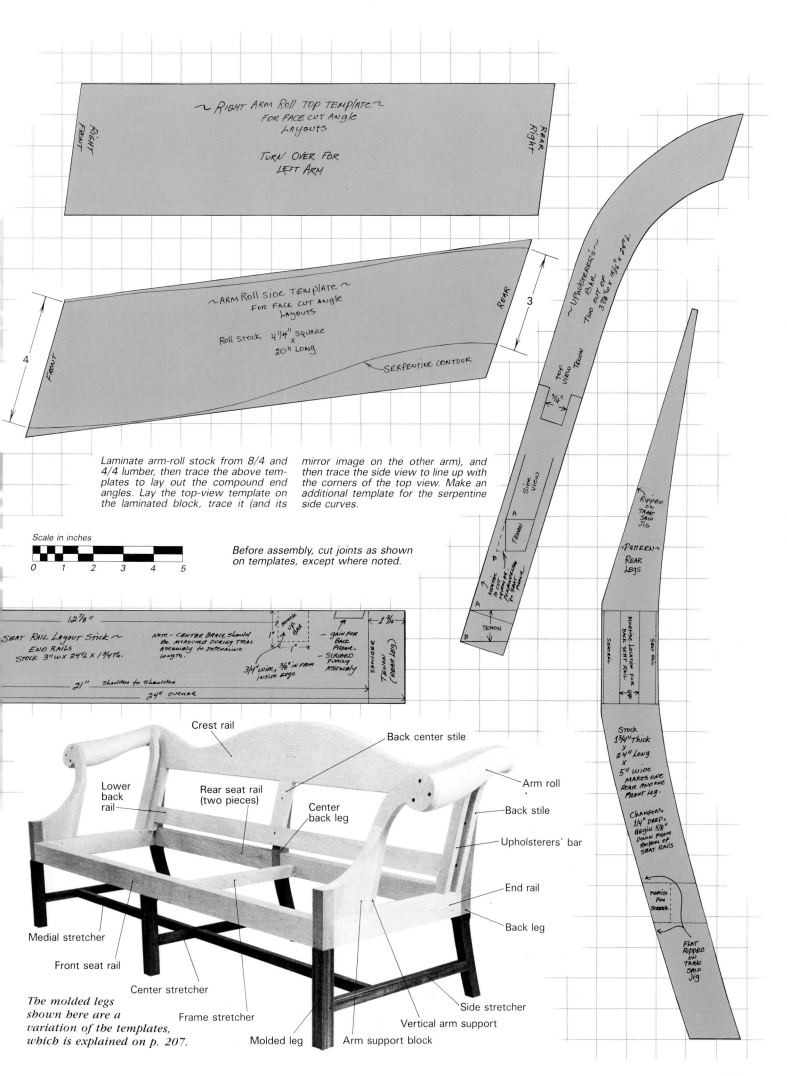

~ RIGHT ARM ROLL TOP TEMPLATE ~
FOR FACE CUT ANGLE
Layouts

TURN OVER FOR
LEFT ARM

RIGHT FRONT

REAR RIGHT

~ ARM ROLL SIDE TEMPLATE ~
FOR FACE CUT ANGLE
Layouts

Roll Stock 4 1/4" SQUARE
x
20" Long

FRONT

REAR

4

3

SERPENTINE CONTOUR

Laminate arm-roll stock from 8/4 and 4/4 lumber, then trace the above templates to lay out the compound end angles. Lay the top-view template on the laminated block, trace it (and its mirror image on the other arm), and then trace the side view to line up with the corners of the top view. Make an additional template for the serpentine side curves.

Scale in inches

0   1   2   3   4   5

Before assembly, cut joints as shown on templates, except where noted.

~ UPHOLSTERERS' BAR ~
Two out of 3 7/8"w x 15/16" x 24"L.

Top View Tenon

Side View

TENON

A

B

TENON

A

B

5/4"

~ Ripped on Table Saw Jig ~

~ PATTERN ~
REAR Legs

SEAT RAIL

Mortise Location for back seat rail

SEAT RAIL

Mortise Location for Back Seat Rail 5/8

Stock 1 3/4" thick x 84" Long x 5" Wide MAKES ONE REAR AND ONE FRONT LEG.

CHAMFERS 1/4" DEEP, BEGIN 5/8" DOWN FROM BOTTOM OF SEAT RAILS

MORTISE FOR Stretch

FLAT RIPPED ON TABLE SAW JIG

~ SEAT RAIL LAYOUT STICK ~
END RAILS
STOCK 3"W x 24"L x 1 3/4 TH.

12 7/8"

NOTE - CENTER BRACE SHOULD BE MEASURED DURING TRIAL ASSEMBLY TO DETERMINE LENGTH.

MORTISE UP BAR

3/4" WIDE, 3/8" IN FROM INSIDE EDGE

GAIN FOR BACK FRAME.
SCRIBED DURING ASSEMBLY

1 3/16

SHOULDER

TENON (REAR LEGS)

21" Shoulder to Shoulder

24" overall

Crest rail

Back center stile

Lower back rail

Rear seat rail (two pieces)

Center back leg

Arm roll

Back stile

Upholsterers' bar

End rail

Back leg

Medial stretcher

Front seat rail

Center stretcher

Frame stretcher

Molded leg

Arm support block

Vertical arm support

Side stretcher

The molded legs shown here are a variation of the templates, which is explained on p. 207.

205

end and a lap joint in the middle). Next make the back frame—the specifics are shown on the crest-rail template. I prefer a single board for the crest rail, as on the originals, but you could glue it up. Size the materials, cut the joints, test-assemble, then glue the frame together. Peg the joints and cut the crest profile with a saber saw.

Glue the back frame to the leg uprights, and, when dry, fasten it securely with #10 or #12 wood screws, driven through the softer wood into the hardwood legs. (Period cabinetmakers usually used clinched nails, and for this reason the legs

on many of the original frames have split.)

With this much of the frame assembled, you can go on to the front arm supports, which consist of a curved vertical upright and a support block. I first cut the support block's straight edges, either with the tablesaw leg jig or with the saw's miter gauge. The block's joints into the leg post and the end rail are critical: a tongue-and-groove at the front leg allows you to slide the block down until its tenon fits in the end-rail mortise. If these joints are not precise, the arm will soon fail. I cut the tenon and the tongue on the table-

saw with the rip fence as a guide, sawing them in length and thickness to fit. Then I bandsaw the block's top curve.

Bandsaw the curved uprights and bevel the bottom edges so they set flat on the end rails. Glue and screw the uprights to the blocks, then fasten the assembled units to the frame with glue and pegs.

For the arm rolls, I always use clear pine, laminated from two pieces of 8/4 stock and one piece of 4/4. Period cabinetmakers used solid pine blocks, but nowadays these are hard to get. The arms meet their supports at compound angles,

Getting a frame upholstered

by Bob McCarthy

First, the bad news: a good upholstery job can cost as much as $1500, and you may have trouble finding a shop that will do it right. Now the good news: if the job is done right—and I'll tell you how to be sure that it is—it will easily last 15 years.

The period sofa: Upholstery and woodworking have both changed a lot since 1780. A true reproduction sofa frame would not have screws, modern glues or upholsterers' bars. There wouldn't be a machine mark anywhere, nor any trace of sandpaper. And a period upholstery job would have no springs or cushion, and would be stuffed with Spanish moss or horsehair. To most people, such a sofa would be very uncomfortable.

Yet modern upholstery methods can recreate the period look—taut, crisp lines—and provide comfort at the same time. As you read on, keep the following basics in mind: A Chippendale camelback sofa should be padded very tightly and never overstuffed. The back should not be padded too thickly or it will push the occupant forward. The seat should slope slightly from front to rear to hold a cushion, if used, in place. Do not allow staples anywhere; someday your sofa will be reupholstered, and staples are difficult to remove without breaking them, which leaves razor-sharp studs sticking up.

Finding the right shop: Many shops specialize in reupholstering and are not qualified to tackle a bare frame, but any large city probably has a shop that can do your job right. Ask a nearby museum for recommendations, check with interior decorators, and keep looking.

Request a list of references from the shop, then take the time to go and look at some of their work. A good shop will cooperate with you in making your sofa what it should be—they will allow you to specify materials and methods, and will put the agreement in writing.

Springs: Springs weren't used in upholstery until the mid 19th century, but they lend support critical to appearance and comfort. Well-tied springs should last for years; webbing alone simply will not, which is why I recommend springs even though they aren't authentic. For the seat, I would insist on coil springs, hand-sewn to the webbing and hand-tied together. For the back, I'd ask for Marshall spring units (light, muslin-covered springs).

Padding: Instead of horsehair, cotton batting commonly is used today. Period materials are hard to acquire, will increase your costs, and won't show anyway. Make certain that muslin is used to hold all padding in place.

Seats: If you want a traditional fabric, you should specify a tight seat, which means one with no cushion. This will look best, and avoids the problem of a cushion that won't stay put, but of course it wears faster. If you want a contemporary fabric, then a single thin cushion wouldn't look bad. The cushion's box (the distance between the edge pipings) should be no more than 3 in. Cover the cushion on both sides so it can be flipped over. Zippers on the back prevent you from flipping it four ways, but are hard to talk upholsterers out of. Use down filling if you can afford it.

Fabric: A 6-ft. camelback sofa with a cushion requires 10 yards of 52-in. wide fabric. A material without a pattern can be "railroaded," that is, run horizontally, thus saving some material.

Documentation for period fabrics can be found in old advertisements and, sometimes, from remnants uncovered during reupholstery. Period fabrics are readily available, and I've listed a few of the best suppliers here. If you have a business letterhead, try to get wholesale prices. Still, be prepared to spend $20 to $50 a yard. It's poor economy to save on fabric or its support, as these are the most obvious fea-

tures of a piece. Damasks were popular on period sofas (a damask is a woven-pattern material, usually with floral motifs, whose design is accentuated by alternating glossy and dull surfaces). Period damasks were wool or silk. Many fine reproduction damasks are available today, in wool, silk or synthetic blends. Another good fabric choice would be wool moreen, a heavy fabric of a solid color embellished with a subtle embossed design. If you're fortunate, you may even find a decorator with some leftover fabric (designers often buy excess material as insurance against running short of a particular dye lot). I've bought such bolt-ends for a quarter of their normal price.

Have the upholsterer pad the rolls slightly to accentuate crisp curves. Ideas for piping, decorative brass tacking and other traditional variations can be seen in antiques books and museums.

If all attempts at locating a qualified local upholsterer fail, do not despair. Learning upholstery is not all that difficult. There are many books on the subject in libraries and bookstores. Few tools are required—mostly patience.

Sources: For traditional fabrics, try Colonial Williamsburg, Box CH, Williamsburg, Va. 23187; Historic Charleston Reproductions, 105 Broad St., Charleston, S.C. 29401; Brunschwig & Fils, Inc., 410 East 62nd St., New York, N.Y. 10021; Cowtan & Tout (chintzes), D&D Building, 979 Third Ave., New York, N.Y. 10022; and Stroheim & Romann, 155 East 56th St., New York, N.Y. 10022. For contemporary fabrics, contact Gretchen Bellinger Inc., 330 East 59th St., New York, N.Y. 10022; and Hasi Hester, 138 South Robertson Blvd., Los Angeles, Calif. 90048. □

Bob McCarthy upholsters period pieces and teaches adult-education courses on the subject. He lives in Columbia, S.C.

both front and back. It's best to cut these angles before shaping the arms. Trace the angles from the side-view and top-view templates on the blanks, taking care that the left and right arms will be mirror images, then cut the angles. You could set up a bandsaw for these cuts, but I find a fine-toothed handsaw easier.

Test-fit the blanks, truing up their ends with a low-angle block plane if necessary. With the blanks in place, trace the circles of the crest rail and the arm supports on their ends as far as you can reach with a pencil. Then remove the blanks and use the two circle templates to complete the end shapes. Bandsaw as much waste as possible, then carve the rolls to shape. I use a drawknife, spokeshave, carving tools and planes.

Preparing for upholstery—On period frames, fabric was tacked directly on the part of the frame it was covering. Most modern upholsterers prefer to pull their material through narrow openings in the frame and tack it down on the back side. On our sofa, the lower back rail is higher than the seat rail, and provides such an opening there. The upholsterers' bar shown on p. 203 provides another opening at the junction of the sides and back frame. Although these bars aren't authentic, they add strength, and a frame with bars *is* easier to upholster.

The bar fits into a gain in the arm, also shown on p. 203. Fair the edges of the bar to the shape of the arm and ease them so as not to strain the fabric. Then relieve all the other sharp milled edges of the frame with a file so the fabric will lie over them smoothly.

The top edge of the crest rail should be rounded toward the front of the sofa. I scribe a line ¾ in. down the face, then round over the edge to this line with a drawknife and spokeshave. Don't bring the top back edge to a sharp point.

After finishing the legs, I seal the entire frame with a coating of two parts boiled linseed oil and one part turpentine. This helps keep dimensional stability, and it also improves the frame's appearance. One of my customers, upon receiving his completed frame, liked the look of it so much that he put off the upholstery job for six months. People like that make the extra touches worthwhile. ☐

Norm Vandal makes period furniture in Roxbury, Vt. He explained how he makes period molding planes in FWW *#37. Black-and-white photos by the author.*

Variations on a theme

The Chippendale sofa frame I've designed is a foundation that can accept many stylistic variations. For instance, I made the classic Philadelphia-style sofa shown in the photo on p. 202 with Marlborough legs, a serpentine seat rail, and peaks on each side of the crest. The sofa frame shown in the photo on p. 205 is a simpler, New England design with molded legs.

Some of these modifications can be accomplished with very few changes in the basic templates. A serpentine front rail, for example, requires a curved template and affects the length of the two stretchers in the center. That's all—everything else can remain the same. Some variations call for more work. If you'd like to change the slope and splay of the arm roll, obviously you'll have to change the template for the vertical arm support as well as the length of the arm-roll templates and their end angles. The arm support block would probably be affected as well.

In the leg designs shown below, I'm recommending that you choose 1⅞-in. stock for the front molded leg. This allows you to reduce the size of the leg post above the carving to 1¾ in., the same size as the post on the Marlborough leg. On my sofas, I do it a little differently, because I like to keep the front and back legs the same overall width. I start with 1¾-in. stock, reduce the post to 1⅝ in., then vary

the end-rail length, front-seat-rail shoulder distance and stretchers to accommodate the smaller post. If you'd like to try this yourself, you'll need to work out gains, chamfers and other minor changes at the front corners so the parts fit neatly. The arm-roll length also shortens by ⅛ in., but this takes care of itself during truing-up.

All the following variations are found on original period pieces.

Legs: Straight, square; straight, molded; tapered, square; blocked-foot Marlborough, plain or carved; ball-and-claw cabriole (no stretchers). Some pieces have eight legs, but six-legged sofas are more common.
Seat rails: Straight; serpentine curved; exposed and ornamented. A 6-ft. length is common; other lengths are options.
Crest rail: Single-hump; peaked to each side of hump; varied in curve.
Arm rolls: Straight, tapered, cylindrical; serpentine; varied in slope and/or flare.
Stretchers: Plain; beaded-edged; relief-carved or with open fretwork.

You'll note that I show no stretchers between the back legs, yet you might see them on many period sofas. Rear stretchers take great abuse from climbing children if the piece is placed near the center of the room. Also, they make it difficult to clean under the sofa. They're not needed structurally, and I prefer to leave them out, but the choice is up to you.   —*N.V.*

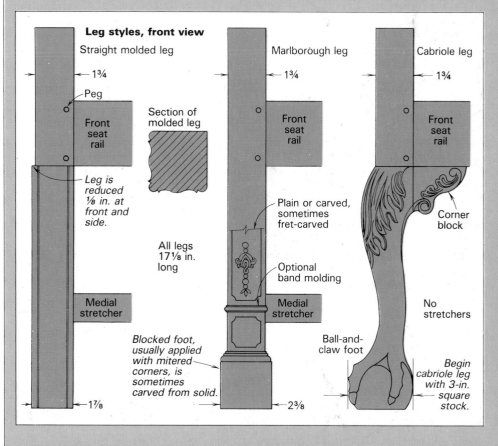

Patchwork Marquetry
Fancy wood, plane geometry

by Mike Peck

Some of the world's most beautiful woods are available only as veneers, and patchwork marquetry is a good way to show them off. These geometric patterns are copied from traditional American patchwork quilts, so any quilt-pattern book is a good place to look for designs. For the small tables and trays that I make, I glue patchwork marquetry to a hardwood-plywood substrate. The techniques I'll describe can be adapted to make decorative panels for many other projects as well.

The designs are created by repeating a simple geometric motif—a triangle, diamond or other polygon—called a design element. With veneers chosen for color and contrast, and variations in the grain direction, the same pattern can range from soft and subtle to flashy and colorful. The possibilities are endless.

To make my patterns, I borrow a quiltmakers' time-saving trick: in assembly-line fashion, quilters cut out the design elements in advance, and later group them together to make the pattern. Instead of stopping to cut each piece individually, I can draw from a stockpile of pre-cut, interchangeable pieces. This way, when I'm putting the design together, I can concentrate on selecting triangles for color and texture.

The design element I use in my tables is a 45° right triangle cut from 1½-in. wide strips of ⅛-in. thick veneer. You can use any type or thickness of veneer, but to minimize sanding, make sure that all the veneers in the same project are about equal in thickness. The size of your design element will determine the finished size of your pattern.

On graph paper, start by laying out your pattern to deter-

mine the total number of pieces, the overall dimensions, and how many species of veneer you'll need to get the effect you want. Next, cut the veneer into strips. To avoid this step, you can use plywood-edging veneer tape, which is sold in ¾-in. to 2-in. widths. It's available at many hardware stores, or by mail from The Woodworkers' Store (21801 Industrial Blvd., Rogers, Minn. 55374) or Constantine's (2050 Eastchester Rd., Bronx, N.Y. 10461). If you want thicker or more exotic veneers, you'll have to cut your own strips. I use the tablesaw jig shown in the box on p. 210 to cut my own strips.

To cut the 45° right triangles from a strip of veneer, you'll need to make the simple masking-tape jig shown in the photo at left below, or you can duplicate the radial-arm saw jig shown on p. 210. To make the masking-tape jig, stick four 10-in. long strips of tape, one on top of the other, to a hardboard or Formica base. With a razor-sharp X-acto knife guided against a steel rule, trim one edge of the tape straight. Hold the blade perpendicular to the work surface while cutting the tape. Next, lay four 3-in. long strips of tape at a 45° angle to the first strips, and trim in similar fashion. Accuracy is critical, so use a good-quality protractor or draftsmen's triangle. Now drive two brads or small nails into the plywood base so that when the steel rule is placed against them, the rule's edge will form the third side of a 45° right triangle.

To use the jig, lay a veneer strip against the longer strip of tape, hold the knife blade perpendicular, and cut a 45° angle on the end of the strip, using the rule as a guide. Never try to cut clear through the veneer on the first pass. Instead, use light pressure on the knife and make several passes. Now flip the strip over and slide the cut end until it stops against the shorter stack of masking tape. Repeat the cut and you'll have your first triangle. Test the accuracy of your jig by cutting four triangles and forming a square with them. There should be no gaps. This is very important, since each small error will multiply itself several times over in the finished marquetry. If there are gaps near the outside of the four-piece square, as

Stacked-up strips of masking tape make a simple jig for slicing 45° right triangles from a strip of veneer. The tape strips form two sides of the triangle; the steel rule, placed across the two nails, forms the third. Adjust the jig by moving the nails.

The patchwork marquetry tray/table shown at left features the traditional 'Ohio Star' quilt pattern in oak, mahogany and birch veneers. To reinforce the show side of a marquetry sheet, tape along the seams of the triangles (above). Overlap the border strips at the corners to miter the veneer border (right). With a razor-sharp X-acto knife guided against a steel rule, cut through both strips at once.

shown at **A**, it means the rule is at an angle greater than 45° to the long strip of masking tape. If there are gaps near the inside of the square, as shown at **B**, the angle is less than 45°. Adjust the angle by repositioning the brads. Adjustment is easiest when the brads are as far apart as the length of your steel rule will allow.

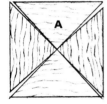
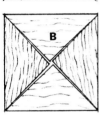

When you've cut out enough pieces, assemble the design on a smooth, flat surface. Hold the triangles together at their corners with small pieces of masking tape. Tape only the show side of the triangles. It may be necessary to move some triangles around to distribute tiny cutting errors—it's almost impossible to make all the triangles fit perfectly. Since there is some elasticity in the veneer, small gaps can be narrowed by gently stretching the veneer to close them up.

Next, reinforce the veneer face by taping over the seams. Then flip the veneer over (taped side down) and use the knife against the steel rule to square up the edges of the sheet for the border, which can be veneer strips 2 in. to 3 in. wide, depending on your design. Flip the panel again (taped side up) and place the border strips around, overlapping the corners slightly. Hold the borders in place with masking tape and cut the miters, going through two border pieces at once. Remember to use light pressure and make several passes, cutting from the inside corner outward. Finally, tape the miters and the joint where the border meets the marquetry. At this point, your project is a flexible sheet of triangles with tape all over the good side and nothing on the backing side.

Hold the marquetry sheet up to a window or other light source and mark any gaps. Fill these with wood putty that matches the wood. Use the putty sparingly, and carefully scrape off any excess. Any putty or dirt caught between the

veneer and the substrate will cause a bump that's easy to sand through. It's a good idea to bond some veneer pieces to a scrap of plywood and test-sand them to see how easy it is to sand through the veneer. If you know what an impending sand-through looks like, you'll know when to stop sanding before it's too late.

Next, glue the marquetry sheet to the substrate, which in my pieces is furniture-grade hardwood-veneer plywood. I know that it's recommended practice to veneer both sides of a panel to eliminate warp and movement, but I buck tradition and veneer only one side. So far, I've had no problems.

Although many veneering experts advise against it, I glue down the marquetry sheet with solvent-based contact cement. It works fine if you apply two coats. I recommend Weldwood Contact Cement. Follow the label instructions faithfully, and note the safety precautions—solvent-based contact cement is extremely flammable.

With a paintbrush or a short-napped roller, apply a uniform coat of cement to both the untaped side of the marquetry and the best side of the substrate. Wrap the brush or roller in aluminum foil while you're waiting for the first coat to dry (which takes about 20 minutes). The cement is dry when a light touch leaves no fingerprint. Apply the second coat, and when that's dry, recoat any dull spots. A properly prepared surface has a uniform, glossy appearance.

Now lay the marquetry sheet taped-side-down on the bench and place ½-in. dowels on the sheet around the edges at 90° to the borders. Invert the substrate panel onto the dowels, being careful to keep the glued surfaces from touching, because once they do, further adjustment is impossible. Align the substrate with the marquetry and slowly pull out the dowels, one at a time, to lower the substrate onto the marquetry. Roll over the entire surface with a wallpaper-seam roller to ensure a good bond. The masking tape can be peeled off now, but be careful to avoid lifting the grain of the veneer with the tape. Fill any remaining gaps with

Jigs speed veneer-cutting

Because I produce lots of patchwork marquetry, I've made two jigs to mechanize the cutting. These jigs are handy for other veneer projects, too. One, shown at right, works on my tablesaw to cut strips of veneer from a large flitch. This jig can also be used for cutting thin stock that would be dangerous to rip on the tablesaw. The other, shown below, fits on my radial-arm saw and produces perfect triangles in large batches.

For power-cutting veneer, I use a 10-in., 200-tooth, thin-rim veneer cut-off blade, and I keep it very sharp. If the veneer is flat, I can cut about 15 sheets of $\frac{1}{28}$-in. veneer at once. If the veneer is wavy or warped, I wet it first, then dry it in a press before cutting.

—M.P.

The tablesaw strip-cutting jig performs two functions. With the two registration pins removed (above), you can joint the edge of an entire flitch with one pass. The jig rides against a piece of plywood to allow room for the flitch. With the pins in place (below) and the jointed edge butted against them, you can rip strips. Strip width equals the distance from the pins to the blade. To vary the width, move the pins to different holes.

Radial-arm saw jig (above and in drawing below) produces triangles in quantity.

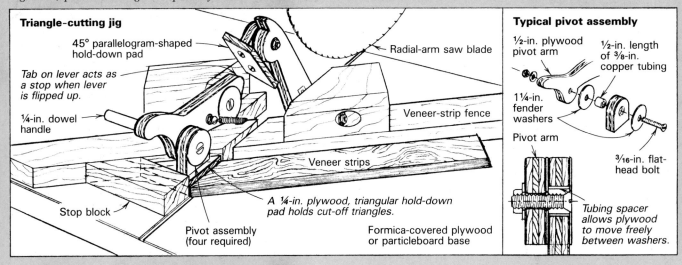

Triangle-cutting jig

45° parallelogram-shaped hold-down pad

Tab on lever acts as a stop when lever is flipped up.

¼-in. dowel handle

Radial-arm saw blade

Veneer-strip fence

Veneer strips

Stop block

A ¼-in. plywood, triangular hold-down pad holds cut-off triangles.

Pivot assembly (four required)

Formica-covered plywood or particleboard base

Typical pivot assembly

½-in. plywood pivot arm

½-in. length of ⅜-in. copper tubing

1¼-in. fender washers

Pivot arm

³⁄₁₆-in. flat-head bolt

Tubing spacer allows plywood to move freely between washers.

---

wood putty, and you're ready to finish-sand.

Before you actually begin sanding, scribble pencil lines over the marquetry. These serve as a reference to help prevent you from sanding through the veneer. Because the grain direction in patchwork marquetry runs in all directions, I just sand with an orbital sander and 220-grit garnet paper. Sand until the pencil lines are almost gone. Go slowly and inspect the surface frequently, especially if you're using thin veneers, such as plywood edging strips. Remove the last traces of pencil with finer paper. I follow up by buffing with 0000 steel wool. A tung-oil and varnish mixture makes a nice finish, but you can use any finish you like. □

Mike Peck designs and builds furniture and hardwood gift items in Atascadero, Calif. Photos by the author. For more on veneering techniques, see pp. 86-89 and pp. 91-95 in this volume. For more on marquetry techniques, see FWW #38, pp. 61-65.

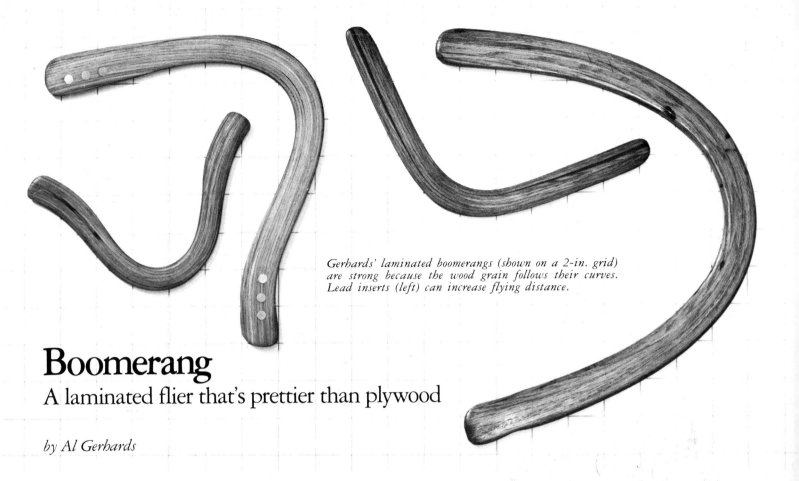

Gerhards' laminated boomerangs (shown on a 2-in. grid) are strong because the wood grain follows their curves. Lead inserts (left) can increase flying distance.

Boomerang
A laminated flier that's prettier than plywood

by Al Gerhards

A boomerang is an exercise in free-form woodworking. No straight lines, no corners to fit, no accurate measurements—just flowing lines and curves. Boomerangs can be made in many different shapes and sizes, besides the traditional shape. They're quick to make, fun to throw, and you can pack one along when you travel. To use it, all you need is a field and a little breeze.

The easiest way to make a boomerang is to cut the shape from 5-ply, ¼-in. birch plywood, then rasp and sand the edges to an airfoil section. I prefer to make a laminated boomerang by gluing up strips of wood on a form to build up not the thickness but the width. You can use any type of hardwood that will bend—so far, I've tried ash, hickory, oak, elm and locust. Where I live, these woods are inexpensive and available from local sawmills.

Since I make my boomerangs in batches, I start with a straight-grained, knot-free board, about 28 in. long, 2½ in. thick and 5 in. or more in width. I can get five of them from a board this size. Allow about ½ in. thickness for each boomerang. If you want to make two, you can start with a board 1 in. thick and 5 in. wide.

On the tablesaw, rip strips about ³⁄₁₆ in. to ¼ in. thick from the edge of the board (see drawing, next page). Eight to ten strips, laminated together, should give you a thickness of 1¾ in. to 2 in. It's a good idea to cut a few extra strips, in case you break some while bending.

My boomerangs have sharp bends—less than 90°—so I steam and pre-bend my strips before gluing and clamping them on a form. If your boomerang doesn't have such a sharp bend, you can omit the steaming step. Place the strips in a preheated steam box for about 30 minutes (*FWW* #40, p. 102). When the strips are pliable, bend them freehand into a "U" shape and immobilize the ends to keep the strips from straightening out again as they dry. On my wall, I nailed lath strips about 16 in. apart, and when I compress the bent "U"

and place the ends between two laths, the bent strip springs back a few inches and wedges in place. You could nail laths on a piece of plywood instead of on a wall. Whatever you do, let the strips dry for about a week.

To laminate the boomerang, you'll need to make a form by gluing and nailing together pieces of plywood or particleboard. You want a block about ½ in. thicker than the width of your strips, and about 4 in. longer than the length of the boomerang you want to make. The outside curve of the boomerang takes its shape from the concave surface of the form. Trace the outer edge of your boomerang pattern onto the plywood block, leaving about 2 in. of block at either end. Cut out the curve with a bandsaw or a bowsaw. Then glue and nail another piece of plywood to the form to make a base. Now you are ready to glue the strips together, but first coat the form with wax so that the glue won't stick to it.

You can get decorative effects by gluing up the strips in different ways. You can reassemble them in the order they were cut from the board, to match the original grain. For a different effect, you can alternate light and dark woods, or cut two long, thin wedges from wood of a contrasting color and slip them between the strips.

Coat both sides of the strips with epoxy (not quick-set epoxy) and allow the glue to cure for about an hour before assembling. This allows the glue to penetrate the pores of the wood and helps prevent a starved joint. I use T-88 epoxy (available from Chem Tech, 4669 Lander Rd., Chagrin Falls, Ohio 44022), but some other brands may set faster, so this technique may not work with all glues. The epoxy should still be tacky when the strips are assembled. Lay the glued-up strips in the form. To even the pressure from the clamps and to prevent them from marring the wood, I use a thin, flexible, steel strap about 2 in. wide and long enough to follow the curve. On a concave form, however, this isn't essential. Place the steel band (if you're using one) against the last

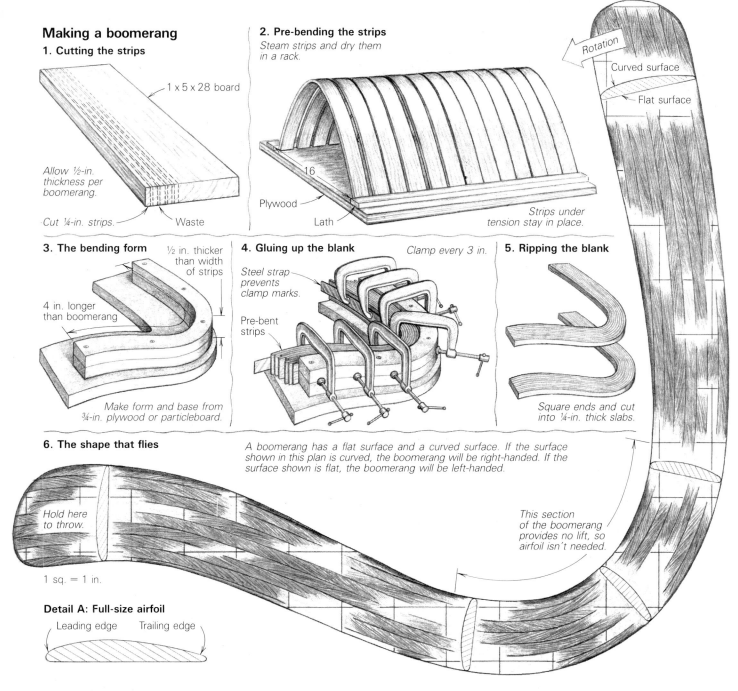

Making a boomerang

1. Cutting the strips

1 x 5 x 28 board

Allow ½-in. thickness per boomerang.

Cut ¼-in. strips.

Waste

2. Pre-bending the strips

Steam strips and dry them in a rack.

16

Plywood

Lath

Strips under tension stay in place.

Rotation

Curved surface

Flat surface

3. The bending form

½ in. thicker than width of strips

4 in. longer than boomerang

Make form and base from ¾-in. plywood or particleboard.

4. Gluing up the blank

Clamp every 3 in.

Steel strap prevents clamp marks.

Pre-bent strips

5. Ripping the blank

Square ends and cut into ¼-in. thick slabs.

6. The shape that flies

A boomerang has a flat surface and a curved surface. If the surface shown in this plan is curved, the boomerang will be right-handed. If the surface shown is flat, the boomerang will be left-handed.

Hold here to throw.

This section of the boomerang provides no lift, so airfoil isn't needed.

1 sq. = 1 in.

Detail A: Full-size airfoil

Leading edge   Trailing edge

---

strip. With a large C-clamp or bar clamp, start pulling in the midsection, snug it up and clamp each side at 3 in. intervals. Allow the epoxy to cure for a day at room temperature.

When the epoxy has cured, remove the laminated block from the form, and square up the sides where the edges of the strips may have slipped out of alignment. You now have a thick block shaped like a boomerang, from which you'll cut individual blanks. I cut mine on the tablesaw, but you can probably do this more safely and waste less wood with a wide resaw blade on the bandsaw. To increase the height of the tablesaw fence, I attach a piece of plywood wide enough to support the blank while ripping. Saw the blanks about ¼ in. thick. The blanks are now ready for shaping and sanding.

Here's how to determine which side gets rounded to form the airfoil. With your throwing hand, hold the boomerang upright by its arm, with the edge of its "elbow" toward your nose. Go through an overhand throwing motion. The side facing your ear is the top surface, which gets curved. The side away from you remains flat. As the boomerang leaves your hand, it spins, and the two edges that cut the wind as it spins

are the edges you want to round. The rounded edge tapers to a thin trailing edge like the cross section of an airplane wing.

When shaping and sanding, I use a boomerang-shaped ¾-in. plywood backup to minimize flexing. Clamp the boomerang blank and the backup in a vise. Using a rasp, shape the top side of the blank into an airfoil shape. After you've roughed out the boomerang, finish it with sandpaper. I use an inflatable-bag drum sander for final contouring.

Every shape and size flies differently, so after flight-testing, you may need to tune your boomerang by slightly changing the shape of the airfoil. To make the boomerang travel farther before it returns, I sometimes epoxy ½-in. dia. lead inserts in holes near the ends of the arms. After the glue sets, I file the lead flush with the wood.

I finish my boomerangs with tung oil or boiled linseed oil, to bring out the wood's natural beauty. A boomerang gets a lot of hard use, and an oil finish is easy to repair.   □

Al Gerhards is a dental technician in Downington, Pa. He's been making boomerangs for 25 years.

Drawing: Lee Hov

Throwing the boomerang

by John Huening

Hold the boomerang so it's nearly vertical and launch with an overhand throw. Snap your wrist on release to give it a good spin.

Rusty Harding took me to a field and considered the air and sky. "A boomerang is a gyroscope without a fixed point of gyration. It describes a circle, or whatever its flight path, depending on the design, velocity, spin, wind direction and thermal air currents."

Harding makes boomerangs for a living. Working in his backyard in Lebanon, Tenn., he produces fanciful, unorthodox shapes—a far cry from the familiar shallow "V" shape developed by the Australian aborigines.

There are right- and left-handed boomerangs, the difference being the location of the rounded edges and the direction the boomerang is thrown into the wind. A right-hander returns in a counterclockwise circle, while a left-hander circles clockwise. Hold the boomerang in your throwing hand, with the flat side against your palm, and imagine it spinning out of your hand, away from you. The rounded edge, like the front edge of an airplane wing, should be the edge that hits the wind first. If it's not, you've got a boomerang designed for the other hand.

"I usually pick up pieces of grass and drop them to see which direction the wind is blowing," Harding told me. "Throw about forty-five degrees into the wind. Stand so that the wind hits your left cheek." Since he's left-handed, Harding let the wind hit his right cheek.

"Spin is important," he continued, "so hold the boomerang as close as you can to the end of its arm. The boomerang should be nearly vertical when launched. Now, pick a target forty to fifty yards away, aim, and throw overhand, snapping your wrist to give the

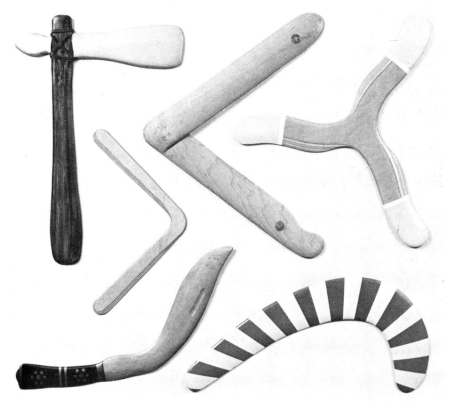

Harding makes his fanciful, unorthodox boomerangs from either hardwood or plywood.

boomerang a good spin."

That first throw was nearly miraculous—the boomerang actually returned and I almost caught it. There was a whirring sound as it cut the air. "Consistency is important," Harding said. "Until you can throw the same way each time, you won't know what you're doing wrong. If the boomerang lands consistently to your left, turn more away from the wind. If it lands to your right, turn more into the wind. Do the oppo-site if you're left-handed. If it lands consistently in front of you, throw a little higher or a little harder. If it lands in back of you, throw a little lower."

Boomerangs were originally used as weapons, and they do have the potential to be dangerous. When throwing one, you should allow between 50 and 75 yards of open space in all directions. □

John Huening is a pipe-organ builder and writer in Seffner, Fla.

Boston Bombé Chest

Bulging drawer fronts are all shaped at once

by Lance Patterson

More than 50 pieces of American bombé furniture made in the last half of the 18th century still exist. Surprisingly, all were built in or around Boston. The kettle-shaped bombé form (the term is derived from the French word for *bulge*) is characterized by the swelling of the lower half of the carcase ends and front, with the swell returning to a normal-size base. This shape is, I think, directly related to English pieces such as the Apthorp chest-on-chest, which was imported to Boston before 1758 and is now at that city's Museum of Fine Arts. Bombé was popular in England for only 10 to 12 years, but remained the vogue in Boston for nearly 60 years.

In America, the carcase ends were always shaped from thick, solid planks of mahogany. In Europe, the ballooning case ends were most often coopered—3-in. to 4-in. pieces of wood were sawn to shape, glued up, contoured and then veneered. Instead of veneering, the Americans worked with sol-id wood. I think the magnificent grain patterns of this shaped mahogany are a major attribute of Boston furniture. The bombé form, I believe, also shows the enthusiasm that 18th-century cabinetmakers must have felt when wide, clear mahogany first became available to them.

There was also an evolution in the treatment of the case's inside surfaces and, consequently, in the shape of the drawers. On the earlier pieces, the case ends are not hollowed out and the drawer sides are vertical. Some transition pieces have lipped drawer fronts, the lip following the curve of the case. The fully evolved form has hollowed-out ends and drawers with sides shaped to follow the ends. Some of the later pieces have serpentine drawer fronts.

I will describe how I built a small bombé chest with four shaped drawers, ball-and-claw feet and a serpentine front. I didn't take step-by-step photos while building, so I'll have to

Patterson's bombé chest, based on an 18th-century design, has four dovetailed drawers and ball-and-claw feet. Side view, right, shows shape of serpentine front.

Fig. 1: Patterson's plans for a Boston bombé chest

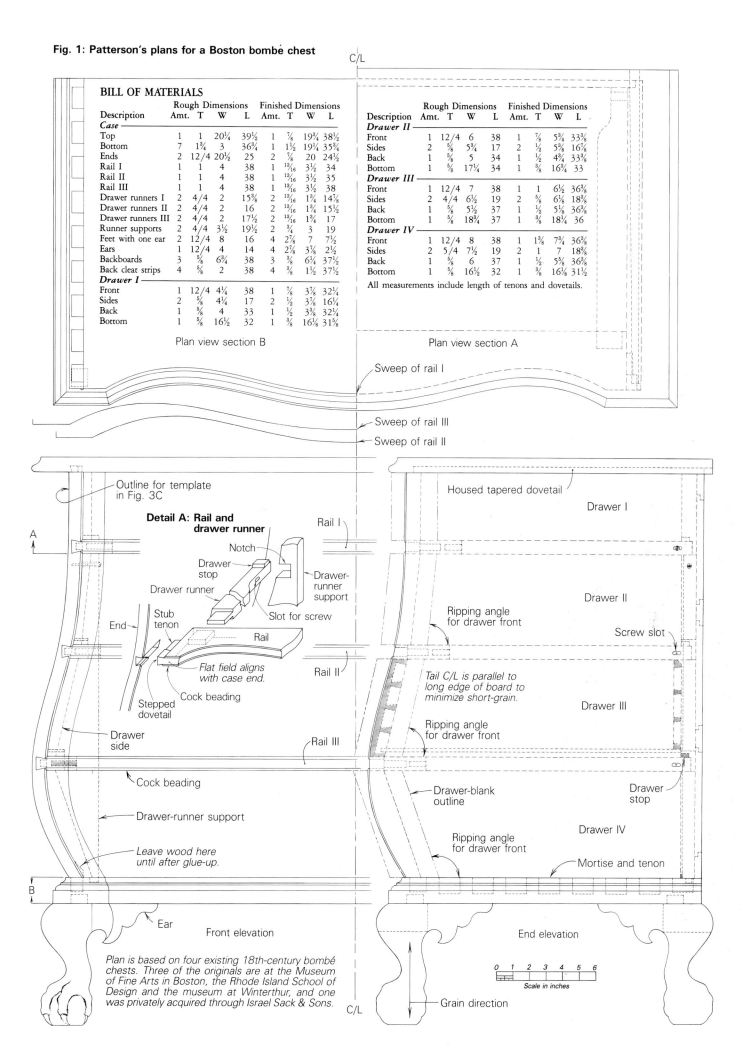

BILL OF MATERIALS

Description	Rough Dimensions				Finished Dimensions			
	Amt.	T	W	L	Amt.	T	W	L
Case								
Top	1	1	20¼	39½	1	⅞	19¾	38½
Bottom	7	1¾	3	36¾	1	1½	19¼	35¾
Ends	2	12/4	20½	25	2	⅞	20	24½
Rail I	1	1	4	38	1	13/16	3½	34
Rail II	1	1	4	38	1	13/16	3½	35
Rail III	1	1	4	38	1	13/16	3½	38
Drawer runners I	2	4/4	2	15⅜	2	13/16	1¾	14⅞
Drawer runners II	2	4/4	2	16	2	13/16	1¾	15½
Drawer runners III	2	4/4	2	17½	2	13/16	1¾	17
Runner supports	2	4/4	3½	19½	2	¾	3	19
Feet with one ear	2	12/4	8	16	4	2⅞	7	7½
Ears	1	12/4	4	14	4	2⅞	3⅞	2½
Backboards	3	⅝	6¾	38	3	⅜	6¼	37½
Back cleat strips	4	⅝	2	38	4	⅜	1½	37½
Drawer I								
Front	1	12/4	4¼	38	1	⅞	3⅞	32¼
Sides	2	⅝	4¼	17	2	½	3⅞	16¼
Back	1	⅝	4	33	1	½	3⅜	32¼
Bottom	1	⅝	16½	32	1	⅜	16⅛	31⅝

Description	Rough Dimensions				Finished Dimensions			
	Amt.	T	W	L	Amt.	T	W	L
Drawer II								
Front	1	12/4	6	38	1	⅞	5⅜	33⅜
Sides	2	⅝	5¾	17	2	½	5⅜	16⅞
Back	1	⅝	5	34	1	½	4⅞	33⅜
Bottom	1	⅝	17¼	34	1	⅜	16¾	33
Drawer III								
Front	1	12/4	7	38	1	1	6½	36⅜
Sides	2	4/4	6½	19	2	⅝	6⅛	18⅜
Back	1	⅝	5½	37	1	½	5⅛	36⅜
Bottom	1	⅝	18¾	37	1	⅜	18¼	36
Drawer IV								
Front	1	12/4	8	38	1	1⅜	7¾	36⅜
Sides	2	5/4	7½	19	2	1	7	18⅜
Back	1	⅝	6	37	1	½	5⅝	36⅜
Bottom	1	⅝	16½	32	1	⅜	16⅛	31½

All measurements include length of tenons and dovetails.

C/L

Plan view section B

Plan view section A

Sweep of rail I

Sweep of rail III

Sweep of rail II

Outline for template in Fig. 3C

Detail A: Rail and drawer runner

Rail I

Notch

Drawer stop

Drawer runner

Drawer-runner support

End

Stub tenon

Slot for screw

Rail

Flat field aligns with case end.

Cock beading

Stepped dovetail

Drawer side

Cock beading

Drawer-runner support

Leave wood here until after glue-up.

Rail II

Rail III

A

B

Ear

Front elevation

Plan is based on four existing 18th-century bombé chests. Three of the originals are at the Museum of Fine Arts in Boston, the Rhode Island School of Design and the museum at Winterthur, and one was privately acquired through Israel Sack & Sons.

C/L

Housed tapered dovetail

Drawer I

Ripping angle for drawer front

Drawer II

Screw slot

Tail C/L is parallel to long edge of board to minimize short-grain.

Ripping angle for drawer front

Drawer III

Drawer-blank outline

Drawer stop

Drawer IV

Ripping angle for drawer front

Mortise and tenon

End elevation

0 1 2 3 4 5 6

Scale in inches

Grain direction

C/L

Don Burkey

Vivid grain patterns are exposed when thick mahogany is shaped. Making the board's bark side convex yields a hyperbolic figure, as in the author's chest, above; cutting into the other side produces elliptical patterns, shown in the photo on p. 218.

illustrate some operations with photos of Jerry de Rham building his bombé desk at Boston's North Bennet Street School, where I teach. His version is of the basic bombé form: the front is not serpentine, but bulges to match the ends.

It's unclear how early cabinetmakers made the shaped drawers, but it probably was done by trial and error, then angle blocks and patterns were made for future reference. There are graphic methods for figuring the angles, and mathematical methods are quick and accurate, too, as explained in the box on p. 219. The same techniques can be applied when designing anything with canted sides and ends, such as a cradle, dough box, or splayed-joint stool or table.

The first step in any project of this scope is to make full-size orthographic drawings, primarily to facilitate making patterns for shaped parts. This also helps you work out joinery dimensions, and preview the actual size and look of the piece. In developing drawings, I like to gather information from all the sources I can find. I know of four original chests similar to mine—one was privately acquired through Israel Sack & Sons, and the others are at the Museum of Fine Arts in Boston, the Rhode Island School of Design, and Winterthur. Measured drawings of the chest at RISD can be found in *Masterpieces of Furniture* by V.C. Salmonsky (Dover Publications). After building the chest, I revised my drawing by adding ½ in. to the bottom drawer height. Because this drawer recedes from the common viewing angles, it appears narrower than it is. Usually I follow the rule of thumb that drawer height plus

The wood for my chest was a 12/4 plank of South American mahogany, 12 ft. by 22 in., and a 4/4 mahogany board, 40 in. by 21 in., with secondary parts of poplar. For effective use of grain, the symmetry of the ends and the continuity of the front are the most important considerations. I laid out the ends book-fashion, with the bulge toward the wider annual-ring pattern (figure 2). Either face of the plank can be used as the outside; both elliptical and hyperbolic annual-ring patterns are beautiful. I chose the bark side of the plank, producing a hyperbolic pattern at the bulge, as shown in the photo at left. De Rham's desk shows the characteristic elliptical pattern of the heart face, best seen in the photo on p. 218.

To avoid conflict between the long grain and the cross grain around the case, and to eliminate applied moldings, I departed from traditional construction. I used a thick mahogany bottom with the base molding cut into it. Thus the end base molding is end grain, but so is the molding on the top's end, and there's a lot of end grain in the serpentine front molding as well. I especially like end-grain molding.

To shape the chest, first rough-saw all the parts according to the rough stock list on p. 215. Note that the final dimensions differ considerably in many cases, but the parts should be cut oversize to ensure that they can be shaped with the setups shown in figure 3. Next, rip the front pieces for the three lower drawers at the angles shown on the side-elevation drawing in figure 1 so that they can be canted to provide the necessary thickness for the serpentine shape. Mark out the rails from the centerline and bandsaw them to shape.

I shaped the front as a unit, the method I recommend for any serpentine or oxbow casework. Mount the drawer fronts and rails on the benchtop jig shown in figure 3A, made with two 2-in. wide supports cut to match the rail and drawer-front profile. I tack-glued the parts to each other at the ends and added two bar clamps for support during shaping.

Using the full-size patterns, trace profile shapes on all four edges of the assembly. These lines, with the bandsawn rails, are your guides for the compound curves. With a large, shallow gouge, I first roughed out the concave areas and then the flat fields at the ends. Now spokeshave to the profile lines, using a square from the end surface to check the front. I used a bandsawn three-dimensional pattern, shown in figure 3C, to draw the line of the corner in to where the flat fields meet the serpentine shape. The rest of the front was shaped from this line. I did most of the gouge work across the grain, following up with spokeshaves, cutting from high to low in various directions. I sawed an inch off the handle of my No. 151 round-bottom spokeshave to reach all the concavities.

The front should be symmetrical and free of lumps,

Fig. 2: Plank-cutting diagram

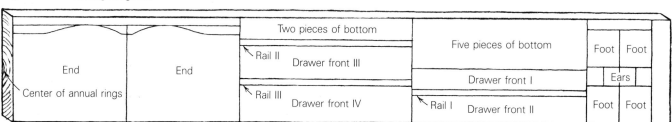

End	End	Rail II Drawer front III	Two pieces of bottom		Five pieces of bottom		Foot	Foot
Center of annual rings		Rail III Drawer front IV			Drawer front I			Ears
				Rail I Drawer front II			Foot	Foot

Most of the major parts were cut from a 12/4 South American mahogany plank, 12 ft. by 22 in. The case ends were laid out book-fashion with the bulge toward the wider annual ring pattern.

Fig. 3: Shaping the curves

A: Contouring the front

A benchtop jig positions all the drawer fronts and rails together so that they can be shaped as a unit. The drawer fronts shown here are in various stages of completion. The two supports are cut to conform to the slope of the backs of the drawer blanks, shown in Fig. 1, and are notched to receive the rails.

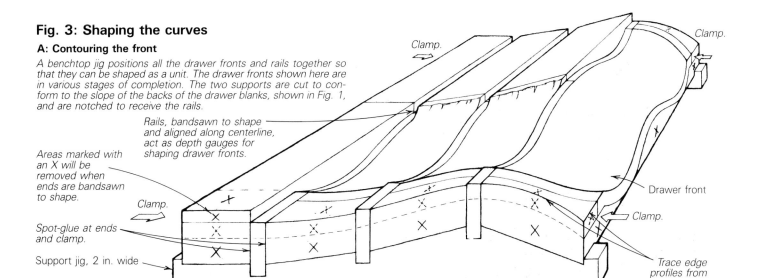

Clamp.

Clamp.

Rails, bandsawn to shape and aligned along centerline, act as depth gauges for shaping drawer fronts.

Areas marked with an X will be removed when ends are bandsawn to shape.

Clamp.

Spot-glue at ends and clamp.

Support jig, 2 in. wide

Drawer front

Clamp.

Trace edge profiles from full-size templates.

B: Shaping the ends

Carcase ends are rough-shaped by making tablesaw cuts every 2 in. about ¼ in. short of the profile lines traced on the edges. These parallel sawcuts allow the waste to be removed quickly with a wide chisel. The contours are smoothed with planes, spokeshave and scraper.

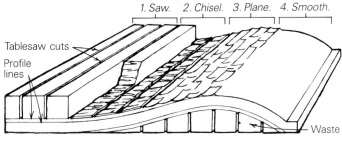

1. Saw.   2. Chisel.   3. Plane.   4. Smooth.

Tablesaw cuts

Profile lines

Waste

C: Matching the curves

Three-dimensional pattern, bandsawn to match chest outline in Fig. 1, allows you to draw a fairly accurate pencil line over the contoured surface to define the corner where the case ends meet the front.

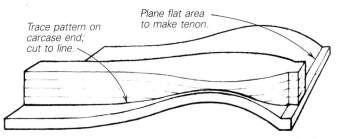

Trace pattern on carcase end; cut to line.

Plane flat area to make tenon.

---

smoothly curved in all directions. The final scraping and adjusting of the field lines can't be done until the case and drawers have been assembled, yet before the cock beading is carved. The gouge work goes quickly and is fun. It's important to stay relaxed, and I try to keep a rhythm to my mallet blows. Hollow the backs of the drawer fronts individually, but leave enough flat area at both ends to pass each piece over the tablesaw, to mark out the dovetails, and to check for any movement after shaping. If there is any winding or other movement, first plane it out of the back of the drawer front, thus making a reference surface for correcting edges and ends.

Now put the front assembly aside, and turn to the case ends. Cut them to their finished width of 20 in., but leave the length and thickness rough. With the flat patterns, trace the shape of the long-grain edges. Rough out the contours by making tablesaw cuts about every 2 in., as in figure 3B. I stopped the cuts about ¼ in. away from the profile line to allow for the inevitable movement: the top of my ends cupped outward, though I suspect that the bulge prevented significant cupping at the bottom. The sawcuts allow the bulk of the waste to be chiseled away quickly, after which it's best to let the wood settle for a couple of days. Then plane the inside areas near the top and bottom edges flat and parallel, and retrace the pattern. Now scrub-plane across the grain down to the line, and finish up with smooth plane and spokeshaves. Place the three-dimensional pattern over the contour and trace the profile of the long edges. Bandsaw the ends to shape, and true up the top and bottom edges.

To join the case, first attach the ends to the top with housed tapered dovetails. When fitting the joint, I tapered the square

side of the half-dovetail with my shoulder plane because I don't have a dovetail plane that will taper the angled side, as is usually done. Otherwise I used traditional methods of sawing, wasting with a chisel, and cleaning up with a router plane. When drawn home, these joints establish the width of the case, and thus locate the mortises in the base.

I made the case bottom from seven pieces, 36¾ in. by 3 in. by 1¾ in., ripped from waste sections of the plank. The thickness lets you shape the base itself, rather than having to use applied moldings. The moldings on the top and base are cut on a spindle shaper, as are the rabbets in the ends. I grind my own cutters. Nine tenons join each end to the base, allowing a lot of grain to run through to the molded edge. There is a short-grain problem inside the case ends between the tenons, so leave extra wood here until after glue-up to prevent a crumbled edge.

Rails on 18th-century Boston cases are typically 4 in. to 6 in. wide, with secondary wood often joined to the primary wood. I think that 3½ in. to 4 in. is wide enough to keep the rails straight. Assemble the case dry, position the rails (aligning the center marks), and cut them to length. Slide the rails in on the stub tenons, scribe the stepped dovetails and cut the mortises for the runners in the rails (figure 1, detail A). The case is ready to be glued up. To avoid friction between parallel edges, the dovetails joining the top and ends must be slid in individually before the rails and base are added.

Glue blocks or screws usually support the runners in bombé cases. To provide support while allowing movement, I used a vertical strip of poplar, notched to support each runner, at the back of the chest. Stub tenons hook these two vertical supports to the base, and screws through slots hold them at the top. The runners are screwed to the case ends through slots at the back. De Rham used oak supports and fastened them both top and bottom with screws, as shown in the photo at right. I didn't glue the runner tenons in until later, after some finish had been applied to the inside of the case.

Bevel dovetails are needed for the lower three drawers, since both their sides and fronts are angled. As discussed in the box on the facing page, cut the drawer parts to length at the proper end and bevel angles, and then before shaping the draw-

Notched vertical members support drawer runners at back.

er sides, cut the dovetails. Next, to fit each drawer front into the case, position it over its opening and scribe the curve of the case ends onto the dovetail pins from inside the case. Trim the pins to the scribe line to get the drawer front started in the opening and to check the fit. Then trim the rest of the drawer front to the pins. The grooves for the drawer bottoms are cut on the shaper wherever possible; the rest is done by hand. Assemble the drawers and plane the drawer sides down to the curve of the drawer-front ends. The drawer bottoms are solid wood, with the grain running from side to side and three sides beveled from underneath to fit the grooves.

With the case on its back, block up the drawers flush with the rails. I established the line of the corner between the flat fields and the serpentine shape by running a compass along the curve of the ends. Scrape the entire front to smooth all the contours, taking care to leave the flat fields at a uniform width that is crisp and clean. Then, after removing the drawers, use a scratch stock to make most of the cock beading on the rails and the case ends. The scratch stock will have to be adjusted for the middle rail, because of the angle of its face. The beading at the corners is carved.

The back of the chest is made of wide and narrow horizon-

tal boards with overlapping rabbets. The narrow boards are screwed into the rabbets at the case ends, but the wide boards are free-floating and can move.

The grain runs vertically in the feet and their ears. I band-sawed each foot with one ear as part of it and the other ear applied. This uses a little more wood, but it eliminates half the glue joints, and the grain match, of course, is perfect. The feet are stub-tenoned to the base, and I put a screw through a sloppy hole in each ear into the base. The feet are carved as large as possible in the 12/4 pieces. (For an article on how to carve ball-and-claw feet, see *FWW #10*, pp. 58-59.) The side toes are angled slightly forward, but the tips of the claw extend to the diagonals of the square blank. I also keep the knuckles of the rear, side and front toes different distances from the floor, to avoid a box-like appearance. The bones of each toe get progressively longer as you go back from the nail, and the number of knuckles is anatomically correct. The ball itself and the claws are smooth, but I left tool marks on the rest of the foot up to the ankle. The case is designed so that the line formed where the flat field ends and the serpentine shape begins runs across the base molding and around the transition as a miter corner, and ends at the point representing the fetlock. I think knee carving suits this design if the mahogany is highly figured. But if the wood is straight-grained, as mine was, then a less fancy style is better.

Bombé chests deserve the best traditionally made hardware: I spent more money for the hardware than for the lumber. My thin cast brasses with separate posts are from Ball and Ball, 436 W. Lincoln Highway, Exton, Pa. 19341. I shaped a pine block to help bend the plates. To seat the posts properly, I drilled post holes perpendicular to the tangent of the curve, then I adjusted the bails to fit the posts. I used #0 by ¼-in. round-head brass screws to attach the keyhole escutcheons, so they are easily removable. All the locks needed 1⅛ in. to the selvage. I used a slant-top desk lock on the lowest drawer and made strike plates for all the locks.

To finish the chest, I gave it one very thin wash coat of orange shellac, to set up the grain for its final sanding, then used boiled linseed oil. If applied in very thin, hand-rubbed coats, linseed displays the grain with depth, clarity and warmth. I don't thin oil greatly with turpentine (never more than 1 part turpentine to 20 parts oil), nor do I apply soaking coats. I don't think these methods significantly increase penetration, and I suspect that not all of the oil oxidizes, so you risk bleed-out problems. I do add a little Japan drier. I store my oil in a colored glass bottle placed in direct sunlight—I think this helps polymerization and drying. It is most important to apply the oil in the thinnest layers possible and to give it adequate time to oxidize between coats. Each coat should be rubbed hard to build up enough heat to force the oil into the pores and to level the surface. Carvings and moldings should be brushed vigorously to remove excess oil. Instead of waxing, I prefer to build up the oil slowly to a high gloss.

Like most 18th-century furniture, each Boston bombé piece is a complete design in itself, independent of its environment. It has character and warmth which are a joy to live with. Its shape continually invites you to run your hand over its curves, or even to tickle its carved feet.   □

Jerry de Rham, a student at North Bennet Street School, scrapes his desk front smooth. Note the alternate traditional design—the front is not serpentine, but matches the curve of the sides.

Lance Patterson is a cabinetmaker and shop instructor at the North Bennet Street School in Boston, Mass.

Photos this page: Brad Mayo

How to make slope-sided boxes

Plans for slope-sided boxes, such as the drawers in the bombé chest on p. 214, aren't in the perspective we're used to. In a front-elevation drawing, the front measures less than its true height because it is tilted out of the plane of the drawing. Here is a method for reading tilted plans, laying the pieces out, and setting the tablesaw to cut the elusive angles involved. In this particular hopper, the front and the back could be cut with the same saw settings, but for clarity, let's consider just the front.

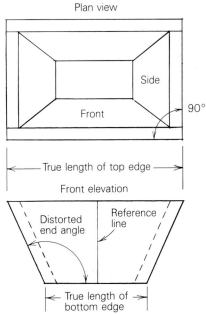

Plan view

Side

Front

90°

True length of top edge

Front elevation

Distorted end angle

Reference line

True length of bottom edge

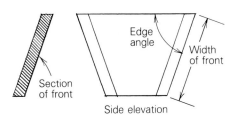

Edge angle

Width of front

Section of front

Side elevation

With no math at all

1. The side elevation, above, shows the true cross section of the board that will be the front of the hopper. Use a bevel gauge to transfer the edge angle to the tablesaw, then rip the front to width.

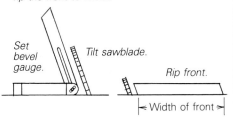

Set bevel gauge.

Tilt sawblade.

Rip front.

Width of front

2. The end angle shown in the front elevation is distorted, but the drawing does show the true length of the top and bottom edges. Measuring out from a perpendicular reference line, transfer the edge lengths to the workpiece. Then connect the edges to draw the true end-cut lines. This method also works for asymmetrical pieces—where end-cut lines are at different angles.

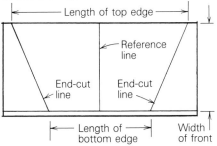

Length of top edge

Reference line

End-cut line

End-cut line

Length of bottom edge

Width of front

3. With a straightedge, set the miter gauge so the end-cut line is parallel to the blade.

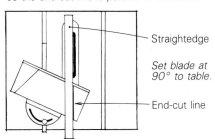

Straightedge

Set blade at 90° to table.

End-cut line

4. As shown in the plan view, above, the cut has to be at 90° to the beveled edge of the workpiece, not at 90° to the face. To determine this tilt angle, place a carpenters' square flat against the beveled edge of the workpiece and crank the blade over until it lies tight against the arm of the square.

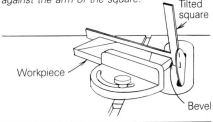

Tilted square

Workpiece

Bevel

5. Lower the blade to a safe height and cut to the line. If the piece is symmetrical, you can switch the miter gauge to the other side of the blade, turn the work over, and saw the other end. If asymmetrical, repeat steps 3 and 4. Repeat all five steps for the other sides.

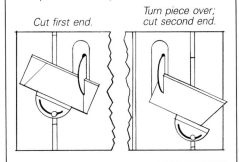

Cut first end.

Turn piece over; cut second end.

The problem of the hopper joint is traditionally solved by projection and measurement on full-size drawings. Lance Patterson derived the mathematics at right from the graphical method, then picture-framer Jim Cummins devised the no-math method shown above. For a photocopy of Patterson's mathematical proof, send a self-addressed stamped envelope to Hopper, c/o *Fine Woodworking*, Box 355, Newtown, Conn. 06470.

The ends of hopper pieces are cut at compound angles by tilting the sawblade and setting the miter gauge. You can use trigonometry to calculate the tangents of the angles, then from the tangents set a bevel gauge with which to set the saw, as follows.

Here's the math

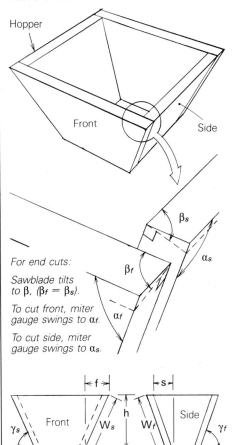

Hopper

Front

Side

β_s

α_s

β_f

α_f

For end cuts:

Sawblade tilts to β, $(\beta_f = \beta_s)$.

To cut front, miter gauge swings to α_f.

To cut side, miter gauge swings to α_s.

f   s

γ_s Front W_s h W_f Side γ_f

Front elevation   Side elevation

On full-size elevation drawings, measure to $\frac{1}{32}$ in. or better:

h = hopper height
f = front 'overhang'
s = side 'overhang'
W_f = width of front face
W_s = width of side face

Now calculate γ_s, the edge angle of the side: $\tan\gamma_s = h \div f$. Calculate γ_f, the edge angle of the front: $\tan\gamma_f = h \div s$.

Then $\tan\alpha_f = W_f \div f$ and $\tan\alpha_s = W_s \div s$.
And $\tan\beta = \tan\gamma_f \div \cos\alpha_f$, or $\tan\gamma_s \div \cos\alpha_s$.
Or $\tan\beta = h\sqrt{f^2 + W_f^2} \div (f \cdot s)$.

Having figured the tangents, you can look up the actual angles in trigonometric tables, punch them on a scientific calculator (arctan or tan-1), or directly set your bevel gauge as below:

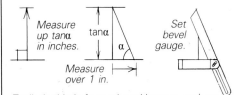

Measure up $\tan\alpha$ in inches.

$\tan\alpha$

α

Set bevel gauge.

Measure over 1 in.

To tilt the blade for a mitered hopper, such as a shadow box, when sides and fronts are of equal thickness: $\beta_m = (180° - \beta) \div 2$.

Author Hanisch renders a contemporary version of the colorful heart motif, a favorite of traditional Pennsylvania-German chestmakers.

Pennsy Painted Chests
Vivid colors brighten the basic box

by Ric Hanisch

I must confess that I don't have a ready answer when people ask me why I started making painted chests. Inspired by the colorful vitality of the old Pennsylvania chests I'd seen, I wanted to explore their potential as a contemporary mode of expression. The simple joinery, the easily worked woods and the fluency of the decoration led me to think that these chests might become an economic cornerstone of my business. I've since found the chests to be a special kind of challenge to my skills as a designer-craftsman.

The painted chests that were popular in the early 19th century in regions of Pennsylvania settled by German immigrants have directly influenced my work. The decorated-chest tradition itself dates to Renaissance Germany and Switzerland, where chests were among the earliest forms of furniture, both for sitting on and for storing household goods such as clothing and linens. In 17th-century Germany, a wealthy merchant could have afforded to commission an elaborate chest, perhaps decorated with bold carving or rich intarsia (a technique in which

pictorial designs are made by inlaying bits of colored wood). While European chests were made by professional cabinet-makers, most Pennsylvania work was probably a sideline for a farmer with diverse skills. Most likely the painting was done by the maker, a member of his family, or some competent member of the community.

The six-board chest (four sides, a bottom and a lid) was a common construction when wide lumber was readily available. The piece was dressed up with trestle, turned or bracket feet and usually a plinth or series of moldings that smoothed the transition from carcase to base. Old chests show a delightful variety of form, from crude, unadorned boxes to refined pieces sporting sophisticated architectural facades. Sizes range from 50-in. long, 24-in. high chests to diminutive boxes less than a foot long. Tulip poplar and white pine were the favored woods because they were easy to get and their mild grain, when hand-planed, provided an excellent surface for painting. Occasionally you'll see chests made of walnut, but

Photos: Ric and Mary Hanisch

these usually were treated with a clear finish, not paint.

As the drawing below shows, constructing a chest is pretty much straight-ahead woodworking. The carcase is dovetailed together and the bottom fitted into a rabbet. The architectural facade, if used, is made up in separate elements and nailed or glued onto the front. Before I assemble a carcase, I plane the inside, which will be left unfinished. I fit the hinges (fabricated to my specifications by a local blacksmith) and fasten them permanently with clinched-over wrought nails. Inside, a small lidded box called a till fits into grooves during carcase assembly. The till is handy for holding valuables and has another practical function: when it's open, it props the main lid at a convenient angle so you can root through the chest's contents.

I like to think of the woodworking portion of making a chest as preparing a three-dimensional canvas. On this blank surface, paint brings an idea to life. The interplay between the chest's form and the paint is an important element in developing a design, so I experiment with proportion and details such as the plinth and feet. For me, this is serious business. I want each successive chest to show greater fluency in paintwork, which comes only with practice. Doors, stools, old chairs, short runs of mirror frames, small boxes, and spoon racks provide places for

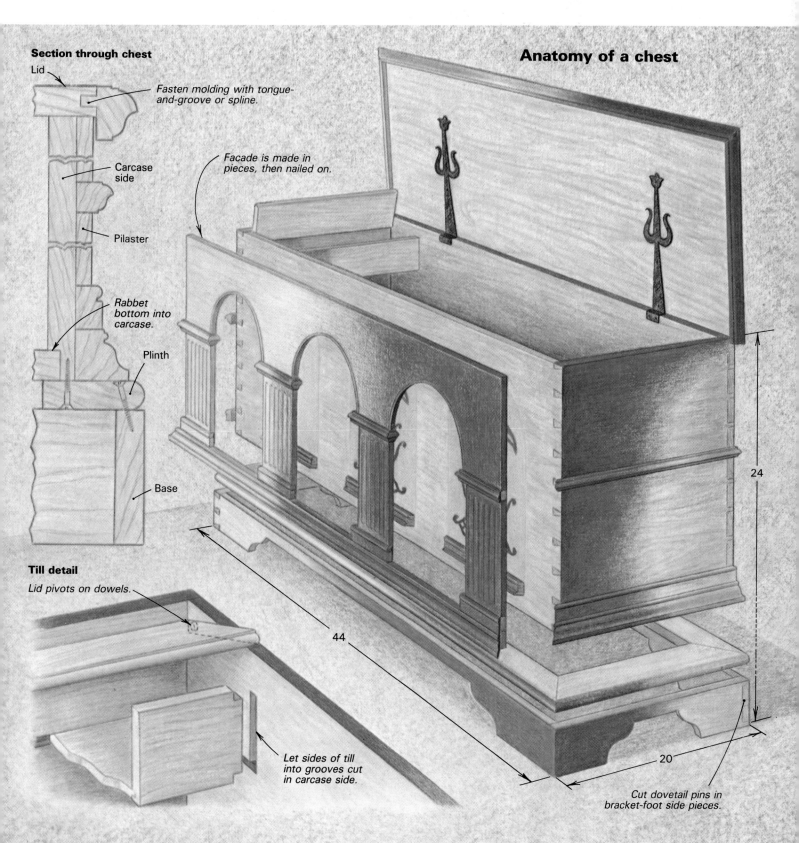

Section through chest

Lid

Fasten molding with tongue-and-groove or spline.

Carcase side

Facade is made in pieces, then nailed on.

Pilaster

Rabbet bottom into carcase.

Plinth

Base

Till detail

Lid pivots on dowels.

Let sides of till into grooves cut in carcase side.

Anatomy of a chest

24

44

20

Cut dovetail pins in bracket-foot side pieces.

Drawing: Lee Hov

me to test painting technique, study color relationships and evaluate materials, thereby broadening the limits of what's possible in a piece.

The painting on traditional chests displays a rich variety of subjects, many dealing with the symbolism and mythology of medieval Europe. Blooming flowers, fanciful birds called *distelfinks,* rearing unicorns, and bold geometric motifs—some reminiscent of the hex signs painted on Pennsylvania-German barns—are quite common. I aim for a more contemporary aesthetic, usually by choosing a strong idea and then organizing the rest of the work to buttress this central theme. Controlling the many variables to achieve a balanced whole takes deliberate effort. As the work proceeds, I carefully review the results. How does it read at fifty feet, at ten feet and at one foot? How does it feel to the touch? Some old chests have remarkable tactile qualities, which the maker produced by manipulating thick coats of wet paint.

Creating a cohesive painted design requires discipline. I like to develop full-size drawings, exploring ideas before taking up the brush. I find that ideas come rather easily; the problem is keeping track of them before they fade from memory. I've taken to

If color is a painted chest's rhythm, texture is its harmony. A paper dauber stabbed into the wet paint stippled the orange background on the chest above. Below, an architectural facade, made separately and nailed on, dresses up a boxy chest front.

filing all my sketches. This rich mine of information provides a practical tool for future projects. And a quick leaf-through also tells me how much time I've spent on the design for a particular project—a figure I need if I expect the price of the work to reflect the effort that went into it. Design time on just the paint for the heart chest (p. 220), for example, totaled about 35 hours, including development of technique and paint tests.

Once I've designed the major elements, I scribe them onto the chest with dividers and a knife so outlines can be seen through the accumulating layers of paint. Then I'm ready to begin painting. The first step is to seal the raw wood with a wash coat of shellac. I make the wash coat from what I call my stock solution—a pound of shellac flakes dissolved in about a quart of alcohol. I filter the stock solution and dilute it by adding one part stock to four parts alcohol.

I apply undercoating next. This coat, which is the background color on which the other designs will be painted, can be a flat oil- or water-based house paint, or a tinted artists' gesso. Since I choose the color to match subsequent opaque coats, or to provide background color for transparent or textured layers, I may have to apply several undercoats on different parts of the same chest. Before working on the actual piece, I prepare sample panels so I can check the color and workability of the paints and brushstrokes I'll be using. After smoothing the undercoats with a Scotch-Brite pad, I seal the surface with shellac to ensure that subsequent coats will be absorbed evenly and to allow mistakes to be wiped off without permanently staining the surface.

For the top layers of paint, I prefer oil-based finishes, either manufactured enamels combined with a tung-oil paint base called Waterlox, or Waterlox mixed with dry pigments or artists' oil paints. Waterlox, available at most paint stores or through Waterlox Chemical and Coating Co., 9808 Meech Ave., Cleveland, Ohio 44105, is a versatile additive. It makes the paint flow more easily and dry more quickly, and the final film is a good deal tougher than that of straight enamel—an important consideration because a chest that's to be used will be subjected to a lot of wear. Another method—which probably is excellent for the beginner—is to mix pigments with shellac, thinned to the appropriate viscosity. Shellac paints are quite thin and flow easily but dry quickly, so they're unsuitable for texturing. They're "one stroke" paints. Using two strokes doubles the paint thickness and intensifies the color.

I've experimented with two kinds of dry pigments: artists' colors and bulk pigments sold as colorants for concrete. The masonry pigments, though cheaper, aren't as finely ground and they come in fewer colors. You sometimes can buy them at local hardware stores for $1.50 to $2.50 per pound. Artists' colors vary widely in cost. Earth colors and titanium dioxide (white) are at the lower end of the scale; vermilion, cadmium yellows and reds, and some blues and greens are at the upper end, costing $36 or more per pound. Pigments also vary in coloring power, ease of mixing, transparency, permanence and toxicity. Some act as catalysts to accelerate drying; some mix up to unusual consistencies (ultramarine gets stringy) or are difficult to disperse in oil. Using a muller or a mortar and pestle helps disperse the pigment in the oil medium. Ralph Mayer's *The Artist's Handbook of Materials and Techniques* (Viking Press, 1981) is a good general reference on this subject.

To mix a color, first add a little oil paint or Waterlox to a small amount of pigment, thoroughly wetting it. Once you've got a homogeneous paste, add more oil until you have the desired color and consistency. A little turpentine will thin the mixture and slow drying, buying you additional time for texturing the surface. Whiting (calcium carbonate) provides bulk without changing the color value appreciably.

To make brushing easier, wipe large areas to be filled with color with a turps-dampened cloth. Brushes vary widely in kind and quality, and choosing the right one is important. When I'm aiming for a particular effect, I may try several brushes, or even modify one by trimming it. Once I've found one that performs a particular function well, I keep it in good condition with careful cleaning. Good natural-bristle brushes are made from the best materials, and even the novice will notice the difference in performance. Also, a good brush will outlast a cheaper one.

In painting a chest design, I start with the broader background colors, then progress to the finer detail. At this point, I might begin adding some texture to the still-wet paint by manipulating it with a brush, dabbing it with a sponge or my finger, or dragging a feather, corncob or perhaps a rolled-up wad of paper through the film. The possibilities are endless. On the heart chest, I textured the green heart with a feather and marbleized the yellow background by dabbing dry color into the wet paint with crumpled paper and Q-tips. Testing paints on a scrap panel is particularly important, however, since each color mixture can be textured only during a critical time period, which varies with daily conditions. If you start too soon, you may find that the paint is too wet to be worked; wait too long and the paint will be too stiff. With a fast-drying paint, I sometimes have a helper do the painting so I can concentrate on texturing.

The safest painting procedure is to allow one color area to dry, then seal it with a shellac wash coat before doing an adjacent color. Flowers, figures, borders and moldings are then painted in to connect the various details. At this point, the reflective qualities of the paints will vary from color to color, depending on the amount of whiting and turps used—both substances tend to flatten the paint surface. To even out surface sheen, richen the colors and give a protective surface film, I rub on a glaze of Waterlox mixed with a tiny bit of whatever pigment brings out the colors best.

I realize that all this will seem rather complicated to someone about to try decorative painting for the first time. In fact, if it had been explained to me this way before I felt the urge to paint, I might not have made the attempt. Confidence, born of ignorance and tempered by experience, kept alive my desire. This is a skill you can teach yourself without enduring years of frustration. Remember, the rural chest decorator of 1750 worked with no formal training and a limited palette, yet was able to achieve results that remain powerful statements of the spirit.

I grew up in a rural New Jersey house built as a church in 1880. There are still traces of the original painted adornments—stenciled fleurs-de-lis on wainscoting and cherubs holding an open Bible. During the 40 years my folks have lived there, most of the flat surfaces carpentered by my father have been enhanced with decorations painted by my mother . . . fish and anemones in the bathroom, mountain scenes down the hall, giraffes and skeletons in the closets, oriental landscapes in the stairwell. Furniture, trays, lamps—nothing was safe. It's strange but true that until a year ago I didn't make the connection that, in fact, I do come from a tradition of decorative painting. And in that way, I am indebted to the past and responsible to my own future. ☐

Ric Hanisch, a member of Guild X in Bucks County, Pa., has a masters degree in architecture and has worked as a builder. He designs and makes furniture in Haycock Township, Pa.

Tubular Table

A router makes the legs round

by Patrick Warner

I've always liked the light and airy configurations of steel tubing in contemporary stools, tables and chairs, but I prefer the look and feel of wood. Using simple joinery and a router, I combined the best of both worlds and came up with the end table shown here.

The construction is straightforward. The end frames are assembled, doweled, then routed round. I used rectangular stock so that after routing, the vertical pieces would appear to bend into the horizontal ones. If you're not interested in this illusion, you can start with square-section stock, and eliminate the rabbeting step (**4**) shown in the drawing. I aligned the end-frame pieces with a routed glue joint for gluing up (**1**), then bored and drove in the dowels after the glue had set (**2**). A simple dowel joint would work just as well; the glue joint alone won't. (I also used the routed glue joint in the top because I like the way it looks. By gluing strips of dark wood on the edges before milling, I made the decorative joint you see in the photo.)

The corner joints are vulnerable to racking stresses in light end frames like these, so I added stretchers to strengthen them. The stretchers can be located almost anywhere along the legs, but bore the relief holes and mortises for the stretchers before rounding the end frames (**3**). Holes for the screws that attach the end frames to the top should be counterbored and oversized to allow the top to expand and contract with humidity changes. Bore these holes before rounding, too. I made the top overhang the base so the screws would be well clear of the rounded edges.

After gluing, doweling and mortising the end frames, plane their faces flush. Then rout the inside surfaces as shown in the drawing (**4**). The piloted rabbet cutter establishes the curve that makes the frame appear to bend around the corners. The straight cutter follows, bearing on the rabbet to clear the rest of the waste.

Curve the outside of each corner by a similar method, but pilot the first cut against a template (**5**). The cutter I use is a TA 170 overhead flush-bearing carbide trimmer, which is sold for $13.50 by OCEMCO, 1232 51st Ave., Oakland, Calif. 94601. The template shown (which can be made of Masonite or plywood) produces an outside curve concentric with the inside one, but you can use whatever curve appeals to you. After the corners have been routed, each frame will be square in section. Figures **6** and **7** show how to round the frames with a flush-piloted, $\frac{5}{8}$-in. radius rounding-over bit. When routing the straight sections, be careful around the screw holes and mortises—if the bearing slips into the holes, the piece will be ruined.

Round the stretchers from 1-in. square stock with a flush-piloted, $\frac{1}{2}$-in. radius rounding-over bit. Cut the stock at least 5 in. longer than needed to give you an end to hold or clamp while routing. I routed the tenons using a rabbet bit with an end-mounted pilot (**8**).

I like a Watco Natural oil finish, wet-sanded during oiling with 400- to 600-grit wet-or-dry sandpaper. I follow this up with a light coat of wax four or five days later when the oil has stopped bleeding. □

The tubular legs of this white oak table were routed round after assembly.

Patrick Warner is a designer/furniture-maker in Escondido, Calif.

Photo: Ernie Cowan and Scott Campbell

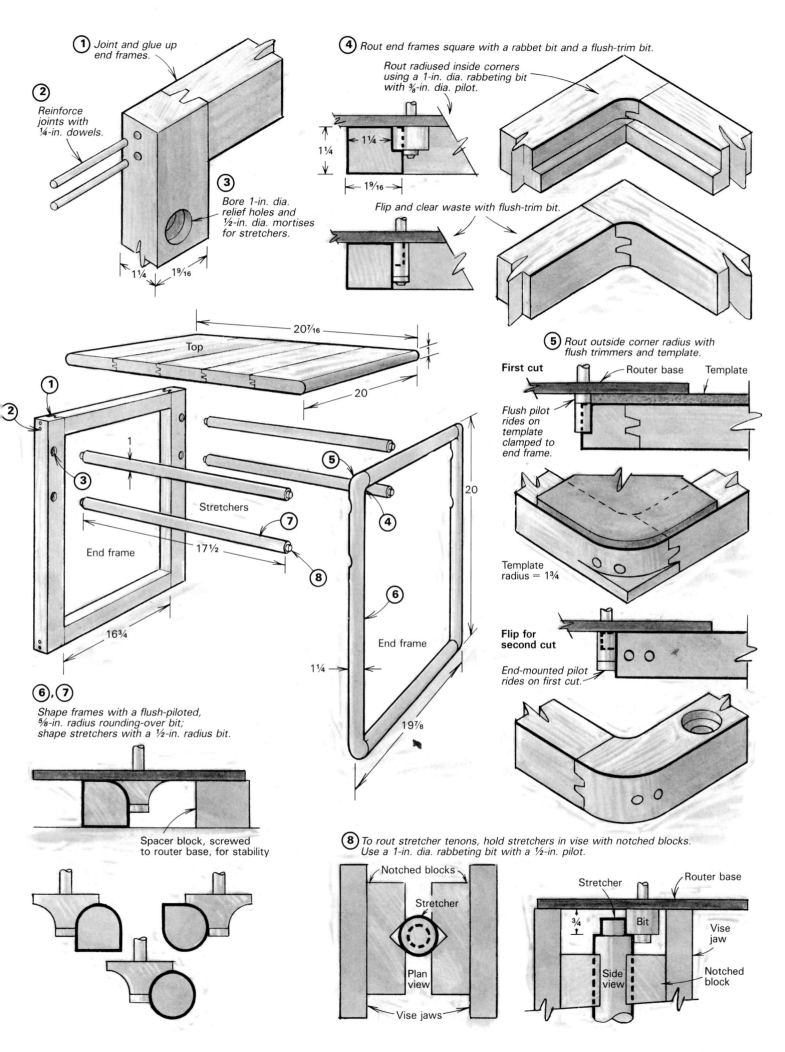

1 *Joint and glue up end frames.*

2 *Reinforce joints with ¼-in. dowels.*

3 *Bore 1-in. dia. relief holes and ½-in. dia. mortises for stretchers.*

1¼   1⁹⁄₁₆

4 *Rout end frames square with a rabbet bit and a flush-trim bit.*

Rout radiused inside corners using a 1-in. dia. rabbeting bit with ³⁄₈-in. dia. pilot.

1¼

1⁹⁄₁₆

Flip and clear waste with flush-trim bit.

20⁷⁄₁₆

Top

1

20

5 *Rout outside corner radius with flush trimmers and template.*

First cut   Router base   Template

Flush pilot rides on template clamped to end frame.

Template radius = 1¾

Flip for second cut

End-mounted pilot rides on first cut.

1

3

Stretchers

End frame

17½

16¾

7

5

4

6

20

End frame

1¼

19⁷⁄₈

8

6, **7**

Shape frames with a flush-piloted, ⁵⁄₈-in. radius rounding-over bit; shape stretchers with a ½-in. radius bit.

Spacer block, screwed to router base, for stability

8 *To rout stretcher tenons, hold stretchers in vise with notched blocks. Use a 1-in. dia. rabbeting bit with a ½-in. pilot.*

Notched blocks

Stretcher

Plan view

Vise jaws

Stretcher   Router base

¾   Bit

Side view

Vise jaw

Notched block

Making Snowshoes
Cold-bending the Indian way

by Henri Vaillancourt

Red paint adds a decorative, personal touch to the lacings of these finely woven snowshoes. The mesh keeps the shoe from sinking into soft snow, but the Indians' sophisticated interlocking design makes this practical device beautiful as well.

For centuries, North American Indians have been using woodbending techniques to turn native hardwoods into snowshoes, canoes and other tools they need for survival. Their nomadic life meant they had to shape and bend wood quickly, without any elaborate steaming, sawing or jigs, and the cold-bending method they devised is as useful today as their snowshoes and canoes are.

The snowshoes are, in fact, one of the Indians' most brilliant inventions, and making a pair is a good way to learn about harvesting and bending green wood. I've always been fascinated by the self-sufficiency of the Indians in the harsh environment of Canada and the northeastern United States. Unfortunately, as youths abandon the ways of their parents, the old skills are in danger of dying out. During the past eight years, I've spent considerable time with various Canadian tribes, learning and recording some traditional snowshoe-making techniques. Here I'll describe the methods used by the Attikamek Indians in central Quebec, who still make a traditional snowshoe with a flat, somewhat angular toe, along with the type of harness once widely used in the northeastern United States and adjacent Canada. Even today winter travel for these people is not a frivolous sport but a rugged necessity—without snowshoes, the Indians would be unable to travel through deep snow to get food or firewood.

The Attikameks' snowshoe is one of the most versatile. It tracks well in open country and is maneuverable in rough or brushy areas. The broad, somewhat square front end gives the shoe a good grip on steep slopes. Since each pair is handmade by eye, no two pairs are exactly alike. Each maker shapes the front and crossbars and weaves the shoe to suit his own personality and tastes. The pair shown above, for example, has a more rounded front and is much larger than the pair shown on p. 229.

To make the snowshoes, the Indians cut down a live tree and then repeatedly split it into riven sections larger than the components of the finished shoes. Using an ax, the maker hews the riven sections into rectangular staves, which he shaves smooth. To make the pieces easier to bend, he whittles the major bending points to thin them, then flexes the stave against his foot or knee until it's pliable enough to be bent and shaped freehand.

The Indians have a choice of four hardwoods that can be split, shaped and bent while green to make frames. Because of its strength and durability, yellow birch is preferred; the softer white birch is the next best. I've found, however, that my local New England birches are brittle and hard to bend. Black ash bends well but wears out quickly, especially in wet or crusty snow. Maple is a durable alternative, but it's difficult to work. White ash, which doesn't grow in Attikamek country, is common in the U.S. Northeast and makes good snowshoes, as does hickory.

The most workable trees are in the 6-in. to 12-in. diameter range. Look for a tree that's straight-grained, fast-growing and free from knots. Remember, you'll be splitting the wood, not sawing it, and the straighter the grain, the better the tree will split and the more unbroken long fibers it will have. A good indication of straight grain is the straightness of the fissures or vertical grooves in the bark of some trees. You can also strip off a length of bark to expose the grain. Fast-growers usually display bushy tops and horizontal or drooping branches. These trees have wider growth rings and a higher percentage of fibers to low-density earlywood vessels, so they're stronger than slowgrowers. The Indians often chop out a chip from the tree's base to check the growth rings: rings about ⅛ in. apart mean that the wood will be easy to cold-bend; closer rings indicate that it will be more brittle and harder to bend.

After you fell the tree, cut an 8-ft. log from the butt end. Split the log in two with wooden wedges, mallets and an ax, then into quarters, eighths or sixteenths, depending on the size of the trunk. You should end up with pieces about 2 in. wide on the bark side. Hew and shave these pieces into rectangular staves, 1 in. by ¾ in., as in figure 1. The Indians hew the staves with an ax or a chainsaw, as shown on p. 228. They use a crooked knife for smoothing, but you might be more comfortable with a drawknife, spokeshave or plane. Dress the staves evenly along their length to ensure symmetrical bending. Following the grain closely, so as not to cut across the long fibers, will minimize fracturing during bending. As no tree is perfectly straight, the dressed stave usually waves or twists, but this unevenness disappears when the snowshoe is given its final form.

To make shoes for an average-size man, cut the staves about

Fig. 1 references photos on p. 228; text references p. 228

Fig. 1: Hewing the staves

Split a 6-in. to 12-in. dia. green tree in half, then in quarters. Continue to split each piece until you have a pie-shaped wedge about 4 in. wide on the bark side. Remove the heartwood from the wedge, then split the remaining sapwood in half along the line shown. The Indian method of trimming and shaping each stave from the riven stock is shown in the photos on p. 228.

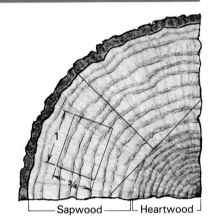

Sapwood ——— Heartwood

Fig. 2: Attikamek pattern

A: Marking a stave

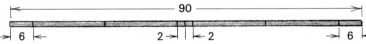

90

6 — 2 → ← 2 — 6

Marks set width of toe, midpoint of stave and length of tail.

Recesses at ends are for shaping tail. Tips can be left full thickness because they will be trimmed after ends are fastened together.

← 8 → ← 8 →

Thin area near toe to make bending easier.

B: Fitting the crossbars

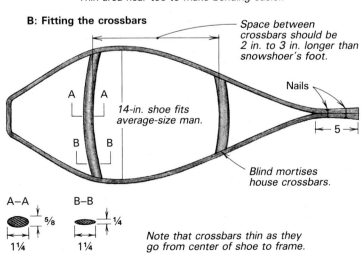

Space between crossbars should be 2 in. to 3 in. longer than snowshoer's foot.

A   A

14-in. shoe fits average-size man.

B   B

Nails

← 5 →

Blind mortises house crossbars.

A–A   B–B

⅝   ¼

1¼   1¼

Note that crossbars thin as they go from center of shoe to frame.

Lee Hov

7½ ft. long (figure 2A). Make a pencil mark 6 in. from each end of the stave where the ends will come together to form the tail—the 6-in. length allows an inch or so to be trimmed off the finished, assembled tail. Make another mark halfway between the two tail marks for the center of the toe. Now draw two more lines 2 in. on either side of this center mark to set the width of the square toe and the placement of the front bends. You should also draw another mark on each side of the stave halfway between the centerline and the tail marks, where a temporary brace will be set while the bent frames dry.

To make it easier to bend the square toe, take a knife and shave the inside face of the stave, the pith side, for about 8 in. on either side of the centerline. The finished thickness should be about ⅜ in. to ½ in. Also shave the stave on either side of the tail marks, but this time on the outside (bark side), as the bend here will be in the opposite direction.

Rather than steaming or boiling the green wood to limber it, you repeatedly bend the stock against your foot or knee. Do the tail sections first. Put your foot near the tail mark, on the bark side of the stave, and flex the stave gently back and forth enough to limber the wood, so it can be bent into the tail shape. You may have to shift your foot several times to produce a smooth curve. Depending on the wood and the skill of the maker, the limbering process can take from 30 seconds or less to several minutes. You'll find that the wood will largely spring back to its original shape when you release it, but that's all right. Limbering bends the stave more than necessary for the finished frame, to make it easier to pull the frame into its final shape.

When you've limbered both tails, bend the sides in the same way, but this time put your knee on the pith side. Bend the stave for 9 in. or 10 in. either side of the brace marks. Flex the stave slightly before moving your knee up or down the stave—too much bending while keeping the pressure in only one position would result in irregular, angular curves. If, in spite of all precautions, the curves are uneven, you can shave the straight sections again to make them more flexible and then rebend them. Like the tails, the sides should be somewhat overbent.

To bend the toe, place your knee at one of the marks on either side of the centerline. Flex the stave back and forth a number of times until you form a sharp bend at that point. Bend the other side of the toe the same way. Splintering often occurs during this process, but the stave is thick enough for you to trim off any slivers after the frame has dried. You could also bind the splinters in place with thread to prevent deeper cracking.

To bend the stave into its final form, place your foot on the flat part of the toe section and pull the two ends of the stave upward until you can insert a stick, or spreader, approximately 14 in. long at the halfway marks (the exact length of this stick depends on the shape desired). Next bend the two sides around this stick and bring the ends together to form a tail. Match the pencil marks indicating the start of the tail and tie the ends securely with twine. Now check if the frame is symmetrical. If it looks uneven, use your knee on the inside or outside of the frame and bend the stave until the curves look right. Bend a second frame to match the first, and tie the pair together with twine to keep them from warping as they dry.

The Indian method of cold-bending takes a fair amount of skill, so those unwilling to practice would be better off using a bending form. Make one from 1-in. boards or plywood cut to the shape of the inside of the snowshoe frame and mounted on a wooden backing somewhat larger than the form. Even though the Indians bend wood cold, I would advise beginners to use hot

Sweat, not steam, is the key to this low-tech method of bending green wood. An Indian needs only a knife, an ax and his body. After splitting a stave out of a live tree, Moise Flamand, an Attikamek from Quebec, hews it with his ax (top left). Then, using his hand as a vise, he shaves the piece with a crooked knife (above). Stepping on the end of the stave, he flexes the piece until it's limber enough to bend (bottom left). To make the sharper front bends, he shaves the area thinner, then uses his knee as a fulcrum for bending the wood (below).

Black-and-white photos: Henri Vaillancourt

A temporary horizontal spreader establishes the characteristic snowshoe shape as the ends of the staves are pulled together. Twine holds the tails together until the green frame has dried.

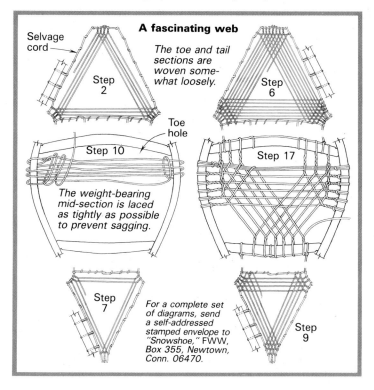

A fascinating web

Selvage cord

The toe and tail sections are woven somewhat loosely.

Step 2

Step 6

Toe hole

Step 10

Step 17

The weight-bearing mid-section is laced as tightly as possible to prevent sagging.

Step 7

For a complete set of diagrams, send a self-addressed stamped envelope to "Snowshoe," FWW, Box 355, Newtown, Conn. 06470.

Step 9

water for the entire bending process—it will make the wood more pliable and easier to handle. Either stand the stave in a pot of boiling water, or hold it over the pot and give the section to be bent a liberal dousing with a ladle for a minute or two. You could also douse the stave with hot water as you wrap it around the form. Then hold it in place with wooden blocks nailed to the backing. First nail a block to hold the toe section, and then simultaneously bend both sides of the stave around the form and fasten them with more blocks. Finally, force the tails together and hold them in place with additional blocks.

After the bent frames have dried for several days, clinch-nail the tail with two nails (any type of nail will do). Next cut the blind mortises for the two crossbars as shown in figure 2B. The two Attikamek crossbars are oval in section and bowed—toward the front and toward the back, respectively. Shaved from the same wood as the staves, they're about 1¼ in. wide and ⅝ in. thick at the midsection, tapering to ¼ in. at the tenons, which have no shoulders. The distance between the bars should be several inches greater than the length of the user's foot.

Next drill the frame for a rawhide or twine selvage cord, which will anchor the weaving in the toe and tail sections. Bore these holes (from 1/16 in. to ⅛ in. in diameter and spaced ⅛ in. to ¼ in. apart) in pairs through the frame from the outside. Place the first pair one above the other about 1½ in. from the ends of the crossbars, and successive pairs on 1½-in. to 2-in. centers. To countersink the cord and protect it from wear, chisel a ⅛-in. deep groove between the holes on the outside edge of the frame. Pass the cord through each pair of holes and knot it on the inside before carrying it to the next pair. You should also loop and run the selvage around the crossbars.

Once the selvage cord is attached, the shoe is ready for weaving. The Attikamek still cut lacings for snowshoes from raw moose or deer hides, but you could substitute untanned cow or calf skin. For those who don't wish to work skins, woven nylon cord from the hardware store is a fair substitute. The ⅛-in. dia. cord is good for both the midsection and the end weave.

The Indians usually leave their snowshoes unfinished, but if you wish, you could give the pair a coat of good spar varnish after you complete the lacing. Some makers, especially those who often travel on wet snow, also varnish the lacings.

To make a harness, the Indians pass a pliable leather strap through the weave near the toe hole of the center section and fasten it around their foot. This harness holds the ball of the foot down, but leaves the heel free to lift. The leather strapping used in commercial harnesses is too stiff for this style harness. Very soft leather is needed, but if you can't get it, you can substitute ¾-in. lampwicking or cotton clothesline.

For snowshoeing, Indians ordinarily wear soft moose or caribou skin moccasins over several pairs of wool socks or liners of wool blanketing or felt. The heelless moccasins don't abrade the lacings, and I find that they let me "feel" the snowshoes and harness. You can readily sense if the harness is poorly adjusted, and how the snowshoe is behaving in relation to your foot. This lets you adjust your stride and balance in subtle ways that are difficult to explain but quickly learned. □

Henri Vaillancourt lives in Greenville, N.H., and is an authority on the traditional crafts of the Northern Woodland Indians. His book, Making the Attikamek Snowshoe, *is available from The Trust for American Cultures and Crafts, Box 142, Greenville, N.H. 03048. The Trust also makes video tapes on Indian technology, including snowshoe-making.*

INDEX